John MacEvilly

An exposition of the Gospel of St. Luke

Consisting of an analysis of each chapter and of a commentary: Critical, Exegetical,

Doctrinal and moral

John MacEvilly

An exposition of the Gospel of St. Luke
Consisting of an analysis of each chapter and of a commentary: Critical, exegetical, doctrinal and moral

ISBN/EAN: 9783337282554

Printed in Europe, USA, Canada, Australia, Japan

Cover: Foto ©Thomas Meinert / pixelio.de

More available books at **www.hansebooks.com**

AN EXPOSITION

OF THE

GOSPEL OF ST. LUKE

CONSISTING OF

AN ANALYSIS OF EACH CHAPTER

AND OF A

COMMENTARY

CRITICAL, EXEGETICAL, DOCTRINAL, AND MORAL

BY HIS GRACE

THE MOST REV. DR. MacEVILLY

ARCHBISHOP OF TUAM

"Go ye into the whole world and preach the Gospel to every creature. He that believeth and is baptized, shall be saved; but he that believeth not, shall be condemned."—MARK xvi. 15, 16.
"And how shall they preach unless they be sent?"—ROM. x. 15.

DUBLIN:
M. H. GILL & SON, 50 UPPER O'CONNELL STREET.

NEW YORK:
BENZIGER BROTHERS, 113 BROADWAY.

1898.

LETTER FROM HIS HOLINESS LEO XIII.

"LEO P.P. XIII.

" VENERABILIS FRATER,—Salutem et Apostolicam Benedictionem—Excepimus tuas litteras et commentaria in sacras Scripturas Novi Testamenti a te elucubrata, quæ ad Nos dono mittere voluisti. Tua quidem volumina, venerabilis frater, utpote Anglico idiomate conscripta delibare non potuimus, at delectati tamen sumus testimonio obsequii erga Nos et hanc Apostolicam Sedem, quod in hoc munere offerendo, nobis, exhibendum censuisti. Dum, itaque, Tibi gratum nostrum animum profitemur commendamus simul pium studium quod in sacris libris perscrutandis impendis, in quibus salutares et inexhausti thesauri veritatis et vitæ reconduntur, et ad virtutem ac fructum pastoralis ministerii adjumenta maxima suppeditantur. Omnia autem quæ nobis obtulisti benevolo excipientes animo, Tibi ex corde adprecamur a Domino, ut ad certandum bonum certamen spirituum sapientiæ et fortitudinis abunde largiatur, ac in auspicium divinæ benignitatis, et in pignus sinceræ dilectionis Nostram Apostolicam Benedictionem peramanter impertimus.

" Datum Romæ apud S. Petrum die 30 Aprilis, An 1879, Pontificatus Nostri anno secundo.

"LEO P.P. XIII.

" Venerabili Fratri, Johanni Episcopo Galviensi,
  Coadjutori Tuamensi, Galviam."

The following is the translation:—

"LEO XIII., POPE.

"VENERABLE BROTHER,—Health and Apostolic Benediction—We have received your letter and the presentation copy of your Commentaries on the Sacred Books of the New Testament, which you were kind enough to send Us. We could not, indeed, do Ourselves the pleasure of perusing your volumes, venerable brother, as they are written in the English language; but We have, nevertheless, been gratified by the evidence of your homage to Us and to this Apostolic See, as conveyed to Us through your present. Whilst, therefore, expressing Our thanks to you, We, at the same time commend your pious and laborious researches in the investigation of the Sacred Scriptures, wherein are hidden the salutary and inexhaustible treasures of truth and life, and which furnish the greatest helps to the fruitful discharge of the duties of the pastoral office. But, in graciously accepting the solemn assurances you have given Us, We heartily pray the Lord to abundantly bestow on you the spirit of wisdom and fortitude to fight the good fight, and as a token of Divine favour, and as a pledge of Our sincere affection, We lovingly impart to you the Apostolic Benediction.

"Given at Rome, at St. Peter's, on 30th April, 1879, in the second year of our Pontificate.

"LEO XIII., POPE.

" To our Venerable Brother, John Bishop of Galway,
  Coadjutor of Tuam, Galway."

THE
HOLY GOSPEL OF JESUS CHRIST,
ACCORDING TO ST. LUKE.

GENERAL INTRODUCTION.

According to Eusebius (Hist. Lib. iii. c. 4), St. Jerome (de Viris Illus.), and indeed nearly all ancient writers, St. Luke, the Evangelist, was a native of Antioch, the capital of Syria. It is almost universally admitted, on the same authority, that he was also the author of the Acts of the Apostles. From the statement made by him in this latter work, wherein he speaks of the language of Palestine—the Syro-Chaldaic—as different from his own, which from his style is acknowledged to be Greek, it is clear that he was not a native of Palestine. St. Chrysostom and St. Jerome (Quæst. in Gen. xlvi 26), relying on the words of St. Paul (Coloss. iv. 11-14), maintain that he was of Jewish extraction. The knowledge he displays of Jewish customs and manners, would warrant the general opinion, that he was a proselyte. This, however, might apply to a convert from Paganism. If he were such a convert, St. Luke might have acquired all this knowledge in his intercourse with the Apostle of the Gentiles.

That he was not one of the seventy-two disciples, as is asserted by St. Epiphanius, nor one of the two disciples at Emmaus (chap. xxiv.), as St. Gregory conjectures (Lib. i., Moral. c. 1), is clearly seen, not only from what has been stated above; but more clearly still, from his own words (chap. i. v. 4) which are hardly consistent with the supposition that he had been at any time an eye-witness of the sacred actions of our Lord. Tertullian (contra Marcion, Lib. iv. c. 2) tells us, that he learned the Gospel from St. Paul, never having been one of our Lord's disciples, or attendant on Him. Hence, St. Jerome (in cap. lxv. Isaiæ) calls him, the spiritual son of St. Paul ; and St. Irænous (Lib. i. c. 20) calls him, the disciple of the Apostles. St. Jerome (de Viris Illust., &c.), and Eusebius (Hist. Lib. iii. c. 4), assure us, on the authority of the old Ecclesiastical writers, that the Evangelist was versed in the healing art. St. Paul (Coloss. iv. 24) terms him, "*his most dear physician*," from which it is inferred that he practised at the medical profession even then. And if we look to the occasions on which St. Luke joins St. Paul for a time — they were separated at intervals—we shall find that this took place in connexion with the bodily illness of the Apostle. We may, therefore, conclude, that it was his attendance on the Apostle, and care of him in his illness, that merited for him the endearing epithet of "*beloved.*" It is remarked by critics, that the precision with which St. Luke employs technical medical terms, when speaking of bodily ailments and their cure, while St. Matthew and St. Mark employ popular terms, when speaking of the same, is owing to the advantage he had over them, in respect to his medical education and practice. (Luke vi. 40—Matthew viii. 16); (Luke v. 31—Matthew

ix. 12); (Luke ix. 11—Matthew xiv. 14, &c.) It is also observed that his intercourse with St. Luke the physician, affected the style of the Apostle himself, as to the use of like technical terms, as in 1 Tim. i. 10 ; vi. 3 ; vii. 6 ; iv. 2, &c., &c. (Patrizzi de Evang. Lucæ. Ep. iii.)

Nicephorus, who died in 1450, speaks of him Hist. Eccles.), and so do other modern Greeks, as excelling in the art of painting, and of having painted pictures of our Lord, and of the Blessed Virgin. This statement of Nicephorus, however, is rejected by many learned critics (Kitto, Cyclopædia).

St. Luke was St. Paul's fellow-labourer in the Gospel Ministry, and the companion of his travels. The first occasion of his association with the Apostle is described (Acts xvi. 10), where he speaks of himself in the *first* person, "*immediately we sought to go into Macedonia.*" After that—as may be seen from his using the *third* person, when speaking of the Apostle's travels and labours—he was, at intervals, living apart from him, until having travelled together from Philippi to Troas (Acts xx. 6), where, likely, St. Luke lived for some time with the Apostle, they remained inseparable up to the second year of the Apostle's imprisonment at Rome, with which the History of the Acts closes (chap. xxviii.), so that during that time, the history of St. Paul is the history of St Luke. And to mark the humility of St. Luke, far from becoming his own panegyrist, he never mentioned his own name in connexion with the labours and trials of the Apostle, in which, doubtless, he must have largely shared, save so far as may be inferred from his having employed the *first* person, "*we*," when speaking of the latter.

The common opinion of the Fathers is, that whenever the Apostle speaks of Luke, in his Epistles, it is to the Evangelist he refers (2 Tim. iv. 11 ; Philem. 24 ; Coloss. iv. 14). Some of the Fathers, Augustine, Jerome, Ignatius (Ep. ad Ephesios) and others, understand the Apostle to refer to him (2 Cor. viii. 19), when speaking of the brother, "*whose praise is in the Gospel*," &c. This is, however, denied by others, as the word "*Gospel*" might mean, not writing a Gospel, but preaching it, through every part of the Church.

After the death of St. Paul, there is nothing known for certain of St. Luke's labours, of the places where he preached the Gospel, or of the manner of his death. He is reckoned among the martyrs by St. Gregory Nazianzen. Eusebius tells us nothing about his martyrdom. Neither is there any notice of it in the Martyrologies. It is stated by others, that he preached the Gospel in Bithynia and died there, and that his remains were transferred to Constantinople by Constantius (Isidore of Seville, c. 82).

HIS GOSPEL—

Its *Integrity*. The integrity of this Gospel was universally admitted by ancient writers, the heretic Marcion alone excepted, who would have expunged the first two chapters, and would commence the Gospel narrative with chapter third, "*Now in the fifteenth year*," &c. Of late years, the spirit of Infidelity that has come forth from the Rationalistic Schools of Germany, following in the train of Marcion, who never doubted the *authenticity* of the Gospel, has called in question the first two chapters, on the ground, that St. Luke had not sufficient testimony, from a human point of view, for the statements he there puts forward. But, abstracting altogether from inspiration, as we know the Blessed Virgin remained on earth after our Lord's Ascension, she was, surely, competent to give testimony respecting the events recorded in these chapters, and it is from eye-witnesses of the events narrated in the Gospel St. Luke tells us he derived his information.

The 43rd and 44th verses of chap. xxii., relating to our Lord's bloody sweat, and the appearance of the angel to strengthen Him in His sacred Passion, were, at one time, questioned, on grounds which, if admitted, would militate against the entire economy of Redemption, against all our Lord's humiliations and sufferings in His Incarnation, and entire life on earth. They are now no longer gainsayed. Indeed, St. Luke, himself a physician, could be quoted as a competent authority on the subject of our Lord's bloody sweat, which has never been proved to be impossible.

DATE OF—

It is not easy to determine anything for certain on this subject. There are two points, however, in connexion with it that may be regarded as certain. First, it has been uniformly held by all ancient writers, that St. Luke wrote his Gospel after those of Matthew and Mark. No ancient writer has questioned the order in which our Gospels are arranged, save Clement of Alexandria (apud Euseb. Hist. Lib. vi. c. 14), who holds that Luke wrote his Gospel before Mark had written his. What his reasons for this strange opinion may have been, as Patrizzi remarks, are utterly unknown to us; secondly, it has been the uniform testimony of antiquity, that St. Luke wrote his Gospel before the Acts of the Apostles. That St. Luke, the Evangelist, was the author of both, hardly admits of any doubt; for, St. Luke himself expressly states this in his preface to the Acts (chap. i. 1-4). If we could ascertain the date of the Acts, it would help, to some extent, in fixing the date of the Gospel, at least in regard to the time after which the Gospel could not have been written. The Acts must have been written after the second year of St. Paul's imprisonment at Rome (A.D. 58), (Patrizzi), as this circumstance is mentioned in the Acts (chap. xxviii. 30, 31); whether immediately after the expiration of that time, or only after the Apostle's martyrdom, cannot be determined for certain. It is likely the History of the Acts was written before the destruction of Jerusalem. This is inferred from St. Luke's silence regarding this great event, so remarkable in connexion with the literal fulfilment of our Lord's prophecies on the subject. Surely, St. Luke would not have been silent regarding this remarkable event, if it occurred at the time he wrote his history. Hence, his Gospel, written before the Acts, must have been written before the year 70, the date of the destruction of Jerusalem. And as St. Mark's Gospel is generally referred to the year 57, before leaving Rome for Egypt, the Gospel of St. Luke must have been written after that; but at what precise period between 57 and 70, cannot be accurately determined.

WHERE WRITTEN—

This, like the preceding point, is involved in uncertainty. The probabilities, greater or lesser, as to the place where it was written, will depend very much on its date. Some hold, it was written in Bœotia and Achaia; others, in Rome, of which Theophylus is supposed to have been a native.

ITS LANGUAGE—

It is universally admitted that it was written in Greek. Its style is more polished than that of the other Gospels. From its contents, it would seem to have been written chiefly for the use of the Gentile converts; so that, as St. Paul was the Apostle of the Gentiles, his disciple, St. Luke, might be justly regarded as the special Evangelist of the same. Hence, we find certain peculiar words and phrases in his Gospel more intelligible to the Gentiles, than the corresponding words employed by the other Evangelists. Thus we have, "*Master,*" for *Rabbi*; "*truly,*" for *Amen*, &c.

Some among the Fathers hold, that whenever the Apostle in his Epistles uses the words, "*my Gospel*," he refers to that written by St. Luke, whence, it is inferred, that it was dictated by the Apostle. This, however, is hardly consistent with St. Luke's own account of his sources of information (chap. i. 1-3), viz., eye-witnesses, among whom St. Paul could not be numbered; nor would St Luke omit stating that he wrote his Gospel at the dictation of St. Paul, if such were the case Considering, however, the wonderful identity of expression employed by both (Luke xxii. 19, 20; 1 Cor. xi. 23), in describing the institution of the adorable Eucharist, it is likely that St. Luke takes, at least, this part *verbatim* from St. Paul, as this latter states that he received his account of the institution of the Eucharist from our Lord Himself.

Among the emblematic figures of the four Evangelists referred to in the prophetic vision of Ezechiel (i. 10), also in the Apocalypse (iv. 6, 7), the ox is said to represent St. Luke, as his Gospel commences with the Priesthood of Zachary, the principal function of which was the offering of sacrifice, the ox being one of the chief victims of the altar.

The Gospel is addressed to "*Theophilus*" (see chap. i. 3, Commentary).

PREFACE TO SECOND EDITION

THE steady sale of the Commentary on the Gospel of St. Luke, published only a few years ago, calls for this Second Edition, in every respect the same as the preceding, with the exception of a few unimportant verbal corrections.

May we hope that this Second Edition will meet with the same consideration and support that have been accorded to the preceding Edition.

It must be left to others to pronounce how far it may have proved useful to the pious reader of SS. Scripture:

☩ JOHN MacEVILLY,
Archbishop of Tuam.

ST. JARLETH'S, TUAM, *January*, 1887.

PREFACE.

ABOUT three years ago, I undertook the publication of a Commentary, in one volume, of the Gospels of St. Matthew and St. Mark, a work which has been received with unexpected favour, as the Second Edition is now nearly exhausted. A second volume containing a Commentary on the Gospels of St. Luke and St. John, together with the Acts of the Apostles, was promised at the time. Those who may have been expecting its appearance, will hardly be surprised that its issue has been so long deferred, if they take into account the arduous and numerous duties of my office, which I could neither neglect nor overlook, and the vast amount of time and labour required for Scriptural researches, particularly with a view to publication. I am now partly redeeming my promise by giving to the public, as a companion volume to the Commentary on the two other Synoptical Gospels of St. Matthew and St. Mark, an Exposition of the Gospel of St. Luke, which may, if so desired, be conveniently bound with the former.

Neither time nor pains has been spared in its composition, according to my humble ability. How far I may have succeeded in my design to produce a useful work, I must leave to others to determine. I purpose publishing, at a future day, should Providence so will it, my notes on the Gospel of St. John and on the Acts.

In the meantime, in the hope that the present work may be received with the same favour that has been accorded to its predecessors, I confidently submit it to the indulgence of the pious Student of Holy Scripture.

☩ JOHN MacEVILLY.

GALWAY, Feast of our Lady, Help of Christians, 1879.

THE HOLY GOSPEL OF JESUS CHRIST,
ACCORDING TO ST. LUKE.

CHAPTER I.

ANALYSIS.

The first four verses of this chapter contain the Preface to the Gospel (see Commentary.) The Evangelist next describes the parentage and sacerdotal descent of the Baptist (5-8). The wonderful apparition of the Archangel Gabriel to Zachary, the father of the Baptist, announcing to him that his wife Elizabeth would give birth to a son, who was to discharge the office of precursor to the Son of God (9-17). The punishment of Zachary's incredulity (18-22). The conception of the Baptist (23-24). The Annunciation made by the Archangel Gabriel to the Blessed Virgin of the birth of our Lord, with all its circumstances (28-38). The Visitation, or the visit of the Blessed Virgin to her cousin, St. Elizabeth, described in detail (39-45). The inspired Canticle *Magnificat* (see Commentary) (46-55). The birth and circumcision of the Baptist, and the wonders which took place on the occasion of it, especially in the miraculous recovery of the use of speech by his father Zachary (57-67). The inspired Canticle (*Benedictus*) of Zachary (68-79) (see Commentary).

TEXT.

FORASMUCH as many have taken in hand to set forth in order a narration of the things that have been accomplished among us;

2. *According as they have delivered them unto us, who from the beginning were eye-witnesses and ministers of the word;*

3. *It seemed good to me also, having diligently attained to all things from the beginning, to write to thee in order, most excellent Theophilus,*

4. *That thou mayest know the verity of those words in which thou hast been instructed.*

COMMENTARY.

1-4. The four first verses of this chapter may be regarded as an Introduction to the Gospel. This form of introduction, common among classical writers, whom St. Luke imitates in this respect, as well as in his polished style of writing, is hardly ever to be met with in the Books of SS. Scripture, save here and in the opening verses of the Acts of the Apostles, from the same inspired penman. While the meaning of each particular word requiring explanation shall be given in each verse in particular, the general meaning of all may be given in the following paraphrase :—" Whereas many have already undertaken to arrange and put together an account of the events regarding which we have the most undoubting faith—the firmest conviction—because they were transmitted to us in our day by those who were themselves eye-witnesses of them, and ministers of the Gospel truth; it seemed fit to me also, who have investigated and ascertained all things that occurred from the commencement of the Gospel history, to write to you, most excellent Theophilus, an account of them, following the general order of events, so that you may fully and securely ascertain the undoubted truth of those things in which you were catechised or instructed by word of mouth.

1. "*Many*," cannot refer to St. Matthew or St. Mark, who were not "*many*." Moreover, Matthew was himself an "eye-witness," and did not, therefore, derive his information from, "eye-witnesses." Nor is it likely Matthew and Mark are referred

A

to with others who with them might constitute "*many*," as St. Luke would hardly class inspired with uninspired writers of the Gospel. Neither is it likely that reference is made to the writers of Apocryphal Gospels, under the names of Matthias, Thomas, Twelve Apostles, &c., as there is no evidence that these were in existence at the time. To whom, then, does St. Luke refer? Probably, to some incompetent, but well-meaning compilers of incomplete and confused histories of the actions and sayings of our Divine Lord, according as they ascertained them from the traditions, which existed at the time, whose motive in undertaking a Gospel History St. Luke neither praises nor censures.

"*Have taken in hand*" (επεχειρησαν). These words of themselves imply neither success nor failure, though generally taken in the latter sense, and very probably they mean it here, as the failure of those referred to in giving a full narrative of the Gospel incidents, and the uncertainty which their confused histories might create in the minds of the faithful, would seem to be put forward by St. Luke as his motive for undertaking a well-arranged, authentic narrative of the doings and sayings of our Blessed Lord.

"*To set forth in order*." The Greek compound—αναταξασθαι—would seem to signify to *re-arrange*, and is so understood by Patrizzi, as if St. Luke referred to men who would fain give a more accurate and orderly account than that of Matthew and Mark. However, it more probably signifies here to give a well-arranged narrative of the events of Gospel History without implying reference to any already existing written records requiring to be put in order.

"*Of the things*," events, embracing doctrinal teachings and external actions.

"*Accomplished*." The Greek word, πεπληροφορημένων, sometimes signifies to *fulfil*, or *accomplish* (2 Tim. iv. 5; Col. ii. 2; Heb. vi. 11), in which sense the Vulgate translator understands it, as if reference were made to the accomplishment of the ancient prophecies and types in the words and actions of our Lord recorded in the Gospel. Sometimes, the word means, *fully credited*, producing a most unhesitating conviction. (Rom. iv. 21; xiv. 5, &c.) This latter would seem to be its meaning here, as appears from the following words, as it was meant, that they had the firmest persuasion, &c., owing to the testimony of "*eye-witnesses*," &c.

"*Among us*," in our time, if "*accomplished*" be taken in the first sense above given; to our knowledge, if taken in the second meaning.

2. "*According as they have delivered them*," &c. There is a diversity of opinion as to the connexion of these with the foregoing words. By some, they are connected with "*accomplished*," or firmly believed, as if in them was assigned a reason for that firm belief, because of the tradition which transmitted them with undoubted truthfulness from sources above all suspicion, viz., the "*eye-witnesses*," among whom we may reckon primarily the Blessed Virgin, the shepherds of Bethlehem, in regard to the earliest incidents, the Apostles from the time of their vocation. The latter were also "*ministers of the Word*," having been divinely engaged in divulging to the world the sacred truths of which it is meant to transmit a well-digested record. Others connect them with the words, "*have taken in hand*," as if it were meant to convey, that the writers in question meant, perhaps, unsuccessfully, to transmit a history of the teachings and actions of our Lord in accordance with the traditions received from "*eye-witnesses*," &c. Others connect them with the words of v. 3, "*in order*," as if St. Luke meant to convey that he undertook to give an orderly account in accordance with the accurate traditions of "*eye-witnesses*," &c. These place a full stop after v. 1.

"*From the beginning*." The origin of the Christian dispensation, the commencement of the events and incidents recorded in the Holy Gospel, viz., the birth and infancy of the Precursor, the birth and infancy of our Lord, &c.

"*Of the Word,*" although sometimes referring to the Increated Word or Eternal Son of God, here most likely refers to the Gospel incidents, embracing our Lord's discourses and actions.

3. "*It seemed good to me also,*" &c., under the impulse and inspiration of the Holy Ghost, which we reverently believe to have guided the hand and pen of St. Luke, preserving him from error in his narrative. To such inspiration, however, St. Luke here lays no claim, when referring to the sources from which, humanly speaking, he derives the incidents of an authentic history, so as to satisfy all reasonable men, even on human grounds, in regard to his claims to be believed.

"*Good,*" in the sense in which "*it seemed good to the Holy Ghost and to us,*" Apostles (Acts xv. 28).

"*Having diligently attained to.*" Accurately investigated and traced out with the greatest diligence and exactness.

"*All things from the beginning.*" All the things that appertained to the Gospel history from the commencement to the end (see v. 2).

"*In order.*" Avoiding all confusion in narrating the series and succession of events in the general complexion of the history. Hence, he puts the account of the conception and birth of the Baptist before that of Christ; the conception and birth of Christ before His baptism; His baptism before His preaching; His preaching and miracles before His death; His death before His Resurrection and Ascension. As our Lord often delivered His instructions repeatedly, and on various occasions, the order in which they were repeated is not strictly adhered to in regard to them, nor in regard to certain minute circumstances. "*Order,*" may refer to subjects rather than dates, to the grouping of events and incidents in cases of similarity rather than to time, regarding which he is less definite than the two other Synoptists, especially in his loose and fragmentary narrative from chap. ix. 51 to xviii. 14, which is exclusively his own, save v. 18, chap. xvi.

"*Most excellent Theophilus*"—literally, *a friend of God, a lover of God*, or *beloved of God*—is not a common name, belonging to the representative of a class, as held by some, or, to a particular Church, as held by others; but a proper name, undoubtedly referring to a particular man. Who he was cannot be fully ascertained. Most likely he was one of St. Luke's converts, distinguished for great moral worth; hence, styled "*most excellent.*" It is, however, more probable still, that this title which the Greeks were wont to bestow on governors, and men occupying high official station, was addressed to Theophilus on account of his exalted rank and high official position. In this latter sense, the same title—κράτιστος—is applied to Felix (Acts xxiii. 26; xxiv. 3) and to Festus (Acts xxvi. 25). He was very likely a Gentile convert of high station, and also an inhabitant of Rome. For, while St. Luke is very particular in topological details, both in his Gospel and in the Acts of the Apostles, when treating of Asia Minor, Palestine, and Greece, he is silent on such matters when he treats of Italy. From this it is inferred that Theophilus was a Roman, in regard to whom it would be superfluous to treat of Italian topography, with which, on this assumption, he must have been thoroughly conversant. But although addressed to Theophilus, we are not to suppose that the Gospel was written for him alone, but for the entire Christian world, to the end of time, of whom Theophilus may be regarded as the representative. Even in our own day, we frequently see writings meant for the public, addressed and dedicated to individuals.

4. "*That thou mayest know*," become thoroughly convinced of, "*the verity*," the secure ground of your belief (ασφαλειαν, security) in.
"*Of those words*." In those things. "*Word*" is a term commonly used by the Hebrews to denote any event or *thing*.
"*Instructed*"—κατηχηθης—*catechised*, instructed orally, or by word of mouth. It was by means of oral, *catechetical* instruction Theophilus was first brought to embrace the faith. St. Luke deems it right to leave a written record, under the influence of inspiration, of the Gospel History, in order to confirm the faith of Christians during all succeeding ages.

TEXT.

5. *There was in the days of Herod the king of Judea, a certain priest named Zachary, of the course of Abia, and his wife was of the daughters of Aaron, and her name Elizabeth.*
6. *And they were both just before God, walking in all the commandments and justifications of the Lord without blame.*
7. *And they had no son, for Elizabeth was barren, and they both were well advanced in years.*
8. *And it came to pass, when he executed the priestly function in the order of his course before God,*
9. *According to the custom of the priestly office, it was his lot to offer incense, going into the temple of the Lord.*
10. *And all the multitude of the people was praying without at the hour of incense.*

COMMENTARY.

5. "*King Herod.*" This was Herod the Great, surnamed ASCALONITES (see Matthew ii. 1), a foreigner from Idumea, upon whom the Romans bestowed the entire of Judea, inhabited by the twelve tribes. After his death, his kingdom was partitioned among his sons (Matthew ii. 22; xiv. 1). St. Luke refers to him here to show, that the period marked out in the prophecy of Jacob, for the coming of the Messiah, in consequence of the sceptre having been transferred from Juda, had arrived, and that it was at that precise time our Saviour was born.
"*A certain priest named Zachary.*" He was not High Priest. St. Luke always calls the High Priest, *Pontifex* (iii. 2; Acts iv. 6). Moreover, the High Priest did not belong to any of the "*courses*" in his ministrations. He might minister in the Temple at any function and at any time he thought proper.
" *Of the course of Abia*," that is, of the rank or priestly family which was bound in its turn to the weekly service of the Temple, of which family Abia was head, according to the distribution made by King David, of the descendants of Aaron into twenty-four ranks or orders. (1 Paralip. xxiv.) The Greek word for "*course*"— εφημεριὰ—means a *daily* service, such as that performed by the Jewish priests in the Temple; and as this daily service was continued by each division for a week, from Sabbath to Sabbath, the word is used to designate the *class*, by whom the daily services were discharged in turn. It is to be observed, that in order to obviate the confusion which might arise in the discharge of the priestly functions in the Temple, owing to the great number of the descendants of Aaron, in the time of King David, this pious king divided the descendants of the two sons of Aaron, viz., Eleazar and Ithamar, into twenty-four *courses* or ranks, who were each to discharge, under the guidance of the chief from whom each family took its name, the priestly functions, and minister for a week in the Temple. The order of precedence was determined by lot. The eighth lot fell on Abia Of these twenty-four orders or *courses*, although

ST. LUKE. CHAP. I. 5

only four returned from the captivity, still, the original division into twenty-four classes, under the ancient name of the family, was retained (1 Esdras ii.; 2 Esdras vii. 39; xii. 1).

"*And his wife was of the daughters of Aaron, and her name was Elizabeth.*" Zachary, if he pleased, might have married into another tribe, as the priests were not bound to take a wife from their own tribe. Neither were women, unless they were heiresses. Hence, Elizabeth might have been cousin of the Blessed Virgin; because, a man of the Tribe of Levi might marry a woman of the Tribe of Juda, and *vice versa*. Zachary, however, not only married into his own Tribe of Levi; but, what was highly deserving of commendation, he took for wife one of the family of Aaron. In commendation of the Baptist, the Evangelist first refers to his noble descent from a holy priestly race, which was the only source of nobility among the Jews; and again, to the great personal sanctity of his parents, next verse.

6. "*Both just before God,*" really just, gifted with real, internal justice, such as commends us to God, and not merely external, so as to be seen by men. "*Justice*" embraces the state of internal justification and the gift of sanctifying grace, together with the possession of the aggregate of all virtues. In this is not implied their exemption from all even indeliberate sins, which faith tells us we cannot avoid during life "without a special privilege of God" (Conc. Trid. ss. vi., Canon 23), but only exemption from gross, mortal sin, which destroys all justice before God.

"*Walking in,*" living in the habitual observance of

"*All the commandments and justifications of the Lord.*" Thus is shown how justice, once acquired, can be preserved, strengthened, and increased, viz., by the observance of all God's commandments, "*factores legis justificabuntur*" (Rom. ii. 13); "*Ex operibus justificatur homo*" (James ii. 24). By "*commandments,*" some commentators understand the *moral* precepts contained in the Decalogue; and by "*justifications,*" the *ceremonial* precepts of the law, having reference to sacrifices and the worship of God.

"*Without blame.*" As the word "*just*" conveys, that they were irreproachable before God, "*without blame,*" conveys that they were irreproachable before men, "*providing good things not only in the sight of God, but also in the sight of men*" (Rom. xii. 17). The words, "*without blame,*" only imply exemption from *grievous* sins or *crimes*, which alone could entail reproach with men.

17. "*No son,*" or offspring, nor any chance of it at this time. For this, two reasons are assigned—first, the natural sterility of Elizabeth; secondly, at the time, they were both too far advanced in life to beget children in the natural course of things. This the Evangelist notes, to convey to us more clearly, that the Precursor was miraculously begotten by a special grace or privilege divinely bestowed by God, as in the case of Isaac (Genesis xviii. 11).

8, 9. It happened, when the week came round for the priestly family of Abia, to which Zachary belonged, to discharge the priestly functions in their turn, "*before God,*" that is, in the Temple, where God is said specially to reside, that among the lots which were cast to determine, in accordance with the usage observed in the exercise of priestly functions, the duties, that were to fall to each ministering priest, the duty of burning and offering up incense every morning and evening, on the altar of incense, fell to him. This was was the most honourable of the priestly functions This altar of incense was in the *sanctum;* but, it opened into the *sanctum sanctorum*, so as to allow the incense to penetrate into it. It was divided by a veil from the *sanctum sanctorum*, in which the Ark was in the time of Solomon. It is manifest the offering of incense here referred to is different from that which the High Priest alone could make within the *sanctum sanctorum*, on the Feast of Expiation, as this latter function could be discharged by the High Priest alone; whereas, here any of the sacerdotal family, to whose lot it fell, could perform it. Hence, Zachary was not High Priest. "*The custom of the priestly office*," refers to what follows, viz., to the custom among the priests of each family to cast lots to determine each one's duty during the week of service; it also refers to the function of offering incense, which was one of the duties it was usual for the priests, as determined by lot, to discharge.

"*Going into the Temple of the Lord.*" By the *Temple* here is meant, in a more restricted sense, the *sanctum*, into which the priests alone could enter. Outside the *sanctum*, or the Temple properly so-called, was the Court of the Priests, which was not covered in; outside this was the Court of Israel, or, of the Jewish people, men and women; outside this, was the Court of the Gentiles.

10. "*All the multitude,*" the great body or bulk "*of the people were praying without.*" When Zachary entered the *sanctum*, where he was concealed from view, to burn and offer up incense, the people were in the outer Court of Israel, as it was called, uniting in prayer with the ministering priest. This may, probably, have occurred on the Sabbath or some minor festival, when the people came in large crowds to pray and worship in the Temple.

"*At the hour of incense,*" that is, at the time the priest offered incense on the golden altar (Exodus xxxi. 8). This happened twice each day, morning and evening.

(For a description of the Temple and its Courts, see Dixon's Introduction, vol. ii. p 95.)

TEXT.

11. *And there appeared to him an Angel of the Lord, standing on the right side of the altar of incense.*

12. *And Zachary seeing him was troubled, and fear fell upon him;*

13. *But the Angel said to him: Fear not, Zachary, for thy prayer is heard; and thy wife Elizabeth shall bear thee a son, and thou shalt call his name John:*

14. *And thou shalt have joy and gladness, and many shall rejoice in his nativity.*

15. *For he shall be great before the Lord: and shall drink no wine nor strong drink and he shall be filled with the Holy Ghost even from his mother's womb.*

16. *And he shall convert many of the children of Israel to the Lord their God.*

17. *And he shall go before him in the spirit and power of Elias; that he may turn the hearts of the fathers unto the children, and the incredulous to the wisdom of the just, to prepare unto the Lord a perfect people.*

18. *And Zachary said to the Angel: Whereby shall I know this? for I am an old man; and my wife is advanced in years.*

19. *And the Angel answering, said to him: I am Gabriel who stand before God; and am sent to speak to thee, and to bring thee these good tidings.*

20. *And behold, thou shalt be dumb, and shalt not be able to speak until the day wherein these things shall come to pass; because thou hast not believed my words, which shall be fulfilled in their time.*

21. *And the people were waiting for Zachary; and they wondered that he tarried so long in the temple.*

22. *And when he came out he could not speak to them, and they understood that he had seen a vision in the temple. And he made signs to them, and remained dumb.*
23. *And it came to pass, after the days of his office were accomplished, he departed to his own house.*
24. *And after those days Elizabeth his wife conceived; and hid herself five months, saying:*
25. *Thus hath the Lord dealt with me in the days wherein he hath had regard to take away my reproach among men.*

COMMENTARY.

11. "*There appeared unto him*," or, as the Greek," Ὤφθη, signifies, *there was seen by him*, in a visible, sensible form, "*an Angel of the Lord*," Gabriel (v. 19), "*standing on the right side of the altar of incense*," which might be regarded as a good omen, to convey that he was the bearer of joyous tidings.

12. On beholding the Angel, Zachary was seized with exceeding great fear, such as fell on Daniel (x. 7) and others (Judges vi. 22 ; xiii. 22), probably owing to the majestic as well as the sudden, unexpected appearance of his heavenly visitor, too overpowering for human infirmity, and also to the idea prevalent among the Jews, that the appearance of an Angel was a certain omen of approaching death.

13. The Angel dispels his fears, telling him that "*his prayer was heard.*" Some, with Maldonatus, think that Zachary had prayed for a son, and that it is to such prayer the Angel refers; for, he subjoins, "*and thy wife Elizabeth shall bear thee a son.*" The common opinion, however, of the Fathers and of Commentators is, that there is question of a prayer offered up for the redemption of Israel and the coming of the Messiah. Hence, the Angel indicates or implies the order in which this was to occur, viz., that the Baptist, to be miraculously born of the sterile and aged Elizabeth, was to precede the Son of God, whom he would one day proclaim as the Lamb that taketh away the sins of the world (vv. 15-17). Zachary himself in the inspired Canticle refers to this order of things (v. 76) "*praeibis ante faciem Domini,*" &c. The doubt expressed by Zachary after the Angel's assurance on the subject (v. 18), for which he was afterwards punished, would seem to show, that he regarded the birth of a son as hopeless; and, hence, it is not likely that what he regarded as hopeless was the object of his prayer. It might, however, be said with some degree of probability, in favour of Maldonatus' opinion, that the Angel may have referred not to his present prayer, but to prayers offered up for this end on former occasions.

"*And thou shalt call his name John.*" We have no instance in the New Testament where a name was given from Heaven to an infant before his birth, save in the case of our Blessed Lord and His Precursor. The word, "*John,*" in Hebrew, *Johanan*, signifies, *the grace or mercy of Jehovah*. It is observed, with reference to the names of John and his parents, that *the oath of God* (the meaning of Elizabeth) and *its memory* (Zachary) begot the "*mercy or gracious gift of the Lord*" (John). To which the words of Zachary in the Canticle, "*Benedictus,*" are clearly allusive, "*memorari Testamenti sui sancti. Jusjurandum quod juravit,*" &c. (vv. 72-73.)

14. "*Thou shalt have joy,*" &c. His birth will be not only a cause of domestic gladness and joy to you, to your friends and neighbours, but of public joy to many, for whose sake he is born, and who, therefore, shall have reason to rejoice spiritually in the great blessings of which he shall be the harbinger, and shall celebrate the Festival of his Nativity with great joy

15. "*For, he shall be great*," &c. This is assigned as a reason for the universal joy, to which the birth of the Baptist shall give rise. For, at present, his friends and neighbours shall see from the extraordinary circumstances of his birth, and future generations, shall see from the knowledge of all that he shall have done, that "*he shall be great*," endowed with superior virtues befitting a Prophet, a Priest, and the exalted ministry of Precursor—and that in a supereminent degree—which, according to a Hebrew idiom, is the meaning of the words, "*before the Lord*" (Genesis x. 9; xiii. 13). Others understand the words, "*before the Lord*," to mean, really great, not only in the sight of men, as hypocrites oftentimes are, but also in the presence of the Lord, who judges according to truth and justice.

"*He shall drink no wine nor strong drink*," indicating that he shall be a perpetual Nazarite, or one consecrated to God. Those who consecrated themselves to the Lord (Numbers vi.) should, during the time of their consecration, abstain from wine and everything that could inebriate. "*Strong drink*." The Greek, σίκερα (Latin, *cicera*) corresponding with the Hebrew, *shecar*, means any inebriating drink not made from the juice of the grape. *Shecar*, is rendered so by St. Jerome (Leviticus x. 9, and elsewhere).

"*And he shall be filled with the Holy Ghost*." Here, we see a clear opposition between being inebriated with wine and being inebriated with the gifts of the Holy Ghost, as in Ephes. v. 18. One is utterly incompatible with the other.

"*From his mother's womb*," meaning, that from his nativity, or after the union of his soul and body, his sanctity shall commence and continue ever after. This indicates the early beginning of that sanctity proceeding from the gifts and grace of the Holy Ghost, which the Baptist displayed ever after. A question is here raised, viz., whether John was cleansed from original sin in his mother's womb, before his birth? The common opinion of the Holy Fathers is, that he was; and they infer it from this passage, and the words of Elizabeth (*v.* 44). Although St. Augustine (in Epist. 57, or 187 ad Damasum) is of a contrary opinion. He maintains, that the sanctification referred to here, as in the case of Jeremias, "*Antequam exires de vulva, sanctificavi te*" [i. 5), merely implies sanctification according to God's predestinating decree. But although his opinion and the reasons adduced by him might be fairly maintained if we look to the context of the passage from Jeremias, they are commonly rejected in regard to the Baptist, whose sanctification in his mother's womb, embracing the remission of original sin, in which he was conceived, and the infusion of the supernatural gifts and virtues through the Holy Ghost, is held by most of the Holy Fathers and theologians of note. Regarding ONE ONLY, the glorious Mother of God, BLESSED above all the rest of pure creatures, does Faith tell us, that, "at the first instant of her conception, she was, by a singular grace and privilege of Almighty God, in view of the merits of Jesus Christ, the Saviour of mankind, preserved free from all stain of original guilt." The particle, "*even*," *adhuc*, ετι, very significantly denotes John's sanctification in his mother's womb, which he demonstrated, while there, on the occasion of the Virgin's visit to Elizabeth (*v.* 44).

16. Thus filled with the Holy Ghost, he shall, in due time, by the example of a holy and austere life, and by his most efficacious preaching, "*turn many of the children of Israel*," to whom alone he preached, "*to the Lord, their God*," by causing them to believe in Him, and give up the ways of sin for a life of sanctity and penance, as we find recorded of him (Luke vii. 29; Matthew xxi. 32). The Angel says, "MANY *of the children of Israel*," not *all*; because, some opposed him and heeded him not (xx. 5).

"*To the Lord, their God*," viz., the true God, adored by the Jews. Hence, Christ is God, since it is of Him, there is question here, as in next verse, "*Shall go before Him*," &c.

ST. LUKE, CHAP. 1   9

17. *" Shall go before Him."* By *" Him,"* is clearly meant our Saviour, of whom John was the Precursor : the same, who in the preceding verse is called *" the Lord God of the children of Israel."* From this, is proved the Divinity of Christ.

" In the spirit, in discharging the *office*—as contradistinguished from the person of Elias—*"and power of Elias,"* displaying the courage, fortitude, resistance to wicked men in the more elevated walks of life, such as was displayed by Elias, when here on earth, in resisting Jesabel and the Prophets of Baal, and is to be hereafter displayed by Him at His second appearance, *" before the coming of the great and dreadful day of the Lord"* (Mal. iv. 5). Hence, there is reference made to the noble deeds of Elias in the past, as well as in the future. Others interpret, *"spirit and power,"* as meaning by a figure of speech (Hendiadis) " the spirit of power." He shall display, while discharging the office of Precursor, the same spirit of fortitude and burning zeal, that was displayed by Elias of old, and is to be still more displayed by him at a future day. when he is to precede the second and glorious coming of the Son of God.

" That he may turn the hearts of the fathers," &c. These words applied in Malachias (iii. 4) to Elias at the *second* coming of our Lord, are by accommodation, applied to the Baptist, who is to discharge the same office of Precursor in regard to the *first*. The meaning of the words is rather difficult. By *"turning the hearts of ths fathers,"* &c., some understand, infusing the faith and virtues of the Patriarchs into their degenerate children, the Jews of his own day. By his preaching of penance and of faith in Christ, John will transfer *" the hearts"* (*i.e.*), the faith and good dispositions of the holy Patriarchs to their children, who shall be of one heart with them, and become perfectly assimilated to them in their thoughts and manner of life. Others understand the words to mean : as the Patriarchs who believed in Christ, although they only saw Him at a distant futurity, and practised sanctity of life, reprobated the conduct of their delinquent and disobedient (απειθεις) children; and ignoring them, turned away from them in disgust—for, *Abraham* knew them not—(Isaias lxiii. 16) ; so, now on seeing their repentance and faith brought about by the preaching and example of the Baptist, they shall turn to them with love and affection, and acknowledge them as their worthy sons and genuine descendants. The same shall be done by Elias, at his second coming, when opposing the persecuting reign of Antichrist. The words spoken of Elias (Eccles. xlviii. 10), *" to reconcile the heart of the father to the son,"* is in favour of the latter interpretation ; for, here as well as in Ecclesiasticus, the Greek word for *"turn"* and *" reconcile"* is the same—επιστρεψαί.

" And the incredulous to the wisdom of the just." This is understood by some to be the same as the second clause of the sentence as given in Malachias (iv. 6), but not quoted here, *" and the hearts of the children to their fathers."* However, as *" turning the hearts of the fathers to their children,"* and *"of the children to their fathers,"* means the same thing, and therefore conveyed in one of the clauses quoted here from Malachias, it is more likely that these words are but an explanation by the Angel of the words, *" turning the hearts of the fathers to their children,"* as if he said, in other words ; he shall display the power and efficacy of that spirit wherewith he will be animated, by prevailing on the unbelieving and on the disobedient, rebellious (απειθεις) generation of his brethren to embrace or practise the wisdom of salvation so prudently adopted and practised by the just of old who went before them ; imbued with their spirit, to practise the virtues for which their fathers were distinguished, and thus securely reach the goal of salvation, which they wisely reached.

" To prepare unto the Lord," &c. The result of this conversion of the hearts of the fathers, &c., will be to prepare, or make ready, by his efficacious preaching and example, so far as he was concerned, for embracing the faith and the precepts of our Lord, a

people whom he imbued with perfect dispositions, for this purpose. The Greek for "*perfect*" is κατεσχευασμενον, *prepared, fitted.* The passage will, therefore, mean : the result of this reconciliation of the fathers to their children, whom John shall induce to walk in the footsteps of the former, both as to faith and obedience, will be, to prepare for the coming and proper reception of our Lord, a people whom he had been already instrumental in imbuing with the dispositions necessary for that purpose.

18. "*Whereby shall I know this ?*" Zachary is considered by almost all the Fathers, to have sinned, at least venially, owing to his doubt or rather mistrust regarding the words of the Angel. Although, in case of doubt, as to whether he was an Angel at all, or an Angel of light, it might be prudent of Zachary to inquire and guard against delusion or deceit; still, in this case, considering all the circumstances, the time, place, appearance of the Angel, &c., he had no reasonable ground for doubting his identity, and therefore, should have believed at once. His doubt, however, did not regard the omnipotence of God, His power to do all things possible. It arose rather from the utter impossibility, humanly speaking, of the promise being fulfilled. "*I am an old man,*" &c. Commentators, observe how different was the case of the Blessed Virgin. She, at once, believes the announcement made. She is only anxious to know *how* the mystery will take place, without any detriment to her virginity. In the case of Abraham and others, who asked for a sign, they did so, not from distrust, for they believed, "*credidit Abraham,*" &c. (Rom. iv. 3, 18-22), but to confirm their faith. Whereas, in the case of Zachary, the doubt proceeded from distrust in the Angel's word (*v.* 20). Hence, whatever may be the similarity in the several cases, if we look to external expression, God, who sees the heart, saw that one believed and the other did not. Zachary's sin, however, is generally considered not to have been grievous ; nor should it be measured by the penalty inflicted on him, inasmuch as it was inflicted not only as a punishment of his hesitancy, but also as a sign of the fulfilment of the Angel's words, which Zachary asked for, "*whereby shall I,*" &c. Indeed, it was quite characteristic of the Jews to seek for signs in such cases (1 Cor. i. 22).

19. The Angel then gives his name, so well known in Jewish history in connexion with the period of the coming of the Messiah (Daniel ix. 25)—a name to which this message had immediate reference—indicating the *Power of God (Gabriel, fortitudo Dei*).

"*Who stand,*" one of those highest angels who are ever next to God, "*one of the seven who stand before the Lord*" (Tobias xii. 15), ever ready to execute His will. Even when sent on an embassy, these still *stand* before the omnipotent God. The Greek is, *stood;* but it may be a Hebraism for, *stand,* as the latter form conveys *perpetual* attendance; or it may mean, *lately stood* before him in heaven, and am now here on an errand to you.

"*And am sent,*" not from myself, nor from any other created power, but on a lofty commission from God, "*to speak to thee and bring thee these good tidings*" regarding the birth of him, who is to go before the Messiah, now near to announce the joyous tidings of the Gospel of peace, and to achieve universal salvation for the entire earth.

20. "*And behold,*" as if indicating something extraordinary—as much as to say, you have asked for a sign, and "behold" it. He gives a sign which also serves as a punishment—a sign of the fulfilment of his promise, and a punishment of incredulity, uniting chastisement and instruction at the same time. "*Dumb.*" The Greek word, σιωπων, is understood by some interpreters to mean, *deaf,* inasmuch as it

would otherwise seem a useless tautology to say afterwards, "*and thou shalt not speak.*" The Greek corresponding word (v. 22) is κωφος, which signifies, *deafness* and *dumbness*, though primarily signifying *deafness*. Deafness is inflicted in punishment of his not hearing and *obeying;* dumbness, for his having contradicted the Angel. It would seem Zachary was deaf also (v. 62). Such is the connexion of dumbness with deafness, that the dumb are generally deaf. Others, however, adhering to the strict signification of the word, say the following are only explanatory, and intensifying the sense, as in Acts xiii. 11, "*Thou shalt be blind, not seeing the sun,*" &c. Thou shalt be dumb (silent), nay, even not able to speak, implying more than the former expression.

"*Until the things shall come to pass,*" viz., the birth of a son, and his giving him the name of John, as commanded by the Angel. The event will show, that he was justly punished, and shall cause him to be released from the punishment inflicted. "*Shall come to pass,*" shows that Zachary's incredulity shall not render God's promise on the subject void.

21. The people who had been praying in the outer Court of Israel, while Zachary was engaged offering incense in the *sanctum* at the appointed time, were awaiting his return to the Court of the Priests, to receive the usual benediction given on such occasions, as had been done by Aaron (Leviticus ix. 23), according to the prescribed form (Numbers vi. 23).

"*And they wondered that he tarried so long,*" &c. The delay was caused partly by the interview, which, possibly, may have embraced more than is recorded here; and partly, by the stupor which continued even after the assurances given to Zachary by the Angel.

22. From the appearance he exhibited (for the effect of converse with heavenly visitors is, to create a change in one's appearance—Exod. iv. 10; Daniel x. 8, 16, 17), and his being deprived of the power of utterance, they knew it was not the result of any sudden attack of illness; and seeing it to be of an extraordinary nature, they concluded he must have seen a vision. "*He could not speak to them,*" so as to give the usual benediction, or explain the cause of his being deprived of the use of speech.

"*And he made signs to them,*" probably expressive of what they suspected, and, possibly, in reply to their inquiries if he had seen a vision, which convinced them more and more that it was so. Likely, also, the "*signs*" may have reference to his mode of officiating during the remaining days of his course, going through his duties in a silent manner, without being able to speak in giving the usual benediction; for it is said (next verse) he waited to discharge the duties of his office during the appointed days.

23. Although deaf and dumb, Zachary did not give over discharging the duties of his ministry during the time assigned to his course for serving in the Temple. The Greek for "*office,*"λειτουργια, originally denoted any public service, civil or military. It now usually denotes priestly functions. On the expiration of his period of office, he left for his home in the mountains of Judea (v. 39). It was after that his wife, Elizabeth, conceived. The Evangelist modestly refrains from any allusion to conjugal intercourse. While on duty in the Temple, the priests lived separated from their wives and families in apartments specially provided for them within the enclosures of the Temple.

24. Elizabeth, after conceiving, *"hid herself five months."* It is generally supposed she did so out of a feeling of modest shame, lest she might expose herself to jeering taunts and ridicule, by appearing pregnant at her advanced age—a thing which the people would regard as ridiculous, until such time as her pregnancy would be beyond all doubt. Thus we find Sara smile at the promise of a son from a like feeling (Genesis xviii. 12). It may be that Elizabeth did so in order to devote herself to prayer and meditation, so befitting one thus singularly blessed by God. Hence, she says, as in next verse,

25. *"Thus hath the Lord dealt with me,"* &c. As if she said, this is the least I can do in thanksgiving for the great blessing of fecundity bestowed on me by God—to whom alone this blessing of fecundity was due—at my advanced period of life. According to the interpretation of others, in these words is assigned a cause for the modest feeling that actuated her in remaining hid, viz., because at this advanced period of life, when it is not usual to conceive children or give any cause for it, God, who would seem to have hitherto turned away from me, has now been pleased *"to regard,"* to look upon me with an eye of mercy, so as to remove, *"in the days"* of my old age, the curse of sterility, considered *"a reproach"* among men, although in His sight who bestows His favours as He wills, *"who killeth and maketh alive, who bringeth down to hell and bringeth back again"* (1 Kings ii. 6, 7), it is often a judgment of mercy and goodness, founded on His prescience of what might occur in case women had begotten children who, in after life, might prematurely bring down their grey hairs in sorrow to the grave. Why sterility should be regarded as a reproach among the Jews, as it undoubtedly was, is differently accounted for. Some say, because it was looked on as a penalty inflicted by God (1 Kings i. 6); others, because it rendered void the end of marriage, which was to beget children; others, because it deprived them of the chance of having the promised Messiah come forth one day from their seed.

TEXT.

26. *And in the sixth month, the Angel Gabriel was sent from God into a city of Galilee, called Nazareth,*

27. *To a virgin espoused to a man whose name was Joseph, of the house of David; and the virgin's name was Mary.*

28. *And the Angel being come in, said unto her: Hail, full of grace, the Lord is with thee: Blessed art thou among women.*

29. *Who having heard, was troubled at his saying, and thought with herself what manner of salutation this should be.*

30. *And the Angel said to her: Fear not, Mary, for thou hast found grace with God.*

31. *Behold thou shalt conceive in thy womb, and shalt bring forth a son; and thou shalt call his name* JESUS.

32. *He shall be great, and shall be called the Son of the most High, and the Lord God shall give unto him the throne of David his father: and he shall reign in the house of Jacob for ever.*

33. *And of his kingdom there shall be no end.*

34. *And Mary said to the Angel: How shall this be done, because I know not man?*

35. *And the Angel answering, said to her: The Holy Ghost shall come upon thee, and the power of the most High shall overshadow thee. And therefore also the Holy which shall be born of thee, shall be called the Son of God.*

36. *And behold thy cousin Elizabeth, she also hath conceived a son in her old age; and this is the sixth month with her that is called barren;*
37. *Because no word shall be impossible with God.*
38. *And Mary said: Behold the hand-maid of the Lord, be it done to me according to thy word. And the Angel departed from her.*

COMMENTARY.

26. The Evangelist minutely describes the circumstances of time, place, persons, &c., in order to gain greater credibility, and more clearly demonstrate the divine origin of the history he is about to give of the adorable mystery of the Incarnation, and of the reparation of the human race.

"*The sixth month,*" is generally computed by interpreters from the conception of Elizabeth. It was usual with the Hebrews, as well as with the Romans, to compute time from some very remarkable epoch or occurrence. The conception of the Baptist, which was the inception of a new order of things, the beginning of a second and more exalted creation, whereby God was to renew the face of the earth, was deservedly regarded as the most remarkable occurrence from which to date the conception of the Son of God. Moreover, God wished that the relations between John the Baptist and his Eternal Son should be so intimate that the years of the latter should be counted in connexion with the former. This "*sixth month,*" is understood as completed, and the order of events so arranged, that John, who was to be our Lord's Precursor, to bear testimony of Him in due time, could commence to do so even from his mother's womb (*v.* 41).

"*The Angel Gabriel.*" The same who had promised Zachary a son (*v.* 13). Although of the highest rank of Archangels, he is still called an *Angel* by St. Luke, as this latter term designates his office of *messenger*, which, in this instance, was the highest privilege he could enjoy. "*Gabriel*," signifies the *strength of God*, well befitting him who was to announce the coming of the *Almighty*. The same messenger who predicted to Daniel the coming of the Son of God at a distant futurity, is now employed to announce His immediate coming in the flesh. To an "*Angel*" was this exalted message to an immaculate Virgin appropriately intrusted.

"*Sent from God,*" *immediately* without the intervention of any higher angelic spirit, as when he was formerly sent to Daniel (viii. 16), to show the great importance of the mission confided to him. "*God*," the Blessed Trinity, this mission being an *actus ad extra*, common to the three Persons of the adorable Trinity.

"*To a city of Galilee named Nazareth.*" It was situated in Lower Galilee, in the Tribe of Zabulon (see Matt. ii. 23).

27. "*To a virgin espoused to a man.*" The Greek word for "*espoused*" (μεμνη-στευμενην), also means, *married*, a signification the word bears (chap. ii. 5), (see Matt. i. 18). The word is meant to convey, that although married, she continued a virgin, free from all carnal intercourse or defilement.

"*Whose name was Joseph.*" The Holy Ghost designates him as "*a just man*" (Matthew i. 19). He was fitly typified by the great Patriarch Joseph, whose affecting history is recorded (Genesis xxvii.—l.) The life of the one may be regarded as the counterpart of the life of the other. Both were singular models of chastity, of patient endurance, and of all supernatural virtues. The Joseph of Egypt, preserving food for his people, plentifully supplied them with bread in the day of dire distress. Our Joseph guarded the *Bread of Life*, which he gave to a famishing world. The power which Pharaoh bestowed on the Patriarch Joseph, though very great, was but a feeble type of the great intercessory power of our Joseph, who, next to his Virgin Spouse, exalted to an inconceivable degree above all created beings, is our most powerful intercessor in the high court of heaven. As Pharaoh of old, when the famishing multitudes cried to him for bread, referred them to Joseph, "*Ite ad Joseph*" (Genesis xli. 55); so does the Almighty refer us in our spiritual necessities to His foster-father, the guardian and protector of His helpless infancy, when he was forced to fly from the wrath of a sanguinary tyrant. To us does he say, as Pharaoh said of old, "*Ite ad Joseph.*"

"*Of the house of David.*" A descendant of David, from whom the Messiah was to spring. Joseph and Mary were both of the family of David (see Matthew i. 16). What the Angel says (v. 32), "*The Lord God shall give him the throne of his Father David,*" was said of our Lord in virtue of His maternal descent, for He had no father on earth. Mary, His mother, must therefore be of the same family of David with her husband Joseph, who is also called elsewhere, "*the Son of David*" (Matthew i. 20), and said to be "*of the house and family of David*" (ii. 4).

"*And the virgin's name was Mary.*" St. Jerome (de nom. Heb.), tells us, that "Mary," in the Greek, Μαριαμ, an indeclinable noun, derived from the Hebrew *Miriam*, signifies, in Hebrew, "*Star of the Sea,*" also, *bitter sea;* and in Chaldaic, *Lady*. Both meanings admirably befitting her who is the glorious Queen of Heaven and Earth, and our *Star* to guide us amidst the storms and darkness of this world to the haven of eternal security and rest. At all times, Christians address the Blessed Virgin with the peculiar title of *Our Lady*. St. Bernard tells us, that of such virtue and excellence is this name, "that the heavens exult, the earth rejoices, and the angels send up hymns of praise when the name of Mary is mentioned" (Hom. *super missus est*); and in the same place this seraphic advocate of Mary calls on those who are in tribulation of mind or body, "to look up to this Star, to call on Mary," &c There is no other name, after the adorable name of Jesus, so venerable, so calculated to inspire all saints and sinners with such hope, such unbounded confidence during life, and especially at the decisive moment of death, when the devil, knowing he has but a short time, puts forth all his strength to compass our ruin. Then it is, that she who is powerful (*ipsa enim potens est*), shall shield her devout children under the protecting shadow of her wing, and put to flight our infernal adversary.

28. "*And the Angel being come in.*" From this it is commonly inferred, and indeed, it is asserted by the Holy Fathers, that the Angel found the Blessed Virgin alone in her private closet. Although there is nothing said here of how she was occupied, it is regarded as certain that she was not idle, but rather occupied with some employment becoming a pure virgin. Not unlikely, she was engaged in prayer, as she is usually represented in all pictures of the Annunciation, and in devotional exercises having reference to the long-expected Messiah, the future deliverer of her people. St. Ambrose (L. 2 in Lucam) remarks, "She was alone in her private closet, where no man could see her, but only an Angel could find her." It is generally supposed that, owing to the angelic gift of subtilty, the Angel having invisibly penetrated the walls of her dwelling, and appearing in a visible form, reverently and on bended knees, saluted as his Queen, Her who was shortly to be constituted Queen of men and angels. Some hold that this occurred in the silence of night, while she was engaged in prayer, before retiring to rest. It was at this hour also Christ was born. It was "*while all things were in great silence, and the night was in the midst of her course, thy omnipotent word leapt down from heaven from thy royal throne*" (Wisdom xviii. 14, 15). Likely, he filled the chamber with heavenly

ST. LUKE, CHAP. I.

effulgence, as happened when the Angels announced the birth of the Son of God to the shepherds (ii. 9).

"*Said to her.*" "*To her,*" should likely be connected not with "*said,*" but with "*being come in, to her,*" or where she was alone in secret (as it is in the Syriac, and found in Holy Fathers, Ambrose, *hic*, and St. Bernard, on the words, *missus est*.) "*Said, Hail, full of grace,*" &c., "*ingressus Angelus ad eam, dixit; ave gratia plena,*" &c., employing the very words communicated by God, when sending him on this most solemn and important message.

"*Hail.*" The corresponding Hebrew form, *shalom lach*, which latter form very likely was used by the Angel, ειρηνη σοι, *pax tibi*, signifies *peace to thee*; or, "*joy to thee,*" and may be either precatory of good, "*may joy or peace be to thee, pax vel gaudium sit tibi,*" wishing her the abundance of all blessings, spiritual and temporal, or congratulatory, on account of the abundant blessings of peace and joy she already possesses, "*pax vel gaudium est tibi.*" In this form, which was usual with the Hebrews at the meeting of friends, the Angel conveys to the Virgin, that his entrance was of a pacific character; that he was a good and not a bad Angel; the bearer of joyous and not of evil tidings, such as the Angels afterwards came to announce, at the birth of the Son of God, "*Peace and tidings of great joy to all the people.*" St. Luke instead of ειρηνη σοι, employs χαιρε, which latter form was more conformable to the idiom of the language then in use. The same is used by our Lord, or rather, His words are so rendered (Matthew xxviii. 9). In this salutation, the Angel accomplished four things:—1. He reverently salutes the Virgin; 2. He propounds the subject of his message (*v.* 31); 3. He points out the mode of its accomplishment (*v.* 35); and thus, 4. He replies to the difficulty (*v.* 34) which presented itself to the mind of the Virgin. Some of the Holy Fathers (Origen, Hom. 6 in Lucam; Bede and Ambrose, *hic*) observe, that the whole message was singular and extraordinary, such as was never before addressed to any human being.

"*Full of grace,*" *gratia plena.* This is the rendering given by all Catholics of the Greek, κεχαριτωμενη, which is the Perfect Passive participle of χαριτοω. This translation is confirmed by the authority of the Fathers, and by the most ancient copies of the Bible. It is the same in the Syriac and Arabic versions. Protestants, while rejecting the Vulgate rendering, differ nearly as widely among themselves on this point as they do from Catholics. Hardly any two of them agree on the precise translation of the word, which is found only in another passage of the New Testament (Ephes. i. 6) εχαριτωσεν ημας, and rendered *gratificavit nos, made us acceptable.* Besides the unanimous consent of the Fathers, the Catholic or Vulgate rendering, *gratia plena*, can be established on intrinsic grounds as well. The word, κεχαριτωμενη, literally rendered, would signify, *one made pleasing* (*gratificata*), which involves (*a*) the state or condition of being thus rendered pleasing; and (*b*) the quality or thing that renders us pleasing. Now, that which makes us pleasing to God, is sanctifying grace; hence sanctifying grace is involved in the word, κεχαριτωμενη. Secondly, the *fulness* of grace is conveyed in the very form of the verb; for, as is known to all Greek scholars, verbs terminating in οω, always denote plenitude, abundance either communicated or received or possessed, according as the verb may be used in the Active or Passive voice, as might be illustrated, if necessary, by numerous examples. Hence, on this principle, κεχαριτωμενη, denotes abundance, fulness of grace. Again, from the Angel's omitting to address the Virgin by the ordinary name of Mary, it is clear he applies κεχαριτωμενη to her as her peculiar title, her distinguishing characteristic epithet, applicable to her alone, and to no one else, as our Lord is called, *the Just One;* Solomon, *the Wise One*, because possessing these qualities in a degree not reached by any other human being. So here the application of κεχαριτωμενη to the Blessed Virgin, never before applied to any one else, shows she possesses the quality or plenitude of grace conveyed in the word, peculiar to herself alone, and distinguishing her from the rest of mankind.

Although "*full of grace*" is applied to our Lord (John i. 17), and to St. Stephen (Acts vi. 8), still we must bear in mind, so far as our Lord is concerned, there can be no parallelism, since the plenitude must be interpreted, having due regard to persons; and hence, in our Lord, the plenitude of grace was, as St. Bonaventure observes, the fulness of the great, inexhaustible fountain, *plenitudo superabundantiæ*, while in the Blessed Virgin was the fulness of the great river next the source or inexhaustible fountain, *plenitudo prærogativæ*, and in all the rest of men, a *plenitudo sufficientiæ*, the rivulets sharing it in a limited degree, sufficient to procure the salvation of them all. As regards St. Stephen, besides that the fulness of grace predicated of him only denotes the grace required for him as minister and witness of God, and in regard to her it denotes the abundance of grace required for her dignity of Mother of God, πληρης χαριτος, is not applied to him as his peculiar designation, as κεχαριτωμενη, is to the Blessed Virgin. That the term, κεχαριτωμενη, is assertive of her present state of acceptableness, owing to the fulness of grace she possesses, and not precatory of good in regard to future favours, is clear from the Greek which is in the passive past tense, and refers to past occurrences, the effect of which remains to the present. In the present instance, there is no limit to the period past; and hence, it implies, that the Virgin was "*full of grace*" from the very first moment of her conception or existence. The words, "*full of grace*," then imply—1st, perfect exemption from all sin, original or actual, even the slightest, and all inclinations to sin, from all passions whatsoever leading to sin; 2ndly, the possession of all virtues, of all graces, in a degree so supereminent, that no virtue, no grace, no gift of the Holy Ghost was ever granted to any one that she did not possess in an eminent degree, although the exercise of them might not always take place. So that every action of her life was virtuous, praiseworthy, and she attained eminence in grace and sanctity to such a degree as rendered her worthy to conceive in her sacred womb and receive within her, the source and fountain of all grace and sanctity, the eternal Son of God Himself (Lucas Brugensis, and Menochius). Suarez, quoted on this passage by A. Lapide, asserts, that at the first instant of her conception, the Blessed Virgin received a greater grace than was ever conferred on the highest angel, and owing to her perfect correspondence and faithful co-operation from her conception till the hour of her death, she acquired such degrees of grace and merit as exceeded that of all angels and men together, and God, therefore, loved the Blessed Virgin more than the entire Church, militant and triumphant, including men and angels.

"*The Lord is with thee.*" This was an ancient form of salutation in use among the Jews (Judges vi. 13; Ruth ii. 4). The words are understood by some commentators of the future abode of our Lord, in her chaste womb, in the mystery of the Incarnation, which it is clear from *v.* 31, did not yet take place. But taken in connexion with the context, and the words, "*full of grace*," "*blessed art thou amongst women,*" which are in the present, the phrase must be understood of her present condition. They express the cause of her being "*full of grace.*" She was so, because "*the Lord was with her.*" These words imply a singular and special assistance on the part of God, which preserved her from all sin, filled her with all grace, and fitted her for the great end for which she was destined. The words, "*the Lord is with thee,*" and the like, both in the Old Testament and in the New, when uttered by God, or by one commissioned by Him, always denote a special assistance on the part of God, and

His presence with the person addressed, for the purpose of effectually accomplishing the end for which such assistance is given (see Murray, de Eccles. vol. i., 200-214). Hence, as the end, for which these graces were conferred on the Blessed Virgin, was the most exalted, that God ever accomplished, viz., the Incarnation of His Son, these graces, which thus fitted her and rendered her worthy, were the greatest ever conferred on any mere creature. The words, however, although denoting the present abundance of grace arising from God's special favour and assistance, very likely, imply also God's special future dwelling in her in His Incarnation, in view of which the present graces were so abundantly given, just as the following words, "*Blessed art thou amongst,*" &c., although referring to the present, clearly have reference to the future Incarnation: for, it is with reference to it, St. Elizabeth addresses the Virgin in these identical words, after she had received the Son of God within her sacred womb (*v.* 42).

"*Blessed art thou among women.*" These words are omitted in some few MSS., the Vatican among the rest. But they are found in most MSS., and generally quoted by the early Fathers. *Blessed* by the Lord, who is with thee. This benediction is subjoined, as the effect of the Divine favour, and implies the amplest gifts and benefits bestowed on her by God at the present moment. It does not refer to the great respect and reverence which the Blessed Virgin was to receive from men in after ages. The form, "benedicta *tu*," is, by a Hebrew usage, equivalent to, "benedicta *es*." For, the Hebrews employed the demonstrative pronoun in place of the verb substantive of the present tense; and she was thus blessed at that moment in the singular graces she then possessed, that rendered her worthy to be the dwelling-place of the Son of God, and of the destination in store for her, to be immediately accomplished.

"*Among women.*" Above all other women. The comparison is not between her and the rest of mankind, but only between her and all other women. Hence our Lord is not included in the comparison. This benediction contains a tacit opposition to the curse pronounced against women in general (Genesis iii. 16); and the special benediction, which distinguishes the Blessed Virgin from all other women, consists in her being a mother and a virgin at the same time; a *virgin*, whose great purity and humility attracted from heaven into her sacred womb, the God of all sanctity; the *mother*, of the Eternal Son of God. She has all the blessings, and none of the losses. She was blessed beyond virgins, widows, mothers; beyond *virgins*, who have the curse of sterility; beyond *widows*, who while gaining the blessing of freedom of mind, suffer the loss of society, while she with the greatest freedom, enjoyed the society of her holy and chaste spouse Joseph; beyond *mothers*, who with the blessing of fecundity, suffer the loss of virginity. Mary had the one without losing the other. From *v.* 31, it is clear, the Incarnation had not yet taken place. Hence, the special blessedness here predicated of Mary, had reference to her future destination to become Mother of God, and to her having been so prepared by God with such an abundance of grace and the gifts of sanctity, as rendered her fit to become His dwelling-place,—an incomparable blessing which was immediately to be conferred on her.

29. "*Who having heard.*" The ordinary Greek has—ιδουσα—*having seen him.* This reading is preferred by St. Ambrose, as if it meant to convey, that the sight of the Angel, his brilliant appearance in the form of a young man—a form to which she was unaccustomed, although, doubtless, often before favoured with visions and conversations of angels—caused this pure virgin uneasiness. "But mark the Virgin by her bashfulness; it is the habit of virgins to tremble and to be ever afraid at the

presence of man, and to be shy when he addresses her. Mary feared even the salutation of an angel" (St. Ambrose). The Greek reading may be easily united with the Vulgate, "*having heard*," and both together will convey the full sense of the passage. The Blessed Virgin was troubled at *seeing* the brilliant form of the young man, but she was still more so, when she *heard* the eulogistic language he addressed to her, which jarred on her humility and modesty. From the text it is clear, that it was the *words* of the Angel that chiefly caused her uneasiness. "*She was troubled at his saying.*" This humblest of virgins was troubled at the praises bestowed on her, while she regarded herself as undeserving of any praise whatsoever. It may be, too, that she had some fears regarding the design and tendency of such language. For, she could not have failed to remember how another Angel, putting on the appearance of light, seduced another virgin, Eve, and entailed on mankind all the ills to which flesh is heir; and very likely this was the train of thought referred to in the words, "*and thought with herself what manner of salutation this should be.*" The Greek for "*thought*," means, "*reasoned*," with herself, with calm deliberation, implying that she retained the full use of her faculties, the disturbance notwithstanding. Unlike Eve (Genesis iii. 2), she prudently refrained from speaking or making any reply until she could more clearly see what was meant, before rejecting or accepting this salutation. "*What manner of salutation this should be*," of which she deemed herself unworthy. She seriously meditated whether it was sincere or deceitful, illusory or divine.

30. "*And*," means, *then*, "*the Angel said to her: Fear not, Mary*," &c. The Angel enlightened by God, saw the thoughts that passed through her mind. He might have divined the same from her countenance, hesitation, &c. Her virginal modesty was disturbed at the sight of a young man suddenly appearing in her presence; her profound humility, at the language of praise addressed to her. Seeing this, the Angel tells her to fear neither his appearance, nor his words. Having addressed her, at the commencement of the salutation, with the high and exalted epithet, of, "*full of grace*," he now addresses her familiarly by her well-known name of "*Mary*," conveying, that she was well known to him, and that she, and she alone, was the person, to whom he was sent on a message from God.

"*For thou hast found grace with God*," and therefore, sure of His Divine protection. In these words is assigned the reason of the high eulogium passed on her, while they would, at the same time, calm her uneasiness. As "*full of grace*," &c., she was acceptable to God, beloved by God—how unworthy soever, she might seem in her own eyes—to whose gratuitous favour, enriching her with all grace and merit, all this was due. In these words, the Angel expresses what was omitted in the words, "*full of grace*," viz., that it was in the eyes of *God*, she was so.

31. The Angel now shows the effect of her being thus singularly pleasing to God, and also furnishes a proof demonstrating how she was blessed beyond all other women. "*Behold thou shalt conceive.*" "*Behold*," points to something new and unexpected, which was to occur at once. It also points to the fulfilment of the Prophecy of Isaias, and conveys that she was the virgin referred to by Isaias seven hundred years before. "*Behold a virgin shall conceive*," &c. (Isaias vii. 14.) "*Thou shalt conceive*," "*Thou shalt bring forth*," "*Thou shalt call*," &c., are the identical words employed in the Prophecy of Isaias, with a change of person.

"*In thy womb*," to show there was question of real, physical conception of Him as a child, whom she had long borne in her heart. It shows, our Lord took real flesh in the chaste womb of the Virgin, as happens in all other conceptions in the womb of a woman.

"*And bring forth a son*," who, in virtue of His conception and birth, shall be really your son, and you really His mother. "*And thou shalt call His name Jesus.*" Thou, preferably to Joseph, as thou art His real mother, and He has no father on earth (see Matthew i. 23).

32. "*He shall be great.*" By the union of the human nature with the Divinity at His conception and Incarnation, "*He shall be great*" by nature; that is, He shall be absolutely and intrinsically, the greatest human being in existence, being Himself God as well as man. Unlike John, who was "*great before the Lord*" (v. 15), He Himself shall be that Lord who conferred limited greatness on John.

"*And shall be called the Son of the Most High.*" He shall really be and shall be recognised and proclaimed, both in life and death, but especially after His glorious Resurrection and Ascension, by angels, men, and devils, the Eternal Son of God.

"*And the Lord God shall give unto Him.*" He shall not obtain it by violence, tyranny, conquest. or unjust means of any kind, but He shall receive from the Lord Himself, "*through whom kings reign*," the peaceable and abiding possession, as legitimate heir, of, "*the throne of David his father*," that is, the throne promised to David, and given to him in his seed, Christ (Psa. cxxxi. 11; 2 Kings vii. 12; Isaias ix. 6, 7 ; Amos ix. 14), not the temporal throne, on which Christ did not sit, now transferred to a stranger, Herod, but the spiritual throne, of which David's temporal throne was a mere type, a mere shadow. Hence, Christ is often called "*David*" by the Prophets (Jeremias xxx. 9; Ezechiel xxxiv. 23; xxxvii. 24, 25; Osee iii. 5). No doubt, the Blessed Virgin was well acquainted with these promises; and hence, as all the Jewish people were at this time expecting the Messiah, who was to restore and raise up the throne of David (Mark xi. 10), that had by this time passed into the hands of strangers, she at once concluded that the Angel referred to His coming. Our Lord was said, in another sense, to sit on the throne of David, inasmuch as His reign was, in the first place, to commence with those, over whom, David, from whom he and they had sprung, had reigned—"*the lost sheep of the house of Israel*"— and from them to extend to all the tribes of the earth.

"*His father.*" Our Lord was the lineal descendant of David. In Him, the promises made to David were to be fulfilled.

"*And He shall reign in the house of Jacob.*" His reign will not be confined to merely two tribes, as happened some of David's successors. It shall comprise the twelve tribes of Israel, the sons of Jacob. It shall also embrace the spiritual Israel, who are to be aggregated to the Church from all nations to the end of time (Apoc. iv. 7-9). Jew and Gentile shall be united under Him (Osee i. 11).

This power was granted the Man-God at His conception, partly, exercised in life, but consummated after His glorious Ascension, when He sat at the right hand of His Father in glory.

"*For ever.*" Unlike David, who reigned only forty years; whose kingdom after him was subject to division, casualties and interruptions, and at length ceased in the days of Herod, He shall reign of Himself, and not through successors like David. The duration of His reign shall be eternal, not waiting to be succeeded by a better. It shall be absolute, and not contingent and conditional, like David's (Psa. cxxxi. 12).

33. "*And of His Kingdom there shall be no end,*" more fully explains and corro-

borates, "*for ever*." It shall never terminate either as to the Ruler or His subjects, either in this world or in the world to come. This was the eternal duration promised to David in his seed, Christ (Psa. lxxxviii. 4, 5, 30, 36, 37; Daniel ii. 44; vii. 14).

34. "*And Mary said to the Angel*"—she now knew him to be an Angel from God— "*How shall this be done?*" This question she puts not from a feeling of unbelief or distrust, like Zachary, who said, "*How am I to know this?*" or, what sign do you give me of this event regarding which I entertain some doubts? Mary did not doubt. She fully believed, "*blessed art thou that hast believed*" (v. 45). She sought for no sign. She only prudently wished to know the order of the compliance which was sought from her (Ven. Bede). She believed the announcement, but only doubted in regard to its accomplishment, consistently with her vow of chastity known to God, of whom Gabriel was the messenger accredited to her.

"*Because I know not man*," viz., her husband Joseph, or any other. These words convey, that she *would not*, or rather *could not*, consistently with her duty to God, know him; otherwise, supposing it to be lawful for her to know him at any time, as it was hereafter she was to conceive, "*thou shalt conceive*," there would be no meaning in her question, since the Angel might rejoin; you can for the purpose of conception know him hereafter. The present tense, "*I know not*," embraces all time, past, present, and future. Thus we say of a man, who resolves not to drink wine either now or at any future time, *he does not drink wine*. In the present instance, the words have a future reference. For, the Angel does not say, "*thou dost now conceive*," but, "*thou shalt conceive*," arising from future agency. The Holy Fathers and Commentators infer from this, that Mary had made a perpetual vow of virginity. Indeed, this is implied in the question, "*how shall this be done?*" since such a vow is the only thing that would make it impossible in a moral sense, that is to say, unlawful for her to conceive of her husband in the ordinary way (there being no precept or law to inhibit it); the only thing that could secure inviolably her firm purpose to observe the virtue of chastity. When it was she made this vow, which is also attested by a most certain ecclesiastical tradition, is uncertain. It is most likely, before her espousals—as is maintained by St. Augustine—and that having apprized the chaste Joseph of it, she engaged in marriage with him on the condition of securing her chastity. It was not the custom with the Hebrews to make such vows. Hence, Mary espoused Joseph, who, far from attempting to deprive her of what she vowed, would rather guard and protect her against any attempts on the part of others. She fully believed the words of the Angel, from whom she clearly learned that she was to be the mother of the long-expected Messiah. She knew that she had vowed chastity to God. She also knew that "*a virgin was to conceive and bring forth a Son.*" (Isaias vii.) Hence, she inquires, not from curiosity, but from an anxiety to know, the order of divine economy in the accomplishment of an event in which she herself was to be prominently instrumental, and also from a feeling of anxiety lest she might suffer in chastity. She continued an Immaculate Virgin, *etiam post partum*. "She read," says St. Ambrose, "behold a virgin shall conceive, but *how*, she had not hitherto read." "How great must have been the Virgin's love for chastity, since for its preservation, she would forfeit the most exalted dignity of Mother of God" (St. Anselm). It was only after the assurance that her virginity would be intact, she consented, "*Ecce ancilla Domini*," &c.

35. The Angel now informs her of the mode in which the mystery can be accomplished without detriment to her virginity, and thus calms her apprehensions on that

head. "*The Holy Ghost*"—whom thou hast already with thee, by the superabundance of grace, producing in thee effects different from fecundity, which He is now to superadd— '*shall come upon thee.*" Shall descend from Heaven, to impart to thee new efficacy, fecundity, and miraculous powers of conception.

"*And the power of the Most High shall overshadow thee.*" These words are explanatory of the preceding, showing the peculiar way in which the Holy Ghost was to descend on her, viz., by His Almighty power, imparting to her the efficacy of conceiving a Son in her womb, without passion or carnal corruption of any kind, chastely supplying the place usually assigned to man in human conception, forming out of the chaste blood of the Virgin a perfect human body, into which was simultaneously infused a created soul, and at one and the same indivisible instant, both body and soul, perfect man, united under one personality to the Divine Person of the Eternal Word. The peculiar metaphorical meaning of επισκιασει, "*overshadow*," as expressive of this wonderful conception by the Virgin through the power of the Holy Ghost, is differently explained by Commentators. Literally, the word means, to *overshadow*, to *surround*, to assist and exert an influence, as here. Some explain it: the Holy Ghost shall invisibly and mysteriously accomplish this in such a way, that no one can perceive it, just as a cloud prevents us from seeing beyond it. Others explain it thus: as the clouds discharge rain and fertilize the earth, so shall the Almighty power of God render thee fruitful, and cause thee to conceive in thy womb. But whatever may be the peculiar reason for using the word, "*overshadow*," one thing is clearly denoted by it, viz., that the Holy Ghost will miraculously cause her to conceive a son in her womb without human intervention or carnal corruption of any sort. Although the Incarnation of the Son of God is common to the entire Blessed Trinity, as being an *actus ad extra*, it is by appropriation ascribed to the Holy Ghost, as being an act of boundless love, just as acts of wisdom are appropriated to the Son; of power, to the Father.

"*And therefore also the Holy, which shall be born of thee,*" &c. The Greek for "*born*" is γεννωμενον, what *is* born or rather conceived; for it is of the conception by the Virgin the Angel is treating. The present is employed, as the conception is to take place immediately, and is virtually present. "*The Holy*" is used in the neuter άγιον, *sanctum*, to convey, that, taken in its total comprehension, this holy offspring, would not merely be man, but God also. (St. Gregory, St. Leo, &c.) The masculine, *qui*, would naturally refer to man. The words mean: therefore, in virtue of this pure operation of the Holy Ghost, without the intervention of man, the Being to be conceived, and, in due time, brought forth in this pure and holy way, free from all corruption and defilement, "*shall be*" in reality in consequence of the union of the Divinity with the Humanity, "*the Son of God*," and "*shall be called*," such, shall be proclaimed and acknowledged all over the world, to the end of time, as the Son of God, the same who was begotten of the Father by an eternal generation.

"*Shall be born of thee.*" The words, "*of thee,*" which express the real conception of our Lord in the Virgin's womb, are generally missing in Greek MSS.

36. "*And behold thy cousin Elizabeth,*" &c. The Angel from himself adduces the example of the supernatural and miraculous conception by Elizabeth of the Baptist, not for the purpose of begetting faith in the Blessed Virgin, who had already believed, but only to strengthen her faith in the still more miraculous and exalted privilege of fecundity conferred on herself. God has shown His miraculous power on Elizabeth, who being beyond the age of child bearing, and moreover, barren, could not therefore, naturally conceive a son. As then Elizabeth, old and sterile

conceived against nature; so, the Virgin's humility ought not to shrink from a similar blessing being conferred on herself. As her kinswoman was blessed; so might she also. The Angel refers to the example of Elizabeth, preferably to the miraculous instances of child bearing in past ages—Sara, Rachel, Rebecca, &c., because the example of Elizabeth was present to her, she could see her pregnancy, and did so in a few days; and moreover, being of a domestic and family nature, it would be more apt to affect her.

"*Thy cousin Elizabeth.*" Elizabeth, whose father was of the Tribe of Levi, "*she was of the daughters of Aaron*" (v. 5), might be cousin to Mary, of the Tribe of Juda, inasmuch as one of Elizabeth's parents in the maternal line, might have married a man of the Tribe of Juda, and *vice versa*, which was not prohibited save in case of heiresses. Thus Joiada, High Priest, married Josebeth, of the Tribe of Juda (2 Paralip. xxii. 11), David married Michol, daughter of King Saul, of the Tribe of Benjamin.

"*This is the sixth month.*" She is advanced in her sixth month of pregnancy, which now cannot be concealed. "*That is called barren*," who has been barren, and has been "*called*," and reputed, and well known to be such, by all, so as to go by the name of the *barren* one. And, as she who was remarkable for her barrenness, has conceived a son, and that at a time, when another natural obstacle intervened, viz., old age; there is nothing repugnant in your becoming a mother, still remaining a virgin; since in both cases, it is the effect of the power of God.

37. "*Because with God no word is impossible.*" By "*word*," some understand His promise; He is able to fulfil everything He promises. Others, understand it of a *thing*; a sense quite common in SS. Scriptures. For, with God to say, is to do. Nothing within the range of possibility exceeds His power. Hence, He can as easily bring about miraculously and supernaturally the conception of a son by a virgin, as by an old woman, who was also naturally sterile. If there be any thing, which God cannot do, such as to *deceive*, to *tell a lie*, these are exceptions from the general assertion regarding God's omnipotence; since they are excepted not only by Scripture itself, but by the very nature of things and their absolute repugnance to the attributes of God. Such exceptions, if included within the range of God's omnipotence, would prove God was not omnipotent, but absolutely impotent; since they would prove Him not to be God at all (St. Augustine de Civitate Dei, c. 10, and contra Faustum, Lib. 26, c. 5).

38. It was only after she was informed that this great mystery was to be accomplished by the operation of the Holy Ghost, without detriment to her virginal chastity, she gives her consent, upon which hung the destiny of the world— a consent which Heaven was awaiting with breathless expectation. For, had she refused assent to the words of the Angel, most probably, the world would never have been redeemed.

"*Behold the handmaid of the Lord.*" "*Behold,*" here I am ready for the divine command—a form usual among the Jews. Behold I am at hand, "*the handmaid of the Lord,*" ready, at His disposal, to be dealt with, as He pleases, placing myself and my services in His hand. *He is my Sovereign Lord*, having full power, control and authority over me; *I am His servant*. All the singular gifts and priceless privileges already conferred, and still destined for me, are His, the gifts of His grace and Sovereign beneficence. I surrender myself into His hands. I give myself over to His will; let Him do with me what He pleases. "*Behold,*" &c., may also mean, I acknowledge myself as the "*handmaid of the Lord,*" and therefore, bound not to disobey or contradict, but to execute His will; or, I offer myself to the Lord, to act as His obedient handmaid. I even wish that what He proposes be done. *"Be it done unto me according to thy word."* In the depth of her humility, she refrains from recounting the things spoken to her by the Angel, so full of her praises: she merely sums up all in the brief phrase, *"according to thy word,"* as thou hast stated or promised, I am ready to become Mother of God, my chastity being secured. Undoubtedly, the Virgin, specially enlightened from above, understood fully the nature of the Angel's announcement and message. What an example of humility the Virgin leaves us here! She is addressed, as *"full of grace,"* destined to become Mother of God; she calls herself, *His handmaid;* of obedience, ready as His handmaid to do what God pleases; of modesty, charity and thorough resignation to the Divine will.

No sooner had she uttered those words of consent, than the Holy Ghost formed out of her pure blood in her chaste womb, a body, perfectly and in every respect organized, which at the same indivisible instant was animated by a created rational soul; and at one and the same instant, this body and soul, perfect man, was united to the Person of the Divine Word, before it began to subsist by human personality. For it subsisted in the Personality of the Son of God alone. It had no human personality, but only the Personality of the Eternal Son of God, who became united not to the human *Person*—for there was no such—but to the human *nature* of Christ. It was *after* the Virgin uttered those words, and not *before*, the mystery of the Incarnation took place, as is clear from the entire context. Almighty God, who disposes all things sweetly, was pleased to await the Virgin's consent, before His Eternal Son took flesh of her. Had she refused, it is hard to say, what might have become of the human race. How the Powers of Heaven must have hung with awful, wonderful suspense upon the expression of the Virgin's consent; and how much are we indebted to her whose consent to the will of Heaven has been instrumental in procuring for us the ineffable blessings of Redemption! At the Almighty's original *"fiat"* the first creation sprang into existence. On the Virgin's *"fiat,"* was made to depend the second and more sublime Creation in the work of Redemption, and reparation of the blighting evils entailed by sin on the original creation.

" And the Angel departed from her," having now successfully discharged his mission, which concluded with the ineffable Mystery of the Incarnation of the Son of God. It is piously believed, that the Angel on bended knees addressed the Virgin; by this reverential posture, paying homage to her, who was in the designs of God, destined to become soon the Mother of God, and Queen of the whole hosts of Heaven.

TEXT.

39. *And Mary rising up in those days, went into the hill country with haste, into a city of Juda.*

40. *And she entered into the house of Zachary, and saluted Elizabeth.*

41. *And it came to pass; that when Elizabeth heard the salutation of Mary, the infant leaped in her womb. And Elizabeth was filled with the Holy Ghost:*

42. *And she cried out with a loud voice, and said: Blessed art thou among women, and blessed is the fruit of thy womb.*

43. *And whence is this to me, that the mother of my Lord should come to me?*

44. *For behold as soon as the voice of thy salutation sounded in my ears, the infant in my womb leaped for joy.*

45. *And blessed art thou that hast believed, because those things shall be accomplished that were spoken to thee by the Lord.*

COMMENTARY.

39. "*And Mary rising up in those days, went with haste,*" &c. "*Rising up,*" means, preparing herself with great earnestness. "*In those days.*" It is commonly thought she did not proceed on her journey immediately after the departure of the Angel, and the Incarnation of the Son of God, but that she devoted a few days to fervent prayer and meditation, and humble thanksgiving for the wonderful things God was pleased to do for and through her. This is conveyed in the words, "*in those days.*" "*Went with haste.*" She did not loiter on the way, or indulge in idle conversations. The words express the burning love and fervent charity which animated her, in the performance of the duty she proposed to herself, "*nesci't tarda molimina gratia spiritus sancti*" (St. Ambrose). The grace of the Holy Ghost knows no such thing as tardy exertions or preparation. "*Into the hill country, into a city of Juda.*" This is generally supposed to be, not Jerusalem, which, though built on a hill, was not in the hilly district, and was in the Tribe of Benjamin; but Hebron, a sacerdotal city assigned to the sons of Aaron (Josue xxi. 11), distant from Nazareth, where the Virgin abode, about 80 miles, or four days' journey. For, Jerusalem was distant from Nazareth three days' journey. Others, with Patrizzi (Lib. iii., Dissert. x. c. 1), say reference is made to *Juta*, a sacerdotal city in the mountains (Josue xv. 55), the difference in the reading, as regards both *Juda* and *Juta*, being very trifling. *Juta* being an obscure place in the time of St. Luke, the locality of it is mentioned, "*the hill country.*" St. Luke invariably puts the proper name of any city he speaks of in apposition to the common noun; thus we have "*the city of Nazareth,*" *i.e.* called Nazareth; "*the city of Joppe,*" *i.e.* the city called Joppe (Acts xi. 5); "*the city of Thalassa*" (xxvii. 8).

This visit of the Blessed Virgin is generally supposed to have for object to congratulate her kinswoman, Elizabeth, on the great blessing conferred on both, and to discharge the pious office of attending on her who was so many years her senior in point of years. It is also supposed, she was impelled to this by the Spirit of God, in order that John might be filled with the Holy Ghost, as the Angel promised (*v.* 15), by the presence of his Lord, and that Elizabeth and John might both testify to the Incarnation of the Son of God. What an example of humility, as well as of charity is set before us here by the Blessed Virgin! The mother of the Creator, the Queen of Angels and of men, visits her inferior and performs the offices of Charity towards her! It was not any doubts she entertained regarding the promise of the Angel, that prompted her to go and see if things happened in regard to Elizabeth, as the Angel declared; nor was it the mere desire to visit a kinswoman, as Theophylact and others seem to maintain; nor was it feelings of curiosity either. No. "She went into the hill country," says St. Ambrose, *hic*—"not as incredulous in regard to the oracle; nor as uncertain regarding the declaration made to her; nor as doubtful in regard to the fact adduced in confirmation of it; but, rejoicing in the accomplishment of her desire, religiously intent on discharging a duty imposed by kindred, and hastening on her way under the impulse of joy." It is conjectured by some, that she was accompanied on her journey by her chaste spouse, Joseph, or at least by some female companion. As the Pasch was close at hand, Joseph likely went up with her as far as Jerusalem, which was on the way from Nazareth to Hebron. It may be, he remained there, and thus did not witness the salutation of Elizabeth, and thereby learn the pregnancy of the Virgin, which cost him afterwards so much mental anguish and uncertainty; or, if he went the whole way to Hebron, God arranged, for His own wise ends, that something prevented him from witnessing the meeting of these singularly holy women.

40. "*The house of Zachary*," which was in the city of Juda, referred to, whether Hebron or Juta, or whatever city it was.

"*And saluted Elizabeth*." The Virgin, as younger in point of years, showed her respect for Elizabeth, her senior, by saluting her first. "The more chaste a virgin is, the more humble should she be, and ready to give way to her elders" (Theophylact). Zachary, being deaf and dumb, was not a subject for salutation. Hence, she saluted Elizabeth, or, Zachary might have been absent.

41. "*And it came to pass.*" The Evangelist uses these words to convey that he was about to relate something unusual and extraordinary.

"*That when Elizabeth heard the salutation of Mary*," &c. The effect caused by the Virgin's salutation was twofold—the infant in his mother's womb, and Elizabeth herself were filled with the Holy Ghost. "She first heard the voice of the Virgin; but, the infant was the first to feel the grace; she heard in a natural way, he leaped with joy on account of the mystery; she perceived the arrival of Mary, he became sensible of the presence of the Lord" (St. Ambrose). He was the more worthy, as being destined to be the precursor of the Son of God; and it was to him, as such, the voice of the Virgin was, by divine impulse, first and chiefly addressed. Now, was verified the promise of the Angel that "*from his mother's womb, he would be filled with the Holy Ghost*" (v. 15), and through him his mother also was filled with the same Spirit. It is clear it is to the same Spirit, viz., Holy Ghost, reference is made in both places. Elizabeth herself attributes this, not to any natural cause, arising from advanced pregnancy; but, to the salutation of the Virgin, and this the Evangelist wishes to convey here. "*When Elizabeth heard the salutation*," the effects described followed.

"*The infant leaped.*" The Greek for "*leap*," ἐσκίρτησεν, means, to "*bound*," as young animals do. But it is afterwards said, he did so "*for joy*" (v. 44). Hence it is commonly held by the Fathers, that this was the effect of miraculous interposition, and not of natural excitement, since it is attributed solely to the salutation and voice of the Virgin—and also, that John was gifted with reason, at least in this passing away, although St. Augustine is of a contrary opinion, and says the effect was produced, "*divinitus in infante, non humanitus ab infante.*" However, the former opinion is the more common, as "*joy*" supposes knowledge. Whether he continued to enjoy the use of reason during the remaining three months in his mother's womb, and during his infancy, must be a mere conjectural matter, regarding which there is a great diversity of opinion. It is commonly held that the Baptist was, on this occasion, cleansed from original sin. The Evangelist carefully notes that the joyous greeting of the infant was prior to the effect it caused in Elizabeth, filling her with the Holy Ghost, which she would seem to have received out of the abundance divinely bestowed on her infant, the order of grace thus reversing the order of nature, in which it is the mother that imparts the vital spirit to the infant shut up in her womb; here, on the contrary, it was from the infant the spirit of grace was communicated to the mother.

"*And Elizabeth was filled with the Holy Ghost.*" The gifts of the Holy Ghost were now bestowed on her in greater abundance—"*filled*," &c. (for, being just, she had the Holy Ghost already residing within her)—and had the effect of bestowing on her a clear knowledge of the cause of the infant's rejoicing and of the Mystery of the Incarnation. They conferred on her also supernatural knowledge (as Ven. Bede remarks, as well as St. Gregory, Hom. i. in Ezechiel) in regard to the past, present and future—the *past*, "*blessed art thou that hast believed*"—evidently showing, she knew the words addressed to Mary by the Angel—the *present*, "*the mother of my Lord*," &c. (v. 43), thus showing, she knew the Son of God was borne in Mary's womb. She also knew the meaning of the exultation of the infant in her own womb; and the *future*, "*those things shall be accomplished*," &c. (v. 45), predicting as certain the accomplishment in due time of the Angel's promises.

42. "*And she cried out with a loud voice*," &c., from the evident impulse and inspiration of the Holy Ghost, with whom she was filled; and from admiration of the wonderful mysteries revealed to her, owing to which she could not contain herself, even in the presence of the Son of God and His Blessed Mother, crying out with a loud voice, in the very words in which the Angel had before addressed the Blessed Virgin, from the inspiration of the same Holy Spirit, "who," as St. Ambrose observes, "never forgets His own words" (Lib. 2, in Lucam). "*Blessed art thou amongst women.*" "*Blessed*" by God, in His wonderful gifts. It does not refer to her future praises by men. "*Amongst*," &c.—before, or above, all other women, as you are virgin and mother at the same time—mother, not of a mere man, but mother of God. The pregnancy of the Virgin, at this early stage, could be known to Elizabeth only from the revelation of the Holy Ghost.

"*And blessed is the fruit of thy womb.*" "*And*," has the force of the causal particle, *because* her blessedness arose from the great privilege of Divine maternity. "*The fruit of thy womb*," shows our Blessed Lord was really conceived and begotten of her, as mother. These words allude to the promise made to David regarding Him—"*De fructu ventris tui ponam super sedem tuam*" (Psalm cxxxi. 11); and she uses this form of expression rather than, Blessed is the Son you have conceived; because this Son was still in her womb. Mary is said to be blessed beyond all other women, but her Son is said to be "blessed" *absolutely*, without any comparison with others, as God, essentially so; as man, owing to the wonderful mystery of his Incarnation, wherein the human nature of our Lord was hypostatically united to the Person of the Divine Word. In these words is shown, that all the blessings conferred on the Virgin were traceable to her having been made Mother of God. From Him, all her blessedness flows. She was blessed and filled with grace in a limited degree, but He, superabundantly—"*Of His fulness we have all received*" (John i. 6). "By a double miracle, the mothers prophesy by the spirit of their infants" (St. Ambrose).

43. "*And whence is this to me?*" &c. How could such wonderful felicity fall to the lot of one so unworthy of it? It is solely the effect of the Divine goodness and condescension. These words by no means argue ignorance on the part of Elizabeth, but only her great humility, and her admiration of the wonderful mystery wrought in Mary, and a deep sense of her unworthiness to be visited by one, who was exalted to the sublimest dignity of Mother of God.

"*That the mother of my Lord,*" &c. That one so exalted "*should come to me*," who am so unworthy of such a privilege. "*Of my Lord*," the Word Incarnate now in her sacred womb. He had been, therefore, by this time united to the human nature. Hence, the Blessed Virgin has been properly called, *Theoticos*. These words of Elizabeth to Mary are very similar to those addressed by the son of Elizabeth to the Son of Mary (Matthew iii. 14). By calling this infant, still shut in his mother's womb, her "*Lord,*" Elizabeth plainly conveyed, that she regarded Him as the Eternal Son of God, as also did David, when he said, "*The Lord said to my Lord*" which is applied by our Redeemer Himself to the Messiah (Matthew xxii. 44).

44. From the exultation of the infant in her womb, the instant the voice of Mary reached her ears, even before she could grasp the meaning of her words, Elizabeth, enlightened by the grace of the Holy Ghost for this end, at once concludes, that the Virgin bore in her womb the Eternal Son of God, whose precursor saluted Him by anticipation from her own womb. While interiorly enlightening the mind of Elizabeth with His grace, which alone could give her the certain knowledge of the great event referred to, the Holy Ghost also wished to give an external corroborative sign, in the leaping of the infant in her womb, which, as Elizabeth conveys, resulted from the salutation of Mary, and was a certain sign of the presence of the Son of God.

45. "*Blessed art thou that believest.*" Hence, unlike Zachary, who was punished for his hesitation and unbelief, with which the faith of Mary is here contrasted, Mary firmly believed all the Angel told her from the beginning. Elizabeth here attributes the blessings to be conferred on Mary to her faith, as the beginning and root of justification; but not to her faith only.

"*Because those things shall be accomplished,*" &c. Some of the things promised her by the Angel were already accomplished. "*Thou shalt conceive,*" &c. This portion was accomplished, as she had now conceived. "*He shall be great,*" &c. This and all the other privileges resulting from it shall be conferred in due time.

"*Spoken to thee by the Lord,*" viz., by the Angel on the part of the Lord, as already referred to in the salutation (vv. 31-33). It is held by some that the words, "*because these things shall be accomplished,*" &c., were the object of Mary's faith, thus immediately connecting them with "*believed*"—she believed that they would be accomplished. Others, more probably, say that they are the *cause* of her blessedness. She was blessed on account of the things which she believed would surely happen. The analogy of ὅτι favours this opinion (See Matthew v. 3-10; Luke vi. 20, 21).

TEXT.

46. And Mary said: *My soul doth magnify the Lord:*
47. *And my spirit hath rejoiced in God my Saviour.*
48. *Because he hath regarded the humility of his hand-maid; for behold from henceforth all generations shall call me blessed.*
49. *Because he that is mighty hath done great things to me: and holy is his name.*
50. *And his mercy is from generation unto generations, to them that fear him.*
51. *He hath shewed might in his arm: he hath scattered the proud in the conceit of their heart.*
52. *He hath put down the mighty from their seat, and hath exalted the humble.*
53. *He hath filled the hungry with good things: and the rich he hath sent empty away.*
54. *He hath received Israel his servant, being mindful of his mercy.*
55. *As he spoke to our fathers, to Abraham and to his seed for ever.*

COMMENTARY.

46. "*And Mary said,*" &c. Seeing the praises bestowed on her by the Angel, and the repetition of the same by Elizabeth, Mary, who was "*full of grace,*" and now bore in her sacred womb, the great fountain of all grace, of whom, therefore, it is not said, on the occasion of the following inspired Canticle, as was said of Elizabeth, that she "*was filled with the Holy Ghost,*" because utterly unnecessary, now, in the fulness of her humility, refers all she possessed, as was meet, to the proper source, Almighty God, from whom all she had was received. As if she said, Elizabeth, you praise me,

you congratulate me on the wonderful things God has been pleased to do for me. But knowing, that of myself, I am and have nothing; that all these come to me from the infinite bounty of God; I do, therefore, in the fulness of truth, and with the deepest feelings of gratitude, extol His goodness and merciful bounty.

This Canticle, the first of the New Testament, and the most perfect ever composed or uttered, is not unlike that of Anna, the mother of Samuel, uttered under similar circumstances: "*My heart hath rejoiced in the Lord, and my horn is exalted in my God*," &c. (1 Kings ii. 1, &c.) It may be said to consist of three parts. In the first, from *v.* 46, to *v.* 50, the Virgin recounts the singular benefits conferred on herself, and blesses God for them, above all, for the conception of the Son of God in her womb. In the second part, *vv.* 50-54, she praises God for the blessings bestowed on the entire Jewish people, at all times, before the advent of the Son of God, making special allusion to the victories of God's people over Pharaoh, and the Chanaanite nations. In the third part, *vv.* 54, 55, she refers again to the mystery of the Incarnation, promised of old to the Fathers.

"*My soul*," that is, I myself. She prefers using the term, "*my soul*," to convey that her praises, and the ardent expression of her gratitude, proceeded from her inmost soul, and all its faculties; from feelings the most intense; from all her strength; from her whole intellect, memory, will; from all the spiritual faculties of her mind; from all the senses of her body; from her tongue, to speak of Him only; her hands, to work for Him only; her feet, to lead and conduct only to Him. In the same sense did David say (Psalm cii. 1), "*Benedic anima mea Domino, et omnia quæ intra me sunt, nomini sancto ejus.*" Some Commentators distinguish between *soul* ("*anima mea*"), and *spirit* ("*spiritus meus*"), next verse, as if the former referred to the inferior faculties of the soul, ψυχη; the latter, to the superior, πνευμα—a signification the words naturally bear (see 1 Cor. ii. 15, Commentary on). Others understand "*soul*," of her intellect; "*spirit*," of her will. But, most likely, they both refer to the same thing, which is repeated in different words, in accordance with Hebrew usage. Hence, they both express the soul, with all its faculties. Nor is there any reason for saying of the "*soul*," that it "*magnifies*," and of the "*spirit*," that it "*exulteth*," since we find it said of the soul elsewhere, that it exulteth, "*anima mea exultabit in Domino*" (Psalm xxxiv. 9), and, "*exultabit anima mea in Deo meo*" (Isaias lxi. 10). It may, however, be that the one refers to the inferior part of the soul, as it considers natural things; the other, to the superior part, as it considers things celestial and supernatural. "*My heart and my flesh have rejoiced in the living God*" (Psalm lxxxiii. 2).

"*Doth magnify*," that is, proclaims His praises, extols His attributes, His sovereign majesty, magnificence, omnipotence, sanctity, wisdom, bounty, &c. As man cannot add to, or take away from, God's greatness, all he can do is to proclaim His attributes to the world, just as His "Name is sanctified" by us; when, on the other hand, God magnifies man, He actually makes him great by bestowing on him honours, riches, extended rule, &c.

"*The Lord.*" The Holy Trinity, to whom alone all praise is due, as it is the Holy Trinity that confers all blessings in the order of nature and grace. The term, "*Lord*," conveys the idea of His majesty and power. All that creatures, however exalted, whether on earth or in heaven, either possess, or expect to possess, whether gifts of nature, of grace, or of glory, are *received*. They come from God alone, from whose heavenly throne above every good gift descends on creatures (St. James i. 17).

47. "*Hath rejoiced*," from the very moment of the Incarnation, and still rejoices, or, as the Greek word, ἠγαλλίασεν, conveys, *bounds*, *leaps* with exultation, not as if

my singular privileges came from myself, but from "*God, my Saviour.*" This is an allusion to Habacuc (iii. 18), "*I will joy in God, my Jesus.*" In the word "*Lord,*" God is represented as exercising power, displaying majesty. Here the Virgin represents Him under a different aspect, as, bountiful, beneficent in bestowing the greatest blessings. He was the Saviour of all men; but, she exhibits Him as bestowing salvation on herself.

48. "*Because He hath regarded,*" &c. Here the Virgin gives the reason of her rejoicing in her God and Saviour, because, He who is the most exalted, the Supreme, Sovereign Being, had, out of His infinite condescension, "*regarded,*" looked upon her with feelings of infinite favour, bestowing upon her such an abundance of gifts, commencing with her Immaculate Conception, and ending with her final, triumphant assumption into glory, as rendered her singularly privileged far beyond the rest of creation, whether on earth or in heaven.

"*The humility of His handmaid,*" which means His most abject handmaid, whose lowly condition, compared with His exalted nature and lofty dominion, is exceedingly great (Genesis xxvi. 32; Esther xv. 2; Judith vi. 15; Philip. iii. 21). The word, "*humility,*" is understood by some, of the virtue of humility, for which the Virgin was greatly distinguished. But, although the Virgin excelled in humility, as opposed to pride, as she did in all other virtues; still, it is unlikely she would credit herself with humility, or make it the subject of boasting. Moreover, the Greek word ταπεινωσιν, means abjection, lowliness of condition. The Greek for humility as a virtue is, ταπεινωφροσυνη. Hence, the Blessed Virgin proclaims her humility not in words, as this might savour of pride; but in deed, by loudly proclaiming her abject unworthiness, which rendered her undeserving of the exalted dignity to which she was now raised by God. For, although she makes no express mention of it, she clearly implies the peculiar way in which God was pleased "to regard" her and exalt her to the sublime dignity of Mother of God. Though full of grace and merits, the Blessed Virgin might still in truth proclaim her unworthiness, looking to her own nature, looking merely to herself, without the grace of God, to which alone every thing good she possessed, was due; and also comparing herself, however exalted, with the supreme, uncreated Majesty of God.

"*The humility of His handmaid,*" then means His most abject, unworthy, handmaid, as if "*handmaid*" did not of itself sufficiently express her lowliness of estate, imitating David, who says, he was not only "*His servant, but the Son of His handmaid*" (Psalm cxv. 7). She uses the word "*humility,*" to express still more, that she was His lowly, humble handmaid. Similar is the form (Apocalypse xvii. 1), "*the condemnation of the harlot,*" meaning the condemned harlot.

"*For behold from henceforth,*" &c. The Virgin here assigns the reason why she should regard herself as specially favoured by God, and raised from a vile, abject, lowly condition, to the most exalted dignity. From this day forward, to the end of time, not only the Angel Gabriel, not only Elizabeth, but all generations of men, Jew and Gentile, without exception or distinction, who are to believe in my Son, as the Eternal Son of the Eternal Father (for, it is of the generations of believers only she speaks) shall, on account of the great dignity of Mother of God bestowed on me, pronounce me "*Blessed,*" shall treat me as such, shall honour me, and confidently have recourse to my powerful patronage in their necessities.

This inspired prophecy of the Blessed Virgin regarding the honour and reverence all generations of believers were to pay her as long as the Church lasts on earth, that is to say, to the final end of all things—"*all generations*"—has been verified from the beginning. Next to her Divine Son Jesus, the Blessed Virgin has been the most cherished and beloved object of Christian love and veneration. The honour and veneration paid to her—while infinitely below the *cultus latriæ* due to God, and to Him alone, as Sovereign Lord and Master—is still far superior to that shown to all the other saints. The worship paid to them is termed *cultus duliæ*—or the worship paid to the *servants*. Hers, *hyperduliæ*, a worship in degree far beyond that paid to them, became proportioned to her exalted dignity of Mother of God, also to her transcendent merits, and to the singular graces bestowed upon her, which far exceeded those of all the angels and saints together.

If, then, it be true, that all generations of believers, of whom alone there can be question here, are to call her Blessed, and treat her as such,—and it must be so, unless the oracles of God are falsified—it follows, as a most necessary logical consequence, that those who dishonour her, who omit reverencing her, whose religious tenets teach them to undervalue her, and not proclaim her singularly "*blessed*," and deserving of the highest honour that can be paid to any creature, must not belong to the generation of believers—and almost all heretics, from the beginning, gloried in decrying the Mother of God. It also follows most logically, that every system of religious teaching must be false which does not enjoin on its followers to honour her,—and this is the leading distinguishing characteristic of all systems of religion outside the Catholic Church. Hence, we may infer that devotion to the Blessed Virgin is, at least, a clear, negative *note* or mark of God's Church. Let those who fail to show the Blessed Virgin due honour and respect, tremble at this prophecy, emanating from the Spirit of God, which excludes them from the society of the faithful followers of Jesus Christ.

49. "*He that is mighty.*" The Greek—ὁ δυνατος—means, the Mighty One, the Almighty, "*hath done great things in me.*" Most Greek copies for "*great*," have μεγαλεια, *wonderful, ineffable* things. She refers to the great and ineffable blessings, the abundant fulness of grace conferred on her, but especially to the crowning favour, the highest of all, in being raised to the singularly exalted dignity of Mother of God. In this, the Virgin assigns the cause, why she is to be proclaimed "*Blessed*," honoured, revered, invoked by all generations, to the end of time. The Virgin chiefly refers to the dignity, lately conferred on her, of bearing in her chaste womb the Son of God. But this, although known to Elizabeth, as it was to be hereafter known to all the faithful followers of her Son, and celebrated by them, was too ineffable for her to give expression to it, in the fulness of her humility and virginal modesty, thus, in a certain sense, verifying the words, "*generationem ejus qui enarrabit*"? (Isaias liii. 8).

"*And holy is His name.*" The *name* of God is the same as God Himself. One of His attributes is essential holiness. This is what the angelic song unceasingly celebrates: "*Holy, holy, holy, the Lord God of hosts*" (Isaias vi. 3). Everywhere the Scriptures proclaim Him as "*the Holy One of Israel.*" Hence, our Lord teaches us always to pray, "*Hallowed be Thy name*" (Matthew vi. 9, see Commentary on). The Blessed Virgin, after referring to the power of God displayed in the great work of the Incarnation and the conception of our Lord in her chaste womb—hence, calling Him "*Lord*," "*Who is Mighty*"—now refers to His great sanctity displayed in connexion with the same great work. Everything in it was pure and holy—the conception from the Holy Ghost, the conception of a pure virgin, "*full of grace,*" sanctified and free from all sin, by His grace. She, therefore, calls Him, "*God, her Saviour.*" As it was a work of power, that the Son of God should become man, conceived in the chaste womb of a virgin, so it was also a work of sanctity to prepare the Virgin for so great an event, and render her pure and undefiled. Therefore, as the Virgin knew, she was to be pronounced "*Blessed*" by "all (future) generations," both on account of the conception of the Son of God, and her own sanctity, she wishes to have all referred to the power and sanctity of God, or, as it may rather be said, that, as the Incarnation of the Son of God and the preparation of the Virgin were both the work of God's power, sanctity, and mercy, the Virgin extols His power, sanctity, and mercy (*v*. 50) in reference to both effects.

"*And holy*," &c. *And*, means, *because*. It is because He is uncreated, essential holiness, He brought about such a wonderful effect of holiness, as that His Son— "*the Saint of saints*" (Daniel ix. 24)—should be conceived in my womb, whom He preserved by His grace from all sin and defilement.

50. This is the second part of the Canticle, wherein the Virgin, after extolling God's wonderful goodness and mercy towards herself, extols His goodness towards the entire world. "*And is from generation*," &c. She extols His great "*mercy*," that is, goodness, beneficence, liberality, manifested not alone in favour of her, but at all times, and to all persons, particularly towards those who "*fear*" and obey Him. The Greek for "*from generation unto generation*," is, "*unto generations and generations;*" that is, countless generations of men at all times. He has displayed in my regard, the boundless mercy exhibited in times *past* to our fathers, and He ceases not to manifest it at all times, *present* and *future* as well.

"*To them that fear Him.*" Fear of God, which is "*the beginning of wisdom*," is naturally inspired by His Holy name, which is also "*terrible.*" This *fear* implies obedience, or the observance of His Commandments. Although "*God's mercy is over all His works*," and is extended even to those who show no reverence for Him; still, it is, in a special manner and effectually, displayed in saving and remunerating in the end, those who *obey* Him ; since, obstinate unbelievers and prevaricators shut against themselves the gate of mercy, which they scorn to enter. The words of this verse are almost identical with those of David (Psalm cii. 17), "*And the mercy of the Lord from eternity unto eternity upon them that fear Him.*"

51. *He hath showed might in His arm.*" Having extolled God's merciful clemency and liberality towards those, who fear and obey Him, the Virgin now extols His severity and justice in regard to those who haughtily resist Him. "*Showed might,*" performed mighty, wonderful deeds. "*In His arm.*" The word "*arm*," is here used metaphorically, to denote God's power, as man's strength is in his arm. There is a diversity of opinion regarding the reference contained in the words of this and the following verses. The most probable interpretation of them is, that, like the words of Anna (1 Kings ii. 4, 5), they are general expressions in praise of God's wonderful power exerted against His enemies in past times, as in the case of Pharaoh, through Moses ; of the Channanites, through Josue and the Judges ; of the Philistines, &c., through David. But, under these deeds of power, most likely, the Virgin, in a prophetic spirit, refers to the great deeds of spiritual power, signified by the former, such as the work of the Incarnation and other achievements of spiritual power, as well as the victories to be obtained by Christ ; so that the past and future works of God are included. Here we have a prophecy expressed, after prophetic usage, in words of the past. Some, by "*arm*," understand the Eternal Son of God, by whom, "*all things were made.*" However, the preceding is the more probable interpretation.

"*He hath scattered the proud in the conceit of their hearts.*" "*Conceit*" means.

thoughts. Hence, the words mean : He hath scattered and brought to nought, those haughty men who, esteeming themselves above every one else, attributed all to themselves, trampled under foot and despised all others (Psalm lxxxviii. 11; Isaias li. 9). The words might also mean, if we connect "*conceit of their heart*" with "*scattered,*" is wont to scatter. He turned their own designs against the proud themselves, and caught, and every day catches the wise in their cunning, as He did in the case of Pharaoh following the Hebrews through the Red Sea, and in the case of Joseph's brethren. The words may refer to the proud Jews, whom after having been rendered incredulous by their intolerable pride, He scattered throughout the globe.

52. "*Put down the mighty from their throne.*" The Greek for "*mighty,*" means *Dynasts*, who enjoyed royal state and power, as conveyed by "*throne.*" . "*Put down,*" has also a present and future signification. He *put, puts,* and *will put,* or it may imply a general allusion to time, *He is wont to put down.* The Greek word, καθεῖλεν, conveys the idea of *routing a vanquished foe.* According to some, reference is here made to Saul, Aman, Nebuchodonozor, Vasthi, &c. ; and, in the next words, "*and hath exalted the humble,*" to David, Mordocheus, Daniel, Esther, &c. Others understand them, of the victory over the devils, so powerful before the coming of Christ ; and by "*humble,*" those harassed by them (Theophylact, Cyril, &c.) ; while others understand them of the humiliation and rejection of the Jewish people from being the chosen and beloved people of God, of the rejection of the Jewish priests from their thrones in the sanctuary ; and of the call to the faith of the Gentiles, hitherto of no consideration, and their election to lofty thrones in the kingdom of God's Church here, and of His eternal glory hereafter. Probably, the Virgin refers in general to the power which God always displays in depressing, and humbling the haughty; and to His great mercy usually displayed in raising up and elevating the humble. Such is the ordinary economy of His providence expressed in the words, "*He resists the proud, and gives grace to the humble.*" "*Every one that exalteth himself, shall be humbled, and every one that humbles himself, shall be exalted.*" Similar are the words of David (Psalm cxii. 6); of Anna (1 Kings ii. 7).

53. " *He hath filled the hungry with good things.*" The idea is similar to that in the foregoing, or connected with it. " *Good things,*" in opposition to "*hungry*" and "*empty,*" has reference to food, of course, understood figuratively. The words of this verse may have reference to the benefits bestowed by God on the Hebrews, whom He fed for forty years with manna in the desert, and introduced into the "*land flowing with milk and honey,*" after expelling the Chanaanites, and suffering them to famish from hunger; to Elias, whom He fed through the ministry of an Angel ; to Daniel in the lion's den, to whom He employed Habacuc to carry food ; to the Virgin herself, hungering and thirsting after justice, whom He fed with the abundance of graces in the Word Incarnate, and also to the countless multitudes of the faithful, whom He feeds daily with the Bread of Life in the adorable Eucharist, so that the words employed in the past tense, as has been already observed, have also a present and future signification and reference. Others understand the words of the Jews, who imagining themselves fully justified by the law, and in consequence, sought not justice, were therefore rejected ; while the Gentiles, destitute of grace and justice, were called to the abundant graces and blessings of the Gospel. It may be, that the Virgin does not refer to any particular instance or fact at all ; but, only expresses, in praise of God's wonderful providence, bountiful liberality and justice, what He is *wont* to do. The same may be also applicable to some of the foregoing

declarations made by her. The words of this verse are very similar to those of Anna (1 Kings ii. 5), and of David (Psalm xxxiii. 11).

54. "*He hath received Israel His servant.*" In this, the third part of the Canticle, the Virgin extols the mercy and goodness of God, in bringing about the great mystery of the Incarnation, in the accomplishment of which the chief instruments were from the Jewish nation, and the chief blessings were primarily intended for the carnal descendants of Abraham, to be afterwards extended to all His spiritual children called from among the Gentiles.

"*Received.*" The Greek word, αντελαβετο, literally means, to lay hold of any thing or person in order to support or prop it up, when on the point of falling. Here, it is employed metaphorically, to signify, to protect, to support, to raise up from a state of abject depression.

"*Israel His servant.*" The ancient Jewish people, whom God was wont to call His Son "*because Israel was a child, and I loved him, and I called my Son out of Egypt*" (Osee xi. 1). The Jewish people, when in great straits, were wonderfully rescued and supported by God. He did so of old in the days of Moses, Josue, Samuel, David, Ezechias, Zorobabel, Machabees, &c. ; but, now when in a most abject state, both in a temporal and spiritual point of view, oppressed by Herod, who seized on the sceptre of David, oppressed and harassed spiritually by their religious guides, the Scribes and Pharisees, God comes wonderfully to their rescue, by sending His Son to take flesh in the womb of a virgin, herself of the family of David, whose throne was to be raised up and perpetuated for ever. No doubt, the Virgin refers also to spiritual Israel, who were to be the spiritual sons of Abraham, imitators of his faith. "*Being mindful of His mercy,*" which, considering the condition of the human race, Jew and Gentile, God would seem to have forgotten. ("*His,*" is omitted in most Greek copies). God is said to "*remember mercy,*" when, in addition to ancient mercies, He gives some fresh and striking instance of mercy and goodness.

"*As He spoke to our fathers.*" These words are, according to some, parenthetical; as the phrase, πρὸς τοὺς πατέρας ἡμῶν, *ad patres nostros,* are in the accusative case, and τῷ Αβρααμ, &c., *Abraham et Semini ejus,* in the dative. Hence, according to these commentators, the connexion should be, "being mindful of His mercy . . . to Abraham and his seed (as He had promised our fathers regarding it")." Others say, the verb, ελαλησεν, "*spoke,*" governs a dative or accusative case. Hence, St. Luke changes the construction, putting "*our fathers*" in the accusative; "*Abraham and his seed,*" in the dative, so that thus, the Virgin points out who "*our fathers*" were, to whom God spoke and made promises of great mercy. These were, Abraham, Isaac, Jacob—to whom He said: "*in thy seed shall all the nations of the earth be blessed*" (Genesis xxii. 18); and David, to whom special promises on this head were still more recently made, "*of the fruit of thy womb, I shall set upon Thy throne.*"

"*For ever,*" may affect "*mercy,*" and mean: He promised everlasting, never-ending mercy; or "*seed,*" and would mean, Abraham's seed, who were to be never-failing, to endure,—at least his spiritual offspring,—to the end of ages, and enjoy never-ending glory for all eternity.

TEXT.

56. *And Mary abode with her about three months : and she returned to her own house.*
57. *Now Elizabeth's full time of being delivered was come, and she brought forth a son.*
58. *And her neighbours and kinsfolk heard that the Lord had shewed His great mercy towards her, and they congratulated with her.*

59. *And it came to pass that on the eighth day they came to circumcise the child, and they called him by his father's name Zachary.*
60. *And his mother answering, said: Not so, but he shall be called John.*
61. *And they said to her: There is none of thy kindred that is called by this name.*
62. *And they made signs to his father, how they would have him called.*
63. *And demanding a writing-table, he wrote, saying: John is his name. And they all wondered.*
64. *And immediately his mouth was opened, and his tongue loosed, and he spoke blessing God.*
65. *And fear came upon all their neighbours; and all these things were noised abroad over all the hill-country of Judea.*
66. *And all they that had heard them laid them up in their heart, saying: What an one, think ye, shall this child be? For the hand of the Lord was with him.*

COMMENTARY.

56. "*And Mary abode with her about three months.*" The word, "*about,*" may denote a period greater or less than the term indicated.

"*And returned to her house.*" She did not loiter idly on the way, but went straight home, after having performed the pious offices of friendship and charity towards her relative. It was shortly after this, that Joseph observing signs of pregnancy, suffered so much in mind on her account (Matthew i. 19, 20). The term of Mary's abode in the house of Zachary was, no doubt, spent in pious conversations regarding the mystery of the Incarnation, and in thanking and extolling the ineffable goodness of God, in thus vouchsafing to visit His people, and in assigning to themselves so prominent a part in this wonderful event. It is warmly disputed here, whether Mary remained till the birth of the Baptist. Some maintain, that she remained only till the term of Elizabeth's delivery was near. Their first reason is, that Mary is said to have remained "*about three months;*" and as Elizabeth was gone with child nearly six months, when she came; she did not, therefore, remain the full time. But this reason proves nothing. For, "*about,*" may as well denote *more* as *less*; besides, in some instances, women bring forth before the nine months of gestation are completed. Again, the advocates of the former opinion, say, it was not becoming in a virgin to be present at the birth of a child. But, in reply, it may be said, that Mary was a mother as well as a virgin, and, at this time, she was carrying in her chaste womb the Son of God; besides, it was not necessary she should be present at the time of parturition. She could have remained in some other chamber in Zachary's house at the time. Again, the former say, the narrative of the Evangelist would seem to indicate, that, it was after Mary's departure, Elizabeth brought forth (*v.* 57). But, the Evangelists are wont often to postpone the order or precise date of events, in order to finish some particular narrative, as may be seen from Matthew xxvi., xxvii. St. Luke, then, having commenced the account of the Virgin's visit to Elizabeth, does not interrupt it even by the narration of events which may have occurred in the meantime, until he concludes by narrating her return home. The opposite opinion, which maintains, that the Virgin did not leave till after the birth of the Baptist, seems by far more probable. It consults more for the friendship and charity of the Virgin, to suppose that having remained, up to the eve of her cousin's confinement, she would wait for the happy event of her delivery. Is it likely, that having gone with haste to congratulate Elizabeth, on hearing of her pregnancy, and having remained till almost the last moment, she would leave her cousin under the circumstances? The Evangelist, in referring to her stay of three months, would seem to convey, that she remained till the birth of the Baptist, as Elizabeth was advanced six months in her pregnancy, when the Virgin arrived. Moreover, is it not very likely, that Mary, who knew the destination of the Baptist as the great Precursor of her Son, whom he saluted from his mother's womb, would be anxious to see and embrace this blessed infant, so closely united to her by so many spiritual relations and ties of natural kindred? Hence, this latter opinion seems by far the more probable.

57. While Mary remained with Elizabeth, the time of the latter for bringing forth had come, and she happily gave birth to a son, on the 8th of the Kalends of June, or 24th of June, as is held by the Church, in accordance with the Angel's promise (v. 13). The Evangelist, before describing this in the precise order of time, first concludes the history of the Virgin's Visitation.

58. Her neighbours and kinsfolk heard of the great mercy the Lord had so signally displayed towards Elizabeth, not only in taking away the curse of sterility in her old age; but also in granting her the blessing of a safe delivery, and also granting her a male offspring. Seeing that God's blessing was rendered perfect by her safe delivery, they "*congratulated with her.*" They came to share in her joy, thus verifying the Angel's prediction, that, "*many would rejoice in his nativity*" (v. 14). The Greek for "*congratulate*," συνεχαίρον, means, *they rejoiced together with her.*

59. "*On the eighth day,*" from the birth, the day prescribed by law for the circumcision of an infant (Genesis xvii. 12; Leviticus xii. 3), "*they came to circumcise the child,*" that is, the priests, the friends and neighbours, who wished to honour the occasion. It is most likely, that this occurred in the house of Zachary. For, the mother, it is clear, was present, and she could not leave the house so soon after childbirth, according to the law of Moses (Leviticus xii. 4). We have several examples in Scripture, of this ceremony being performed at home as well as in the synagogues, where infants are circumcised according to modern Jewish usage. See examples of Abraham (Genesis xvii. 23-26), of the son of Moses by Sephora (Exodus iv. 25), of the Jewish people in the desert circumcised by Josue (Josuo v. 3). Many of the Holy Fathers held that one of the effects—nay, the chief effect—of circumcision was, the remission of original sin in the male descendants of Abraham, which was, of course, accompanied with the infusion of sanctifying grace. This opinion seems warranted by Genesis xvii. 14. It was held by St. Augustine (Lib. 16, c. 17 de Civitate Dei; Lib. 4 contra Donatistas, c. 24, Ep. 57, contra Dardanum); Ambrose (Lib. 2 in Lucam); Basil (Hom. 13); Bernard (Sermo 1, de Circumcis. Domini); Innocent III. (C. Majores, &c.)

"*And they called him*"—the Greek, εκαλουν, *were calling*, in the imperfect, is expressive of an attempt, which did not take effect—"*by his father's name, Zachary.*" From this, it appears to have been customary with the Jews to give names to the infants at circumcision, as is done with us at Baptism. Among other reasons, circumcision being a sign of God's covenant, to convey, that they were then aggregated to, and numbered amongst the people of God. God Himself, at circumcision, changed the name of Abraham (Genesis xvii. 5). It also appears, that they were wont to give them the names of their parents, or of some one among their friends or relatives. The Church recommends to give infants the names of saints at Baptism, whose virtues they should imitate, in order to become, one day, sharers in their glory.

60. "*And his mother answering.*" His father being deaf and dumb, she was probably on this account, asked, or, she may have overheard the conversation among her neighbours and friends on the subject.

"*Not so, but he shall be called John.*" This she conveyed in this imperative form, without consulting her friends, or neighbours, or giving them any voice in the matter, because it was enjoined by God (*v.* 13). She may have learned from her husband in writing an account of the Angel's vision and injunctions; or, more probably, she learned it from the inspiration of the Holy Ghost. (For meaning of the word, "*John,*" see *v.* 13.)

61. At this period, it was usual to give the circumcised infants the name of their parents or relatives, although, at the beginning of creation, and afterwards, in the days of the Patriarchs, it was usual, perhaps, owing to the paucity of men and names to be transferred, to impose a name derived from some remarkable event or occurrence connected with those to whom names were to be given. Thus, Adam's first-born was named Cain (Genesis iv. 1), "*quia possedi hominem per Deum.*" Another, Seth, for a similar reason (Genesis iv. 26); Noe (Genesis v. 29); Isaac (Genesis xxi. 4-6). Manasses and Ephraim, Joseph's sons, were so called for similar reasons (Genesis xli. 51, 52).

62. "*And they made signs to his father,*" &c., who, as appears from this, was deaf as well as dumb; otherwise, instead of addressing him by "*signs*" and gestures, they would have spoken to him. "*And,*" signifies, *therefore*. They wished Zachary to settle the matter by interposing his paternal authority. Likely, those present might dread, that the name so imperatively suggested by Elizabeth might not prove agreeable to him.

63. "*A writing-table,*" πινακιδιον, means, a small tablet, waxed or whitened over, or prepared in some other way, to be written on by the *stylus*, or iron pen, in use at the time.

"*He wrote, saying,*" a Hebrew form of expression, which is not uncommon in the Greek also, as in the Septuagint of 2 Kings (xi. 15), 1 Kings (x. 1-6), Josephus (Antiq. xiii. c. 4, &c.) The phrase means: he wrote, conveying in words written, but not spoken by word of mouth. In this case, it is clear, Zachary was yet dumb. For, it was immediately *after* this, his tongue was loosed (*v.* 64).

"*John is his name.*" "*Is,*" not, *will be,* to convey that he did not give him the name. It was given him by God, whose will no man shall dare contravene. Hence, all discussion on the subject should at once cease.

"*And they all wondered,*" at the strange and unexpected coincidence between his wishes and those of his wife on the subject.

64. "*And immediately,*" on his writing these words, "*John is his name,*" in accordance with the injunctions of the Angel, which shows, that it was owing to his having thus written, the use of speech was restored, as Origen observes (Hom. 9), "*his mouth was opened, and his tongue loosed,*" that is, he began to speak. The Greek simply is: *his mouth was opened, and his tongue. Loosed* is added in our English version. It is not in the Vulgate, "*apertum est os ejus et lingua ejus.*" There is hardly any necessity for adding the word, *loosed*. For the Greek word for "*opened,*" Ανεωχθη, is often used to signify, *loosed*. The first use he made of his tongue was in "*blessing God,*" for His wondrous mercy shown him. This may have reference to the praises contained

in the Canticle (68-79), of which a portion is taken up with the praises of God. At all events, it is very likely, Zachary's "*blessing of God*," was in the strain expressed in the inspired Canticle in question, and had reference to the Incarnation, the chiefest of God's favours.

65. "*Fear,*" φοβος, a feeling of reverential awe and wonder seized on all the country and neighbours, owing to the wonderful things that took place in connexion with the birth of the child—Elizabeth, old and barren, conceived; his father, struck dumb, and afterwards wonderfully recovering the use of his speech, &c. "*All these things.*" The Greek and Latin copies have, *all these words.* But the term, "*words*," means, *things*, as expressed in the English version.

66. "*Laid them up in their hearts*"—a Hebrew idiom, signifying, they treasured them up—seriously reflecting and pondering on them (as in chap. ix. 44, &c.)
"*Saying, what then shall this child be?*" How great a prophet shall he not be? What a wonderful distinction must be in store for him, whose very conception and birth have been rendered illustrious by so many miracles?
"*For the hand of the Lord was with him.*" These are the words of the Evangelist, and form a portion of the narrative, but not the words of the people who said, "*What then shall this child be?*" In some Greek copies, instead of "*for*," we have, και, *and.* But, *and*, has a *causal* signification, as if the Evangelist meant to convey, not without cause did they reason thus. *For*, the power of the Lord was displayed in regard to this child and all the events connected with him. In the Vatican MS. it is και γαρ. "*The hand of the Lord,*" means chiefly His power and His providence, His special care and favour. These were notably displayed in everything connected with the birth of this wonderful child.

TEXT.

67. *And Zachary his father was filled with the Holy Ghost: and he prophesied saying:*
68. *Blessed be the Lord God of Israel: because he hath visited and wrought the redemption of his people:*
69. *And hath raised up a horn of salvation to us, in the house of David his servant.*
70. *As he spoke by the mouth of his holy prophets, who are from the beginning.*
71. *Salvation from our enemies, and from the hand of all that hate us.*
72. *To perform mercy to our fathers; and to remember his holy testament.*
73. *The oath which he swore to Abraham our father, that he would grant to us,*
74. *That being delivered from the hand of our enemies, we may serve him without fear,*
75. *In holiness and justice before him, all our days.*
76. *And thou child, shalt be called the prophet of the highest: for thou shalt go before the face of the Lord to prepare his ways.*
77. *To give knowledge of salvation to his people, unto the remission of their sins.*
78. *Through the bowels of the mercy of our God, in which the Orient, from on high, hath visited us.*
79. *To enlighten them that sit in darkness, and in the shadow of death: to direct our feet into the way of peace.*
80. *And the child grew, and was strengthened in spirit; and was in the deserts until the day of his manifestation to Israel.*

COMMENTARY.

67. "*And Zachary his father was filled with the Holy Ghost,*" not merely for the effect of sanctification (for in regard to that, he had the Holy Ghost already, "*being just*

before God," *v.* 6), but for the purpose of exercising the gift of prophecy. Hence, as if to show, how he was filled with the Holy Ghost, and for what purpose or end he was so favoured, it is added:

"*And he prophesied saying.*" The following Canticle of Zachary—the second of the New Testament—is chiefly a prophecy, although some of it is taken up with the praises of God, which are so many ornaments of the prophecy. It commemorates past events relating to our Saviour—His Incarnation, and several other things accomplished regarding Him, as predicted in the ancient prophecies. These *past* occurrences he mentions in a prophetic spirit, as *future*; and penetrating their spiritual sense, he shows, they have reference to the remission of sin and to spiritual blessings; and he prophesies several things regarding his infant son to be accomplished at a future time. However, we need not regard the word, "*prophesy*," in the strict sense of predicting *future events*. It is often employed to signify, expressing the Divine mind, explaining the Scriptures in an extraordinary way, as the result of inspiration at the moment (see 1 Cor. xiv., Commentary on). In this Canticle, the chief thing is prophecy, in the sense of predicting future events. The other matters are accessory ornaments. Hence, Zachary may be said to have "*prophesied*," in the strict sense of the term. In the first part of the Canticle, *vv.* 68-76 he chants the praises of God for the Mystery of the Incarnation in the Virgin's chaste womb, and for the great blessings of Redemption thus accomplished, and for all the abundance of grace flowing therefrom. From *v.* 76 to *v.* 79, he continues the praises of God, and addressing his son, the infant Baptist, he proclaims aloud his office of Precursor to the Incarnate Son of the Most High God.

68. "*Benedictus Dominus Deus Israel*," &c., "*Blessed be*," may "*the Lord God of Israel*," be for ever praised and extolled, as He is deserving of all praise and glory. Zachary, following the usage observed by sacred writers, opens his prophetic Canticle with the praises of God. "*The Lord God of Israel*," the true God of heaven, in contradistinction to the false gods of the Gentiles, who are only devils, "*omnes Dii gentium, Dæmonia*" (Psa. xcv. 5). Although He is the Lord God of all mankind, He is specially said to be the "*God of Israel*," of the entire Jewish race, descendants of Abraham, Isaac, and Jacob, because by that people only was He known and honoured. He was to them specially a Father, and they were His children. They were types of the spiritual Israel, who were to be Abraham's children by faith. They were made the chief instruments in the accomplishment, of the great work of redemption, to which Zachary chiefly refers in this Canticle. To them was it first announced. Hence he subjoins,

"*Because He hath visited*," &c. The visitation to which Zachary here refers, in a prophetic spirit, is the Incarnation of the Son of God in the Virgin's womb. This he knew from the inspiration of the Holy Ghost. In Scriptural language "*visit*" means to bestow some great benefit on one. It is also taken sometimes in an unfavourable sense, to signify the infliction of punishment. Here, Zachary shows that it is used in a favourable sense, by adding,

"*And wrought the redemption*," &c. Although the death of the Son of God, whereby the redemption of the human race was effected, and full atonement made to God, was as yet future; still, Zachary employs the past, "*wrought*," according to some, in accordance with prophetic usage, in describing future events as past, on account of the certainty of their accomplishment. According to the more probable opinion of others, he regarded the work of redemption, which was to be fully accomplished by the death of Christ, as now commenced in the Incarnation of the Son of God. The Greek word for "*Redemption*"—λυτρωσιν—shows how this was brought about, viz., by paying the price and making full compensation. It was in this way, He redeemed mankind from the captivity of Satan and slavery of sin.

"*Of His people.*" This primarily refers to Israel, to whom He was specially promised, whom He was sent to save, "*oves quæ perierunt domus Israel,*" whom He personally visited and instructed—the nations were evangelized by the Apostles— it also includes spiritual Israel; nay, the entire human race, whom He came to save.

69. "*And hath raised up a horn of salvation to us,*" &c. The words, "*raised up,*" have reference to the depressed condition of the Jewish people, and to the destruction of the Royal power of the House of David, which was, at this time, utterly prostrated, and transferred to Herod, a foreigner.

"*A horn of salvation,*" that is, a powerful saving kingdom or king, "*for us.*" Zachary identifies himself with the Jewish people. The word, "*horn,*" is allusive to animals whose power or strength for defence or aggression is in their horns. The word is frequently employed metaphorically in Scripture to denote strength, power, principality (Lamentations ii. 3-17 ; Psa. lxxiv. 11, also Psa. cxxxi. 17), to which latter passage, the words of this verse are clearly allusive. This verse conveys more than the preceding. Not only did He rescue us from our enemies ; but, He has established and raised up a firm bulwark to save us from future assaults and subjection, and an invincible power to war successfully with our enemies, and cause their utter discomfiture.

"*In the house of His servant David,*" from whose royal house the Messiah, according to the promises of God, was to spring. In magnificent terms, the prophets announced, beforehand, the glory of His reign, which would date its commencement, from the time that the sceptre had been transferred from the Tribe of Juda; and Zachary employs words almost identical with, or, at least, very similar to the language of the ancient prophets on the subject. They spoke in the primary sense of the temporal kingdom of David and Solomon ; under this, however, they principally meant the spiritual kingdom of the Messiah, of which the former was a mere type and figure. They did so in accommodation to the prevailing notions and expectations of the Jewish people regarding the temporal glories of the Messiah's reign, just as we often see in Scriptures, certain qualities attributed to God in accommodation to popular notions, such as God having hands and feet, being agitated by passion, the stars being gifted with intelligence, brute beasts with reason, &c. Our Redeemer did not correct these ideas entertained even by the Apostles themselves on this subject of the coming glorious temporal reign of the Messiah ; He reserved their correction for the period after His resurrection, and the coming down of the Holy Ghost.

"*David His servant,*" who, being a man after God's own heart, just in the administration of his kingdom (Psalm lxxvii. 70-72)—on which account he received a promise that his Kingdom would be eternal—(Psalm lxxxviii. 36-38), was an expressive figure of our Lord. So much so, that, in many passages of Scripture, our Lord is called David (Jeremias xxx. 9 ; Ezechiel xxxiv. 24 ; xxxvii. 24).

70. "*As He spoke by the mouth of His holy prophets.*" Those words may be connected with the preceding, "*He raised up a horn,*" &c., as He promised to do, "*by the mouth*" of those who are His "*prophets,*" who are also "*holy ;*" hence, entitled to credit on both grounds. The word, "*holy,*" distinguishes those from the false prophets, who appeared from time to time. Zachary, in referring to the "*holy prophets,*" conveys, that what he was after uttering was neither novel, nor from himself—that he is only

repeating the utterances of the ancient prophets on the subject. They may be connected with what follows, "*as He spoke* (or promised) *salvation from our enemies.*"
"*Who are from the beginning,*" of the world. For, all the prophets from the beginning prophesied regarding Christ. Adam (Genesis ii. 24), "*Wherefore shall a man leave father and mother,*" &c.; which words St. Paul (Ephes. v. 31) applies to Christ and His Church; Moses (John v. 46); and so did all the rest. Or the words may mean, *ancient*—"*as he spoke by the mouth of the* ANCIENT *prophets.*" Some include this verse in a parenthesis, and place, "*salvation from our enemies*" (v. 71), in apposition to "*horn of salvation,*" thus, "*a horn of salvation*" (v. 69), who is a Salvation or Saviour, to rescue us from our enemies (Bede, Enthymius). But as it would seem a harsh construction to say, "He raised up salvation," it is, therefore, better connect it with "*He spoke,*" or promised (Jansenius). Others, however, say, as "*salvation*" means, *a Saviour*, there is no harshness in saying, "He raised up *a Saviour*" (Barradius).

71. "*Salvation from our enemies.*" This is dependent on, "*as He spoke,*" or promised. "*He raised up a horn of salvation* . . . *as He spoke,*" &c., or in accordance with and in fulfilment of His promises, uttered by His prophets, that He would grant is salvation from our enemies. There is reference here to our spiritual enemies, viz., the Devil, with his hosts; the flesh, with its wicked passions; the world, or wicked men, whose bad example and vicious, corrupting principles withdraw us from God. From these enemies Christ rescues our souls here, and our souls and bodies hereafter (see Colossians ii. 13, 14; i. 13, 14; 1 John iii. 5). In this verse Zachary, under the influence of the Holy Ghost, interprets or explains the words spoken by the ancient prophets, relative to the salvation of the Jews from the hands of their enemies, and to their salvation from their spiritual enemies, also, as more fully and more clearly expressed in *vv.* 75, 77.

"*And from the hands of all that hate us.*" This is a repetition, in other words, for greater emphasis, of the idea conveyed in the preceding words, *our enemies*, which is very common in Sacred Scriptures. Reference is made to our spiritual enemies "*who hate us,*" who ever war against us, and strive to compass our spiritual and eternal ruin. The liberation, which Zachary ascribes to the Son of God, will bring about "*the remission of our sins*" (v. 17), and enable us by the spiritual conquest achieved, to live "*in holiness and justice all our days.*" (v. 75).

72. "*To perform mercy to our fathers,*" &c., may be connected with "*horn of salvation,*" thus, "*He raised up a horn of salvation*" for the purpose of performing "*mercy to our fathers,*" or, with "*salvation,*" He promised salvation from our enemies, in order "*to perform mercy to our fathers.*" The "*mercy to our fathers,*" conveys, that the Patriarchs were sharers in the mercy shown their children on their account. God showed mercy to all; to the Patriarchs, to whom, out of pure mercy, He promised Redemption and the graces afterwards bestowed by Christ; to their remotest posterity, also, whom His Son came to redeem and visit. Zachary may be said to refer, in a special way, to the mercy shown their fathers, because, by the coming of Christ, they were brought forth from prison. "*By the blood of thy Testament, Thou hast sent forth thy prisoners, out of the pit, wherein is no water*" (Zacharias ix. 11).

"*And to remember His holy covenant,*" to show Himself mindful, after a long delay, which would seem to savour of utter oblivion, of the covenant or pact, (this is the meaning of "*covenant*," here,) He made with Abraham, regarding the birth of Christ from His seed (Genesis xxii. 17, 18), which is clearly explained and applied (Acts iii. 25). Zachary would seem to say, that God visited His people, and raised up a horn of salvation, for three ends. First, to fulfil the promises made through His prophets; secondly, to show mercy to the Fathers; thirdly (here), to declare Himself mindful of His covenant with Abraham, regarding the benediction of all nations in his seed, a commencement being made with "*the lost sheep of the house of Israel.*" The Vulgate, "*ad faciendam misericordiam . . . . et memorari Testamenti sui sancti,*" should, following the Greek, be, "*facere misericordiam . . . . et memorari,*" ποιησαι ελεος . . . . και μνησθηναι διαθηκης.

73. "*The oath which He swore to Abraham,*" &c. The word, "*oath,*" is connected by some with "*holy covenant,*" as if He said, which holy covenant is "*the oath which He swore,*" &c., thus placing the word, "*oath,*" in apposition to "*covenant;*" and, although "*oath*" and "*covenant*" are in different cases, "*covenant*" (testamenti—διαθηκης), in the genitive; "*oath*" (*jusjurandum*, ορκον), in the accusative; still, the advocates of this interpretation say, the Greek word for "remember," governs both cases. Hence, in the Syriac, it is put very clearly, "*memorari testamenti . . . et jurisjurandi.*" Origen reads it, ορκου, in the genitive. Beelen takes ορκον, for ορκου, in the genitive, in apposition to διαθηκης, as attracted into the case of the relative, ὅν, which follows (Grammat. Græc., c. 11, § 24. Others, with A. Lapide, connect "*oath,*" with "*to perform*" (v. 72), as if he said, "*He raised up a horn of salvation,*" among other reasons, to perform, or observe, the oath He made to "*Abraham, our father,*" recorded Genesis (xxii. 16), and elsewhere, regarding the multiplication of his spiritual children, and the benediction of all nations in his seed.

"*That he would grant us,*" has reference to what follows, viz., "*that being delivered,*" &c. (v. 74). This appears from the Greek construction, του δουναι ημιν.

74. "*That being delivered,*" &c., has reference to deliverance from our spiritual enemies, the world, the flesh, and the devil. This, already expressed in v. 71, "*salvation from our enemies,*" is repeated here, as connected with what follows. "*We may serve Him without fear,*" without any *excessive*, torturing fear. For, we are commanded "*to work out our salvation with fear and trembling.*" Here there is question of *immoderate* fear of those enemies who are vanquished by Jesus Christ (John xvi. 33; Col. ii. 13; Jeremias xxiii. 6); of fear of death, which is only the portal of eternal life (Heb. ii. 13). In this, and the following verses, Zachary, no doubt, has also in view eternal life, to which, as its reward, and consummation, a life of persevering sanctity in this world surely conducts; and in which, according to Isaias (xxxii. 18), "*God's people shall sit in the beauty of peace, and in the tabernacles of confidence, and in wealthy rest.*"

"*Serve.*" The Greek word, λατρευειν, denotes the supreme worship due to God alone. "*Him,*" who rescued us from the servitude of sin, that we might become the servants of justice and of God (Rom. vi. 18-22).

"*In holiness and justice before Him.*" "*Holiness,*" denotes our duties towards God, as expressed in the *first table* of the Decalogue. "*Justice,*" our duties towards ourselves and our neighbour, as expressed in the *second table*. "*Before him,*" real, true justice and sanctity. So that here is expressed the faithful observance of all God's Commandments, with sincerity of heart, which alone is pleasing to Him, and approved by Him. Likely, there is an opposition and comparison instituted here between the Law of Christ and the Old Law. The latter only conferred external justice, the justifications of the flesh; the former brought with it and conferred real interior justice and sanctity.

"*All our days,*" implies, perseverance in the service of God, in the practice of justice and holiness; in a word, in the observance of God's Commandments to our last expiring breath, since it is those alone who persevere to the end, that shall be partakers of the blessings of Redemption referred to by Zachary—and shall obtain the crown of eternal life. The words may also imply a contrast with the Old Law, which was temporary, and ceased; whereas the New was to continue to the end of ages. The passing, temporary duration of one, is contrasted with the permanent, never-failing continuance of the other.

76. "*And thou child shall be called,*" &c. This is the second part of the Canticle, wherein Zachary, feelingly addressing the infant, predicts the dignity, office, and successful mission of the Baptist, and points to the effects and privileges of the Gospel, as also to the conversion of all men, Jews and Gentiles. "*Shalt be called,*" shalt be in reality, and proclaimed, "*a prophet of the Highest.*" John was "*a prophet, and more than a prophet,*" according to the testimony of truth itself (Matthew xi. 9-11, see Commentary on). "*Of the Highest,*" has reference to our Blessed Lord, as in the following words, "*For thou shalt go before the face of the Lord,*" which latter words are clearly allusive to the words of Malachias (chap. iii. 1), and prove the Divinity of Christ. He whom John was to precede is called, "*Lord, the Highest.*" Some of the Fathers are of opinion, that the child who, from his mother's womb, saluted the Son of God in the womb of the Virgin, retained the use of reason with which it is commonly supposed, he was then miraculously imbued. Others, without having recourse to this hypothesis, explain the words of Zachary as apostrophizing his infant son, under the influence of strong emotions, as we often find, in Sacred Scripture, inanimate objects feelingly addressed, "*Audite cœli, quæ loquor*" (Deut. xxxii.), "*Montes Gelboe,*" &c. (4 Kings xxi.), Josue addresses the sun and moon (Josue x. 12). Moreover, Zachary addresses his infant son, for the instruction of those present, who, on afterwards seeing John acting as the Precursor of our Lord, and, pointing Him out to the people as infinitely superior to himself, would be confirmed in their faith, by the remembrance of the prophecy, now uttered by Zachary on the subject.

"*Thou shalt go before the face of the Lord,*" who, though clad in human nature, is also God and Lord of all things.

"*To prepare His ways,*" contains an allusion to a prevalent usage, especially in the East, whenever a king visited any remarkable place in his dominions, to have a herald go before him, and point him out to his people; and also to have every obstacle, every unsightly object, that might retard his journey, or cause any disagreeable feeling, removed out of the way. John prepared the ways of our Lord, by teaching the Jews the true faith, and inculcating the practice of penance, as in following verse.

77. He shall prepare the ways of the Lord, and remove all disagreeable objects and obstacles by imparting to God's people, the saving "*knowledge,*" whereby they shall be taught the ways of justice and of truth, shall be brought to Him, who is "*the Way, the Truth, and the Life,*" and shall know Him to be the Saviour promised to them, who shall bestow the salvation, of which John shall impart the knowledge, to be the Eternal Son of God, who came to redeem and rescue them from the slavery of sin and Satan; and by preaching, by word and example, the necessity of penance, to dispose them for "*the remission of their sins.*" This remission of sin can be obtained solely through the merits of our Lord, in the first instance, in the regenerating waters of Baptism, to which the Baptism of John served as a type and preparation.

The Greek has, "*in the remission of their sins,*" and will mean, that the "*salvation,*" preached by John, and imparted by Christ, consists in "*the remission of sin,*" or, if we follow the Vulgate, "*in remissionem peccatorum,*" &c., we can interpret it, procured through the remission of sins. For, by a Hebrew idiom, "*in,*" signifies, *by*, "*per,*" whether construed with an Ablative or Accusative.

78. "*Through the bowels of the mercy of our God.*" This remission of sin, and all the other blessings connected therewith, were the result of God's tenderest, most intense feelings of mercy and commiseration for our miseries. It is to God's tenderest mercy alone, we are indebted for all the blessings resulting from the Incarnation of His Son—this, "*Horn of Salvation of the house of David.*"

The "*bowels of mercy,*" mean intimate, intense feelings of mercy, such as a mother feels for her offspring in distress. Thus we find it said of the mother in the judgment of Solomon (3 Kings iii. 26), "*her bowels were moved upon her child.*" Similar, also, is the meaning of the word "*bowels*" (1 John iii. 17).

"*In which,*" "*bowels of mercy,*" or through the strong impulse of which tender feelings of merciful love.

"*The Orient from on high visited us.*" It was owing to His exceeding great love for the world, that God gave up for it His only, His well-beloved Son. It was the same intense love, that moved the Eternal Son Himself to assume flesh, to visit us in person, and not through His prophets, as of old, and to come down from the highest heavens, for our sakes. "*Qui propter nos, homines, et propter nostram salutem, descendit de cœlis.*"—Nicene Creed. This love of God is heightened by the circumstance so clearly referred to by the Apostle, in commendation of it, that, "*When we were yet sinners, Christ died for us. When we were enemies, we were reconciled to God, by the death of His Son*" (Romans v. 8, 10). The words, "*from on high,*" are to be connected with, "*visited us,*" by coming down from heaven, and assuming flesh in the chaste womb of the Virgin, in order to accomplish the work of Redemption.

"*The Orient.*" This is a noun—ανατολη. The corresponding Hebrew word, *Tzemah*, is universally regarded as denoting the Messiah, or Christ; and hence, in the Chaldaic Paraphrase, or Targum of Jonathan, it is rendered, not literally, but as signifying, the *Messiah*.. The Greek interpreters, in one passage only (Jer. xxxiii. 15), translate, *Tzemah*, βλαστος, *germen*, "*a bud.*" In several others, ανατολη, or, "*Orient*" (Jer. xxiii. 5; Zach. iii. 8; vi. 12). St. Jerome, in his translation from the original Hebrew, renders *Tzemah* into Latin, in some passages, *germen*, or *bud* (Isaias iv. 2; Jer. xxiii. 5; xxxiii. 15), and in other passages, *Orient* (Zach. iii. 8; vi. 12). In both significations, of "*bud*" springing forth, and of "*Orient*" darting forth its rays of light (and the precise signification of *Tzamar*, the root from which *Tzemah* is derived, is to *shoot forth*, applicable to a *bud*, or light alike), the word is very applicable to Christ; as a bud, it is very applicable to "*the rod out of the root of Jesse, a flower out of his root*" (Isaias xi. 1), who, when the house of David seemed to be destroyed for ever, and to have gone into utter oblivion, unexpectedly sprang from the family of David, and re-established the glory of His throne for ever. As a light darting forth its rays, it is equally applicable to our Lord, "*the True Light that enlightens every man coming into this world*" (John i. 9). Himself, "*the Light of the World*" (John viii. 12), "*The Sun of Justice to them that fear His name*" (Malachias iv. 2), "*The Bright and Morning Star.*" And it is in this latter signification of the word, as appears from the following (*v.* 79) "*to enlighten,*" &c., it is here applied to our Lord.

79. "*To enlighten them*," &c. This was the end for which the Orient came to visit us. The image conveyed in the words of this verse is allusive to the wretched condition of those who are forced to dwell and spend their lives in darksome dungeons or sepulchres, into which the cheering light of day is never permitted to enter. "*Shadow of death*" intensifies the word, "*darkness*," and both mean *darkness the most intense*. The corresponding Hebrew word, *Salmaveth*, denotes the colour which death on its immediate approach impresses on the face and entire countenance of a man. Hence, it points to dense darkness from which one cannot emerge, and to the condition of extreme danger usually followed by destruction. The words, "*shadow of death*," are commonly used in this sense in the Sacred Scriptures, and often applied to the darkness of the grave and of hell (Job iii. 5; x. 21, 22).

The words, "*darkness and shadow of death*," in the moral and spiritual sense intended here, denote the great ignorance and sinfulness in which the human race was plunged before the coming of Christ. As sunrise over the hills dissipates the mists and lights up the lowliest valleys; so, Christ dispelled this ignorance by teaching the truths of faith, by revealing those mysteries of grace and glory concealed hitherto from the children of men (Ephes. iii. 5-9); thus clearing away the shocking errors regarding God's Divine nature and attributes, regarding man's origin and ultimate destiny which disfigured the face of the earth, and destroying the empire of Satan and sin, by meriting the grace whereby sin was remitted and cancelled, and by permanently instituting these channels of Divine grace—the sacraments of His Church, which were to subsist to the end of time. Some include among those enlightened by Christ, even the departed souls of the just shut up in the gloomy prison of Limbo, to whom Christ went, in the interval between His Passion and Resurrection, to announce their near deliverance (1 Peter iii. 19). But, most likely, the words exclusively refer to the living, as explained above.

"*To direct our feet*," &c. In removing the darkness of ignorance and sin, our Lord pointed out the way of justice and peace in which we should walk in future, after having culpably deflected from it in the past. He, at the same time, helps us, by His abundant grace, to walk in this road, and to direct all our affections and actions towards the performance of the works of justice, and the observance of His commandments, which alone could insure for us true peace here, with God and man, and eternal peace in the enjoyment of everlasting happiness hereafter, according to the words of Isaias (xxxii, 17, 18), "*And the work of justice shall be peace, and the service of justice quietness, and security for ever. And my people shall sit in the beauty of peace, and in the tabernacles of confidence, and in wealthy rest.*"

The word "*peace*," by a Hebrew idiom, denotes the possession of all things desirable.

80. "*And the child grew*," &c. The Evangelist wishes to convey that the after life of the Baptist fully corresponded with these wonders recorded in connexion with his birth and circumcision. He "*grew*" in *bodily* stature and age. "*And was strengthened in spirit.*" His *soul* advanced in virtue and grace, plentifully bestowed on him by the Holy Ghost. The same or similar words are applied to our Lord in a still more exalted sense (chap. ii. 40).

"*And was in the deserts*" (see Matthew iii. 1, Commentary on). John retired into the desert, according to some, to escape Herod, who, on hearing of the wonderful events connected with his birth and circumcision, would have regarded him as the Messiah, the born King of the Jews, afterwards referred to by the Magi. He would thus be exposed to the indiscriminate slaughter of the holy innocents. The

Baptist found the serpents of the desert less formidable than a tyrannical king, as St. Jerome remarks (contra Lucifer.). He retired also, in order to be less liable to be influenced in after life, by favour or partiality in regard to the vices of the Jews, which he denounced with prophetic and apostolic firmness; also to give an example of the penance which he preached, and to secure greater credit for his testimony in favour of our Lord, regarding whom, he could have derived knowledge from God alone and His holy angels.

"*Until the time of His manifestation to Israel.*" God, who had illustrated his birth and circumcision by so many wonders, did not fail to protect him in the desert, and exert a miraculous providence, if necessary, in his regard, whom He had destined to be in due time, the herald to announce the presence on earth, of His Eternal Son.

"*Manifestation,*" &c., when he was to make his appearance publicly to exercise the function of Prophet, which, among the Jews no one was allowed to do before attaining the age of thirty (see Matthew iii. 1)—and to discharge the duties of his exalted office, as Precursor to the Son of God.

CHAPTER II.

ANALYSIS.

In this chapter we have an account of the birth of our Lord, and of certain remarkable events connected with it. Its announcement to the shepherds by the Angel. The celestial hymns sung on the occasion by a multitude of the heavenly army (1-14). The visit of the shepherds to the crib (15-19). Their return after having witnessed the truth of the joyous announcement made to them by the Angel (20). The circumcision of our Lord. The purification of his Virgin Mother (21-24). The timely arrival in the Temple of Simeon, no doubt, providentially arranged, to bear testimony to our Lord (25-28). Simeon's inspired Canticle, and prophecy, relating to our Lord, and His Blessed Mother (29-35). The testimony borne by the saintly prophetess, Anna (36-38). Our Lord's return to Nazareth, after His circumcision (39-40). The finding of Him in the Temple, after a diligent search made for Him during three days, by His disconsolate parents, on the occasion of His going up with them, at the age of twelve, to assist at the Paschal solemnity (41-50). His hidden life at Nazareth, and His obedience to His parents.

TEXT.

A ND *it came to pass that in those days there went out a decree from Cesar Augustus; that the whole world should be enrolled.*

2. *This enrolling was first made by Cyrinus the governor of Syria.*

3. *And all went to be enrolled, every one into his own city.*

4. *And Joseph also went up from Galilee out of the city of Nazareth into Judea, to the city of David, which is called Bethlehem: because he was of the house and family of David,*

5. *To be enrolled with Mary, his espoused wife, who was with child.*

6. *And it came to pass, that when they were there, her days were accomplished, that she should be delivered.*

7. *And she brought forth her first-born son, and wrapped him up in swaddling clothes, and laid him in a manger: because there was no room for them in the inn.*

8. *And there were in the same country shepherds watching, and keeping the night watches over their flock.*

9. *And behold an Angel of the Lord stood by them, and the brightness of God shone round about them, and they feared with a great fear.*

10. *And the Angel said to them: Fear not; for behold I bring you good tidings of great joy, that shall be to all the people:*

11. *For this day is born to you a Saviour who is Christ the Lord, in the city of David.*

12. *And this shall be a sign unto you. You shall find the infant wrapped in swaddling clothes, and laid in a manger.*

13. *And suddenly there was with the Angel a multitude of the heavenly army, praising God, and saying :*

14. *Glory to God in the highest : and on earth peace to men of good-will.*

COMMENTARY.

1. "*And it came to pass*," not by mere chance or accident, but it was so arranged by the over-ruling providence of God. "*That in those days.*" Shortly, or immediately after the birth and circumcision of the Baptist, described in the preceding chapter. "*There went out a decree from.*" A decree was promulgated by "*Cæsar Augustus.*" Julius Cæsar, who was assassinated, was the first Roman Emperor ; "*Augustus*," who immediately succeeded him, was the *second*, in the forty-second year of whose reign, Christ was born. "*Cæsar*," was the title generally given to all the Roman Emperors. The title of "*Augustus*," was given by the Roman Senate to this Cæsar, whose reign, so long and prosperous, lasting for fifty-seven years, gave rise, partly to the saying, "*Augusto felicior, Trajano melior.*"

"*That the whole world should be enrolled.*" There is no mention made of this enrolment by Pagan historians. Hence, some Expositors understand by the words, "*whole world*," Judea only, a signification they bear sometimes in SS. Scripture. These say, that Augustus had for object in taking this census in that part of his Empire, to ascertain the amount of aid he might expect, in case of emergency, from Herod, who was the mere creature of the Romans. They assign as a reason for using the words in this restricted sense, the mention of "*Cyrinus, as Governor of Syria*," in connexion with it, which would have no meaning, if there were question of the vast Roman Empire, the enrolment of which could not be committed to Cyrinus. However, the mention of Cyrinus, as Governor of Syria, might be accounted for, even if there were question of a general enrolment of the Empire ; because, it was the enrolment, which, so far as it regarded the Syrian part of the Empire, had immediate connexion with the wonderful event now about to be recorded. It was owing to the decree of enrolment in this part of the Empire, that Christ was born in Bethlehem, the place marked out for His birth in the ancient prophecies. If the above restricted sense of the words be adopted, the silence of profane historians is perfectly intelligible, as an event occurring in so remote a corner of the Empire would be beneath their notice. However, the words are commonly understood, of the habitable quarters of the globe, then subject to the Roman Empire, πᾶσαν τὴν οἰκουμένην, a sense, which the words, "*whole world*," sometimes bears, as the Roman Empire at the time embraced the greater part of the habitable globe. This is held by many, with Paulus Orosius, Ven. Bede, &c.

"*Should be enrolled.*" Whether this enrolment, or census, of the subjects of the whole Empire, its provinces and dependencies, with an account of its population and resources, was ordered without any view to taxation, and solely out of a feeling of vain-glory, on the part of Augustus—an opinion maintained by some, chiefly on the ground, that if taxation were in view, each one would be enrolled, not in the place whence his family had sprung, as in this case, but where his possessions were (Patrizzi, Dissert. xviii., Lib. 31); or whether it was ordered by Augustus, with a further view to taxation, in order to recruit the Imperial Treasury, exhausted by long wars, as is stated by Josephus (De Antiq. Lib. 18, c. 1), is uncertain; although, the latter opinion seems the more probable. One thing, however, is quite certain, viz., that it was ordained by the all-ruling providence of God, for the verification of His prophecies regarding the birth of His Son in Bethlehem. It might seem strange, at first, considering that Herod was at this time King of Judea, that the general enrolment decreed by Augustus, whether from motives of vanity, or with a view to taxation, should include his kingdom. But, it is to be borne in mind, that Herod held his kingdom at the good-will of the Romans; and, hence, he could not safely object to their taking a census of a kingdom which was tributary to them. Josephus informs us (Antiq. xvi. c. 9), that Herod had at this time, owing to grave accusations preferred against him, incurred the displeasure of Augustus, who threatened, "instead of treating him any longer as his friend, to treat him in future as his subject." Hence, his dominions, regarded as subject to Augustus, were now included in the general census of the Roman Empire. It is supposed by many, that Augustus had in view to impose a tribute, or capitation tax, levied on all, men and women. Therefore, the Blessed Virgin accompanied Joseph to Bethlehem. After ascertaining the number of his subjects, most likely, the tax imposed in Judea was similar to that contributed for the necessities of the Temple (see Matthew xvii. 23). We are informed by historians, sacred and profane, that at this period, the whole world enjoyed a profound peace, as an indication of which, the Temple of Janus was now closed a third time by Augustus. All this was well suited to greet the entrance into this world of Him, who was "*the Prince of Peace*," who came to reconcile God to man, by making atonement to His outraged Majesty by the plentiful effusion of His most sacred blood; and to establish the firmest bonds of union between men themselves, by breaking down the middle wall of partition, that divided Jews from Gentiles (Ephes ii. 14).

2. "*This enrolment was first made by Cyrinus,*" &c. This general enrolment of all the subjects of the entire Empire was the first of the kind that was made, or could be made, owing to continucus wars (although there might possibly have been several partial or local ones), and so far as the portion of the Empire connected with the extensive province of Syria, including Judea, was concerned, it was made by Cyrinus, who was President of Syria, vested with supreme vicarial authority. The more probable opinion is, that Cyrinus or Quirinus acted as extraordinary commissioner on this occasion, being invested with this high office by Augustus, in reward for his public services, especially for having utterly destroyed the Homodanenses—a savage tribe in the neighbourhood of Mount Taurus, who proved very troublesome to the Roman authorities in these distant dependencies. The ordinary Governor of Syria— the most important of the Roman Provinces—was at this time Sentius Saturninus, (Tacitus Annal., Lib. iii.) Cyrinus associated him with himself in taking the census in the province of Syria, and, on this account, Tertullian (Lib. iv., c. 7, adv. Marcion), referring to the Roman Archives in proof of our Lord's nativity and its circumstances, says (c. 19), that the census was taken by *Sentius Saturninus*, as he was the ordinary Governor of Syria at the time, whom Cyrinus had associated with himself, in this important business. Cyrinus only is mentioned by St. Luke, because eleven years afterwards he returned as ordinary Governor of Syria, when, after the banishment of Archelaus, Judea was annexed to the province of Syria. It is likely our Lord was registered, at least, on the octave day of His nativity, when He was circumcised and returned on this census. For, Justin Martyr addressing Antoninus Pius, appeals to the Roman census under Cyrinus, and Tertullian (*ut supra*), to their own archives, in proof of our Lord's nativity. The Greek, omitting the particle "*by*," merely has—ἡγεμονεύοντος τῆς Συρίας Κυρηνίου—*Cyrinus being President of Syria*.

Some understand, "*first*," of the census made by Cyrinus as extraordinary Commissioner, in the life-time of Herod, in opposition to a *second* made by the same Cyrinus, eleven years after this, when, on the banishment of Archelaus, his kingdom was annexed to the Roman Province of Syria, of which Cyrinus was then appointed ordinary Governor (Josephus, Antiq., Lib. 15, c. 1); and a tax levied, which gave occasion to the unhappy rebellion of Judas of Galilee (Acts v. 37). St. Luke refers to the former census; Josephus to the latter. Or "*first*" may mean the first census of Judea made by the authority of the Romans, who committed it to Cyrinus, Governor of Syria (Justin Martyr adv. Typhon). Some Expositors, in order to remove more fully still, the chronological difficulties raised here, say "*first*" means, *before*, a signification the word, πρωτη, bears in other parts of the Gospel; this census was made *before* Cyrinus was Governor of Syria; while, by others, the words are understood to mean, this enrolment was perfected and its object carrried out, viz., the levying of a tax by Cyrinus, when he was President of Syria, eleven years after this.

3. "*And all went to be enrolled.*" This was the tenor of the decree as regarded Judea; "*Every one (went) into his own city.*" The usual system of enrolment practised among the Jews was, to commence with the tribe; then, to descend to the family; and then, to the individuals comprised in each family (Josue vii. 14; 1 Kings ix. 21; 2 Kings xxiv. 2). Augustus wished the same order to be observed on this occasion. Whether any similar arrangement was made in regard to the Gentiles is not ascertained. Livy (Lib. xlii. 10) makes mention of some such arrangement having been made by order of the Consul in regard to the taxing of the allied cities, or the *Socii Latini Nominis.*

"*Into his own city*," not the city of His birth, nor where He dwelled; but, the city whence the head of His family had sprung, as in the present case, Bethlehem was the city of David.

4. "*Joseph also went up*"—because Judea was higher in point of situation than Galilee—"*to the city of David, which is called Bethlehem,*" to distinguish it from the citadel of Sion, which David built, after having taken it from the Jesubeans, and dwelling there, made the seat of his kingdom. Hence, in several parts of the Book of Kings, it is called "*David's city;*" but, he was born in Bethlehem. Bethlehem was six miles to the south of Jerusalem, and about seventy from Nazareth, in Galilee, a long and wearisome journey for the Virgin, under the circumstances. It is supposed that it was made on foot.

"*Because he was of the house and family of David.*" "*House and family*," mean one and the same thing, although some Expositors mean by "*house,*" the several heads of each household; by "*family,*" the several distinguished members of each tribe. Both words convey, that Joseph sprang from the family, of which David was the distinguished head.

5. "*To be enrolled with Mary,*" &c. "*With Mary,*" may be joined with "*enrolled,*" or, "*went up*" (v. 4), or rather with both, as both occurrences took place. He went up with her, and he was enrolled with her. Women, as well as men, were enrolled at every such census, particularly with a view to the capitation tax, which, most likely, was the chief or ultimate object Augustus contemplated in ordering it. Nor can we see why Mary, in an advanced state of pregnancy, would have undertaken so toilsome a journey from Nazareth to Bethlehem, unless in obedience to the law

requiring her to be enrolled. So that she might say with her Son, "*We must fulfil all justice*," particularly as she was an heiress of the Tribe of Juda, and family of David (see Matthew i. 16, Commentary on). All this was regulated by the all-wise providence of God, in view of the birth of His Son in Bethlehem, as had been long before predicted by the prophets (Micheas v. 2).

"*His espoused wife.*" The word, "*espoused*," is used to show, that although married to Joseph, she was, still, an Immaculate Virgin.

"*Who was with child*," on the point of giving birth to a child, at the time of their arrival in Bethlehem, now referred to.

6. "*And it came to pass,*" not by chance, but by the ordination of God's providence.

"*That when they were there,*" which some Commentators, (Maldonatus, Toletus, Lucas Brugensis, Jansenius, &c.,) understand to mean, having tarried there some days after their arrival; either waiting for their turn to be enrolled, or, after being enrolled, awaiting the event, which they knew would certainly come to pass there. Others (with Silveira, &c.), understand the words to mean, immediately on their arrival. These quote a revelation made to St. Brigid (Lib. 7; Revel. c. 21), that the Blessed Virgin brought forth our Lord the night she reached Bethlehem.

"*Her days were accomplished,*" that is, fully nine months—the natural period of gestation—commencing with the conception of our Lord, on the 25th of March, and His birth, on the 25th of December, which, "the authority of the Church keeps, taking up the tradition of the ancients on the subject" (St. Augustin de Trinitate, Lib. iv. c. 5). "*Sicut a majoribus traditum suscipiens Ecclesiæ custodit auctoritas.*" It is thus shown, that our Lord was born in the fulness of time, having been carried in His mother's womb, like other children, thereby proving He was true man, no less than true God, begotten of the Father by an eternal generation.

7. "*And she brought forth her first-born Son.*" She gave Him birth, as other women do to their offspring. But she did so, unlike them, without any detriment to her virginal integrity, being, as Catholic faith teaches, a spotless Virgin, "*ante partum, in partu, post partum.*" He emanated from her, just as His glorious body penetrated the apartment in which His Apostles were assembled after His resurrection, the door remaining shut; and as the rays of the sun penetrate glass, without any fracture of its component parts. She also brought Him forth without pain, or lassitude, or weakness of any sort, being free from the curse entailed on other mothers by sin, "*in dolore filios paries*" (Genesis iii. 16). Commentators observe, that while of Elizabeth it is said, "*she brought forth a son*" (chap. i. 57); of Mary, it is said, "*she brought forth her Son,*" as if to convey, that she was the mother of her Son, in the strictest sense of the word; and even might be called the mother of her Son, on a title still stricter than applies to other mothers; because *her* Son had no father on earth, unlike other children; and His mother alone, without the co-operation of an earthly father, supplied the substance of His sacred body. Now, as this Son is also God, having a Divine Person only; hence, Mary is justly termed, the *Mother of God*.

"*First-born.*" For meaning, see Matthew, chap. i. *v*. 25.

"*And wrapped Him up in swaddling clothes,*" as is commonly done to infants, to prevent distortion of the limbs. Although this was not needed in the case of our Blessed Lord; still, the Blessed Virgin acted in His regard, as mothers commonly see done in regard to their new-born babes, and wrapped Him in the swaddling clothes she had provided, in view of the approaching birth of the Divine Infant, of which she was fully aware. From the activity and pious offices performed by the Blessed Virgin, herself in person, requiring no assistance, as ordinary mothers do, immediately on giving birth to the children of sin, it is clear, she brought forth, without pain, or lassitude, which, in other mothers, are the allotted punishment of sin.

"*And laid Him in the manger,*" which implies, that our Lord was born in a stable. This manger was the most befitting place in the stable for receiving the Divine Infant on His entry into this world. Tradition has it, that, at the time, an ox and an ass were tied to the manger, to which allusion is made (Isaias i. 3), "*The ox knoweth his owner, and the ass his master's crib,*" as explained by St. Gregory of Nyssa (Serm. de Nativitate), and also, in the Septuagint version of Habucuc (iii. 2), which, instead of the words, as rendered by St. Jerome, "*in the midst of the years, thou shalt make it known,*" has, "*in the midst of two animals, thou shalt be known,*" "*in medio duorum animalium cognosceris.*" This manger is now religiously preserved in the Basilica of St. Mary Major, at Rome, and made the object of pious veneration.

"*Because there was no room for them in the inn.*" Either on account of their having arrived late, the inns, or places of public reception—caravanseries, as they are called in the East—were crowded by the concourse of people coming from all quarters, to be enrolled at Bethlehem. Hence, no room for Joseph and Mary; or even if they arrived, as most likely they did, in time, they were obliged, on account of their poverty, to make way for more favoured and more welcome guests, especially as there might be some reluctance in receiving a woman evidently far gone in pregnancy. Thus "*there was no room for them.*" They were, therefore, forced to take shelter in a stable, where the King of Heaven and Creator of the Universe, to whom belongs the earth and its fulness, was to be born. There is a diversity of opinion among Commentators regarding the site of this stable. Some hold, that it was a kind of outhouse attached to the inn, in the little town of Bethlehem. Others, however, who explored the Holy Land, and among them St. Jerome (Ep. ad Marcellam ; Bede, de locis sanctis) maintain, that it was at the extreme eastern side of the town, a cave hewn in a rock, whither the shepherds were wont to drive their cattle as a place of protection against the inclemency of the weather.

What a mystery of love and humiliation. The God of heaven, the Almighty Creator of the universe, the Eternal Son of God, becoming a weak babe and born in a stable, although His "*was the earth and its fulness.*" What excess of love. "*God so loved the world*" (and this world His enemy by sin, sunk in the depth and mire of sinful degradation), "*as to give up for it His only begotten Son*" (John iii. 16), "*and evidently great is this mystery of godliness, manifested in the flesh,*" &c. (1 Timothy iii. 16.)

What a moving example of humility, austerity, poverty, penance, and above all, of charity, does He not leave us in the stable. While "*the foxes had their dens, and the birds of the air their nests, He had not whereon to lay His head.*" Born in a stable, living in a workshop, dying on a gibbet "*being rich, He became poor, for our sakes, that through His poverty we might be made rich*" (2 Cor. viii. 9). From the pulpit of the crib, He addresses us—I, "*who measured the waters in the hollow of my hand . . . and poised with three fingers the bulk of the earth, and weighed the mountains in scales, and the hills in a balance*" (Isaias xl. 12); who created the heavens and the earth out of nothing, the King of glory, and Lord of majesty, before whom "*the pillars of heaven tremble*" (Job xxvi. 11), "*and under whom they stoop, that bear up the world*" (Job ix. 13), in order to save you, wretched worms of the earth, and out of pure love, to rescue you from the unquenchable flames of hell, and bring you to the happiness of heaven—"*came leaping over the mountains, skipping over the hills*" (Cant. ii. 8). From heaven and my Father's bosom, I leaped to the Virgin's womb; from her womb, to earth; from earth, to the cross; from the cross, to the lower regions; thence, I leaped back to earth; from earth, to heaven, to convey you thither. By the bowels of my mercy, I visited you rising from on high; and I united heaven to earth, God to man, by the closest personal union. I became flesh, to make you God; and when you became like the horse and mule, and without understanding, like unto the brute beasts, I was born between two brute animals, to rescue you from this miserable servitude (A Lapide).

8. Having described the circumstances of our Lord's birth, His poverty and humility, St. Luke now describes the kind of people first favoured with the joyful tidings. "*In the same country*," surrounding Bethlehem and its immediate proximity, St. Jerome (Lib. de locis Hebraicis) says, it was the place of the Flock Tower, or Tower of Eder (Genesis xxxv. 21), where Jacob dwelt with his flocks on his return from Mesopotamia, and where Rachel died and was buried. Ven. Bede (Lib. de locis Sanctis) says, they were three in number, as were the Magi also in number, three.

"*Shepherds watching.*" The Greek word for "*watching*," αγραυλοῦντες, properly signifies, *dwelling in the fields*, either in the open air, or covered with tents. David formerly cared his father's sheep as shepherd, probably in the very same place near Bethlehem.

"*And keeping the night watches.*" Watching for a fixed portion of the night, till relieved by others, who spent their allotted portion of time, when they, in turn, were relieved. In this, there is allusion to the division of the nights into four watches, at that time observed by the Jews in imitation of Roman usage (see Matthew xiv. 25). The Greek literally means, "*watching the watches of the night*," or nightly watches, "*over their flock*," to guard them against wolves or robbers.

Some writers, with Scaliger, infer from this, that our Lord's birth occurred not in the end (25th) of December—as the weather would be then too cold for shepherds to tend their flocks out at night; but, in September, when the shepherds could live out at night, watching their flocks. But, the constant tradition of the Church has always been, that our Lord was born at night, on the 25th December; and, as regards the reason adduced to the contrary by Scaliger, it is of no weight if it be borne in mind, that, in hot climates, flocks are fed out on the pastures at night even in mid-winter, or in huts, such as most likely were erected around the "*Flock Tower*" or Tower of Eder, for sheltering flocks in case of great severity of weather (A. Lapide).

9. "*And behold,*" as a matter of unusual occurrence, coming on them, quite unexpectedly.

"*An Angel of the Lord,*" generally supposed to be Gabriel, who had been already entrusted by God with such an exalted commission in connexion with the Incarnation. (Tertullian, Lib. de carne Christi; Cyprian, de Nativitate, Bede, &c.)

"*Stood by them,*" probably, in a visible, human form, which was now assumed by the King of Angels Himself. The Greek, επεστη, would signify also, to stand *over* them, as if gliding down from heaven; and this rendering would be in perfect accordance with what is said of "*the multitude of the heavenly army*" (*v.* 13), who accompanied "*the Angel*" referred to, and were no doubt aloft in the air.

"*And the brightness of God.*" Some divine effulgence reflected from the glorious majesty of God, such as was reflected from our Lord in His glorious transfiguration on Thabor. when "*His face shone as the sun.*"

"*Shone round about them,*" enveloping them, and diffusing a bright light on every side, so as to dispel the surrounding darkness, and show it was divinely sent.

"*And they feared with a great fear,*" as men usually do, when there is question of the supernatural. Among the Jews, it was thought, that whosoever saw an angel, would die (Judges vi. 22, 23; xiii. 22).

The Greek for "*the brightness of God,*" has "*the brightness of the Lord,*" δόξα τοῦ κυρίου. And the Angel calls our Redeemer, "*Lord,*" "*Christ the Lord*" (v. 11), as if the Evangelist meant to convey, that it was the same Christ, our Lord, who was laid obscurely in a manger, that as Sovereign King of heaven, despatched His angels and shed a heavenly effulgent light around the shepherds.

Several reasons are assigned why our Lord appeared first to the poor shepherds, the chief of which are—1st, because He wished, in His humility and poverty, as He had selected a poor stable to be born in, to show a preference for the poor and humble, since "*His communication is with the simple*" (Prov. iii. 32), making them His first Evangelists, as He made fishermen His Apostles; and, because in the whole economy of Redemption, while forwarding the new order of things, which He came to establish on earth, He made use of "*the weak to confound the strong, the foolish to confound the wise . . . and the things that are not, to bring to nought the things that are*" (1 Cor. i. 28), thus removing all grounds for boasting on the part of creatures. He, therefore, hid these things from the wise, the Scribes and Pharisees, and the princes who would have derided Him (Matthew xi. 25; Luke vii. 30); 2ndly, because the shepherds were, in their occupation, very like the Patriarchs, themselves shepherds, to whom were made the promises regarding the future Incarnation of the Son of God; 3rdly, because their occupation resembled His own, who was "*the good Shepherd,*" and was to lay down His life for sheep; 4thly, to convey, that He was one day to be offered up as the Lamb, who was to take away the sins of the world, and had by the retrospective merits of His future Passion, remitted sins in all former ages, being the Lamb slain from the beginning of the world, "*agnus occisus ab origine mundi*" (Apoc. xiii. 8).

It is remarked by Ven Bede, that never in the Old Testament is it said of angels, that they appeared surrounded with light, as is said here; because now a light has risen for those who are upright of heart, "*exortum est in tenebris lumen rectis.*"

10. The Angel dispels the fear caused by his presence and the heavenly effulgence which accompanied him.

"*For, behold I bring you good tidings.*" I announce "to *you,*" and not to the great ones of the earth, excellent tidings regarding a subject, which will cause "*great joy,*" not only to you, but "*to all the people*" of Judea, to whom it is announced first, and "*to all the people*" and nations of the earth, and to all generations of men, who shall have cause to rejoice for it for all eternity, in the priceless blessings and solid good which they shall derive from it, both in time and eternity.

11. "*For this day is born to you a Saviour,*" absolutely called so, because He rescues us from all sin, its guilt and eternal liability; and all this He shall one day perfect in the general resurrection of the just. This was the subject of the "*great joy*" whereby the Angel wished to dispel their fears and calm their apprehensions. It was a subject not only of great joy, but of the greatest joy ever communicated to the human race.

"*This day*"—showing the cause of joy to be present—this very hour of midnight, when we are on the point of entering on a new day, "*is born,*" a perfect man, after having assumed human nature "*to you*" Israelites, to whom He was promised in the first place, "*parvulus natus est nobis; filius datus est nobis*" (Isaiah ix. 6) or, "*to you,*" as representatives of the human race: for, it was not for Angels, who needed Him not, He was born; but, for lost man. "*Born for you,*" as your Saviour, in His *second* generation, as Man God, who in His *first* generation from the Eternal Father, was begotten as God, the Creator, "*per quem, omnia facta sunt.*"

"*Who is Christ the Lord,*" thereby implying His divine nature, as His human nature was implied in the preceding, "*born to you.*" "*Christ,*" the Messiah, *anointed* in virtue of the hypostatic union, to be Prophet, Priest and King (see Matthew i. 1), "*anointed with the oil of gladness, beyond His fellows.*"

"*In the city of David,*" conveys, that He was the blessed seed referred to by the prophets, as springing from the seed of David, and that He was born in the place indicated and foretold by the Prophet Micheas (v. 2), viz., Bethlehem. The words, "*city of David,*" are used preferably to *Bethlehem*, to point out Christ's descent, as had been foretold, from David (John vii. 42).

In order to estimate at their full value, the magnitude of the blessings contained in the words, "*born to you a Saviour,*" we have only to consider the state of the world, the miserably hopeless, spiritual condition of the human race, progressing daily from bad to worse, at the time of the birth of our Redeemer. St. Paul graphically describes it in reference to the Gentile world (Rom. i. 23-32), and in reference to the Jews, (ii. 19-24), and in reference to both together (iii. 11-19). Out of this miserable state, which would, in all probability, have become worse every day, as it had been progressing in evil up to that, only the grace of our Lord Jesus Christ could have rescued them. Hence, the necessity of His coming; and when He did come, to establish a new order of things, to institute a new creation, whereby He renewed the face of the earth, the abundance of grace and gifts He bestowed far exceeded the evil entailed by sin. "*Where sin abounded, grace abounded still more*" (Rom. v. 15-20). Hence, the birth of the Son of God, in accordance with the economy of Redemption decreed by the Almighty, was a subject "*of great joy to all the people,*" to all generations of men, who were to exist on earth to the end of time.

12. "*And this shall be a sign unto you.*" If you wish to go and pay your homage to your new-born Saviour, in order to distinguish Him from others, this will serve as a distinctive sign. Others say, the Angel meant by the words, "I give you a proof and confirmatory argument of the truth of my announcement, that the long expected Saviour is born, and that He is Christ the Lord." It is quite usual in Scripture for divinely commissioned messengers to give signs, as proofs of the truth of what they assert. Thus, Gabriel gave it to Zachary (i. 20); to the Blessed Virgin (36); the Angel to Gideon (Judges vi. 36, 37); Samuel to Saul (1 Kings x. 2). Most likely, however, the Angel primarily refers to a distinctive sign for knowing the infant and distinguishing Him from others; and it may be also, in a certain sense, confirmatory of the truth of what he announced, by showing he could divine future contingent things, and tell beforehand what would happen. The holy Virgin might have changed the position of the infant, and instead of having Him "*laid in a manger,*" at the advent of the shepherds, she might have him clasped in her blessed arms. The Angel, to prove his divine mission and credibility, states the exact position of affairs on their arrival.

"*You shall find the infant,*" if you mean to go and pay Him your homage, not in a royal palace, in regal splendid attire, but, "*wrapped in swaddling clothes, and laid in a manger.*" His first advent amongst us was in humility and poverty, thus the more effectually to elevate, by being the first Himself to enter on it, the new order of things

He came to establish, viz.: to exalt poverty, humility, beyond riches, pride, worldly comfort, so much prized by men, who were fast going along the broad road that leads to perdition.

Some say, "*the manger,*" and "*stable,*" referred to here, were commonly known to the shepherds, as celebrated all over the country; otherwise the Angel would not have given the shepherds sufficient information, if there were many such places in Bethlehem. Others hold, the Angel probably pointed out the direction in which the manger lay—a circumstance omitted in his narrative by the Evangelist—and that the grace of God, interiorly enlightening them, guided them securely thither

13. "*And suddenly,*" unexpectedly, as soon as the Angel ceased to speak, after making the joyous announcement.

"*There was with the Angel,*" either, at that moment descending from heaven, as Ven. Bede, &c., hold, or, then only heard and seen, although present with the Angel from the beginning of the joyous announcement of our Saviour's birth, as is held by others. It is commonly held, they were seen as well as heard by the shepherds.

"*A multitude of the heavenly army.*" That is, a countless number of angels, who came to corroborate the testimony of the Angel, who announced the birth, so that there would be more than *one* witness, and all doubt might be removed from the minds of the shepherds. It is very likely, the Heavenly Father sent all the angels of heaven to adore His Incarnate Son on this occasion, to which reference is made in the words, "*Adorate eum omnes angeli ejus*" (Psalm xcvi. 8), "*et cum iterum introducit primogenitum in orbem terræ, dicit, et adorent eum omnes Angeli Dei*" (Hebrews i. 6). The angels are called "*an army,*" on account of their number, on account of their orderly, hierarchical division, on account of their great power, and their readiness ever to obey the commands of their great Leader in heaven, mighty in battle, who is so often termed, "*Deus virtutum, Deus exercituum, Deus Sabaoth,*" the number of whose soldiers is beyond counting (Job xxv. 3).

"*Praising God,*" with songs of exquisite, angelic melody, thanking Him for the ineffable manifestation of His goodness, displayed in the birth of His Eternal Son; and the priceless benefits resulting from it to earth and heaven. If, at the *first* creation, "*the morning stars praised Him together, and all the sons of God made a joyful melody*" (Job xxxviii.), with how much greater reason should all heaven now resound with shouts of joy and jubilee at the birth of His Son—the greatest of all His works, the *second* and more exalted creation, by which He renewed the face of the earth?

14. "*Glory to God in the highest: and on earth peace to men of good will.*" According to this reading, adopted by the Vulgate—"*pax hominibus bonæ voluntatis*"—there are but *two* members in the sentence. According to the ordinary Greek reading, there are *three* members. "*Glory to God . . . and on earth peace, good will in men,*" και επι της γης ειρηνη, εν ανθρωποις ευδοκια. In the Vatican MS., the reading is, ευδοκιας, *bonæ voluntatis*, which is followed by the Vulgate, and by the most ancient Latin writers, by Origen (Hom. 13 in Lucam), Chrysostom (Hom. de Nativitate); by the Codex Cantabrigensis, by St. Irænaeus, SS. Cyril of Jerusalem, Ambrose, Jerome, Augustine, &c. The antithesis between "*God in the highest heaven,*" and "*men on earth,*" is better sustained by rendering the sentence, *bimembris;* for, between "*men,*" and "*earth,*" there is hardly any distinction; since, it is only of men there is question when "*earth*" is spoken of. Another question arises as to whether the words are *assertive* or *optative.* The former seems more likely; inasmuch, as, the praises of the

angels seem to extol God for what has been mercifully accomplished by Him. The result of the birth of Christ is, "*Glory to God,*" of which He had been hitherto robbed, when man impiously transferred to senseless idols, what was His inalienable due. His power, wisdom, goodness, mercy, and other attributes are now displayed in the birth of His Son, and proclaimed, as due to Him, "*in the highest*" heavens. These words may be joined immediately with "*God,*" who dwells in the highest heavens; or, with "*Glory,*" which is rendered in the highest heavens to God, by the angels who surround His throne, and sing a new song of joy in praise of His infinite perfections, now so resplendently manifested in the Incarnation and birth of His Son.

"*And on earth peace to men of good will.*" "*And*" may mean, "*because.*" Glory to God, &c., *because*, on earth peace is established, which was so long desired. The word "*peace,*" according to a Hebrew usage, means every description of blessings. It may mean, "*peace,*" reconciliation with God, which is soon to be effected by the blood of His Son, who is to reconcile sinful man to His Father, offended by sin, and pay the price of his ransom, and make full satisfaction and atonement; or, "*peace*" between man and man, who were hitherto held asunder. This peace Christ came to establish, breaking down, by His blood, the middle wall of partition, which kept asunder for ages Jews and Gentiles. He came to establish true peace between all the tribes of the earth, by meriting for them the grace to overcome their dreadful feelings of mutual enmity and desires of revenge, which corrupt nature of itself could not overcome; and by substituting in their place, the sweet law of charity, forgiveness of injuries, and brotherly love.

"*Men of good will,*" is understood by some to mean, that while Christ came to establish peace for all, and to tender to all the blessings of peace; it was only men of good will, men well-disposed to profit by the graces and blessings thus offered, that would actually enjoy the priceless blessings of this peace, which He came to establish.

Others, looking to the meaning of the Greek word for "*good will,*" ευδοκια, which, although sometimes understood of men (Romans x. 1), generally, and almost always, in Sacred Scriptures is understood to refer to God, to His benevolence, favour, gracious designs of mercy towards men (as Psalm cxlix. 4, 7; Ephes. i. 5), interpret the words in connexion with "*peace*" thus, "*and on earth, peace of good will,*" which results not from men's merits or deserts; but is purely the effect of God's merciful designs "*in,*" or towards, "*men,*" elected by God to salvation, according to the purpose of His good will (Ephes. i. 5), and merciful designs in regard to them.

TEXT.

15. *And it came to pass, after the angels departed from them into heaven, the shepherds said one to another: Let us go over to Bethlehem, and let us see this word that is come to pass, which the Lord hath showed to us.*

16. *And they came with haste: and they found Mary and Joseph, and the infant lying in the manger.*

17. *And seeing, they understood of the word that had been spoken to them concerning this child.*

18. *And all that heard wondered: and at those things that were told them by the shepherds.*

19. *But Mary kept all these words, pondering them in her heart.*

20. *And the shepherds returned, glorifying and praising God, for all the things they had heard, and seen, as it was told unto them.*

COMMENTARY.

15. "*After the angels*," having discharged their commission, "*departed from them into heaven*," in an invisible form, unto God, by whom they were sent. This shows they were good angels.

"*The shepherds said one to another: Let us go over to Bethlehem and see this word,*" &c. "*This word,*" this *thing*. "*Word,*" in Sacred Scripture, is used, by a Hebrew phrase, to mean any *thing*. "*Which the Lord hath showed to us.*" It was "*the Lord*" who "*showed*" it to them, preferably to the Scribes and Pharisees, and great ones of the earth; because it was He that commissioned the angels. He "*showed,*" that is, *revealed* it, and gave signs for ascertaining it, thereby inviting them to go see for themselves, and learn experimentally the truth of what was said. The shepherds at once obey the heavenly call, and correspond with the Divine inspirations. While the Angel instructed and invited them externally, the grace of God, no doubt, aided and impelled them interiorly to leave their flocks, and visit this Divine Infant in His crib. The same divine grace enlightened them fully as to the Divinity of Him, whom they resolved to visit, and before whom they, doubtless, fell down in prostrate adoration, with mingled feelings of faith, love, and awe.

16. "*With haste,*" from a burning desire, inspired by the grace of God, to see their infant Saviour, and then to return at once to their flocks.

"*They came.*" The cave, it is supposed, was a mile distant. "*They came in haste.*"

"*They found Mary*"—who brought Him forth in full vigour of health—"*and Joseph,*" the guardian of His birth, both spending the night in holy contemplation and prayer, "*and the infant lying in the manger,*" as they had been told beforehand by the Angel. What a consoling spectacle, to behold, for the first time, the Holy Family, Jesus, Mary, and Joseph. How the souls of the shepherds must be inflamed with divine love, at beholding this Trinity of persons on earth, who most faithfully represented the Trinity of the Godhead in heaven. Happy we, if in spirit, we often visit the Holy Family, and merit to be visited by them, at the awful and decisive moment of death.

17. "*And seeing, they understood of the word that had been spoken to them.*" "*Understood,*" may mean, they saw, with their own eyes, that the "*word,*" or announcement, made to them by the Angel was literally true, just as St. John says, "*That which was from the beginning, which we have heard, which we have seen with our eyes, which we have looked upon,*" &c. (1 John i. 1).

The Greek word for "*understood,*" εγνωρισαν, may also mean to divulge, to noise abroad, which sense accords well with what follows. The shepherds, doubtless, told, not only Mary and Joseph, of the Angel's announcement, and the hymns of celestial melody chanted in the skies by multitudes of angels, but others also, as appears from the words of following verse, "*And all that heard wondered,*" &c.

18. "*And all that heard wondered.*" It is likely, that many on hearing the accounts given of what occurred, went themselves to the stable, and saw with their own eyes, the truth of what was narrated. Some, probably, believed whom God enlightened; others, probably, remained in their incredulity, offended by the lowly appearance and condition of the Divine Infant.

"*And at those things that were told them,*" &c. The Greek and Syriac have not "*and.*" Of those who retain it, some understand it to mean, "*that is,*" at the things, &c. Others, understand it literally, and interpret the words thus, they admired the event of the birth of the Son of God, *and*, the other circumstances connected with it, which had been told them by the shepherds, such as the announcement made to them by the Angel, and the appearance of multitudes of angels praising God, &c

19. "*Mary kept all these words.*" While all others were loud in speaking of the wonderful things they saw and heard, and, probably, Joseph too spoke of what he himself knew, as well from the declaration of the Angel regarding the Divinity of the child, as also from what he himself knew in connexion with His birth, thus strengthening the faith of the shepherds, and others who came to the crib ; "*Mary*," as modest in regard to her tongue, as she was in body, displaying consummate prudence and humility.

"*Kept all these words.*" that is to say, things spoken of in her heart. "*Pondering them*," *putting them together* (Bloomfield), comparing the past with the present, the oracles of the prophets regarding the birth of the Saviour from a virgin, and in a determinate place, and other oracles regarding Him, with their full accomplishment ; the announcement made to herself by the Angel, regarding the Son to be born of her, with that made to the shepherd, regarding His actual birth. These things she pondered over, and derived from them fresh arguments, to confirm her faith, and "*kept them in her heart*," treasured them up in her memory, to be disclosed, at God's appointed time, to the world, to be made known to His Apostles, and especially to the Evangelist, St. Luke, by whom they are here recorded in detail.

20. "*The shepherds*," after being fully satisfied from the testimony of their own senses of the truth of the announcement made by the Angel, now "*returned*" to the discharge of their duty of tending their flocks, "*praising and glorifying God, for all the things they had heard*," and had not only heard, but "*seen as it was told to them.*" These latter words, "*as it was told*," &c., affect the words, "*had seen.*"

TEXT.

21. *And after eight days were accomplished that the child should be circumcised ; his name was called Jesus, which was called by the Angel, before he was conceived in the womb.*
22. *And after the days of her purification according to the law of Moses were accomplished, they carried him to Jerusalem, to present him to the Lord.*
23. *As it is written in the law of the Lord, Every male opening the womb shall be called holy to the Lord.*
24. *And to offer a sacrifice according as it is written in the law of the Lord, a pair of turtle doves, or two young pigeons.*

COMMENTARY.

21. "*And after eight days were accomplished that the child should be circumcised.*" The words, "*after eight days*," do not convey, that the period of eight days had elapsed, and after that, circumcision took place. For, it was on the *eighth day*, after the birth of a child, this was to take place according to the law of Moses ; and here, the words, "*that the child should be circumcised*," or, as was appointed by law for His circumcision, show, there is reference to the eighth day *commenced* but not *ended*. It is usual in SS. Scripture, to describe as happening after a time, what took place towards the close of it, and before the time had expired. Thus, of our Lord it is said, that "*He was to rise after three days ;*" although, from the context, it is clear it was meant, that this would happen on *the third* day. So also (Genesis xli. 18, 19, 20), where a thing is said to occur "*after three days*" (18, 19), which occurred "*on the third*" (v. 20). Here, then,

the words mean, after seven days had passed and the eighth had arrived, on which, according to law, the child was to be circumcised. The Evangelist does not expressly say, *He was* circumcised; but, he implies it, by a reference to the time and law of circumcision, which Ho submitted to, who came *" to fulfil all justice."* Our Lord voluntarily submitted to the painful rite of circumcision; although, not bound to do so, being Himself the legislator; and moreover, the reason of its application to Him did not exist at all, as He was free from all sin, of which circumcision was the type. He submitted to it, however, for several reasons, viz., to give an example of obedience; to take away every pretext from the Jews of rejecting Him, as not being a true son of Abraham; to show, that He assumed a real body on this earth; to approve of the rite of circumcision; to submit to the law, that being *"made under the law, He would redeem those who were under the law."* (Gal. iv.)

It is likely, He was circumcised in the stable, not by Joseph, but by some Priest or Levite, so that there would be an authentic record of the fact. See chap. i. v. 59.)

"His name was called Jesus," by Mary and Joseph, according to the command given from Heaven to both (Matthew i. 21; Luke i. 31.) The Greek has, *"And* His name was called Jesus." *"And"* may mean, *also,* or *then.* It is omitted by the Vulgate interpreter as superfluous. *"Which was called by the Angel,"* enjoined on them by the Angel to bestow on Him.

"Before He was conceived in the womb." It was only after the close of the Annunciation, and the consent of the Virgin, that our Lord was conceived in her sacred womb. It was also given Him *after* He was conceived (Matthew i. 21).

For the meaning and derivation of the word *"Jesus"* (see Matthew i. 21). The rite of circumcision was most painful to the Divine Infant, who began to suffer thus early for our sakes. It was also most humiliating, even more so still, than His birth in a stable. In the latter case, He took on Himself the form of a man; in the former, of a sinner. But, in reward for this humiliation, He received an exalted name, at the sound of which every knee in heaven, earth, and hell, must bend. And, indeed, in almost every case, where our Lord endured any signal humiliation, His Heavenly Father bestowed on Him some compensation and mark of honour. In the stable, the angels sang hymns of praise; here, He received the most exalted of names; when the Scribes blasphemed His Divine works, the people would exalt Him; at His final humiliation and death, all nature, the sun, the rocks, the very dead, did Him honour, to convey to us, that if we wish to be exalted, we must first be humbled. Such is the disposition of Divine economy established in the present order of things. It is only in the adorable Sacrament of His abiding love on our altars, when He is truly a *hidden God,* and where He permanently submits to the greatest outrages for our sakes to the end of time, that He receives no proportionate sensible compensation from His Heavenly Father. Hence, the obligation on the part of His faithful, to whom His Heavenly Father intrusts Him, to make, as far as possible, some reparation to Him in this Divine institution, where He is our food during life, our solace at death, the last friend we hope to accompany us, when all others must leave us, our Viatic, guide and support when entering the gates of Eternity, whence we are never to return.

22. *"And after the days of her purification according to the law of Moses were accomplished."* This means, as explained already in reference to the words, *"and after eight days,"* &c. (v. 21), when the days filling up the interval between the birth of the child and the day appointed in the law of Moses for the purification of a woman had passed, and the day itself was partially over, for, it was on that day the rite of puri-

ST. LUKE, CHAP II.

fication took place. A similar form is used (Leviticus xii. 6). There is reference in these two verses to a threefold law enacted by Moses. The *first* (Leviticus xii.) having reference to a woman after child-birth. In case of a *son*, she should be unclean *seven* days, during which, anything she touched or came in contact with, was legally unclean. She should remain thirty-three days, besides, in the blood of her purification. During these thirty-three days, she was forbidden to enter the Sanctuary; but, she might not have kept so much aloof from others, as during the preceding seven days. After the lapse of these forty days, she was to be purified according to a certain rite, in the Temple. If she gave birth to a *female* infant, she was to remain unclean, *fourteen* days, in the strictest sense, so as to keep aloof from all, as was usual during the *seven* days succeeding the birth of a *male* child, and she should remain *sixty-six* days more —in all, eighty days, double the number of days enjoined in case she gave birth to a male child—in the blood of her purification. During the latter sixty-six days, she was only prevented from entering the Sanctuary. It is to this law, reference is here made by St. Luke, "*When the days of her purification according to the law of Moses*," which, in regard to a male child, was forty days. The following words, "*and they carried Him to Jerusalem*," have no essential connexion with this law, as the law, having reference to the offering of a male infant was quite distinct from that regarding the purification of the mother, although, usually, the legal process of declaring the mother purified and offering the child took place at the same time.

The *second* had reference to a sacrifice which the mother, whether in case of the birth of a son or daughter, was bound, by the law of Moses, to offer, on the occasion of her being declared purified. If the parties were rich (Leviticus xii. 6-8), they should present a lamb of a year old for holocaust, and a turtle or young pigeon for a sin-offering, which they were to deliver to the priest; if poor, two turtles, or two young pigeons, one for a holocaust, and the other for sin-offering. To this, reference is made by St. Luke (*v.* 24), "*and to offer a sacrifice, &c.*," and as the Blessed Virgin was, from her condition in life— the wife of a carpenter—reckoned among the poor, St. Luke only cites the portion of the Divine ordinance that had reference to the offering on the part of the poor. It is to be observed, that the words (*v.* 24), "*and to offer*," &c., are not joined with, "*they carried Him to Jerusalem;*" but, with the words, implied and understood, viz., *they went to Jerusalem*, since the presence of the child was not necessary at the offering of turtles, &c., for, this offering took place, whether there was question of either a male or female child; and in the latter case, the child was not present at all.

The *third* (Exodus xiii.) had reference to an ordinance requiring the Jews, in the case of the first-born male, whether of man or beast, that it should be given and consecrated to the Lord, in commemoration of the preservation of the Hebrews, and the slaying of the first-born of the Egyptians by the destroying Angel in Egypt. In case of the first-born of a clean animal, it was offered up as a victim; of an unclean, it was to be redeemed (Numbers xviii. 15); the first-born of an ass to be exchanged for a sheep; if not redeemed, to be killed (Exodus xiii. 13). In the case of man, as the Lord had chosen the sons of Levi in place of the first-born male children of His people (Numbers iii.), he was to be redeemed at a price (Exod. xiii. 15) of five sicles. It is to this ordinance St. Luke refers in the words, "*They carried Him to Jerusalem to present Him to the Lord, as it is written . . . every male opening the womb shall be called holy*," that is, shall be dedicated and set apart from profane uses, and thus "*holy to the Lord*." Although St. Luke makes no mention of it, it is likely our Lord who came "*to fulfil all justice*," was redeemed for five sicles.

It is commonly held, that the Blessed Virgin was not strictly bound by the law of Leviticus xii., prescribing the rite of purification; because she brought forth her child, a pure virgin, without any physical, or moral defilement either. But she complied with this law, to avoid scandal; as her Son, for the same reason, submitted to the knife of circumcision, and paid the tribute. As regards the precept of (Exodus xiii.) having reference to the offering of the first-born, some hold, the Blessed Virgin was not bound; because the words of the law, "*opening the womb*," could not apply to her offspring, who was born of her, without opening her womb, because, she remained a pure virgin. Hers was, therefore, according to these, an exceptional case, not comprehended in the law, relative to the opening of the womb. However, some interpreters understand the words to mean, the *first-born* of a mother. At all events, as in the preceding case, she offered her Son to avoid scandal, and to give an example of humility and obedience.

The same applies to the offering of two turtles or two young pigeons (the Evangelist does not say which), one offered for a holocaust in thanksgiving for the happy deliverance of the mother; and the other, for a sin-offering. With this also she complied, to give an example of obedience and humility, and to avoid scandal, although, not strictly bound by the precept on this subject.

TEXT.

25. *And behold there was a man in Jerusalem named Simeon, and this man was just and devout, waiting for the consolation of Israel: and the Holy Ghost was in him.*

26. *And he had received an answer from the Holy Ghost, that he should not see death, before he had seen the Christ of the Lord.*

27. *And he came by the Spirit into the temple. And when his parents brought in the child Jesus, to do for him according to the custom of the law,*

28. *He also took him into his arms, and blessed God, and said:*

29. *Now thou dost dismiss thy servant, O Lord, according to thy word in peace.*

30. *Because my eyes have seen thy salvation,*

31. *Which thou hast prepared before the face of all peoples:*

32. *A light to the revelation of the Gentiles, and the glory of thy people Israel.*

33. *And his father and mother were wondering at those things, which were spoken concerning him.*

34. *And Simeon blessed them, and said to Mary his mother: Behold this (child) is set for the fall, and for the resurrection of many in Israel, and for a sign which shall be contradicted.*

35. *And thy own soul a sword shall pierce, that out of many hearts thoughts may be revealed.*

COMMENTARY.

25. "*And behold.*" it being a matter well deserving of attention. The Evangelist wishes to convey, that testimony was rendered to our Lord, by two saints of both sexes, venerable for their years, and edifying conduct; both imbued with a prophetic spirit. Hence, their testimony was of the greatest weight.

"*There was a man in Jerusalem named Simeon.*" Some say, he was a priest; because he blessed Joseph and Mary (*v.* 34). But, it is most likely, if he were a priest, St. Luke, who mentions other qualities in commendation of him, would not have omitted this. He might have blessed Mary and Joseph, in the capacity of a venerable old man.

"*Just and devout.*" These qualities first assigned in commendation of him, are calculated to add weight to his testimony. "*Just*," owing to the inherent justice and sanctification permanently residing in him, and showing this in his relations with his fellow-men. "*Devout*" (ευλαβης) towards God, whom he reverenced and feared to offend.

"*Waiting for the consolation of Israel*," anxiously looking forward to and expecting the advent of Him, who was to bring consolation to Israel, under the temporal and spiritual bondage and misery, from which they suffered. They suffered great temporal evils from the Romans and Herod, and great spiritual tyranny from the Scribes and Pharisees (Matt. ix. 36). Christ was looked forward to as the consoler of Israel. (Isaias xl. 1; li. 3; lxi. 1, 2). Simeon inferred from the several prophecies—the sceptre having passed away from Juda—the fulfilment of the seventy weeks of Daniel, and other prophecies, that the time of the Messiah had arrived. Simeon was more anxious about the public good than his own.

"*And the Holy Ghost was in him*," by sanctifying grace, as he was "*just*," and also by the gift of prophecy which he possessed, a sense in which the words are often taken in SS. Scripture. They are thus used (Luke i. 35) in reference to the conception of a Son by the Blessed Virgin, and (i. 45) in reference to Elizabeth, who, under this influence, began to prophesy. The Evangelist probably mentions this, to show now it is he received an answer; because, God's Spirit had resided in him.

26. "*And he had received an answer*." The Greek word—κεχρηματισμενον—means, to receive an oracular or divine admonition, as in Matthew (ii. 12). How it is this admonition was communicated, whether orally, or by dream, or by internal inspiration, or otherwise, the Evangelist does not say.

"*See death*," means, by a Hebrew idiom, *to die*.

"*The Christ of the Lord*." For the meaning of "*Christ*," and its application to our Lord (see Matthew i. 1; Psalm xliv. 7, 8; Heb. i. 9). The Evangelist ascribes the foregoing qualities to Simeon, to add greater weight to his testimony regarding our Lord.

27. "*By the Spirit*," under the inspiration and guidance of the Spirit that "*was in him*."

"*His parents*." Joseph was the reputed father of our Lord (*v.* 48).

"*To do for Him according to the custom of the law*." Offering Him up to God as first-born male child (*v.* 23); and, probably, paying the ransom of five sicles, usually paid in such cases.

28. "*He also took Him*." "*Also*," &c., may mean, that He as well as His mother, who carried Him, or the priest who offered Him, to be returned to His parents on paying the ransom of five sicles. It may also mean, *then*, or, perhaps, it may be redundant.

"*Took Him into his arms*," embracing Him with all faith and devotion, in which he had the advantage over the prophets of old, who only saw Him at a distant futurity, and were gladdened in their exile. The same Holy Spirit that guided and inspired Simeon to enter the Temple, also revealed to him, our Lord as the Redeemer of mankind and Consoler of Israel. We can conjecture, says Origen (in Luc., Hom. 15), what graces Simeon received, who took the Son of God into his arms, when we read of the favours bestowed on the woman who merely touched the hem of His garment. "*And blessed God*," thanking Him for having fulfilled His promise, that he would see his Saviour before he died; thanking Him also for the great mystery of the Incarnation of His Son.

29. "*Now, O Lord*," who art master of life and death, "*who killeth and maketh alive, bringeth down to hell, and bringeth back again*," (1 Kings ii. 6). "*Dost dismiss*." Greek—απολυεις—means to loosen, to dissolve, as if he meant to loosen the bonds

whereby the soul is detained in the body, away from its native, eternal home. Some read the words, imperatively, "*now dismiss;*" others, in the future, "*thou shalt dismiss.*" Better give it a present signification; "now, O Lord, whenever it pleases Thee to take me out of life, Thou doest so *in peace*," leaving me no cause of regret, nothing to bind me to earth. All my desires are satiated. The words, "*in peace*," are to be joined to "*dost dismiss.*" "*Peace,*" among the Jews, meant the quiet possession of all blessings. Here, the fulness of satiety without any want or cause for regret. The words of Simeon are similar to those of Jacob on beholding Joseph (Genesis xlvi. 30), "*Now shall I die with joy, because I have seen thy face.*"

"*Thy servant.*" He speaks of himself in the third person, out of humility.

"*According to Thy word,*" or promise made, that before death I would see my Salvation. This promise being now enjoyed by me, there is nothing else to bind me to this earth. I can, therefore, depart contentedly out of life, the only thing to keep me anxiously in it, to bind me to it, being to see your promise fulfilled. But, now, this promise fulfilled, I depart cheerfully at any moment Thou mayest fix upon.

30. "*Because my eyes have seen Thy salvation.*" This is addressed to God, the Father, whose Son, sent by Him—"*Thy salvation*"—for the salvation and redemption of His people, is frequently in SS. Scripture called "*Salvation*" (Genesis xl. 8; Psalm l. 14; lxxxiv. 8; cxviii. 81, &c.; Isaias xxxii. 10; Habacuc iii. 18). Simeon is now willing to die, because with his corporal eyes, he saw Him present, whom with the eyes of his soul, he believed to be the Eternal Son of God, and who was only seen in spirit by the Patriarchs at a distant futurity.

31. "*Which*" ("salvation," or) Saviour, "*Thou hast prepared,*" by an Eternal decree, and sent in time, not to a remote corner of Judea; but, "*before the face of all peoples,*" Jews and Gentiles alike, whom He was to redeem; and who by knowing Him, and looking on Him by faith, conceived from the preaching of His Apostles and their successors were to obtain eternal happiness and full redemption from all evils here and hereafter. Here holy Simeon refers to the calling of the Gentile world, and their full participation in these spiritual blessings, of which the Jews alone were hitherto the depositaries (Romans iii. 2; ix. 1, 2).

32. "*A light,*" that is, Thou hast prepared Him to be "*a light.*" It is put in apposition to "*salvation*" (v. 30). A light to enlighten the Gentiles sunk in the densest darkness of error, unbelief, and sin, "*sitting in darkness and the shadow of death*" (i. 79), and to be the glory of the Jewish people, to whom it was a source of particular glory to have Christ born of them, according to the flesh; to have all His miracles during life performed in their midst, not excepting His glorious Resurrection and Ascension; to have His Apostles first sent amongst them. Although the Gentiles derived great glory from the birth of Christ, and the Jews received great light, still, *light* appropriately applies to the Gentiles, on account of the darkness of Paganism, out of which they were rescued by Christ.

"*Father.*" Joseph was reputed in public, to be the father of our Lord, being the spouse of His mother, as men are frequently called the fathers of the children they adopt.

"*Were wondering,*" because, although they knew the Divine Infant to be the Son of God, the destined Saviour of mankind; still, they did not know in detail the things said here of Him by Simeon and Anna; such as, that He was to be the light of the Gentile and the glory of the Jew; that He would be "*for the ruin as well as for the resurrection of many, &c.*"; that "*the sword of sorrow would pierce her soul, &c.*" For, what is said in the following verses formed the subject of admiration on their part, just as well as what precedes.

34. While holding Jesus in his arms, "*Simeon blessed them,*" His parents. We cannot for a moment suppose he would presume to bless Him whom he knew to be the Son of God. The form of sacerdotal blessing is given, (Numbers vi. 24, 25, &c.) Simeon's blessing of them here, according to St. Bonaventure, consisted in congratulating them; *Mary*, in having given birth to the source of all good; *Joseph*, in being charged, as reputed father, with His education; and, in wishing them the increase of all blessings. Before treating of His future Passion and Mary's sufferings on His account, Simeon "*blessed them,*" to prepare them for the bitter cup in store for them.

"*And said to Mary His mother.*" These words he addresses to her in particular, because they concerned her; and, in all probability, Joseph was not alive when these prophetic words were verified in her regard. It is likely, Joseph died before our Lord's manifestation to Israel, and was not on earth to be looked upon by men as the reputed father of Jesus, when He publicly called God His Father. Epiphanius (Hæresi 71, contra Antidicomarianatas). Simeon, after congratulating her, on the wonderful things God did for her, now predicts the sufferings of herself and her Son.

"*Behold,*" as a matter deserving of all attention, "*this*" (*child*), whom I have proclaimed to be a Saviour in the face of all peoples, will still be the occasion, through their own perversity, of the eternal ruin of many.

"*Is set for the fall and resurrection of many in Israel.*" Our Lord was set as the foundation in the spiritual edifice of the Church, *indirectly*, for the fall and spiritual ruin of many in Israel, being its occasion, owing to their own perversity, and obstinate rejection of His preaching and mission; but He was set *directly*, "*for their resurrection,*" their resuscitation from the grave of sin and infidelity, to a new life of grace, truth, and sanctity here, and a life of eternal glory hereafter. This was directly intended by God, as the effect of Christ's coming.

This is allusive to Isaias (viii. 14; xxviii. 16), quoted by St. Paul (Rom. ix. 33; 1 Peter ii. 6; Acts iv. 11; Matthew xxi. 42).

"*And for a sign which shall be contradicted.*" Holy Simeon here corroborates what he had already said regarding our Lord being set up "*for the ruin of many,*" who shall perversely oppose Him, by word and act; and who by blasphemous charges and persecutions shall oppose and make Him the mark, at which they shall level all the arrows of their cruel hate and malignity. In several parts of SS. Scripture our Lord is referred to, both as a "*sign to be set up*" (Isaias viii. 18; xi. 10; Lament. iii. 12, 13; Job xvi. 13), and as an object of contradiction. (Psa. xvii. 44; Heb. xii. 3, &c.) The idea is borrowed from archers, who level their arrows at some mark they set up, and cease not till by perforation in all parts it is rendered perfectly valueless. So, this prophecy of Simeon is seen thoroughly verified from the history of our Lord's life, in the calumnies, the expressions of hatred, malevolence and envy He suffered at the hands of the Jews, and the persecution they subjected Him to, throughout the whole course of His sacred mission, until finally they raised Him aloft on the cross, thus contradicting or rather persecuting Him to the very death. While the "*sign of contradiction*" includes all the sufferings of our

Redeemer through life; it is likely, it contains special reference to His elevation on the cross, with marked allusion to the brazen serpent raised up by Moses in the desert, which was a figure of our Lord's crucifixion (John iii. 14). It was at the time of our Lord's crucifixion the following words of Simeon regarding the "*sword*" of sorrow, &c., were specially verified.

The Greek for, "*shall be contradicted,*" is in the present, αντιλεγομενον, but the Vulgate interpreter gave the sense in the future tense; or, the Greek word may mean, that He was a sign liable to contradiction, as some of the Holy Fathers have it, *signum contradicibile*.

35. "*And thy own soul,*" as well as the soul of your Son, "*a sword shall pierce.*" It shall penetrate His soul and body, and cause His death; and, by the same stroke, while killing Him, it shall wound her soul, and transfix it to its inmost depths. By the "*sword,*" is meant, the contumelious language, ["*lingua eorum gladius acutus*" (Psalm lvi. 5); "*exacuerunt ut gladium linguas suas*" (Psalm lxiii 4)] addressed to her Son, both in life, and particularly, at His death, and the torments inflicted on Him especially during His cruel Passion. She suffered in her soul the most intense grief, which may be measured by her intense love for her suffering Son; by the dignity of His person; by the atrocity and duration of His torments; by His utter dereliction, "*ut quid dereliquisti,*" &c. Simeon predicts these, in order to fortify the Virgin against them, by preparing her to bear them, as she did, with the greatest sense of dignity and heroic patience.

"*That out of many hearts thoughts may be revealed.*" These words are commonly connected with the preceding verse, and the intervening words, "*a sword shall pierce thy own soul,*" read parenthetically, "*behold this child is set for the fall . . . to be contradicted*" (*and thy own soul . . .*) "*that out of many hearts, &c.,*" as if it were meant to convey, that the *consequence* of His being "*set for the fall and resurrection of many,*" was, that "*out of many hearts, &c.;*" or, the *cause* ("*that*") signifying either cause or consequence, or both), of His being thus contradicted, was, to elicit the latent thoughts of many regarding Him. Some affecting great love for justice, a great longing desire for the advent of their Messiah, regarding whom, however, they entertained erroneous notions, scornfully rejected Him, and rejoiced in His ignominy and death; others, who were in heart and soul true believers, now openly avowing their convictions, resolved to sacrifice everything for His sake. In truth, at all periods of the Christian dispensation, our Lord's presence in this world, as a sign rejected by many, would be the test for disclosing men's innermost thoughts, for showing, on the one hand, who were His humble followers, that were to be numbered among His elect; and, on the other, who, the obstinate unbelievers were, that perversely rejected Him

Others, who reject the idea of the preceding words, "*a sword,*" &c., being included in a parenthesis, hold, that these words are to be connected immediately with the preceding, and mean, that the sight of the Virgin, transfixed with sorrow at the foot of the cross, would have the effect of causing many to associate themselves with her, and openly and fearlessly proclaim their belief in our Lord (John xix. 38; Mark xv. 14). Thus, we see Nicodemus, the holy women, St. John, and others, who fled from fear, now rally round the Blessed Virgin in the hour of her intense sorrow and openly proclaim their faith and feelings.

TEXT.

36. *And there was one Anna, a prophetess, the daughter of Phanuel, of the tribe of Aser; she was far advanced in years, and had lived with her husband seven years from her virginity.*

37. *And she was a widow until fourscore and four years; who departed not from the temple, by fastings and prayers serving night and day.*

38. *Now she at the same hour coming in, confessed to the Lord; and spoke of him to all that looked for the redemption of Israel.*

COMMENTARY.

36. The Evangelist now adduces a second witness to our Lord's divinity—since our Lord came to repair and redeem both sexes—so that, "*in the mouth of two witnesses every word might stand.*" He mentions certain qualities pertaining to this witness, "*Anna,*" which served to add greater weight to her testimony. Her name "*Anna,*" which signifies, *grace;* her parent, "*Phanuel,*" well known for his goodness at the time; "*the tribe*" from which she sprung, "*Aser,*" thus distinguishing her from others of the name who might have lived at the time.

"*A prophetess,*" filled with the spirit of prophecy, as appears (*v.* 38); probably, she may have been regarded as such by common repute.

"*Far advanced in years,*" not likely to be carried away by youthful enthusiasm.

"*And had lived with her husband seven years from her virginity.*" In these words she is commended for her virginal and conjugal chastity. She reached puberty and got married about the 15th year of her age.

37. "*She was a widow until fourscore and four years.*" In this, she is commended for her continency in the state of widowhood, not again seeking second nuptials Some, with St. Ambrose, understand these words to embrace the period of time she was a widow, so that according to them, she must have reached about the 106th year of her age, during fifteen of which she was a virgin; seven, a married woman; 84 a widow. From the Greek reading, it is commonly inferred that the term 84, comprises the number of years she lived up to this time. "*Who departed not from the Temple,*" spent a great part of her time there. Some say, she lived in the Temple, or in the apartments set aside for devout females in the Temple, "*who watched at the door of the tabernacle*" (Exodus xxxviii. 8).

"*By fastings and by prayers*"—these kindred virtues, which serve as wings to raise up the soul to God, to whom they have been from the beginning in all dispensations, and are still and shall be, so acceptable, "*bona est oratio cum jejunio.*" (Tobias xii.) "*Serving.*" The Greek word, λατρευουσα, signifies, offering the homage of divine worship. This she did almost constantly, "*night and day,*" by means of prayer and fasting. Fasting and prayer are recommended in the Old Testament and the New, as specially agreeable to God. Fasting disposes for prayer; excessive indulgence renders us unfit for it. "*Qui corporali jejunio . . . mentem elevas*" (Præf. Missæ). What then are we to think of those who, boasting of their Christian profession, decry by every means, this Christian exercise of fasting, so much commended throughout the SS. Scriptures?

38. "*Now she at the same hour,*" at the time Simeon holding our Lord in his arms spoke of Him, as above. "*Coming in,*" not by chance, but under the guidance and impulse of the same Holy Spirit that directed Simeon to the Temple at the time (*v.* 27). "*Coming in,*" Greek, επιστασα, would signify, *coming up.* Probably, leaving the place in the Temple where she was engaged in prayer, she came up to the portion of it in which the child and His parents were.

"*Confessed to the Lord,*" gave thanks and praised His eternal mercies in having now, at His appointed time, sent His Son into the world, and exhibited Him now in

His holy temple. The Greek word, ανθωμολογεῖτο, would imply, that she did so in *turn* on her own part, in response to the praises uttered by Simeon.

"*And spoke of Him.*" She acted discreetly by not speaking of Him to every one, who cared little for His coming, and might spurn her profession; but, "*to all that looked,*" with sincere and anxious minds, and a spirit of true faith and piety, "*for the redemption of Israel*"—the coming of the promised Messiah, now present, who was to be for them, a Saviour to rescue them from sin and its temporal and eternal consequences. The Greek has, "*the Redemption in Jerusalem,*" and some Greek MSS., viz., Vatican, "*of Jerusalem.*" However, it does not much affect the sense. In the latter reading, "*of Jerusalem,*" there is mention of a part, the most prominent and conspicuous, of the Jewish nation, whose capital city was Jerusalem, the seat of their religion—so a part is used for the whole; the other reading, "*in Jerusalem,*" would either mean, that they were expecting this redemption would be accomplished in Jerusalem, or that she spoke to such as expected the Messiah in Jerusalem. It may be, that the Evangelist wrote both, viz., "*all who were expecting the salvation of Israel in Jerusalem.*"

TEXT.

39. *And after they had performed all things according to the law of the Lord, they returned into Galilee, to their city Nazareth.*

40. *And the child grew, and waxed strong, full of wisdom; and the grace of God was in him.*

COMMENTARY.

39. "*And after they had performed all things according to the law of the Lord,*" in regard to the purification of the mother, the presentation of a pair of turtles, or two young pigeons; the offering of the child, and His redemption, as first-born, for five sicles.

"*They returned into Galilee,*" &c. (See Matthew ii. 13, as to the time at which this occurred, and the order of events connected with it.) St. Luke passes over the flight into Egypt, the visit of the Magi, probably, because St. Matthew had already fully described these occurrences. Some say, they proceeded from Judea to Egypt, as it was to Judea Joseph afterwards was about returning from his exile. Others say, from Nazareth. Others, from Bethlehem, whither they went directly from the Temple, with the view of returning to Nazareth. Nothing certain is known regarding it.

40. "*And the child grew,*" in stature, "*and waxed strong,*" His limbs becoming more firm and robust, as He grew in bodily size. The common Greek has, "*waxed strong in spirit,*" having reference to His soul, which was filled with all the gifts of the Holy Ghost, by whom He was conceived.

"*Full of wisdom,*" with which His soul was full, arising from the hypostatic union, from the moment of His Incarnation. The Greek reading—πληρουμενον σοφιας—would convey, that He gradually acquired experimental knowledge, or, it may mean, that while *interiorly* filled with all knowledge and wisdom, which, according to some, was incapable of increase or augmentation, as, "*in Him were hidden all the treasures of wisdom, &c.*" (Coloss. ii. 3), He, *externally*, to the eyes of men, became more and more perfect in the exhibition of all virtues, being thoroughly free from all these faults and imperfections, to which children and youth are commonly subject.

"*And the grace of God was in Him,*" or, as the Greek—επ'αυτο—has it, "*upon Him,*" that is to say, the favour, unchangeable complacency, and benevolence of

His Heavenly Father, who was always well pleased with Him, ever guided and regulated all His movements and actions. By saying, "*the child grew, and waxed strong,*" &c., the Evangelist wishes to note the reality of His assumed nature ; while, at the same time, he indicates that there was something more to be seen in Him, being free from all imperfections, He every day showed advancement in perfection.

TEXT.

41. *And his parents went every year to Jerusalem, at the solemn day of the pasch.*

42. *And when he was twelve years old, they going up into Jerusalem according to the custom of the feast,*

43. *And having fulfilled the days, when they returned, the child Jesus remained in Jerusalem ; and his parents knew it not.*

44. *And thinking that he was in the company, they came a day's journey, and sought him among their kinsfolks and acquaintance.*

45. *And not finding him, they returned into Jerusalem, seeking him.*

46. *And it came to pass, that after three days they found him in the temple sitting in the midst of the doctors, hearing them and asking them questions.*

47. *And all that heard him were astonished at his wisdom and his answers.*

48. *And seeing him, they wondered. And his mother said to him : Son, why hast thou done so to us? behold thy father and I have sought thee sorrowing.*

49. *And he said to them: How is it that you sought me? did you not know, that I must be about my Father's business?*

50. *And they understood not the word, that he spoke unto them.*

51. *And he went down with them, and came to Nazareth : and was subject to them. And his mother kept all these words in her heart.*

52. *And Jesus advanced in wisdom and age, and grace with God and men.*

COMMENTARY.

41. "*And His parents went every year,*" &c. The men were commanded by the law of Moses (Exodus xxiii. 14-17 ; xxxiv. 23 ; Deut. xvi. 16) to go to the Temple three times in the year, viz., at the solemn festivals of the Pasch, Pentecost, and Tabernacles. It was not enjoined on the women; the Blessed Virgin, however, out of devotion, accompanied her husband. Whether Joseph himself went up on these three occasions, or, only at the Pasch—the greatest solemnity of all—and whether Mary accompanied him on these three occasions, with the child Jesus, is disputed. Some hold, Joseph went up only at the Pasch, from which there was no dispensation ; and that, on account of the great distance of Jerusalem from Nazareth, he was dispensed from going to the two other feasts. It is, however, more commonly held, that Joseph attended on all three occasions each year; and that his holy Virgin spouse accompanied him on these several occasions; and, as it is most unlikely, they left their heavenly charge behind them ; it is, therefore, commonly held that our Lord always accompanied them. Moreover, in this, they would give a lesson to parents as to the practical early teaching of children in the duties of religion. But, St. Luke refers only to their annual attendance at the Pasch, as it was only at the Pasch, the following wonderful occurrence, in the Temple, where our Lord showed He was "*full of wisdom,*" took place. He does not deny it regarding other occasions. And, although the cruel Archelaus still reigned in Jerusalem, the dread of whose cruelty caused Joseph to give up all idea of dwelling in Judea (Matt. ii.); still, the parents of the child naturally expected He would pass unnoticed in the crowd that flocked to Jerusalem on these solemn festivals. Besides, they had great

trust in Providence, for whose honour and service they underwent this risk, and they dreaded offending God, by neglect, more than the danger they incurred from Archelaus, which was diminished by their immediate return home on each occasion. Some hold, that our Redeemer did not go to the Temple till he was twelve years old, when, according to them, Archelaus, in the tenth year of his reign, was banished by Augustus, and sent into exile. Hence, no danger from him.

42. To the end of this verse should be added, in order to complete the sense, the words, "*the child also went up with them.*"

43. They religiously remained till the Octave day, although not bound to remain, at Jerusalem; and then, returned home, while "*the child Jesus remained in Jerusalem.*" Some say, He rendered Himself invisible on this, as He did on subsequent occasions (Origen in Luc., Hom. 19). He assigns Himself the reason of His remaining (v. 49).

"*And His parents knew it not.*" Some Greek copies have, "*Joseph and His mother knew it not.*" Very likely, He concealed His design from His parents, lest if He asked their permission, which they probably might refuse, He would seem guilty of disobedience by remaining; and He also may have in view to show, He had a more exalted Parent in heaven, whose glory and business He should promote, independently of all earthly relations and considerations. He wished, by remaining, to give a glimpse of the glory concealed within Him, and to prepare men for its manifestation in due time, marked out in the decrees of His Eternal Father. He "*remained,*" not by accident, but, by the all-ruling designs of Providence. The parents may be freed from the charge of negligence regarding Him, if it be borne in mind, that those of the same neighbourhood and kindred returned in companies; those of one household being mixed up with those of another, till, at evening, they were to be recognised at the place of public entertainment. Probably, the *men* formed one company apart; and the *women*, another. Thus, Joseph might have supposed that the Divine Infant was with His mother's company; and, His mother, that he was with Joseph. This is held by St. Bernard (Serm. infra Octav. Epiph.), by Ven. Bede, St. Bonaventure, &c. However, the Evangelist seems to favour the former supposition, viz., that the persons of the same neighbourhood used to travel in companies without minding the distinction of families, or household, on their journey, till they halted at evening. For, he says, His parents thought, "*He was in the company,*" among whom they searched for Him in the evening.

44. "*They came a day's journey.*" Nazareth was three days' journey from Jerusalem. "*And sought Him,*" when they reached the term of their day's journey, at the place of common resort. The Evangelist would seem to exculpate Mary and Joseph, as the practice of allowing children to travel with the members of the same company was probably quite common, and it may be, that our Lord did so on former occasions when He went up, in company with them, to attend the festival celebrations at Jerusalem.

45. "*They returned to Jerusalem,*" as they got no tidings from any one regarding His having been seen leaving it. "*Seeking Him,*" inquiring regarding Him on their way thither.

46. "*After three days,*" or on the third day after they left. It is quite common in Sacred Scriptures to say that a thing occurred after a day on which it took place

(*v.* 21 ; also Mark viii. 31). One day was spent on their way home ; a second, on their return to Jerusalem. On the third, they found Him. "*They found Him in the Temple,*" engaged in His Father's business, in His Father's house, and not in places of public diversion or entertainment. Probably, the "*Temple*" here means, a court of it, in which the doctors sat for the purpose of public instruction.

"*Sitting in the midst of the doctors,*" not that the child took His place among them. This His own modesty would forbid, and the pride of these learned teachers would not submit to it. It only means, that He was sitting in their presence, as a hearer, listening to them treating of the Divine law.

"*Hearing them and asking them questions.*" He so managed His questions, which He proposed modestly, not by way of disputation, as to convey knowledge ; and, in turn, elicited from them questions, to which He replied with marvellous wisdom and knowledge. It was wonderful to see this child of twelve, answering and proposing questions connected with the Law of God to these learned doctors, which elicited the admiration of all. It is very likely, He managed to turn their attention to the great question of the coming of their Messiah, and to the fulfilment of all the prophecies that had reference to Him, viz., the passing away of the sceptre from Judah—the seventy weeks of Daniel, &c. Very likely, He proved the Messiah must now have come. His personal appearance showed His human nature ; the maturity of His judgment and knowledge, and wisdom, at that age, showed He was something more than man. He thus early gave a passing proof of what He was. He darted forth a ray of His Divinity in order to prepare men for a fuller manifestation of it, when He would, at no distant day, enter on His public mission, and the instruction of the world.

47. "*His wisdom and His answers,*" that is, the wisdom of His answers.

48. His parents "*seeing Him, wondered.*" Not that it caused them surprise to see Him, whom they knew to be the Eternal Son of God, display such knowledge. But as He never before *publicly* acted thus—very likely in *private*, He might have given proofs of His latent Divinity—they were surprised at His doing so now, for the first time, the more so, as it was these very doctors who had been consulted formerly by Herod the Great as to the place of His birth (Matthew ii. 4), and this wonderful display on the part of so young a child might make them suspect, He was the very Messiah referred to.

"*His mother said to Him,*" not in a spirit of rebuke or reproach, but, from a feeling of sorrow that had hitherto overwhelmed her and her blessed spouse, she lovingly addresses Him—"*Son,*" specially confided to my care by your Heavenly Father, "*why hast Thou done so to us ?*"—to leave us without knowing it, and thus overwhelm us with unspeakable sorrow at your loss and absence, and the fear lest through any fault of ours, we should have the unspeakable misfortune of losing you for ever. Joseph, who knew he had no claim of paternity, save that he was His reputed father, the husband of her who gave Him birth, observes a guarded and respectful silence, though, he also was oppressed with grief at the loss of the child.

"*Behold Thy father,*" commonly reputed such by men, "*and I have sought Thee sorrowing,*" fearing lest we might be guilty of any neglect, or have merited the punishment of losing you. It is likely, the Virgin thus spoke to Him apart, after they left the meeting of the doctors in the Temple, and she lovingly gives Joseph a share in their common sorrow and anxiety concerning Him. St. Augustine here notes the singular modesty and humility of the Virgin, in putting Joseph before herself, "*Thy father and I,*" thus giving an example of the respect wives should never fail to show their husbands.

49. "*How is it that you sought Me?*" as if He said, It is a wonder you, who knew who I am, viz., the Eternal Son of God, did not reflect, that My departure and absence for a time, was not the result of mere accident; that it was arranged by the all-ruling providence of My Eternal Father. In this, He by no means censures or blames them, since they did only what it was right and natural for them to do. They were guilty of no fault, and therefore gave no cause for blame or censure. It was great natural affection, and a laudable pious solicitude and fear for the safety of their heavenly charge, that prompted them in what they had done.

"*Did you not know that I must be about My Father's business?*" The Virgin mother had spoken of His putative father on earth; He refers to His true and Eternal Father in heaven. This Father sent Him to earth to redeem mankind. It was to this all His thoughts and actions were to be referred; it was to this, His appearing on this occasion in the Temple was to be attributed. These are the words recorded in the Gospel as the first spoken by our Lord, and they convey to us the most important of all lessons, viz., that we should be always engaged in the business of our Heavenly Father, and the advancement of His glory. In them, He also conveys, that while subject in all His merely human actions, to His earthly parents, still, when aims and objects of a higher order interfered, He ceased to be subject to them, or to be influenced by any human feelings or affections whatever. In regard to His mission, He was to be guided, solely by the good-will and pleasure of His Eternal Father in heaven, to have no dependence on flesh or blood; to know neither father nor mother on earth. These words, though apparently reproachful, convey not a reproof, because such was undeserved; but only instruction to His parents regarding His relations towards them, His utter independence of them, whenever the work of God was to be done, and His Father's precept urgent; and consolation also, by intimating that it was solely on account of the loftier duties that devolved upon Him, He was forced as it were, to ignore them, and cause them the sorrow and pain they lately endured.

Whenever in the Gospel, there is mention of any interference on the part of friends in what was peculiarly the business of His Eternal Father, and the action of His Divine nature, our Lord employs language apparently reproachful, (though really not so, because unmerited, as in this case) for the instruction of children in all ages, as to how they are to act whenever their parents, or feelings of natural affection, would interfere with what is clearly their duty towards God; as for instance, should parents unreasonably oppose their children's entrance into religion, when clearly called to that state by God. In such a case, ordinarily speaking, the higher call of duty to God is to be preferred

50. "*And they understood not,*" &c. Although the parents of our Redeemer, especially the Holy Virgin, knew our Lord to be the Eternal Son of the Father, and that He was sent into this world to save mankind, and promote His Father's glory; still, they did not fully comprehend the meaning of His words. They did not see what connexion His withdrawal from them, His appearing at that age in the Temple and disputation with the doctors had with this general object. No doubt, the Blessed Virgin was at this time perfect in *charity*; but, we need not suppose her perfect in the *gift of knowledge*. God gradually developed the fulness of this gift in her, and left her nescient of several details connected with her Son, which she knew in

course of time. Although Mary and Joseph did not fully understand our Lord's words, they devoutly and reverently acquiesced in all He said without asking further questions, without entertaining or expressing any doubts regarding them, fully resigning themselves to the Divine will, perfectly satisfied with having found and received Him back again.

51. "*And was subject to them.*" Having for a moment displayed His Divinity, and after showing in what things children are not subject to their parents, He now returns to His usual occupations, and gives an example of obedience to His earthly parents in their home at Nazareth, which all children are strictly bound to follow, under pain of being deprived of the special reward promised to dutiful children, and of being excluded from the inheritance, or land which the Lord God is to give them. The Evangelist, probably, adds this to let us see, that the passing manifestation of His Divine origin did not exempt Him from the duty of obedience, which, as man, He felt to be due to His parents in human and domestic affairs. It is likely, He laboured as a carpenter, and assisted Joseph in his workshop. Hence, called "*a carpenter*" (Mark vi. 3), as well as "*the carpenter's Son*" (Matthew xiii. 55). From these words we see the great merit of obedience, the entire private life of our Lord, from the age of twelve to thirty, being briefly summed up in these words, "*et erat subditus illis.*" This is the abridgment of Christian duty. The spirit of religion is a spirit of submission; its practice is the practice of obedience. On these words, St. Bernard (Sermo 1, super missus est), cries out, *Who* was subject? God. To *whom?* To men. He, whom the powers of heaven obey, was subject to Mary, and not to Mary only; but to Joseph. On both sides, an astounding wonder. On both sides, a miracle. That God would obey a woman, is an instance of unexampled humility. That a woman should rule a God, of unequalled sublimity. Blush, proud ashes, a God humbles Himself; and dost thou exalt thyself? A God subjects Himself to man, and dost thou anxiously wish to prefer thyself to the Author of thy being? Learn therefore, man, to obey; learn, O earth, to be subject; and thou, O dust, to submit.

"*His mother kept all these words in her heart.*" She constantly meditated on all the words and acts and events connected with her Son, whom she knew to be God, thus nourishing her piety, acquiring a more certain knowledge of all the mysteries of His life, which she might be enabled to communicate with undoubting certainty to the Apostles and Evangelists, who were, at the appointed time, to announce them throughout the world. It is likely, it was from her, St. Luke obtained the information he here gives regarding the Incarnation, birth and infancy of our Redeemer.

We have no further mention of Joseph in the Gospel. It is likely he passed to his reward, before our Lord entered on His public mission. No doubt, with Jesus and Mary presiding at his death bed, the approach of death only revealed to him, by anticipation, the unspeakable joys in store for him. We find no mention of him even at the first public manifestation of our Saviour at the marriage feast of Cana in Galilee. (John ii., &c.)

52. "*And Jesus advanced in wisdom and age,*" &c. Hitherto the Evangelist called Him "*the child,*" παιδίον; but, henceforth, after His having displayed so much wisdom, he calls Him "*Jesus.*" Nothing more is recorded of Him, than that He was subject to His parents, probably toiling in His workshop with His reputed father (Mark vi. 3), and discharging faithfully all the other offices of a dutiful son. "*And He advanced in wisdom and age.*" The word "*age,*" may mean stature, ἡλικία, as it is rendered (Luke xii. 25). How it is He "*advanced in wisdom,*" in whom, from His Incarnation, from

the moment of the hypostatic union, when the Holy Ghost anointed Him with "*the oil of gladness beyond His fellows,*" were "*hid all the treasures of knowledge and of wisdom*" (Col. ii. 2); "*who was full of grace and of truth*" (John i. 14), has caused a difference of opinion among Commentators. The usual modes of explaining this point are—First, He advanced in the external manifestation of hidden wisdom, by words and acts proportioned to His advancing age, which, before men, were indications of greater wisdom; from wise words and acts, progressing to acts and words wiser still; the interior habit, however, or fund of infused wisdom which was perfect from the Incarnation in a finite degree, of which alone the soul of Christ was capable, received no real increase; just as the sun, according to its position above the horizon, increases not in itself, as it is always the same; but, in its effects, in its light and greater brilliancy in regard to us. In SS. Scripture, words and external acts emanating from wisdom, are called "*wisdom.*" Thus, "*The queen of the south came to hear the wisdom of Solomon*" (Luke xi. 31; Matthew xii. 42). Thus it is said, "*we speak the wisdom of God*" (1 Cor. ii. 7). Secondly, He *increased* in wisdom, as to a new mode of acquiring it, viz., experimentally, He advanced in acquired experimental knowledge, which He had not before, and which could result from experience only, just as is said of Him, "*And whereas, indeed, He was the Son of God, He learned obedience by the things which He suffered*" (Heb. v. 8).

"*And grace with God and man.*" As regards *men*, all His acts, His entire demeanour procured Him greater favour and acceptability with them, conciliated more and more the esteem and love of all. This has reference to His *private* hidden life. In His *public* missionary life, many, for whose ruin He was set, were found to find fault with Him, owing to their own perversity.

In regard to *God*, He increased in grace, inasmuch as its external manifestation before men was genuine, and not affected, but real in the sight of God, who felt complacency in this external manifestation of it before men. While His body grew in stature, His soul grew in wisdom and grace, not as to the internal habit, but, as to its external manifestation in acts before men, which was not affected but real, emanating from the internal habit, as seen by God and pleasing in His sight.

CHAPTER III.

ANALYSIS.

In this chapter, the Evangelist, before recording the preaching and baptism of John the Baptist, with a view to determine its precise date, refers first, to the civil and ecclesiastical authorities that governed Judea and the adjacent districts at the time (1-2). He then describes the baptism and preaching of the Baptist (3-18). His imprisonment (19-20). The baptism of our Lord and His genealogy (21-38)

TEXT.

NOW in the fifteenth year of the reign of Tiberius Cesar, Pontius Pilate being governor of Judea, and Herod being tetrarch of Galilee, and Philip his brother tetrarch of Iturea and the country of Trachonitis, and Lysanias tetrarch of Abilina,

2. Under the high-priests Annas and Caiphas: the word of the Lord was made unto John the son of Zachary, in the desert.

3. And he came into all the country about the Jordan, preaching the baptism of penance for the remission of sins;

4. As it was written in the book of the sayings of Isaias the prophet: A voice of one crying in the wilderness. Prepare ye the way of the Lord, make straight his paths.

5. *Every valley shall be filled; and every mountain and hill shall be brought low: and the crooked shall be made straight, and the rough ways, plain:*

6. *And all flesh shall see the salvation of God.*

7. *He said therefore to the multitudes that went forth to be baptized by him : Ye offspring of vipers, who hath shewed you to flee from the wrath to come ?*

8. *Bring forth therefore fruits worthy of penance, and do not begin to say, We have Abraham for our father. For I say unto you, that God is able of these stones to raise up children to Abraham.*

9. *For now the axe is laid to the root of the trees. Every tree therefore that bringeth not forth good fruit, shall be cut down, and cast into the fire.*

10. *And the people asked him, saying : What then shall we do ?*

11. *And he answering, said to them: He that hath two coats, let him give to him that hath none; and he that hath meat, let him do in like manner.*

12. *And the publicans also came to be baptized, and said to him : Master, what shall we do ?*

13. *But he said to them: Do nothing more than that which is appointed you.*

14. *And the soldiers also asked him, saying : And what shall we do ? And he said to them: Do violence to no man, neither calumniate any man; and be content with your pay.*

15. *And as the people was of opinion, and all were thinking in their hearts of John, that perhaps he might be the Christ :*

16. *John answered, saying unto all: I indeed baptize you with water ; but there shall come one mightier than I, the latchet of whose shoes I am not worthy to loose; he shall baptize you with the Holy Ghost and with fire :*

17. *Whose fan is in his hand, and he will purge his floor : and will gather the wheat into his barn, but the chaff he will burn with unquenchable fire.*

18. *And many other things exhorting did he preach to the people.*

19. *But Herod the tetrarch, when he was reproved by him for Herodias his brother's wife, and for all the evils which Herod had done,*

20. *He added this also above all, and shut up John in prison.*

COMMENTARY.

1. "*Now in the fifteenth,*" &c. Having passed over the long intermediate period, comprising about eighteen years, between our Redeemer's return to Nazareth, at the age of twelve, and His appearance in public to preach to the people,—among the Jews, this was not allowed till one reached the age of thirty—the Evangelist now determines the precise period of His public appearance. This he does in accordance with the usage observed by the prophets, and other sacred writers of the Old Testament, who usually, at the commencement of their sacred writings, make mention of the reigning sovereigns, and the respective dates of their reign. St. Luke, here, fixes the date of the Baptist's preaching, and our Redeemer's mission, by a reference to the civil and ecclesiastical authorities that then governed Judea. "*Now in the fifteenth year of the reign of Tiberius Cæsar.*" The several difficulties and objections advanced against the veracity of the sacred text by infidels, who assert that the respective dates assigned here by St. Luke are in direct contradiction to the most undoubted historical records, are at once set at rest, by counting the years of Tiberius given here, not from the death of Augustus, when Tiberius succeeded him as sole supreme ruler, A.U.C. 767, but from the time that Tiberius, after having triumphed over the Pannonians and Dalmatians, and having put an end to the wars in Germany, was associated by Augustus, as partner, with equal authority in the administration of the armies, and of the provinces of the Empire, Judea among the rest. This partnership

in power and in administration, was conferred on Tiberius by the Roman Senate at the express desire of Augustus, about the year U.C. 764 or 765, as we are informed by Velleius (Hist. Rom. Lib. ii. 121); Suetonius (Tiberius, § 20, 21), thus making the fifteenth year of Augustus, the year U.C. 778, and the year of our Lord's birth 748, or 749 U.C. It was by no means unusual to date events from the beginning of a proconsular reign. Here, the Greek word for "*reign*," ἡγεμονία, which is applied to governors and procurators in general, as it is to Pontius Pilate, in this very passage, would imply that the date is not from the beginning of the occupation of the Imperial throne by Tiberius solely, in succession to Augustus, which would be expressed by αρχη; but, from his association with Augustus in the Government. "*Collega Imperii et consors Tribuniciæ potestatis adsumptus*" (Tacitus Annal. Lib. i. c. 3). (See Patrizzi, Lib. iii. Dissert xxxix.; also, Dr. MacCarthy, in *hunc locum*.)

"*Pontius Pilate being governor of Judea.*" The Evangelist fixes another date to determine the time of the Baptist's preaching. After Archelaus, to whom was assigned the one half of his father's dominions, with the title of Ethnarch, by Augustus, who confirmed Herod's will, had been banished to Vienne, in Gaul, on account of his cruelties and proven misconduct, his dominions were reduced to a Roman province, with a governor or procurator dependent on the governor of Syria, and subordinate to him. In this office, Pontius Pilate was the sixth in succession since the banishment of Archelaus. He governed Judea for ten years (Josephus Antiq. xviii. 5), when he was sent to Rome by Vitellius, governor of Syria, to justify himself against the charge of cruelty alleged against him by the Samaritans. He arrived there after the death of Tiberius. Now, Tiberius died A.D. 37; so, Pilate's procuratorship commenced A.D. 27. He was condemned to perpetual exile by Caius, Tiberius's successor, and died by his own hand.

"*Governor of Judea.*" The Vulgate renders this more clearly, "*Procurante Judæam.*" For at this time, Vitellius, a Consular senator, was governor of Syria; and Pontius Pilate, a Roman knight, was procurator of Judea, which was dependent on the province of Syria.

"*Herod* (Antipas) *being tetrarch of Galilee*," the same by whom our Lord was mocked at His Passion, and the Baptist beheaded.

"*Philip, his brother, tetrarch of Iturea*," &c. Whether this Philip, whom Herod the Great, begot of Cleopatra, was the former husband of Herodias, at whose instigation the Baptist was beheaded, is disputed. Some say the husband of Herodias was another Philip, son of Herod the Great, by Mariamne, daughter of Simon the high-priest. This latter Philip was not mentioned in his father's will, and was altogether excluded from any share in his inheritance; he must, therefore, have lived in a private station (see Commentary on Matthew, pp. 260-62).

"*Lysanias, tetrarch of Abilina.*" Some maintain that this Lysanias was son of Herod the Great, on account of his having been called "*tetrarch*," with Herod's sons. This is commonly rejected as unfounded and improbable. Josephus makes no mention of any such person among Herod's sons, which he would have done, if it were the case. The most probable opinion seems to be, that this Lysanias was son, or a descendant of another Lysanias, son of Ptolemy, and grandson of Mennæus—ruler of Colchis, contemporary with Cleopatra—who ruled sixty years before the period here referred to. This Lysanias, who was put to death by Antony, at Cleopatra's instigation, in the year 34 before Christ, was never styled, "*tetrarch*." For, it was only after Herod's death, the tetrarchal division of Palestine and the neighbouring districts was made, nor did he ever rule at Abila or Abilina.

"*Abilina*," so called from the chief city of the district. *Abila*, seems to have included the eastern declivities of Anti-Libanus, and to be bounded on the south by

Mount Hermon. The Emperor Claudius, as Josephus informs us (Antiq xix. 5), " bestowed on Agrippa, grandson of Herod the Great, Abila of Lysanias."

2. "*Under the high-priests, Annas and Caiphas.*" As, according to Jewish law, there could be only one ministering high-priest at the same time, Commentators are perplexed in endeavouring to explain, why two are mentioned here by St. Luke with the same designation, and, seemingly, with equal authority. Some, with Maldonatus, hold that, in consequence of the corruption induced by the Romans, the office of high-priest, which the law conferred for life, became venal; that the Romans set it up to the highest bidder, and, hence, it became a temporary office, to be exercised at the will and pleasure of their Imperial masters. These hold, that Annas and Caiphas exorcised its functions alternately, which is implied by St. John (xi. 47-49); when treating of our Lord's Passion, he says, "*Caiphas was the high-priest of that year,*" implying that somebody else exorcised it some other year. Others, hold, that either Annas was deputy to Caiphas, or Caiphas, to Annas. Hence, both are mentioned. Caiphas was, certainly, high-priest, the year of our Lord's Crucifixion. Annas was father-in-law of Caiphas, and enjoyed the greatest influence with him. Hence, our Lord is led to Annas before He is brought to Caiphas. (John xviii. 13). Annas had been appointed high-priest by Quirinus, president of Syria, and exercised the office for eleven years. He was most successful in life, and having once been high-priest, he ever after retained the title, and was called by that name. He was held in the greatest veneration among the Jews, with whom, as well as with the high-priest, he had the greatest influence. He is mentioned by St. Luke in connexion with Caiphas, his son-in-law, who, no doubt, was guided greatly by him in the administration of his office. Different other reasons are assigned by different Expositors, but, those given above seem the more probable, in a matter, regarding which, at this period, there can be no absolute certainty.

" *The word of the Lord came to John,*" &c. This is a phrase peculiar to the Prophets, signifying that the Lord spoke to him, and implying that the person thus spoken to went forth to announce the will of God, not of himself or self sent, but armed with a heavenly mandate and divine mission, without which John would not venture to exercise the ministry of baptizing and preaching.

Probably, this " *word of the Lord,*" points to a divine inspiration moving John to go forth and preach "*in the desert*" (see Matthew iii. 1).

3. "*He came,*" promptly obeying the divine mandate, from the interior of the desert, where he dwelt from his infancy, till the time of life before which no one was allowed to exercise the office of preaching among the Jews, viz., the age of thirty.

" *Unto all the country about the Jordan,*" the country on each side of the river and contiguous to it, so that the Baptist had always an abundant supply of water to exercise his ministry.

" *Preaching* "—and administering—" *the baptism of penance,*" that is to say, his own baptism, which, as a profession of penance, was a protestation of the necessity of performing the penitential works that accompanied it (see Mark i. 4). It also served as a preparation for " *the remission of sin* "—of which the bodily ablution was a sign—to be conferred by the baptism of Christ, the superiority of which, over his own, John never ceased to proclaim. This "*remission of sin*" was one of the blessings of " *the kingdom of heaven,*" which John announced as near at hand. (For the distinctive qualities and effects of John's baptism, compared with that of Christ, see Matthew iii. 6-11, Commentary on.)

4. "*As it is written,*" &c. (See Matthew iii., &c.) The words mean, that John did this in accordance with, and in fulfilment of, the Prophecy of Isaias, regarding him, "*Prepare ye the way,*" &c.

5. "*Every valley shall be filled.*" Here as well as in the following sentence, the future is employed, by a Hebrew idiom, for the imperative. *Let* every valley be filled; *let* every mountain, &c. The prophet perseveres in the allusion to the Eastern custom of preparing and making smooth the ways on the occasion of the coming of princes to visit their subjects. St. Luke in this and the following verse quotes from the prophet more fully than is done by either Matthew or Mark, and enlarges more on the Eastern allusion, as he wrote in a special way for the Gentiles, to whom it was necessary to give the assurance, as is here given at the close of the quotation, that they were to be sharers in the salvation announced by the Gospel, as well as the Jews, who hitherto were alone the chosen and favoured people of God.

6. "*All flesh shall see,*" &c. The words of this verse, although, according to some Expositors, literally and primarily referring to the return of the Jews from the Babylonish captivity, under the protection of Cyrus, refer in a secondary sense, principally intended by the Holy Ghost, to the good tidings of Redemption, proclaimed by the Baptist as now at hand. They have also a moral signification, and denote the removal of every thing that might prove disagreeable in the eyes of the coming King, of all obstacles to the operation of grace, and to the full effect, on their souls, of the preaching of Christ, the mortification and destruction of the passions and vicious habits, the avoidance of sin and its occasions, the practice of penitential works, and the cultivation of the opposite virtues, for which penance disposes us in future; while, it serves as a reparation and satisfaction for past transgressions. All this served to prepare men for the Gospel of Christ, to level the hills and fill up the valleys, —words which are here clearly used in a metaphorical sense. "*And all flesh,*" &c. "*And*" signifies *for*, giving a reason for this preparation. "*All flesh,*" every man, be he Jew or Gentile, without distinction ; or, rather, many men of every description, of every rank and tribe, "*shall see,*" by faith, and some shall see with the eyes of the body, "*the salvation of God,*" the salvation which God will accomplish; or, they shall see the Saviour, the Eternal Son of God, Himself true God, who assumed human flesh to redeem the entire human race. For, "*God Himself shall come and save you*" (Isaias xxxv. 4). In Isaias, quoted in this passage, the reading, according to the Vulgate, is (Isaias xl. 5), "*And all flesh together shall see, that the mouth of the Lord hath spoken.*" In the Septuagint it is "*All flesh shall see the salvation of God, because the Lord hath spoken.*" But, the sense in all is substantially the same. The prophetic quotation (v. 5), "*Every valley, &c.,*" is the same as the words of the Baptist, "*do penance,*" and (v. 6) the same as the other words of the Baptist, "*the kingdom of heaven is at hand.*" Men of every class shall see and feel within themselves the grace and salvation brought by Christ.

7-10. (See Matthew iii. 7-10, Commentary on.)

10. "*And the people asked him.*" The Scribes and Pharisees, whom John had reproached so sharply, "*had despised the counsel of God*" (vii. 30), and therefore, paid no heed to John's preaching; but, "*the people,*" who were well affected, touched by his preaching, "*asked him, what shall we do?*" what works of penance shall we perform? what fruits, worthy of penance, shall we produce, in order to evade the

threatened ruin, and be worthy to enter the kingdom of heaven, which you announce as near?

11. "*He that hath two coats*," &c. The Baptist specially enjoins works of mercy, and alms-deeds, among the most deserving fruits of penance. Not that they are alone to be performed; but, because they commend themselves most to us. They wonderfully commend us to God, and incline Him to show mercy to us in turn, "*peccata tua eleemosynis redime*," &c. He refrains from inculcating severe penitential works, in the first instance, for fear of scaring the multitude away from the way of perfection. He inculcates the exercise of mercy, which will obtain of God abundant grace, to perform these painful works of penance with alacrity, "*Quod superest, da Eleemosynam, et ecce, omnia munda sunt vobis*" (Luke xi. 41). "*That hath two coats*," and one of them superfluous, let him give the superfluous one to him who wants it, "*that hath none*." The same is inculcated on the man, who hath meat to spare, let him give it to his neighbour, who wants it. Under these two works, clothing the naked, and feeding the hungry—the two things most necessary, before everything else, for sustaining human life—are included all the other works of mercy, corporal and spiritual. The words of this verse clearly demonstrate the necessity of exercising the corporal works of mercy, in relieving our indigent brethren; and the Baptist inculcates it on the multitude without distinction, as a precept binding on all classes of persons.

12. "*And the publicans also came to be baptized*." Who the *publicans* were (see Matthew ix. 11). The Greek, τελωνης, is not accurately rendered by the Vulgate, *publicanus*, the publicans being men of rank among the Romans, who farmed the revenue. Here, the word means a tax-gatherer, employed by the *Publicani*. Among the Jews, the collector of taxes, especially if he were a Jew, was regarded as an extortioner and apostate, and classed with the worst description of sinners, *peccatores ex officio* (Tertullian de Pudicitia, c. ix) Their occupation was not, of itself, illicit. For, if it was licit for rulers to impose, it must also be for others, to collect taxes. Hence, the Baptist here does not tell them to give up this calling in life, which he would do, in the first instance, if it were unlawful. But, owing to their excessive and unjust exactions, their grinding oppression of the poor, the publicans, as a class, were regarded in the light of public sinners; and they are regarded by our Redeemer frequently in the Gospels, as outside the pale of salvation. Here, touched with the preaching of the Baptist, they come to be baptized; thus verifying the words of our Lord, "*the publicans and the harlots will go before you into the kingdom of God*" (Matthew xxi 31).

13. They asked John what they were to do, in order to avoid the wrath to come. He only tells them, "*Do nothing more than that which is appointed for you.*" The Greek word for "*do*"—πρασσειν—means also, to *exact*, the meaning it has here. He tells them, in collecting taxes, to exact no more than is assessed on the people, in each case, by the legally constituted authorities. In this, it is not implied, that cessation from unjust exactions was sufficient for them, or fully constituted the fruits of penance he required them to bring forth. He only imposes this on them, in the first instance, to avoid the sin to which they were particularly liable, and which was ordinarily committed by them, from a belief that their fidelity in this respect, would merit for them grace to do the other things required of them in common with all; to practise works of mercy among the rest. The first thing to be enjoined on all is, the mastery over their predominant

passion, and the performance of the peculiar duties of their state. This, however, though necessary for all, is not sufficient; they must, in addition, fully observe the precepts of avoiding evil, and of doing good. From the words of the Baptist, it is clear, the office of Publican was not bad, save in its abuse. He does not enjoin on them to *exact nothing*, but only to exact *nothing beyond their due*.

14. "*The soldiers*," as a class, though there are many saints among them, are most indifferent, not very susceptible of religious impressions, and greatly exposed to sin. These also are cautioned or warned by John against three vices to which they are subject, viz. :—1st, violence, or, the violent use of the arms which, put into their hands against the enemy, are sometimes employed by them in oppressing their fellow-subjects, for the purpose of unjust exactions ; 2ndly, calumny, in falsely accusing their innocent neighbours of crimes against the State, and giving false information against them, in order to partake of their confiscated property ; 3rdly, pillage, to support the extravagance and dissipated habits for which their ordinary pay was unequal. The Baptist here taxes the vices peculiar to the military state; inculcates their avoidance, with the firm hope, that if military men overcame themselves in this respect, they would ultimately practise the virtues, which are obligatory on all men, and avoid the vices condemned in all, by the law and commandments of God. From the words of John here it is legitimately inferred, that warfare is a lawful profession to engage in. The Baptist only tells them to avoid the vices incident to that calling. The same is fairly inferred from our Lord's treatment of the Centurion (Matthew viii. 10), and from Peter's conduct towards Cornelius (Acts x. 36), neither of whom tells those whose faith they praise to abandon the profession of arms.

The Greek word for "*calumniate,*" συκοφαντησητε—from συκον, *a fig*, and φαινω, *to declare*, strictly denoting, *to inform against the exporters of figs*, is allusive to the law prohibiting the exportation of figs in Attica during seasons of scarcity. When there was a plentiful harvest, the law was useless. Still, as it was binding at all times, in consequence of not having been repealed, ill-natured and malicious people took occasion from it to accuse all persons transgressing the letter of the law. Hence, all busy informers, have ever since, been branded with the odious name of *sycophants*. With an accusative of the person, as here, it signifies, to oppress any one, to annoy him by frivolous accusations, especially under pretence of law. With a genitive of the person and an accusative of the thing (Luke xix. 8), it signifies, to take away any thing from a man on the same pretences (Parkhust, Greek Lexicon; Potter, Antiquities, Book i. c. 21).

15. "*And as the people were of opinion,*" &c. The end of the Baptist's mission was twofold—to preach penance, in order to dispose the people for receiving the Gospel; and to preach faith in Christ, and render Him testimony. He had already performed the first part, and now he enters on the second object of his mission. The Greek for "*opinion,*" προσδοκωντες, means, *desiring, hoping*. On considering John's wonderful birth, life, preaching and baptism, which was to be instituted in a new form by the Messiah (Ezechiel xxxvi. 25) ; being also aware that the period of our Lord's coming was near —the sceptre having passed from Juda, and the seventy weeks of Daniel having been accomplished—the people began to hope, that John might have been the desired Messiah. They were revolving these thoughts in their hearts, when John, either informed by his disciples, of the opinion currently circulated regarding him, or being inspired by the Holy Ghost; or, if we make the testimony rendered by him here to be the same as that given (John i. 20) and rendered on the same occasion, being

interrogated on the subject, at once rejecting the high prerogative falsely ascribed to him, proclaims the Divinity and infinite superiority of our Lord over himself. This public declaration of John given "*to all*," was providentially deferred until John himself having been reputed to be the Messiah, his testimony regarding our Lord would carry with it greater weight, and would seem still more to proclaim the glory and Divinity of the Son of God. It is disputed whether St. Luke here refers to the occasion described (John i. 20). If both occasions be identical, then, St. Luke and the other synoptists must have described it by anticipation, since, they describe it as occurring before our Lord's baptism; John thus supplying, as was his wont, what they omit; namely, the circumstances of the deputation from Jerusalem, to whom our Lord rendered this testimony. If both occasions be different—and the words of the Baptist, addressed to the deputation (John i. 26), "*there hath stood one in the midst of you, whom you know not.*" . . . "*The same is He that shall come after me,*" &c. (John i. 27) would favour this opinion; for, he spoke of our Lord as Him of whom he before had said, "*that He was to come after him*")—then, John learned their feelings from inspiration or from his Disciples.

16, 17. (See Matthew iii. 11, 12.)

18. By these and other similar discourses full of grace and holy unction, the Precursor announced beforehand the glad tidings of redemption by Christ which was soon to be accomplished; and by exhorting the people to penance, and announcing the Gospel truths beforehand, he disposed them for faith in the coming Redeemer, of whom he was the Precursor.

19. The Evangelist records, by anticipation, this imprisonment of the Baptist which took place after our Lord's baptism; because he wished to finish the Acts and history of John before proceeding to other subjects.

"*Herod the tetrarch,*" &c. (See Matthew xiv. 8, &c.; Mark vi. 17, &c.)

"*And for all the evils which Herod had done.*" St. Matthew and St. Mark represent the Baptist as reproaching Herod, with truly apostolic firmness, only for the crime of living in scandalous incest with his brother's wife. From St. Luke here, it would appear, he reproached him for other crimes too, of which no doubt Herod was guilty, to which our Lord refers in His description of him (xiii. 32), "*Go, tell that fox,*" and which afterwards caused the Emperor Caius to consign him to perpetual banishment, after having deprived him of all his power and property.

TEXT.

21. *Now it came to pass, when all the people was baptized, that Jesus also being baptized and praying, heaven was opened:*

22. *And the Holy Ghost descended in a bodily shape as a dove upon him: and a voice came from heaven: Thou art my beloved Son, in thee I am well pleased.*

23. *And Jesus himself was beginning about the age of thirty years; (being as it was supposed) the Son of Joseph, who was of Heli, who was of Mathat,*

24. *Who was of Levi, who was of Melchi, who was of Janne, who was of Joseph,*

25. *Who was of Mathathias, who was of Amos, who was of Nahum, who was of Hesli, who was of Nagge,*

26. *Who was of Mahath, who was of Mathathias, who was of Semei, who was of Joseph, who was of Juda,*

27. *Who was of Joanna, who was of Reza, who was of Zorobabel, who was of Salathiel, who was of Neri,*

28. Who was of Melchi, who was of Addi, who was of Cosan, who was of Helmadan, who was of Her,

29. Who was of Jesus, who was of Eliezer, who was of Jorim, who was of Mathat, who was of Levi,

30. Who was of Simeon, who was of Judas, who was of Joseph, who was of Jona, who was of Eliakim,

31. Who was of Melea, who was of Menna, who was of Mathatha, who was of Nathan, who was of David,

32. Who was of Jesse, who was of Obed, who was of Booz, who was of Salmon, who was of Naasson,

33. Who was of Aminadab, who was of Aram, who was of Esron, who was of Phares, who was of Judas,

34. Who was of Jacob, who was of Isaac, who was of Abraham, who was of Thare, who was of Nachor,

35. Who was of Sarug, who was of Ragau, who was of Phaleg, who was of Heber, who was of Sale,

36. Who was of Cainan, who was of Arphaxad, who was of Sem, who was of Noe, who was of Lamech,

37. Who was of Mathusale, who was of Henoch, who was of Jared, who was of Malaleel, who was of Cainan,

38. Who was of Henos, who was of Seth, who was of Adam, who was of God.

COMMENTARY.

21, 22. (See Matthew iii. 16, 17.)

23. "*And Jesus Himself was beginning about the age of thirty years.*" The translation of the words given by Kenrick is more in accordance with the Greek, and better expresses the sense, "*And Jesus Himself beginning, was about thirty years old.*" He places "*was*" after "beginning," and not *before* it. The Greek, literally rendered, would run thus, "*And Jesus Himself was about thirty years old, beginning.*" So that the word, "beginning," refers to His "*beginning*" or commencing His ministry, after His baptism by John, as in Acts (i. 22; x. 37), where the Greek, as here, is αρξαμενος, and not to His beginning to be thirty years old (see Beelen, Gramm. Græc., p. 381). For, if it meant the latter, the particle, ωσει, would have been absurdly introduced.

"*About the age of thirty.*" No one was allowed among the Jews to exercise the office of Doctor till he reached that age; hence, our Lord began, or was "*beginning,*" His public ministry at this age appointed among the Jews for the exercise of the teaching ministry.

"*Being (as it was supposed) the Son of Joseph, who was of Heli,*" &c. (For an explanation of this passage, and the probable mode of reconciling the genealogy of our Lord, as given here by Luke, with that given by Matthew, see Matthew i. 16, Commentary on.)

CHAPTER IV.

ANALYSIS.

In this chapter, we have an account of the temptation of our Lord (1-13). His preaching in Galilee and in His own native place, Nazareth. The contemptuous rejection of Him by His own countrymen (14-32). The casting out of a devil in the synagogue at Capharnaum (33-37). The healing of Peter's mother-in-law and of others (38-41). His preaching throughout Galilee (42-44).

TEXT.

AND Jesus being full of the Holy Ghost, returned from the Jordan, and was led by the Spirit into the desert,

2. For the space of forty days; and was tempted by the devil. And he ate nothing in those days; and when they were ended he was hungry.

3. And the devil said to him: If thou be the Son of God, say to this stone that it be made bread.

4. And Jesus answered him: It is written: "that man liveth not by bread alone, but by every word of God."

5. And the devil led him into a high mountain, and showed him all the kingdoms of the world in a moment of time;

6. And he said to him: To thee will I give all this power, and the glory of them; for to me they are delivered, and to whom I will, I give them.

7. If thou therefore wilt adore before me, all shall be thine.

8. And Jesus answering said to him: It is written: "Thou shalt adore the Lord thy God, and him only shalt thou serve."

9. And he brought him to Jerusalem, and set him on a pinnacle of the temple; and he said to him: If thou be the Son of God, cast thyself from hence.

10. For it is written, that "he hath given his angels charge over thee, that they keep thee:

11. And that in their hands they shall bear thee up, lest perhaps thou dash thy foot against a stone."

12. And Jesus answering said to him: It is said, "Thou shalt not tempt the Lord thy God."

13. And all the temptation being ended, the devil departed from him for a time.

COMMENTARY.

1-13. (See Matthew iv. 1-11, Commentary on.)

TEXT.

14. And Jesus returned in the power of the Spirit into Galilee, and the fame of him went out through the whole country.

15. And he taught in their synagogues, and was magnified by all.

16. And he came to Nazareth where he was brought up: and he went into the synagogue according to his custom on the sabbath-day; and he rose up to read,

17. And the book of Isaias the prophet was delivered unto him. And as he unfolded the book, he found the place where it was written:

18. "The spirit of the Lord is upon me, wherefore he hath anointed me, to preach the gospel to the poor he hath sent me, to heal the contrite of heart.

19. To preach deliverance to the captives, and sight to the blind, to set at liberty them that are bruised, to preach the acceptable year of the Lord, and the day of reward."

20. And when he had folded the book, he restored it to the minister, and sat down. And the eyes of all in the synagogue were fixed on him.

21. *And he began to say to them: This day is fulfilled this scripture in your ears.*
22. *And all gave testimony to him; and they wondered at the words of grace that proceeded from his mouth, and they said: Is not this the son of Joseph?*
23. *And he said to them: Doubtless you will say to me this similitude: Physician, heal thyself: as great things as we have heard done in Capharnaum, do also here in thy own country.*
24. *And he said: Amen I say to you, that no prophet is accepted in his own country.*
25. *In truth I say to you, there were many widows in the days of Elias in Israel, when heaven was shut up three years and six months, when there was a great famine throughout all the earth.*
26. *And to none of them was Elias sent, but to Sarepta of Sidon, to a widow woman.*
27. *And there were many lepers in Israel in the time of Eliseus the prophet; and none of them was cleansed but Naaman the Syrian.*
28. *And all they in the synagogue, hearing these things, were filled with anger.*
29. *And they rose up and thrust him out of the city, and they brought him to the brow of the hill, whereon their city was built, that they might cast him down headlong.*
30. *But he passing through the midst of them, went his way.*
31. *And he went down into Capharnaum a city of Galilee; and there he taught them on the sabbath-days.*
32. *And they were astonished at his doctrine: for his speech was with power.*

COMMENTARY.

14. "*And Jesus returned in the power of the Spirit to Galilee.*" He "*returned*" to Galilee, whence He had come, to the part of the Jordan where He was baptized by John; "*in the power of the Spirit,*" under the strong impulse and influence of the Holy Ghost. He now displays and externally manifests in His preaching and wondrous works, the power of the Holy Ghost, with which He was filled from His Incarnation, which He possessed without measure, and with which He was anointed in the unction of the hypostatic union. The Evangelist now wishes to have us to understand, that in all the words and actions of our Lord about to be narrated, He was always guided by, and always acted under the influence and power of, the Holy Ghost. This was the *second* return of our Lord into Galilee, since His fast and baptism. John (i. 43), records His *first* return. Hence, the Evangelist passes over several events in the life of our Lord, which occurred before the return referred to here, viz., His coming to John (John i. 29), who speaks of Him in the most exalted terms; the marriage feast of Cana; the wonders performed at Capharnaum (v. 23, here); His going up to Jerusalem at the Pasch (John ii. 13); the time spent by Him in Judea, baptizing (John iii. 22); the intimation He received that John was imprisoned, which occasioned His going to Galilee, as recorded here (see Matthew iv. 12, Commentary on).

"*And the fame of Him,*" on account of the wonderful things He did and said, "*went out through the whole country,*" viz., Galilee and the adjacent districts, Samaria, Phœnicia, Syria, &c.

15. "*And,*" is interpreted by some to mean, "*for,*" "*He taught in their synagogues.*" This was the chief cause of His being so celebrated among them. "*And was magnified* (extolled) *by all,*" on account of what He taught, and His authoritative mode of teaching. "*He was teaching them, as one having authority, and not as their Scribes and Pharisees*" (Matthew vii. 29).

(For meaning of "*synagogue,*" see Matthew iv. 23, Commentary on).

16. "*And He came to Nazareth*," which He passed by on a former occasion (Matthew iv. 13), "*where He was brought up.*"

"*Nazareth*" was His native place, where He spent the period of boyhood and youth.

"*He went into the synagogue according to His custom*," &c. It was usual with the Jews to assemble on Sabbath and festival days in their synagogues for devotional exercises, such as, reading and hearing the Word of God, as also, prayer. "*His custom*," may signify the custom He observed from infancy, of frequenting the places of devotion on Sabbath days; or, His custom of frequenting the synagogues since He commenced His mission, for the purpose of expounding the SS. Scriptures. Our Lord taught everywhere, all those who came to Him for instruction; and He availed Himself of every befitting occasion, especially when He wrought miracles, to expound His heavenly doctrines. But, on Sabbath days, He availed himself of the religious meetings in the synagogues to instruct the assembled people.

"*He rose up to read*," and expound the SS. Scriptures. It was usual with the Jews to have a certain portion of the Pentateuch read for the people in the synagogue on Sabbath days, to which was subjoined a section from the prophetical books bearing in sense on the passage read from the Pentateuch. Any one learned in the law, might be invited to read and expound such passages. See Acts (xiii. 15), where "*the reading of the law and the prophets*" is referred to, also Acts (xv. 21). Our Lord "*rose up to read*," thereby intimating, that He had "*an exhortation to make to the people*" (Acts xiii. 15). He read the SS. Scriptures in a standing posture, not only to be better heard, but chiefly out of reverence for the Word of God.

17. The Book of the Prophet Isaias was delivered to Him by "*the minister*" of the synagogue (v. 20). This, although humanly speaking, apparently accidental, was arranged by God's providence, to afford Him an opportunity of showing His Divinity and Divine mission, from the writings of their own prophets.

"*Unfolded the book.*" Unlike our modern form of books, the parchment was folded round a roller, in the form of a map—whence the term, Volume—and on unfolding it off the roller, "*He found the place where it was written.*" He lighted, doubtlessly, by the deliberate guidance of God's providence, on the following passage (Isaias xli. 1). This passage is quoted by St. Luke, according to the Septuagint version, save that Luke himself adds to the passage, according to that version, the words, "*to set at liberty them that are bruised,*" probably taken from Isaias (lviii. 6), where these words are used in the Septuagint, in the imperative mood.

18. "*The Spirit of the Lord is upon me.*" In Isaias (lxi. 1, 2), the Lord promises the Jewish people a Redeemer; some say, the Prophet primarily refers to the deliverance of the Jewish people from the Babylonish captivity, under Cyrus, which mystically and principally signifies their spiritual deliverance through Christ —"*He shall come like a violent stream which the Spirit of the Lord driveth on*" (lix. 19). In the passage quoted here by St. Luke (Isaias lxi. 1), the Prophet represents the Deliverer or Redeemer as having already come, and saying, "*the* (promised) *Spirit of the Lord is upon me,*" or as is said elsewhere (Isaias xi. 2), "*rests upon Him.*" I am filled with His gifts, which are bestowed upon me without stint or measure. This Spirit our Lord received at His Incarnation and from the hypostatic union. This Spirit guided and influenced all His actions.

"*Wherefore He*"—the Hebrew has, "*the Lord, hath anointed me.*" "*Anointed*" is allusive to the rite employed in consecrating Kings, Prophets, and Priests. Here Christ is the *Messiah* or *Anointed*. It is because He had the fulness of all Divine gifts given Him without measure, at His Incarnation, therefore did the Lord anoint Him with the oil of gladness at His baptism; by this unction consecrating and preparing Him for the great office of preaching the Gospel. The words, *"the Spirit of the Lord is upon me,"* have reference to His Incarnation; and the words, *"wherefore He hath anointed me,"* to His baptism. The former is the cause of the latter. Some Commentators connect the words, *"He hath anointed me"* with, *"to preach to the poor,"* this being the office for which He was anointed and consecrated, to fit Him for it. *"He hath anointed me to preach the Gospel to the poor,"* and these connect the words, *"sent me,"* with *"to heal the contrite,"* &c., *"He sent me to heal the contrite of heart."*

"The poor." This is the Septuagint rendering. The Hebrew has, *"to the meek"* (see Matthew xi. 4). *"To heal the contrite of heart,"* whose hearts are heavily bruised with the heavy load of sin. These words are wanting in some Greek copies.

19. *"To preach deliverance to the captives,"* captive in the bonds of sin. *"Deliverance,"* from their chains, and also the providing of means for effectively accomplishing such deliverance.

"And sight to the blind." To bestow the light of faith and truth on those who are sitting in darkness and the shadow of death, and open the eyes of their understanding to the light of faith, against which they have been hitherto shut.

"To set at liberty them that are bruised." These words would seem to signify the same as the words, *"to heal the contrite of heart."* Hence, some Expositors regard one or the other as redundant; and as the words, *"to set at liberty, &c.,"* are not found either in the Hebrew, or Chaldaic, or Greek, it is, most likely, the redundant phrase. A similar sentence is found in Isaias (lviii. 6), *"let them that are broken go free."* Probably, St. Luke inserted these words in the quotation here, taken from chap. lxi. 1 of Isaias, as illustrating the benefits conferred by our Redeemer, and more fully explaining the sense of the passage.

The Hebrew phrase, *Laasurim Poqach*, signifies, *Laasurim*, *"those bound,"* and *Reqach*, *"an opening."* St. Jerome then rendered the words, *"clausis apertionem,"* *"deliverance to them that are shut up."* But the Septuagint rendered them, τυφλοις αναβλεψιν, *"sight to the blind."* For, *assurim* signifies, *those bound*. This is true of the blind, whose eyes are bound, and *Peqach* signifies, *an opening*. The blind, when restored to sight, have their eyes opened; hence, the Septuagint rendering of the words.

"To preach the acceptable year of the Lord." *"Year,"* is put for time. There is manifest allusion here to the year of Jubilee, which occurred every fiftieth year among the Jews, when slaves were set at liberty, and the possessions that were sold, reverted to their original owners. This Jubilee year among the Jews, and the blessings it brought with it, were a type of the entire period of the Christian dispensation, a period of time productive of the greatest blessings to mankind, when they are rescued from the slavery of Satan and sin; the greatest gifts of grace are conferred on them, and they are restored to their lost inheritance of heaven. Our Lord proclaimed this as present, *"appropinquavit regnum, &c."* (Matthew iv. 17.) This is the period of benevolence on the part of God; of His good-will towards man. This shall continue now to the end of the world. Hence, the Apostle says, *"Ecce nunc tempus acceptabile; ecce nunc, dies salutis"* (2 Cor. vi. 2). Our Lord was sent to announce these glad tidings of a year of jubilee and perpetual reconciliation of God with man. *"Pascha nostrum immolatus est Christus"* (1 Cor. v. 7.)

"And the day of reward." St. Jerome renders the Hebrew, *Jom naquam*, *"diem ultionis,"* *"the day of vengeance,"* which some understand of the last day of general judgment, when the Lord, while rewarding the good, shall take vengeance on His

enemies. Others, seeing that the entire prophetic quotation regards the benefits to be conferred by Christ on the children of the New Law, understand "*vengeance*," of the evil spirits, the enemies of men's souls, on whom our Lord will take signal vengeance, by publicly exposing them, to public view, to grace His triumph (Coloss. ii. 15); judging the Prince of this world and casting him out. To this, reference is made in Isaias (xxxv.), "*Behold your God shall bring the revenge of recompense; God Himself will come and will save you*" (xxxv. 4). It is the same as the acceptable year. "*Acceptable*," as regards God's servants; "*the day of vengeance*," as regards His and their enemies.

20. "*And when He had folded the book*," on the roller round which it was folded, "*He returned it to the minister*," the person who was in attendance on the chief officer of the synagogue, and had charge of the sacred books. "*He sat down*," as was usually done in such cases before delivering a discourse on the subjects read previously in a standing posture by the speaker.

"*And the eyes of all in the synagogue were fixed on Him.*" Probably, on seeing Him read who had not learned letters. It may be also that a Divine effulgence shone from His countenance; and as the Jews knew, that the prayer read had reference to the Messiah, they were anxious to know, if He might not Himself be the Messiah considering the wonders wrought by Him elsewhere (*v.* 23), and the fame that went abroad regarding Him.

21. "*This day is fulfilled this scripture in your ears.*" "*In your ears.*" A Hebrew phrase for, *in your hearing*. This oracle of the prophet, which, as you know, regards your expected Messiah, is now fulfilled in me, whom you see preaching to the poor, and of whom you heard it stated, that He performed elsewhere the works described by the prophets, as the distinguishing characteristics of the Messiah. He thereby, without expressly stating it, insinuated that He Himself was the Messiah spoken of by Isaias.

22. "*Gave testimony to Him;*" not exactly that He was the Messiah, as appears from their calling Him "*the son of Joseph*," and their attempt at precipitating Him down the hill; but, they testified to the superior way in which He acquitted Himself, as expressed in the following words, "*and wondered at the words of grace, &c.*," the graceful, eloquent words that were uttered by Him, full of persuasiveness, so calculated to move and convince. "*He spoke like one having authority, not as their Scribes and Pharisees*" (Matthew vii. 29).

"*Is not this the son of Joseph?*" (Matthew xiii. 55). The son of a poor carpenter, Himself a carpenter, brought up in our midst, without influence or consideration or education of any kind. Hence, their wonder. Likely with this, at least in some of them, were mixed up feelings of scorn at His low extraction and humble occupation. "*They were scandalized in His regard*" (Matthew xiii. 57).

23. *Doubtless you will say to me this similitude: Physician, cure thyself;*" a trite proverb, sometimes addressed to physicians, whose powers in the healing art benefit strangers without proving of any service to themselves or theirs; and generally applied to such, as attending to the concerns of others, neglect their own "*Physician*," confine not the advantages of your skill and healing powers to strangers; make yourself and your friends sharers in them. In thus divining the thoughts of their hearts, and their latent objections to Him, to which He replies in the following verse, He displays His Omniscient Divinity.

"*As great things,*" &c. Here, the proverb is applied to Him, in regard to His fellow-citizens. The people of Nazareth were scandalized or offended at two things in our Redeemer—First, His humble extraction. To this, He replies in verse 24; secondly, the fewness of His miracles among them. To this, He replies in verses 25-27, and He illustrates His own mode of acting on account of their unworthiness, by example of a similar line of acting, from the same causes, on the part of the ancient prophets. If He did not perform a greater number of wonders among them, they had to blame themselves as the guilty cause. From this passage, it is clear our Lord had been in Galilee performing wonderful works and miraculous cures. The visit, therefore, referred to in verse 14, was His *second* visit. For, on the first occasion, He passed by Nazareth (Matthew iv. 13), and proceeded to Capharnaum, which He made His place of abode, and the centre of His missionary labours. The Nazarites, our Lord's fellow-citizens, wished that He would favour His own people, who naturally had greater claims than strangers had, with these miraculous wonders that He was reported to have performed elsewhere.

24. In this, He taxes their depreciation of Him, as their fellow-citizen, and shows that He scanned the inmost thoughts of their minds. He assigns in this verse, a reason for not favouring them with His miracles, of which, from their pride and contemptuous depreciation of Himself, they would be unworthy (see Matthew xiii. 58).

25. Again, He shows that their incredulity rendered them unworthy of what they wished for; and hence, following the example of the most celebrated prophets of old, He withheld from them the miracles which were performed in favour of strangers, who proved themselves not undeserving of such blessings. St. Matthew says, "*He performed not many miracles, because of their unbelief*" (xiii. 58).

"*When heaven was shut up three years and six months.*" This is not mentioned in the SS. Scriptures of the Old Testament. Hence, our Lord know it by His omniscient intelligence, or from Jewish tradition, from which source St. James (chap. v.) must have learned it, or from the revelation of our Lord. In the 3rd Book of Kings (chap. xvii. 1) there is no mention made of the prayer of Elias, that a drought would come; but only that he proclaimed that a drought would prevail. But St. James supplies what is omitted there, when he tells us it was at Elias' prayers it was done (chap. v. 17). Indeed, it was always the custom with the Prophets and Apostles and our Lord Himself to commence important events with prayer. In 3 Kings (xviii. 1), it is said, that it was *in the third year*, the word of the Lord came to Elias about "*giving rain upon the face of the earth.*" But this "*third year,*" may denote the third year completed; others reconcile the words of the Old Testament, by saying that the years there referred to are to be computed, not from the beginning of the drought; but, from the time Elias came to Sarepta. Others say, the "*third year*" is to be computed from the commencement of the famine, which began to be felt nearly a year after the drought commenced.

27. By these two examples well known to the Jews, our Lord wishes to convey, that as their celebrated prophets of old, by the command of God—"*to none of them was Elias sent*"—refused performing miraculous cures among their countrymen, on account of their unbelief, while they exercised the same in favour of strangers, who proved worthy of such blessings; so, might the people of Nazareth blame themselves, if He did not work many miracles among them. This was owing to their unworthiness and unbelief.

28, 29. Perceiving the force of His rebuke, when charging their own pride and incredulity with the fewness of the miracles performed by Him in their midst, the Nazarites were "*all in the synagogue filled with anger.*" Even those, who before admired His graceful words and His eloquence, are now suddenly changed. Their pride was such at finding themselves corrected by Him, at being told of their envy and incredulity, which rendered them more undeserving of His miracles than the rest of their countrymen, nay, than the very Pagans themselves; that, notwithstanding the cures they saw Him perform among them; notwithstanding the sacredness of the Sabbath, and their natural feelings of consideration for a fellow-citizen, who had already done so much to reflect honour on their hitherto despised district of Nazareth; they are prepared for the last extremity, and mean to compass His death.

30. "*But He passing through the midst of them.*" Some say He rendered Himself invisible; others, that He changed their wills, so that they no longer meditated His death; others, that He so stupified them and restrained their hands and feet, that seeing Jesus, they could not or dare not lay hands on Him. His hour had not come. The mode in which He was to die was different from that kind of death, with which He was now menaced; hence, He exerted His power to prevent it. "*Went His way,*" fearing no one. No one could harm Him save by His own free will and consent.

31. "*And He went down into Capharnaum, &c.*" Capharnaum was in a lower situation than Nazareth. Hence, the Evangelist says, "*He went down.*" This was not His first visit to Capharnaum (v. 23). Nor is this visit to be confounded with that recorded (Mark i. 21), since on this latter occasion He did not "*descend.*" He only came there from the maritime coasts, although the miracle here recorded is mentioned there also.

"*And there He taught them on the Sabbath days.*" He taught them assembled in the synagogue on Sabbath days, principally; but, He, at the same time, taught all who came to Him, and made frequent missionary excursions into the country, and sometimes performed miracles on these occasions.

"*And they were astonished.*" The Greek word, εξεπλησσοντο, means, they were *wonderfully struck and enraptured,* "*at His doctrine.*"

"*For, His speech was with power*" (see Matthew vii. 28-29).

TEXT.

33. *And in the synagogue there was a man who had an unclean devil, and he cried out with a loud voice,*

34. *Saying: Let us alone, what have we to do with thee, Jesus of Nazareth? art thou come to destroy us? I know thee who thou art, the Holy one of God.*

35. *And Jesus rebuked him, saying: Hold thy peace, and go out of him. And when the devil had thrown him into the midst, he went out of him, and hurt him not at all.*

36. *And there came fear upon all, and they talked among themselves, saying: What word is this, for with authority and power he commandeth the unclean spirits, and they go out?*

37. *And the fame of him was published into every place of the country.*

38. *And Jesus rising up out of the synagogue, went into Simon's house. And Simon's wife's mother was taken with a great fever, and they besought him for her.*

39. *And standing over her, he commanded the fever, and it left her. And immediately rising, she ministered to them.*

40. *And when the sun was down, all they that had any sick with divers diseases, brought them to him. But he laying his hands on every one of them, healed them.*
41. *And devils went out from many, crying out and saying: Thou art the Son of God. And rebuking them he suffered them not to speak, for they knew that he was Christ.*
42. *And when it was day, going out he went into a desert place: and the multitudes sought him, and came unto him: and they stayed him that he should not depart from them.*
43. *To whom he said: To other cities also I must preach the kingdom of God: for therefore am I sent.*
44. *And he was preaching in the synagogues of Galilee.*

COMMENTARY.

33-37. (See Mark i. 23-28, Commentary on.)

38-40. (See Matthew viii. 14-16.)

41. (See Mark i. 34.) "*Devils went from many,*" by our Lord's command. At this time there were many demoniacs among the Jews, either because the devils had a presentiment of our Lord's coming, whose presence caused them the greatest torture; or, because God wished to give His Son an opportunity of showing His power over demons by expelling them forcibly from the bodies of the possessed.

42. "*When it was day,*" at the early twilight. St. Mark (i. 35), has "*very early.*" "*Going out,*" from the house where He spent the night and from the city. "*He went into a desert place,*" probably, for the purpose of prayer (Mark i. 35), and to avoid the crowd and show His indifference in regard to human applause.

"*The multitudes,*" attracted by His miraculous cures, coming to Peter's house, where He stayed, and not finding Him, went in search of Him into the desert place, and desired Him to remain with them. St. Mark (i. 36) says, the Apostles found Him first, and received the answer there recorded (i. 38), and the multitude afterwards found Him, and received the answer recorded here, next verse.

43. "*To other cities also,*" where the Gospel has not yet been preached. "*The kingdom of God*" (see Matthew iii. 2). "*For therefore,*" viz., the preaching of the Gospel, "*am I sent.*" The object of His mission by His Heavenly Father was not precisely to work miracles. They were only subsidiary to the other end. They were only means to be employed to confirm the truth of the Gospel.

44. "*He was preaching.*" He now discharged the function of preaching, continuously, unremittingly. Now, that the Baptist, His Precursor, had passed away, after discharging his office of bearing testimony; our Redeemer, who had during John's lifetime, preached only in a partial way, now preaches everywhere, publicly and privately, throughout Galilee and Judea, filling every place with the blessings of the Gospel. Hence, at His Passion He is charged with stirring up commotions everywhere, "*commovet populum docens per universam Judæam, incipiens a Galilea usque huc*" (Luke xxiii. 5). As the sun rises gradually, and emerging by degrees, diffuses its light only in a gradual way, and following the day star, diffuses its full light and heat when the latter disappears; so was it with our Lord's preaching; while the Baptist, who preceded Him, like the day star, pointing to the coming sun, was engaged in preaching and bearing testimony to Him, He did not suddenly appear. But, when the Baptist had diffused the light of his testimony and dis-

appeared; then, the Sun of Justice appeared in all His splendour, diffusing the heat of Divine grace, and the light of heavenly truth everywhere around Him.

CHAPTER V.

ANALYSIS.

In this chapter, the Evangelist records the first miraculous draught of fishes—the call of Simon Peter, and the two sons of Zebedee, most likely, to the Apostleship (see Matthew iv. 18, Commentary on) (1-11). The cure of a leper (12-16). The cure of the paralytic at Capharnaum (17-26). The call of St. Matthew to the Apostleship. The murmurs of the Scribes and Pharisees on the occasion of the feast given by St. Matthew to our Lord (27-32). Our Lord's teaching on the subject of fasting (33-39).

TEXT.

AND it came to pass, that when the multitudes pressed upon him to hear the word of God, he stood by the lake of Genesareth,

2. And saw two ships standing by the lake; but the fishermen were gone out of them and were washing their nets.

3. And going up into one of the ships that was Simon's, he desired him to draw back a little from the land. And sitting he taught the multitudes out of the ship.

4. Now when he had ceased to speak, he said to Simon: Launch out into the deep, and let down your nets for a draught.

5. And Simon answering, said to him: Master, we have laboured all the night, and have taken nothing; but at thy word I will let down the net.

6. And when they had done this, they enclosed a very great multitude of fishes, and their net broke.

7. And they beckoned to their partners that were in the other ship, that they should come and help them. And they came, and filled both the ships, so that they were almost sinking.

8. Which when Simon Peter saw, he fell down at Jesus's knees, saying: Depart from me, for I am a sinful man, O Lord.

9. For he was wholly astonished, and all that were with him, at the draught of the fishes which they had taken.

10. And so were also James and John the sons of Zebedee, who were Simon's partners. And Jesus saith to Simon: Fear not; from henceforth thou shalt catch men.

11. And having brought their ships to land, leaving all things they followed him.

12. And it came to pass, when he was in a certain city, behold a man full of leprosy, who seeing Jesus, and falling on his face, besought him, saying: Lord, if thou wilt, thou canst make me clean.

13. And stretching forth his hand he touched him, saying: I will. Be thou cleansed. And immediately the leprosy departed from him.

14. And he charged him that he should tell no man, but, Go, show thyself to the priest, and offer for thy cleansing according as Moses commanded, for a testimony to them.

15. But the fame of him went abroad the more, and great multitudes came together to hear, and to be healed by him of their infirmities.

16. And he retired into the desert and prayed.

17. And it came to pass on a certain day, as he sat teaching, that there were also Pharisees and doctors of the law sitting by, that were come out of every town of Galilee and Judea and Jerusalem; and the power of the Lord was to heal them.

18. And behold men brought in a bed a man who had the palsy; and they sought means to bring him in, and to lay him before him.

19. *And when they could not find by what way they might bring him in, because of the multitudes, they went up upon the roof, and let him down through the tiles with his bed into the midst before Jesus.*

20. *Whose faith when he saw, he said : Man, thy sins are forgiven thee.*

21. *And the scribes and Pharisees began to think, saying : Who is this that speaketh blasphemies ? Who can forgive sins, but God alone ?*

22. *And when Jesus knew their thoughts, answering he said to them : What is it you think in your hearts ?*

23. *Which is easier to say, Thy sins are forgiven thee ; or to say, Arise and walk ?*

24. *But that you may know that the Son of man hath power on earth to forgive sins (he saith to the sick of the palsy) I say to thee, Arise, take up thy bed, and go into thy house.*

25. *And immediately rising up before them, he took up the bed on which he lay ; and went away to his own house, glorifying God.*

26. *And all were astonished : and they glorified God. And they were filled with fear, saying : We have seen wonderful things to-day.*

COMMENTARY.

1-11. The call of the Apostles, and the miraculous draught of fishes, recorded here, took place before the miracles, recorded verses 33, 39, 41, &c. of the preceding chapter. The Evangelists proposed to themselves to describe the leading events of our Redeemer's life, without exactly observing in their narrative, the order in which they occurred. This is particularly true of St. Luke, who gives a more detailed account of our Lord's actions, without attending to the order in which they took place ; while St. Matthew is more exact in observing the order of events ; but not so circumstantial in detailing the events themselves. Hence, in this passage, St. Luke describes the call of the principal Apostles and the miraculous draught *after* the cure of the demoniac, and Peter's mother-in-law, although occurring *before* them.

"*And it came to pass,*" &c. Whether the occurrences recorded (*v.* 1-11), are the same as those described in Matthew (iv. 18-22), is disputed. It seems, however, notwithstanding some difference in details, that they are the same. St. Luke here narrates certain circumstances connected with the vocation of the four Apostles, which are only passed over by St. Matthew ; but, not denied by him ; and everything described by St. Luke is perfectly consistent with the narrative of St. Matthew (see Matthew iv. 18-22, Commentary on).

12-14. (See Matthew viii. 12-14.)

15. The more our Lord desired to labour, unknown and unobserved, the more the fame of His wonderful deeds was noised abroad, which attracted vast multitudes to Him to be cured of their infirmities and bodily ailments.

16. To avoid all incentives to vain glory, and leave us an example in this respect, our Lord, after performing miracles which redounded to His glory, used to retire to a desert place, and there communicate in prayer with His Heavenly Father, to whom He referred all the glory of His actions.

17. "*On a certain day, while He sat*"—the posture usually observed by teachers—the Pharisees and doctors of the law (in *v.* 21, called "*Scribes*"), who were attracted from every town of Galilee and Judea and Jerusalem by the fame of His miracles and teaching, sat by Him for the purpose of hearing Him and narrowly watching all His

words and actions; "*and the power of the Lord*" permanently resided in Him to heal the Jews, who laboured under corporal infirmities. Kenrick (*hic*) observes that this latter clause regarding our Lord's healing power would naturally follow, or be immediately connected with *v.* 15. In the Greek for "*sat teaching*," it is *was teaching*.

18-26. (See Matthew ix. 2-8, Commentary on.)

TEXT.

27. *And after these things he went forth, and saw a publican named Levi, sitting at the receipt of custom, and he said to him: Follow me.*
28. *And leaving all things, he rose up and followed him.*
29. *And Levi made him a great feast in his own house; and there was a great company of publicans, and of others, that were at table with them.*
30. *But their Pharisees and scribes murmured, saying to his disciples: Why do you eat and drink with publicans and sinners?*
31. *And Jesus answering, said to them: They that are whole, need not the physician: but they that are sick.*
32. *I came not to call the just, but sinners to penance.*
33. *And they said to him: Why do the disciples of John fast often, and make prayers, and the disciples of the Pharisees in like manner; but thine eat and drink?*
34. *To whom he said: Can you make the children of the bridegroom fast, whilst the bridegroom is with them?*
35. *But the days will come; when the bridegroom shall be taken away from them, then shall they fast in those days.*
36. *And he spoke also a similitude to them: That no man putteth a piece from a new garment upon an old garment; otherwise he both rendeth the new, and the piece taken from the new agreeth not with the old.*
37. *And no man putteth new wine into old bottles: otherwise the new wine will break the bottles, and it will be spilled and the bottles will be lost.*
38. *But new wine must be put into new bottles; and both are preserved.*
39. *And no man drinking old, hath presently a mind to new: for he saith, The old is better.*

COMMENTARY.

27-38. (See Matthew ix. 9-17, Commentary on.)

39. This is an additional reason, recorded by St. Luke alone, adduced by our Lord to justify His mode of acting towards His disciples. It is very hard at once to overcome the force of habit, just as men accustomed to old wine cannot be induced to wish for the new wine, or choose it all at once, although stronger and more substantial. "*He saith, The old is better*," more palatable, and more agreeable for use. It is not "*presently*," or all at once, but gradually, he gives it up. So, our Redeemer does not at once enjoin on His followers to embrace the austerities of the New Law, to which they were hitherto unaccustomed. Making every allowance for the force of habit, He only requires it of them gradually. He compares the New Law and its austerities to new wine, which is stronger, and produces an effect sooner than the old. By saying, they cannot be brought to it "*presently*," or all at once, He implies that this would be done by degrees, as happened later on. "*When the bridegroom is taken away . . . then they shall fast in those days*" (*v.* 35).

CHAPTER VI.

ANALYSIS.

In this chapter, we have an account of the plucking of the ears of corn on the Sabbath, and our Lord's reply to the malevolent animadversions of the Pharisees in relation to it (1-5). The healing of the man with the withered hand, and our Lord's defence of his mode of acting regarding it (6-11). The calling of the twelve Apostles (12-16). The sermon on the Mount (17-49).

TEXT.

*A*ND it came to pass on the second first sabbath, that as he went through the corn-fields his disciples plucked the ears, and did eat rubbing them in their hands.

2. And some of the Pharisees said to them: Why do you that which is not lawful on the sabbath-days?

3. And Jesus answering them, said: Have you not read so much as this, what David did, when himself was hungry and they that were with him:

4. How he went into the house of God, and took and ate the bread of proposition, and gave to them that were with him, which is not lawful to eat but only for the priests?

5. And he said to them: The son of man is Lord also of the sabbath.

6. And it came to pass also on another sabbath, that he entered into the synagogue, and taught. And there was a man, whose right hand was withered.

7. And the scribes and Pharisees watched if he would heal on the sabbath; that they might find an accusation against him.

8. But he knew their thoughts; and said to the man who had the withered hand: Arise, and stand forth in the midst. And rising he stood forth.

9. Then Jesus said to them: I ask you, if it be lawful on the sabbath-days to do good or to do evil; to save life, or to destroy?

10. And looking round about on them all, he said to the man: Stretch forth thy hand. And he stretched it forth: and his hand was restored.

11. And they were filled with madness; and they talked one with another, what they might do to Jesus.

12. And it came to pass in those days, that he went out into a mountain to pray, and he passed the whole night in the prayer of God.

13. And when day was come, he called unto him his disciples; and he chose twelve of them (whom also he named Apostles:)

14. Simon whom he surnamed Peter, and Andrew his brother, James and John, Philip and Bartholomew,

15. Matthew and Thomas, James the son of Alpheus, and Simon who is called Zelotes,

16. And Jude the brother of James, and Judas Iscariot who was the traitor.

17. And coming down with them, he stood in a plain place, and the company of his disciples, and a very great multitude of people from all Judea and Jerusalem, and the sea-coast both of Tyre and Sidon,

18. Who were come to hear him, and to be healed of their diseases. And they that were troubled with unclean spirits, were cured.

19. And all the multitude sought to touch him, for virtue went out from him, and healed all.

20. And he, lifting up his eyes on his disciples, said: Blessed are ye poor: for yours is the kingdom of God.

21. Blessed are ye that hunger now: for you shall be filled. Blessed are ye that weep now: for you shall laugh.

22. Blessed shall you be when men shall hate you, and when they shall separate you, and shall reproach you, and cast out your name as evil, for the son of man's sake.

23. Be glad in that day and rejoice; for behold, your reward is great in heaven. For according to these things did their fathers to the prophets.

24. But wo to you that are rich: for you have your consolation.

25. Wo to you that are filled: for you shall hunger. Wo to you that now laugh: for you shall mourn and weep.

26. Wo to you when men shall bless you: For according to these things did their fathers to the false prophets.

27. But I say to you that hear: Love your enemies, do good to them that hate you.

28. Bless them that curse you, and pray for them that calumniate you.

29. And to him that striketh thee on the one cheek, offer also the other. And him that taketh away from thee thy cloak, forbid not to take thy coat also.

30. Give to every one that asketh thee, and of him that taketh away thy goods, ask them not again.

31. And as you would that men should do to you, do you also to them in like manner.

32. And if you love them that love you, what thanks are to you? for sinners also love those that love them.

33. And if you do good to them who do good to you; what thanks are to you? for sinners also do this.

34. And if you lend to them of whom you hope to receive; what thanks are to you? for sinners also lend to sinners, to receive as much.

35. But love ye your enemies; do good, and lend, hoping for nothing thereby; and your reward shall be great, and you shall be the sons of the Highest; for he is kind to the unthankful, and to the evil.

36. Be ye therefore merciful, as your Father also is merciful.

37. Judge not, and you shall not be judged. Condemn not, and you shall not be condemned. Forgive, and you shall be forgiven.

38. Give, and it shall be given to you: good measure and pressed down and shaken together and running over shall they give into your bosom. For with the same measure that you shall mete withal, it shall be measured to you again.

39. And he spoke also to them a similitude: Can the blind lead the blind? do they not both fall into the ditch?

40. The disciple is not above his master; but every one shall be perfect, if he be as his master.

41. And why seest thou the mote in thy brother's eye: but the beam that is in thy own eye thou considerest not.

42. Or how canst thou say to thy brother: Brother, let me pull the mote out of thy eye, when thou thyself seest not the beam in thy own eye? Hypocrite, cast first the beam out of thy own eye; and then shalt thou see clearly to take out the mote from thy brother's eye.

43. For there is no good tree that bringeth forth evil fruit; nor an evil tree that bringeth forth good fruit.

44. For every tree is known by its fruit. For men do not gather figs from thorns; nor from a bramble bush do they gather the grape.

45. A good man out of the good treasure of his heart bringeth forth that which is good; and an evil man out of the evil treasure bringeth forth that which is evil. For out of the abundance of the heart the mouth speaketh.

46. And why call you me Lord, Lord: and do not the things which I say?

47. Every one that cometh to me, and heareth my words, and doth them, I will show you to whom he is like.

48. He is like to a man building a house, who digged deep, and laid the foundation upon

a rock. And when a flood came, the stream beat vehemently upon that house, and it could not shake it; for it was founded on a rock.

49. But he that heareth, and doth not; is like to a man building his house upon the earth without a foundation: against which the stream beat vehemently, and immediately it fell, and the ruin of that house was great.

COMMENTARY.

1-5. (See Matthew xii. 1-8, Commmentary on.)
6-10. (See Matthew xii. 9-14.)

11. "*Filled with madness,*" fury and rage, at being unable to reply to our Lord. Hence, their wicked, murderous thoughts regarding Him.

12-38. (See Matthew v., vi., vii.)
39. (Matthew xv. 14.)
40. (Matthew x. 24, 25.)
41-44. (Matthew vii.)
45. (Matthew xii. 34, 35.)
46-49. (Matthew vii. 24-29.)

CHAPTER VII.

ANALYSIS.

In this chapter, are recorded the healing of the Centurion's servant (1-10). The raising to life of the son of the widow of Naim (10-17). The embassy from John; our Lord's teaching in connexion with it, and His panegyric on John (18-35). The anointing of our Lord by the penitent woman, and our Lord's declaration in reply to the strictures of the proud Pharisee in regard to it (36-50).

TEXT.

AND when he had finished all his words in the hearing of the people, he entered into Capharnaum.

2. And the servant of a certain centurion, who was dear to him, being sick, was ready to die:

3. And when he had heard of Jesus, he sent unto him the ancients of the Jews, desiring him to come and heal his servant.

4. And when they came to Jesus, they besought him earnestly, saying to him, He is worthy that thou shouldest do this for him.

5. For he loveth our nation; and he hath built us a synagogue.

6. And Jesus went with them. And when he was now not far from the house, the centurion sent his friends to him, saying: Lord, trouble not thyself. For I am not worthy that thou shouldest enter under my roof.

7. For which cause neither did I think myself worthy to come to thee: but say the word, and my servant shall be healed.

8. For I also am a man subject to authority, having under me soldiers: and I say to one, Go, and he goeth; and to another, Come, and he cometh; and to my servant, Do this, and he doth it.

9. Which Jesus hearing, marvelled; and turning about to the multitude that followed him, he said: Amen I say to you, I have not found so great faith even in Israel.

10. *And they who were sent being returned to the house, found the servant whole who had been sick.*

11. *And it came to pass afterwards, that he went into a city that is called Naim; and there went with him his disciples, and a great multitude.*

12. *And when he came nigh to the gate of the city, behold a dead man was carried out, the only son of his mother; and she was a widow: and a great multitude of the city was with her.*

13. *Whom when the Lord had seen, being moved with mercy towards her, he said to her. Weep not.*

14. *And he came near and touched the bier. And they that carried it, stood still. And he said: Young man, I say to thee, arise.*

15. *And he that was dead, sat up, and began to speak. And he gave him to his mother.*

16. *And there came a fear on them all: and they glorified God, saying: A great prophet is risen up among us: and God hath visited his people.*

17. *And this rumour of him went forth throughout all Judea, and throughout all the country round about.*

18. *And John's disciples told him of all these things.*

19. *And John called to him two of his disciples, and sent them to Jesus, saying: Art thou he that is to come; or look we for another?*

20. *And when the men were come unto him, they said: John the Baptist hath sent us to thee, saying: Art thou he that art to come; or look we for another?*

21. *(And in that same hour, he cured many of their diseases, and hurts, and evil spirits: and to many that were blind he gave sight.)*

22. *And answering, he said to them: Go and relate to John what you have heard and seen: The blind see, the lame walk, the lepers are made clean, the deaf hear, the dead rise again, to the poor the gospel is preached:*

23. *And blessed is he whosoever shall not be scandalized in me.*

24. *And when the messengers of John were departed, he began to speak to the multitudes concerning John: What went you out into the desert to see? a reed shaken with the wind?*

25. *But what went you out to see: a man clothed in soft garments? Behold they that are in costly apparel and live delicately, are in the houses of kings.*

26. *But what went you out to see? a prophet? Yea, I say to you, and more than a prophet.*

27. *This is he of whom it is written: "Behold I send my angel before thy face, who shall prepare thy way before thee."*

28. *For I say to you: Amongst those that are born of women, there is not a greater prophet than John the Baptist. But he that is the lesser in the kingdom of God, is greater than he.*

29. *And all the people hearing, and the publicans, justified God, being baptized with John's baptism.*

30. *But the Pharisees and the lawyers despised the counsel of God against themselves, being not baptized by him.*

31. *And the Lord said: Whereunto then shall I liken the men of this generation? and to what are they like?*

32. *They are like to children sitting in the market-place, and speaking one to another, and saying: We have piped to you, and you have not danced; we have mourned, and you have not wept.*

33. *For John the Baptist came neither eating bread nor drinking wine; and you say He hath a devil.*

34. *The son of man is come eating and drinking; and you say: Behold a man that is a glutton and a drinker of wine, a friend of publicans and sinners.*
35. *And wisdom is justified by all her children.*

COMMENTARY.

1-10. (See Matthew viii. 5-10.)

11. "*And it came to pass afterwards.*" Maldonatus holds that the following miracle, which St. Luke alone records—we have no mention of it by the other Evangelists—did not occur immediately after the cure of the Centurion's servant, recorded in the preceding verses. He thinks, that the occurrences mentioned in chaps. viii., ix., x. of St. Matthew, took place between the two miracles narrated here. For, he remarks, all the Evangelist says is, that this miracle of the resuscitation of the young man of Naim occurred "*afterwards,*" and St. Matthew (chap. xi.) says, that after directing and instructing His disciples, our Lord proceeded to preach and teach in their cities; in Naim, where this miracle occurred, among the rest. It is, however, commonly held that the word, "*afterwards,*" in Latin, "*deinceps,*" means the following day, as the Syriac version has it. And, indeed, the progressive description of still increasing wonders was very natural on the part of St. Luke. It was wonderful, that a man, who was present, should be cured by our Lord at once, of a loathsome leprosy; and that, by a single word; more wonderful still, to cure an absent man, at the point of death; but most wonderful, to raise to life a man, undoubtedly dead, and carried out to be buried. For, some might say that the Centurion's servant might have naturally recovered, even though our Lord had not interposed. But, in the last miracle, no evasion or denial could be admitted.

"*Naim,*" in Greek, *Nain*, was not far from Capharnaum, about two miles from Thebor (St. Jerome, in loc. Hebracis). St. Luke is the only Evangelist that records this miracle.

"*His disciples.*" The ordinary Greek has ικανοι (many of) "*His disciples.*" The word is not found in the Vulgate version or Vatican MS.

12. "*And a great multitude,*" who accompanied Him, owing to His teaching and miracles.

"*The gate of the city,*" generally a crowded place. "*A dead man was carried out,*" to be buried. The Jews had their cemeteries outside the towns and villages, for sanitary purposes. "*The only son.*" The Greek means, "*the only-begotten child,*" which, naturally, made the grief of his bereaved mother more intense. "*And she was a widow,*" another circumstance, that made her condition more pitiable, as she lost her only prop and support.

"*And a great multitude of the city,*" who testified their respect and sympathy, "*were with her.*" These, together with the crowd who accompanied our Lord, bore ample testimony to the truth of the miracle. Humanly speaking, our Lord's going to Naim, and meeting the funeral procession, under such circumstances, might seem casual or fortuitous; but, it was all arranged by the over-ruling providence of God, to give His Son an opportunity of performing this great miracle on so public an occasion.

13. Our Lord was moved with compassion at the sad condition of this desolate widow; and, to leave us an example of how we are to treat the afflicted, He consoles her, not only by words—"*weep not*"—which might afford a cheap and barren sympathy; but, by act.

14. He shows His sympathy by act. *"He touched the bier, and they that carried it stood still,"* and our Lord at once, by the sole exercise of His power, by His word alone, without any prayers, any ceremony, such as were resorted to by Elias, Eliseus, and St. Peter, to show His omnipotence, perfectly restores to life the young man, who was undoubtedly dead.

15. *"Rose up and began to speak."* Our Lord, to show that it was pity and compassion for his mother that induced Him to perform the miracle, *"gave him to his mother."* The consequence of this wonderful miracle was, that the people were seized with *"fear,"* a feeling of awe at so wonderful and unusual an event.

16. *"They glorified God,"* for having sent so great a Prophet among them, and for having *"visited His people,"* by sending the great Prophet, promised them of old, by Moses (Deut. xviii. 15). For a long time, no prophet appeared among them; and now God shows His ancient love for His people, by sending this great Prophet, who wrought more brilliant miracles than ever were performed before. Most likely, they did not regard Him as the Messiah, but only as a great Prophet. Zachary used the words, *"visited His people,"* in his canticle, but, probably in a higher sense than was meant here; for, he spoke under the influence of inspiration; and he adds, as if referring to the Incarnation of the Son of God, *"and wrought the redemption of His people"* (i. 68).

The resuscitation of the young man of Naim has also an allegorical and moral meaning. The bereaved widow represents the Church, who bewails over each of her sons, by mortal sin dead to God, as if he were an only child. She weeps over them, and employs the multitude of her children to intercede for them. Jesus touched with compassion for the wailing of this bereaved spouse, at once speaks to their hearts. He employs the power and unction of His heavenly grace, He raises them mercifully to life and restores them to their now rejoicing mother to care them, and save them from wandering any more in the ways of sin and death. The three miracles now recorded, represent three classes of sinners; some not altogether abandoned, or so sunk in sin, as not to be able themselves to approach our Lord by prayer, and obtain remission and cure, as did the leper; others, the entire faculties of whose souls are so utterly benumbed from habits of sin, that, like the paralytic servant of the Centurion, they must employ intercessors; and, a third class so utterly abandoned and insensible, that it will require still greater efforts, still greater miracles of divine grace to rouse and restore them. St. Ambrose says, the three dead persons raised by our Lord to life, represent three classes of sinners—the daughter of Jairus lying dead at home, represents those who grievously sin inwardly; the young man here publicly carried out, those who commit external grievous sins; and Lazarus, three days dead and corrupting, those, who are the slaves of evil habits and are buried in sin.

18. John was now in prison (Matthew xi. 2).

19-29. (See Matthew xi. 2-13.)

29, 30. *"And all the people hearing,"* &c. Some say the words of these two verses are written by the Evangelist and thrown in, as it were, parenthetically, between the preceding discourse of our Redeemer and its continuation (v. 31, &c). They ground this interpretation on the words (v. 31). *"and the Lord said."* But, these words are wanting in many editions and versions. Hence, others maintain that the words of these verses are the words of our Lord; and the consequence which He draws (v. 31), "*whereunto then, &c.*," they maintain, favours their construction, as our Lord would not ground this consequence which naturally results from the assertions contained in these verses, (29, 30) on the words of the Evangelist. In this construction, our Lord says, as He says in almost similar terms (chap. xxi. 31, 32), that the ignorant people, and the greatest sinners, on hearing John's preaching, "*justified God*," glorified and praised Him for His goodness in sending so great a Prophet; declared Him provident, veracious in all His promises; merciful, as announced by John; and in proof of their belief in John's words, they received the baptism he preached, as a preparation for penance; or "*justified*," might mean, they proclaimed God, as the author and source of justice, and received the baptism of John, as a proof of their belief in all he announced, and of their sincere desire to embrace the course of penance, which he pointed out, as necessary. Our Lord depicts in brighter colours, the perversity of the Pharisees and those learned in the law, viz., "*the Scribes*," by contrasting them with the ignorant people and the most notorious sinners. "*They despised the counsel of God, against themselves*," that is, spurning the preaching of John, and refusing to receive his baptism, they spurned the gracious designs of God regarding them, and this "*against themselves*," to their own condemnation; or, "*against*" might mean "*in*," "*within*," in their own hearts, they despised God's beneficent designs of mercy in their regard. This is said of the Pharisees in *general*; as, no doubt, *some* of them did follow the teachings of John, as *some* of the people and publicans turned a deaf ear to his preaching. Hence, our Lord, or the Evangelist, speaks of both classes in *general* terms, as likely there were some exceptions among both, in the way of following or rejecting "*the counsels of God.*"

31-35. (See Matthew xi. 16-19.)

TEXT.

36. *And one of the Pharisees desired him to eat with him. And he went into the house of the Pharisee, and sat down to meat.*

37. *And behold a woman that was in the city, a sinner, when she knew that he sat at meat in the Pharisee's house, brought an alabaster box of ointment;*

38. *And standing behind at his feet, she began to wash his feet with tears, and wiped them with the hairs of her head, and kissed his feet, and anointed them with the ointment.*

39. *And the Pharisee, who had invited him, seeing it, spoke within himself, saying: This man, if he were a prophet, would know surely who and what manner of woman this is that toucheth him, that she is a sinner.*

40. *And Jesus answering, said to him: Simon, I have something to say to thee. But he said: Master, say it.*

41. *A certain creditor had two debtors, the one owed five hundred pence, and the other fifty.*

42. *And whereas they had not wherewith to pay, he forgave them both. Which therefore of the two loveth him most?*

43. *Simon answering said: I suppose that he to whom he forgave most. And he said to him: Thou hast judged rightly.*

44. *And turning to the woman, he said unto Simon: Dost thou see this woman? I entered into thy house, thou gavest me no water for my feet; but she with tears hath washed my feet, and with her hairs hath wiped them.*

45. *Thou gavest me no kiss; but she, since she came in, hath not ceased to kiss my feet.*

46. *My head with oil thou didst not anoint; but she with ointment hath anointed my feet.*

47. *Wherefore I say to thee: Many sins are forgiven her, because she hath loved much. But to whom less is forgiven, he loveth less.*

48. *And he said to her: Thy sins are forgiven thee.*

49. *And they that sat at meat with him began to say within themselves: Who is this that forgiveth sins also?*

50. *And he said to the woman: Thy faith hath made thee safe, go in peace.*

COMMENTARY.

36. *And one of the Pharisees.*" His name was "*Simon*" (v. 40), whether the same as "*Simon the leper*" (Matthew xxvi. 6), is disputed. Although the anointing of our Lord, mentioned here, as occurring *two years* before our Lord's Passion, must be different from that recorded, as occurring immediately on the eve of His Passion, by Matthew xxvi. 5; Mark xiv. 3, &c.; John xii. 3, &c., all of whom refer to the latter anointing, and say nothing of that recorded here by St. Luke, who, in turn, omits all mention of the anointing recorded by them; still, it is held by many, that the Simon mentioned here, is the same as "*Simon the leper*." This they infer from the identity of name, and also from the familiar intimacy and friendship which existed between Simon and "*the woman*," who discharged this great office of piety in regard to our Lord, at his house; otherwise, she would hardly have obtruded herself on the occasion of supper, in the presence of the assembled guests. St. Augustine holds, they are different, as this anointing occurred at Galilee, probably, in Naim; the other, at Bethany, where our Lord stopped before His Passion. It is all but certain, that the woman who anointed our Blessed Lord on both occasions, was the same, viz., Mary Magdalen, the sister of Martha and Lazarus. (See Matthew xxvi. 7, &c.) The approbation by the Church of this opinion, while ascribing the occurrence here recorded to Mary Magdalen, in the office of her festival, (July 22,) together with the words of our Lord, that wherever the Gospel would be preached, this woman's act would render her celebrated, which is verified in regard to Magdalen, furnish a most powerful argument in favour of this opinion. (Jans. Gandav. c. xlviii.)

37. "*Behold,*" a wonderful example of penance.

"*In the city,*" where the Pharisee resided, probably Naim, mentioned immediately in the foregoing. "*A sinner,*" publicly noted for her immoral course of life. A sense of propriety would forbid her acting the part she did towards our Blessed Lord, save in public, and in the house of her friend, with whom she was manifestly on friendly terms. On having heard of our Lord being in the house of the Pharisee, she approached Him, not like others, who only sought for bodily cure, but in the spirit of true penance, to obtain the cure of her soul from Him, of whom, she heard it said, that He was "*the Lamb that taketh away the sins of the world.*"

38. *Standing,*" may signify any posture. It means, simply, being there, in a kneeling or prostrate posture.

"*Behind His feet.*" She did not venture to come forward, from a deep sense of humiliation and shame. It may also be allusive to the mode in which the Orientals sat at table, reclining on couches, their head and face turned to the table, with their feet in an outward direction. It was by being behind Him, she could anoint His feet, which were exposed, the sandals being laid aside.

"*To wash His feet with tears.*" "*Wash,*" may mean, to *bedew, moisten,* so as to remove the dust that adhered to them. This shows her great sorrow for sin, and her deep penitential spirit.

"*And wiped them with the hairs of her head,*" shows, how she trampled all worldly vanity and self-love under foot, by soiling that portion of her person, viz., her hair, about which women in general are so solicitous. She probably made the decking out of her hair, the means of attracting others to commit sin. Now, she makes the same hair, the instrument of penance (Rom. vi. 19). This was also a great mark of the profoundest reverence, it being customary with persons in exalted stations, of old, after washing their hands, to dry them on the flowing hair of some attendant slave.

"*Kissed His feet,*" in token of penitential love, and self-humiliation, and of desire of reconciliation and peace; a "kiss" being a sign of peace. Kissing one's feet, a great proof of love and humility.

"*And anointed them with ointment.*" The ancients were wont to employ ointments, that is, odorous liquors, at their banquets, usually for anointing the head, so as to diffuse a fragrance all around. (Matthew xxvi.; Psalm xxii.) It was generally applied by females (1 Kings viii. 13). Hence, Magdalen fearlessly rushes into the house of her friend, for the purpose of performing this office towards our Blessed Lord, and of showing her love for Him. In this, she also gave proof of her faith in her Lord, His power to remit sin—a power granted to none of the prophets. Hence, she believed in *Him* as Man God. She displayed, in the plentiful effusion of her tears, a heroic, a penitential spirit. By anointing His feet, she displayed her great humility, as if unworthy to approach His head; though, it is held by some, that she anointed, not only His feet, of which there is mention here; but His head, also, of which the Evangelist here omits all mention.

39. "*A prophet,*" one sent from God, and gifted with knowledge of hidden and supernatural things.

In the foregoing we have an illustrious example of a truly humble penitential spirit. Here, we have an example of the supercilious arrogance of the Pharisee, who, instead of admiring the humility and penitential spirit displayed by the sinful woman, who shed such copious tears—a proof of her conversion and penitential spirit—in the midst of a festive scene, and ought to render thanks to God's grace, which inspired it; on the contrary, haughtily sits in judgment on our Lord, and while he should praise His merciful clemency, in rejecting no one, however unworthy, questions His claims to be considered a prophet, and doubts His clear insight into hidden things, with which, it was supposed, He ought, as a prophet, to be gifted. In this the Pharisee displayed his ignorance; since it formed no part of a prophet's gift to know all hidden things, save as far as it may please God to enlighten him; and He often conceals hidden things from His prophets (4 Kings iv. 27). He also erred, in supposing, that if our Lord knew her to be a sinner, He would not allow her to touch Him, as if contact with a sinner would defile the soul, which was a gross error. For, even where contact with unclean objects was prohibited by law, it only regarded external bodily defilement (Levit. xiv. 15). Nay, the very fact of knowing her to be a sinner, was the reason why He, who came to save and rescue sinners, would mercifully attract her to Himself. The Pharisees themselves, brought to our Lord the adulterous woman (John viii. 3).

"*Who and what manner of woman she is that toucheth Him.*" He did not censure the fact of her anointing Him—a thing usual at feasts—but His allowing her to touch Him, as if it would defile Him. "*That she is a sinner,*" well known, even notorious for her sinful, disorderly life.

40. Our Lord showed Simon, that He knew the character of the sinful woman in question, and still more, that He knew more than prophets in general ever know, viz., the inmost thoughts of man's heart.

"*Answering*," is a Hebrew form for beginning to speak without reference to any previous question; or, here it might mean, "*answering*," the objection or rash judgment passing through the mind of the proud Pharisee. "*Simon*"—supposed by many to be the same as Simon the leper of Bethania, where Magdalen anointed our Lord's feet six days before His Passion (v. 36). Likely, this Simon, touched with the penance and piety of Magdalen, who was clearly a friend of his, from her entering his house at dinner hour, may have transferred his abode from Galilee, to Judea, where she stopped with Martha and Lazarus.

"*I have something to say to thee.*" Our Lord, while reproving and correcting His host, does so in a very considerate way; thus sparing his feelings, by first presenting the case in the form of a parable. In this, He leaves to all in authority, when about to exercise the duty of correction, an example of consideration for the feelings of others.

41. "*A certain creditor.*" The Greek word (δανειστης) means, either a creditor a usurer, or, money lender. Here, it means a creditor; because the sum credited, as the application implies, was given gratuitously. "*Five hundred*," "*fifty*," denote sums of lesser and greater magnitude.

42. "*He forgave them both*," a manifestly gratuitous act, without any claims to forgiveness on their part. This is particularly true of the application of the parable, as regards the remission of our sins, which is done gratuitously by God, without any claims on our part.

"*Loveth him most*," or ought in duty, and was in gratitude bound, to exhibit greater marks of affection for his generous benefactor. Or, which of them showed the most affection, which induced the creditor gratuitously to forgive his debts? This is said in allusion to the conduct of Magdalen, and the intense affection displayed by her on the present occasion. It also implies, that a very large debt had been remitted to her by Him; and also, that being now fully cleansed from her sin, she was not the loathsome sinner, unworthy of approaching or touching the Son of God, which the proud Pharisee erroneously supposed her to be. The Greek is in the future, "*shall love Him*," as if it referred to the manifestation of love subsequent to the remission of sin. Some understand it of the love manifested beforehand, which induced the creditor gratuitously to forgive; for, in the case of the remission of sin, love is one of the dispositions required in order that God may gratuitously remit it.

43. "*He to whom He forgave most*," should be more lavish of the manifestation of gratitude proportioned, in some measure, to the magnitude of the benefit conferred, of the debt remitted, or expected to be remitted.

"*Thou hast judged rightly.*" Our Lord approves of Simon's judgment, and then applies it, as coming from Simon himself, to the present subject, of the affection shown by Magdalen to our Lord Himself, regarding which the Pharisee had previously judged erroneously.

44. "*Turning to the woman*," who knelt behind His couch. Our Lord applies the similitude in the clearest and most delicate way. There is a striking antithesis between Simon's not furnishing Him with common water, nor getting any of the domestics

to wash His feet, and her washing His feet with her very tears, and wiping them with, what women prize most, the hairs which ornament their head.

45. Secondly, between Simon's omission to give Him the ordinary kiss, the sign of friendship and peace, common among the Jews, and her kissing His feet; and that, not once, but repeatedly and unceasingly. "*Hath not ceased to kiss My feet.*" What a proof of humble love. She did this, from the moment she perceived Him to enter the house. She probably was there before Him.

46. Thirdly, between ordinary oil, and precious ointment, which she profusely poured on His sacred feet. It may be that, on this as well as on a later occasion, she anointed His head also, though St. Luke here makes no mention of it. Our Redeemer, by thus contrasting her services and pious offices with what Simon had done and omitted, wishes to convey to him, that he need not regard her as one to be shunned, and to be prohibited all contact with Himself; that, she had proved herself more deserving than the Pharisee himself, with whom, though less worthy than she was, our Lord did not disdain to come in contact; nay, even to become his guest, and familiar, and take food at his house.

47. "*Therefore,*" having given such proof of her intense, ardent love—on account of this—"*I say to thee, Many sins are forgiven her*"—for which she was indebted to me as creditor—"*because*"—like the debtor referred to in your judgment approved of by me—"*she hath loved much.*" Would not this seem to be the inverse of the conclusion of which the parable and the judgment of Simon were naturally suggestive, viz., that the debtors to whom a larger amount was remitted had, as a *consequence* of such remission, loved much, in gratitude for the favour bestowed by the creditor? For, the parable supposes the creditor to have remitted the debt, owing to the incapacity of the debtors to pay; and then, the question regards the gratitude due for such a favour. In truth, from the parable, would it not seem, that the manifestation of greater love was *consequent* on the remission of the greater debt; whereas, in our Redeemer's conclusion, the inverse is inferred, viz., that the remission of the debt was consequent on the exhibition of sincere love, and, in some measure, caused by it? In the second instance, however, in regard to the debtor, who owed *less*, to whom *less* was remitted, we see that our Lord draws the conclusion naturally suggested by the parable. "*But, to whom less is forgiven, he loveth less.*" In order to solve this difficulty, caused by the apparent opposition between the parable and the conclusion derived from it, by our Redeemer, in the first part, regarding the greater debtor, some Expositors give "*because,*" "*quoniam,*" the meaning of, *idcirco, quapropter,* "*on that account;*" as if our Lord said, Many sins are forgiven her, "*because,* (or, *therefore*), *she loveth much;*" making the exhibition of love consequent on the remission of her sins; in this way, they solve the difficulty, and make the conclusion to accord perfectly with the parable. These say, the Greek word for *quoniam, because*—ὅτι—has frequently the meaning of, "*therefore,*" or "*on that account,*" in SS. Scripture. (John viii. 29; xiv. 17, &c.) This interpretation disposes, at once, of the difficulty, and makes the conclusion to be perfectly in accordance with the parable and with the judgment of Simon, approved of by our Lord, which supposes that the person to whom a greater debt was remitted feels and manifests greater love, out of gratitude for the benefit received and in consideration thereof. In a word, that the exhibition of grateful love was consequent on the remission of a heavy debt gratuitously granted to Magdalen, when she had no claim on such remission. Speaking of this construction, which gives

"*quoniam*" the meaning of *idcirco, therefore*, Calmet observes (*in hunc locum*), "*ita omnes hujus loci ambages et antilogiæ solvuntur.*"

The above construction, however convenient for solving the difficulty, is rejected by most Commentators, as a violent and unauthorized rendering of, ὅτι, in this passage. Hence, the Vulgate rendering, "*because she loved much*," is the one more commonly adopted and approved of. According to this reading, the exhibition or manifestation of love precedes the remission to which it served, in some measure, as a *cause*. If the love referred to, be the perfect love of charity, perfecting Magdalen's contrition and sorrow for sin; then, it obtained from God, the remission of her sins; because perfect charity, the perfect love of God above all things, remits sin; charity being the formal cause of justification, holding the same relation to justification that heat does to calefaction (Jans. Gandav. c. 48). If there be question of charity not so intense; then, it is one of the dispositions, or, essential conditions disposing us for justification. For, among the other conditions required as dispositions for justification, such as faith, hope, &c., a necessary condition on the part of sinners is, *initial* charity, that, "*they begin to love God, as the fountain of all justice*" (Con. Trid. ss. vi. c. vi.) Following the Vulgate rendering—"*quoniam dilexit,*" &c., to which the Greek, οὗ χαριν, "*wherefore*"—an inference drawn from the exhibition of love by Magdalen, preceding the remission granted to her—adds some degree of probability, and considering that Magdalen's exhibition of love took place before she knew her sins were remitted,—for, it was afterwards our Lord assured her of it,—it may be said, that in these words, "*quoniam dilexit,*" &c., our Lord has regard, in the first place, to the great love and penitential spirit that animated Magdalen before she reached the banquet hall, and prompted these acts of penance and humility, which occasioned the rash judgment of Simon, and induced Him to grant her the abundant remission expressed here; and in the next place, He omits referring to her love perfected by the remission of her sins, and consequent on it. He refers to her love before the remission of her sins, as it was one of the dispositions for their remission, "*quoniam dilexit multum,*" and He omits all express allusion to the love she showed *after* their remission, as an expression of her gratitude, just as in the second member of the sentence, He speaks only of the *lesser* degree of love which followed the remission of a *lesser* debt, omitting all express allusion to the less intense love which preceded such remission, and which, as, *initial charity*, formed one of the essential conditions for securing it.

He omits all allusion to the love which followed the remission of the greater debt, expressing only that which preceded it, although, existing in both cases; in the former, as a *cause;* in the latter, as an *effect*, or, grateful recognition; to convey to us, that the remission of sin is differently effected from that of a pecuniary debt. In the latter case, love on the part of the debtor, does not ordinarily operate as a disposing cause, influencing the creditor; whereas, it is different, as regards the remission of sin, where love is one of the essential dispositions for obtaining it. Love is the *cause* of remission and its *effect*. Our Lord conveyed this in both sentences. The former in the remission of the larger debt, which it *caused;* the latter, in the remission of the lesser debt, as its *result* and grateful recognition. In inverting, as it were, the conclusion, and in the application of the parable, our Lord wishes to show, not only that Magdalen's sins were remitted; and hence, that she was not the loathsome creature Simon judged her to be; but, He also wishes to show how her heavy sins were remitted.

"*But, to whom less is forgiven, he loveth less.*" Here, our Lord refers to the less degree and manifestation of love consequent on the remission of the lesser debt.

In this, He refers to Simon, whose love was manifestly less intense than that of Magdalen; because he fancied, that our Lord had not much to remit in his case. The expression of gratitude was less demonstrative, as we see, every day, those who are released from a lesser amount of sin not so fervent or brimful of gratitude as those are, who obtained the forgiveness of very great and numerous sins.

Some maintain, that the words, "*less is forgiven*," mean, "*nothing is forgiven;*" and that to Simon,—who, according to them, had been guilty of a grave sin of incredulity, "*If this man were a prophet,*" as also of rash judgment, in regard to the penitent woman,—*nothing* was remitted. "*Loving less*" means, not loving *at all*. (The Greek for "*less*," in both cases, is—ολιγον—*little*.) According to them, our Lord uses the word, "*less*," instead of nothing, in allusion to the opinion the haughty Pharisee had of his own comparative sinlessness, and also out of urbanity and consideration for the feelings of His host; for the same reason, He uses the third person. These also say, our Lord uses the latter sentence, as ornamental in the application of the second part of the parable relative to the lesser debtor, who owed only "*fifty pence*" (v. 41). Simon's invitation did not, according to them, arise from any supernatural faith or love — essential conditions for the remission of sin. He did not invite our Lord in order to obtain the remission of his sins—the motive which influenced Magdalen to approach Him with faith and love. He did so, from human motives, seeing the high repute in which our Lord was held by the people.

48. "*And He said to her: Thy sins are forgiven thee.*" Some Commentators are of opinion, that it was only after these words were uttered, Magdalen's sins were remitted, and the words of verse 47, "*Many sins are forgiven her,*" verified, as much as to say: because these sins are to be immediately forgiven, as (in verse 48), I, by one continuous action, announce this, and actually forgive them (as in verse 48).

It seems, however, more probable, that the sins of Magdalen had been already forgiven, at the time our Lord declared this regarding her, owing to her perfect sorrow for sin, which embraced or included perfect love of God. The words (v. 47), "*are forgiven,*" are in the past tense in the Greek—αφεωνται—"*have been forgiven,*" and now (v. 48) our Lord Himself publicly and in the hearing of all, remitting her sins a second time, pronounces absolution over them. 1. To make her sure of the remission of her sins, and of her having obtained what she sought. 2. To indicate to the Pharisee that he rashly judged her. 3. To show He was God. We find it to be an approved practice at all times, to have absolution pronounced repeatedly for sins already confessed, and already remitted, whether by valid absolution or perfect contrition.

The Priest, in pronouncing absolution, in the Tribunal of Penance, for sins already remitted. "*Ego te absolvo,*" means, "*Ego tibi confero et communico sanctitatem et gratiam ex se remissivam omnis culpæ.*" St. Thomas (3 Part, Quæst. 84, Art. 3 ad 3); Suarez (Tom. 4 ad 3 Part, Disput. 19, Sectione 2, n. 15).

Hence, our Lord repeats the same a third time (v. 50), "*Thy faith hath made thee safe.*"

49. "*They that sat at meat with Him,*" His fellow guests, "*began to say within themselves;*" they durst not speak openly, for fear of being, like Simon, reprehended by our Lord. Instead of being touched with His great mercy and humanity, they only murmured within themselves and censured Him.

"*Who is this that forgiveth sins also?*" *Who* is not merely content with admitting a sinful woman into His presence, and with working miracles; but, arrogates the divine power of forgiving sins. Similar are the blasphemous murmurings referred to. (Matthew ix. 3, &c.)

50. *"Thy faith hath made thee safe."* Faith being *one* of the essential dispositions for justification, just as charity is assigned as the cause of Magdalen's justification, as being *another* of the necessary dispositions. Faith is the primary disposition. It is *"the foundation and root of justification"* (Conc. Trid.)

"Go in peace," free from all apprehension of punishment for your past sins, which are now fully remitted, both as to guilt and the punishment due to them. Peace and tranquillity of conscience are among the fruits of penance.

CHAPTER VIII.

ANALYSIS.

In this chapter, we have an account of our Lord's ministry and attendants (1-3). The Parable of the Sower and its explanation (4-15). The arrival of our Lord's blessed mother and brethren from Nazareth, and His teaching relative thereto (19-21). The stilling of the storm at sea (22-25). The healing of the Geraseno demoniac (26-39). The raising to life of Jairus' daughter, and the healing of a woman with an issue of blood (40-56).

TEXT.

AND it came to pass afterwards, that he travelled through the cities and towns, preaching and evangelizing the kingdom of God; and the twelve with him.

2. *And certain women who had been healed of evil spirits and infirmities; Mary who is called Magdalen, out of whom seven devils were gone forth.*

3. *And Joanna the wife of Chusa, Herod's steward, and Susanna, and many others who ministered unto him of their substance.*

4. *And when a very great multitude was gathered together and hastened out of the cities unto him, he spoke by a similitude.*

5. *The sower went out to sow his seed. And as he sowed, some fell by the way side, and it was trodden down, and the fowls of the air devoured it.*

6. *And other some fell upon a rock, and as soon as it was sprung up, it withered away because it had no moisture.*

7. *And other some fell among thorns, and the thorns growing up with it, choked it.*

8. *And other some fell upon good ground; and being sprung up, yielded fruit a hundredfold. Saying these things, he cried out: He that hath ears to hear, let him hear.*

9. *And his disciples asked him what this parable might be.*

10. *To whom he said: To you it is given to know the mystery of the kingdom of God; but to the rest in parables, that seeing they may not see, and hearing may not understand.*

11. *Now the parable is this: The seed is the word of God.*

12. *And they by the wayside are they that hear; then the devil cometh, and taketh the word out of their heart, lest believing they should be saved.*

13. *Now, they upon the rock, are they who when they hear, receive the word with joy: and these have no roots; for they believe for awhile, and in time of temptation they fall away.*

14. *And that which fell among thorns, are they who have heard, and going their way, are choked with the cares and riches and pleasures of this life, and yield no fruit.*

15. *But that on the good ground, are they who in a good and very good heart, hearing the word keep it, and bring forth fruit in patience.*

16. *Now no man lighting a candle covereth it with a vessel, or putteth it under a bed; but setteth it upon a candlestick, that they who come in may see the light.*

17. *For there is not any thing secret, that shall not be made manifest; nor hidden that shall not be known and come abroad.*

18. *Take heed therefore how you hear. For whosoever hath, to him shall be given; and whosoever hath not, that also which he thinketh he hath, shall be taken away from him.*

19. *And his mother and brethren came unto him; and they could not come at him for the crowd.*

20. *And it was told him : Thy mother and thy brethren stand without, desiring to see thee.*

21. *Who answering said to them : My mother and my brethren, are they who hear the word of God, and do it.*

22. *And it came to pass on a certain day, that he went into a little ship with his disciples, and he said to them : Let us go over to the other side of the lake. And they launched forth.*

23. *And when they were sailing he slept; and there came down a storm of wind upon the lake, and they were filled, and were in danger.*

24. *And they came and awaked him, saying : Master, we perish. But he arising, rebuked the wind and the rage of the water, and it ceased, and there was a calm.*

25. *And he said to them : Where is your faith? Who being afraid, wondered, saying one to another : Who is this (think you) that he commandeth both the winds and the sea, and they obey him?*

COMMENTARY.

1. "*He travelled through the cities and towns,*" of Galilee. This was our Lord's second journey through Galilee, "*preaching and evangelizing the kingdom of God,*" announcing the joyous tidings regarding the near approach of the kingdom of heaven. For meaning of "*kingdom of heaven*" (see Matthew iv. 22). We are informed (Matthew ix. 35), that on this occasion our Lord was also "*healing every disease and every infirmity,*" doubtless, with the view of proving the truth of His sacred doctrines. This occurred after the decollation of John the Baptist. Our Lord, very likely, now wished to attach to Himself, and count among His followers, the disciples of the Baptist, who were left without a guide to direct them, after John's death.

For, "*through towns and cities,*" the Greek is, "*through town and city,*" used, in a distributive sense, to denote several towns and cities. Hence, the meaning is expressed in our version.

"*And the twelve were with Him.*" He wishes them to accompany Him in order to give them an idea of the hardships of the Apostolic office, and to point out the mode of labouring successfully hereafter, for the salvation of souls.

2. "*And certain women who had been healed of evil spirits and infirmities.*" Corporal obsession and possession by demons was at this time very common, and bodily infirmities were often caused thereby. Our Lord, as we find it frequently recorded in the Gospels, exercised His power over demons, by expelling them from the bodies of those whom they possessed. The women, of whom there is question here, being freed from evil spirits, and cured of their bodily distempers, attached themselves to Him out of feelings of gratitude and devotion; and, probably, from a dread, if He were absent, of being again subject to their former afflictions. These women also furnished our Lord and His Apostles with the necessary means of support, out of their temporal substance, accompanying them on their missions—a usage quite common among the Jews, as we learn from St. Jerome on chap. xxvii. St. Matthew. Hence, it was not wondered at by any one; nor was it a subject of scandal or of wonder to any one among the Jews, to see these devoted and pious women attend on our Lord and His Apostles. (See 1 Cor. ix.)

Among these pious women, the first-mentioned is, "*Mary who is called Magdalen.*" It is generally supposed, that she was Mary, the sister of Martha and Lazarus, the same spoken of (chap. vii. 37) as "*a sinful woman of the city,*" who, "*anointed our Lord's feet with ointment*" (John xi. 2). (See Matthew xxvi. 7.) She is called "*Magdalen,*" from *Magdala,* a town or castle in Galilee, to whose proprietor she was married. St. Augustine holds, that she was not only a public sinner, but an adulteress (Hom. 23, int. 50). It is deemed more probable by many interpreters, that she was not by birth a Galilean, that she came from Judea, her native place being Bethania, where her brother and sister lived. She was in Galilee when our Lord entered on His mission, and being converted by Him, and freed from evil spirits, she followed Him; hence, was among those who followed Him from Galilee, ministering unto Him (Matthew xxvii. 55); and thus, through her, our Lord became intimate with her brother and sister, honouring their house with His personal abode (Luke x. 38). Others maintain, that the Mary, who was sister of Martha and Lazarus, is a different person from Magdalen referred to here, by St. Luke, and by St. Matthew xxvi. This they infer from the different accounts given here and in chap. x. 40. It would be hard for one, after reading St. Luke's account of the woman here, to suppose he referred to the same in chap. x. 39, &c. The former opinion, however, which holds that the sinful woman (Luke vii. 37), Mary Magdalen and Mary the sister of Lazarus, refer to one and the same person, is far the more probable, and accords best with the sense of the Church as expressed in the Roman Breviary and Missal in the Office and Mass of Mary Magdalen. (July 22.)

"*Seven devils were gone forth.*" Mark (xvi. 9) says, "*out of whom He had cast seven devils.*" By these some understand seven grievous sins, passions or capital vices of which she was cured by her conversion. But the more probable opinion seems to be, that there is question of evil spirits who were permitted to possess and torment her in punishment of her wicked, disorderly life. Of these our Lord mercifully freed her. The word "*seven,*" according to Scriptural usage, denotes a large number. We find elsewhere that a whole *legion* of evil spirits possessed one man (v. 30).

3. "*Joanna, the wife of Chusa, Herod's steward.*" It may be that her husband was dead, or that having become himself a follower of our Lord, he permitted his wife, out of gratitude for the cure performed on her, to follow Him. She would hardly have done so, without her husband's sanction. There is question of "Herod," tetrarch of Galilee. What office is designated by "*steward*" (in Greek, επιτροπον) is not agreed upon. It may mean, guardian, lieutenant of a province, treasurer, land or house steward. It denotes, at all events, some office to which large emoluments were attached, which enabled Joanna to act a liberal part in the support of our Lord and His disciples.

"*Who ministered*" (Greek, διακονουν, *supplied the necessaries of life*) "*unto him.*" Some Greek copies have "*unto them,*" but the Vulgate reading is the best supported by critical evidence. Our Lord permitted such of those as were able, to supply Himself and His Apostles with the necessaries of life, in order not to be a burden on the poor among whom He was preaching.

4-15. (See Matthew xiii. 2-23.)
16. (See Matthew v. 15; Mark iv. 21, &c.)
17. (See Matthew x. 26; Mark iv. 22.)
18. (See Matthew xiii. 12; xxv. 29.)
19-21. (See Matthew xii. 46; Mark iii. 31.
22. (See Matthew viii. 18.)

TEXT.

26. And they sailed to the country of the Gerasens which is over against Galilee.

27. And when he was come forth to the land, there met him a certain man who had a devil now a very long time, and he wore no clothes, neither did he abide in a house, but in the sepulchres.

28. And when he saw Jesus, he fell down before him; and crying out with a loud voice, he said: What have I to do with thee Jesus, Son of the most high God? I beseech thee, do not torment me.

29. For he commanded the unclean spirit to go out of the man. For many times it seized him, and he was bound with chains, and kept in fetters; and breaking the bonds, he was driven by the devil into the deserts.

30. And Jesus asked him, saying: What is thy name? But he said; Legion: because many devils were entered into him.

31. And they besought him that he would not command them to go into the abyss.

32. And there was there a herd of many swine feeding on the mountain; and they besought him that he would suffer them to enter into them. And he suffered them.

33. The devils therefore went out of the man, and entered into the swine; and the herd ran violently down a steep place into the lake, and was stifled.

34. Which when they that fed them saw done, they fled, and told it in the city and in the villages.

35. And they went out to see what was done; and they came to Jesus, and found the man, out of whom the devils were departed, sitting at his feet, clothed, and in his right mind, and they were afraid.

36. And they also that had seen told them how he had been healed from the legion.

37. And all the multitude of the country of the Gerasens besought him to depart from them; for they were taken with great fear. And he going up into the ship, returned back again.

38. Now the man, out of whom the devils were departed, besought him that he might be with him. But Jesus sent him away, saying:

39. Return to thy house, and tell how great things God hath done to thee. And he went through the whole city, publishing how great things Jesus had done to him.

40. And it came to pass; that when Jesus was returned, the multitude received him: for they were all waiting for him.

41. And behold there came a man whose name was Jairus, and he was ruler of the synagogue: and he fell down at the feet of Jesus, beseeching him that he would come into his house,

42. For he had an only daughter almost twelve years old, and she was dying. And it happened, as he went, that he was thronged by the multitudes.

43. And there was a certain woman having an issue of blood twelve years, who had bestowed all her substance on physicians, and could not be healed by any;

44. She came behind him, and touched the hem of his garment: and immediately the issue of her blood stopped.

45. And Jesus said: Who is it that touched me? And all denying, Peter and they that were with him said: Master, the multitudes throng and press thee, and dost thou say, Who touched me?

46. And Jesus said: Some body hath touched me; for I know that virtue is gone out from me.

47. And the woman seeing, that she was not hid, came trembling, and fell down before his feet; and declared before all the people for what cause she had touched him, and how she was immediately healed.

48. But he said to her: Daughter, thy faith hath made thee whole, go thy way in peace.

49. *As he was yet speaking, there cometh one to the ruler of the synagogue, saying to him, Thy daughter is dead, trouble him not.*

50. *And Jesus hearing this word, answered the father of the maid: Fear not; believe only, and she shall be safe.*

51. *And when he was come to the house, he suffered not any man to go in with him, but Peter, and James, and John, and the father and mother of the maiden.*

52. *And all wept and mourned for her. But he said: Weep not, the maid is not dead, but sleepeth.*

53. *And they laughed him to scorn, knowing that she was dead.*

54. *But he taking her by the hand cried out saying: Maid, arise.*

55. *And her spirit returned, and she rose immediately. And he bid them give her to eat.*

56. *And her parents were astonished, whom he charged to tell no man what was done.*

COMMENTARY.

23-26. (See Matthew viii. 23-28.)
27-34. (See Matthew viii. 28-33.)
35-39. (See Mark v. 15-20.)
40-56. (See Matthew ix. 18-26.)

CHAPTER IX.

ANALYSIS.

In this chapter are recorded the mission of the twelve Apostles and the instructions given them (1-6). The perplexity and doubts of Herod regarding our Lord (7-9). The miraculous multiplication of five loaves and two fishes, so as to satiate the cravings of five thousand (10-17). Peter's confession of our Lord's Divinity—our Lord's prediction of His Passion—His teaching on the subject of carrying our cross after Him (18-27). His Transfiguration (28-36). The cure of the lunatic child (37-42). The prediction of our Lord's death and resurrection (43-46). The inhospitable treatment received from the Samaritans, and our Lord's reply to the vengeful spirit of the Apostles in reference thereto (51-56). His instructions to such as mean to be among His true followers (57-62).

TEXT.

THEN *calling together the twelve apostles, he gave them power and authority over all devils, and to cure diseases.*

2. *And he sent them to preach the kingdom of God, and to heal the sick.*

3. *And he said to them: Take nothing for your journey, neither staff, nor scrip, nor bread, nor money, neither have two coats.*

4. *And whatsoever house you shall enter into, abide there, and depart not from thence.*

5. *And whosoever will not receive you, when ye go out of that city, shake off even the dust of your feet for a testimony against them.*

6. *And going out they went about through the towns, preaching the gospel and healing everywhere.*

7. *Now Herod the tetrarch heard of all things that were done by him; and he was in a doubt because it was said*

8. *By some, that John was risen from the dead: but by other some, that Elias hath appeared; and by others, that one of the old prophets was risen again.*

9. *And Herod said: John I have beheaded; but who is this of whom I hear such things? And he sought to see him.*

10. *And the apostles, when they were returned, told him all they had done: and taking them he went aside into a desert place apart, which belongeth to Bethsaida.*

11. *Which when the people knew they followed him, and he received them, and spoke to them of the kingdom of God, and healed them who had need of healing.*

12. *Now the day began to decline. And the twelve came and said to him: Send away the multitude, that going into the towns and villages round about, they may lodge and get victuals; for we are here in a desert place.*

13. *But he said to them: Give you them to eat. And they said: We have no more than five loaves and two fishes; unless perhaps we should go and buy food for all this multitude.*

14. *Now there were about five thousand men. And he said to his disciples: Make them sit down by fifties in a company.*

15. *And they did so. And made them all sit down.*

16. *And taking the five loaves and the two fishes, he looked up to heaven, and blessed them; and he broke, and distributed to his disciples, to set before the multitude.*

17. *And they did all eat, and were filled. And there were taken up of fragments that remained to them, twelve baskets.*

18. *And it came to pass; as he was alone praying, his disciples also were with him; and he asked them saying: Whom do the people say that I am?*

19. *But they answered, and said: John the Baptist; but some say Elias; and others say that one of the former prophets is risen again.*

20. *And he said to them: But whom do you say that I am? Simon Peter answering, said: The Christ of God.*

21. *But he strictly charging them commanded they should tell this to no man,*

22. *Saying: The son of man must suffer many things, and be rejected by the ancients and chief priests and scribes, and be killed, and the third day rise again.*

23. *And he said to all: If any man will come after me, let him deny himself and take up his cross daily, and follow me.*

24. *For whosoever will save his life, shall lose it; for he that shall lose his life for my sake, shall save it.*

25. *For what is a man advantaged, if he gain the whole world, and lose himself, and cast away himself?*

26. *For he that shall be ashamed of me and of my words, of him the son of man shall be ashamed, when he shall come in his majesty, and that of his Father, and of the holy angels.*

27. *But I tell you of a truth: There are some standing here that shall not taste death, till they see the kingdom of God.*

28. *And it came to pass about eight days after these words, that he took Peter and James and John, and went up into a mountain to pray.*

29. *And whilst he prayed, the shape of his countenance was altered; and his raiment became white and glittering.*

30. *And behold two men were talking with him. And they were Moses and Elias,*

31. *Appearing in majesty. And they spoke of his decease that he should accomplish in Jerusalem.*

32. *But Peter and they that were with him, were heavy with sleep. And waking, they saw his glory, and the two men that stood with him.*

33. *And it came to pass that as they were departing from him, Peter saith to Jesus: Master, it is good for us to be here; and let us make three tabernacles, one for thee, and one for Moses, and one for Elias: not knowing what he said.*

34. *And as he spoke these things, there came a cloud, and overshadowed them: and they were afraid, when they entered into the cloud.*

35. *And a voice came out of the cloud, saying: This is my beloved Son, hear him.*

36. *And whilst the voice was uttered, Jesus was found alone. And they held their peace, and told no man in those days any of these things which they had seen.*

37. And it came to pass the day following when they came down from the mountain, there met him a great multitude.

38. And behold a man among the crowd cried out, saying: Master, I beseech thee, look upon my son, because he is my only one.

39. And lo, a spirit seizeth him, and he suddenly crieth out, and he throweth him down and teareth him so that he foameth, and bruising him he hardly departeth from him.

40. And I desired thy disciples to cast him out, and they could not.

41. And Jesus answering said: O faithless and perverse generation, how long shall I be with you and suffer you? Bring hither thy son.

42. And as he was coming to him, the devil threw him down and tore him.

43. And Jesus rebuked the unclean spirit, and cured the boy, and restored him to his father.

44. And all were astonished at the mighty power of God: but while all wondered at all the things he did, he said to his disciples: Lay you up in your hearts these words, for it shall come to pass that the son of man shall be delivered into the hands of men.

45. But they understood not this word, and it was hid from them, so that they perceived it not. And they were afraid to ask him concerning this word.

46. And there entered a thought into them, which of them should be greater.

47. But Jesus seeing the thoughts of their heart, took a child and set him by him.

48. And said to them, Whosoever shall receive this child in my name, receiveth me; and whosoever shall receive me, receiveth him that sent me. For he that is the lesser among you all, he is the greater.

49. And John answering, said: Master, we saw a certain man casting out devils in thy name, and we forbade him, because he followeth not with us.

50. And Jesus said to him: Forbid him not: for he that is not against you is for you.

51. And it came to pass when the days of his assumption were accomplishing, that he steadfastly set his face to go to Jerusalem.

52. And he sent messengers before his face: and going they entered into a city of the Samaritans, to prepare for him.

53. And they received him not, because his face was of one going to Jerusalem.

54. And when his disciples James and John had seen this, they said: Lord, wilt thou that we command fire to come down from heaven and consume them?

55. And turning, he rebuked them, saying: You know not of what spirit you are.

56. The son of man came not to destroy souls, but to save. And they went into another town.

57. And it came to pass as they walked in the way, that a certain man said to him: I will follow thee whithersoever thou goest.

58. Jesus said to him: The foxes have holes, and the birds of the air nests; but the son of man hath not where to lay his head.

59. But he said to another: Follow me. And he said: Lord, suffer me first to go, and to bury my father.

60. And Jesus said to him: Let the dead bury their dead: but go thou, and preach the kingdom of God.

61. And another said: I will follow thee, Lord, but let me first take my leave of them that are at my house.

62. Jesus said to him: No man putting his hand to the plough, and looking back, is fit for the kingdom of God.

COMMENTARY.

1-6. (See Matthew x. 1, &c.)
7-10. (See Matthew xiv. 1-12.)
10-17. (See Matthew xiv. 13-21.)
17-25. (See Matthew xvi. 13-26.)
26. (See Matthew x. 32, 33; xvi. 27.)
27. (See Matthew xvi. 28.)
28-36. (See Matthew xvii. 1-9.)
37-43. (See Matthew xvii. 14-17.)
44-46. (See Matthew xvii. 21; Mark ix. 31.)
47, 48. (See Matthew xviii. 1-5; xx. 26, 27.)
49, 50. (See Mark ix. 37-39.)

51. "*The days of His assumption*" (αναληψεως). "*Assumption*" means, His Ascension, His being taken up into heaven, when "*He was to pass out of this world unto the Father*" (John xiii. 1). Similar is the term (Acts i. 2-11; Mark xvi. 19). The Evangelist refers to His Ascension rather than to His Passion, though the latter event was nearer; because, in their journey, our Lord had before His eyes, His glory, rather than His suffering, "*qui proposito sibi gaudio sustinuit crucem*" (Hebrews xii. 2). "*Were accomplishing*," were approaching their accomplishment, εν τω συμπληρουσθαι, an interval of over six months was yet to elapse.

"*He steadfastly set His face*." This form of words is often employed in Scripture to denote a firmness of purpose in carrying out one's resolves (Ezechiel iv. 3; xiv. 8; Jerem. xxi. 10). By His countenance, gait, language, &c., which caused surprise to His Apostles (Mark x. 32), our Lord showed His determined, unwavering purpose in going straightway to Jerusalem, without looking back or deflecting from the direct road, in order to preach or instruct, as was His wont. It showed His firm resolution to embrace death voluntarily for our sakes, which He knew He was to suffer in Jerusalem. This occurred about the Feast of Tabernacles (*Scenopegia*). Our Lord did not suffer on this occasion, nor was He assumed till after the Feast of the Passover, six months later on. In the meantime, He went about Judea, preaching, as He had hitherto done in Galilee. The Evangelist conveys here, that He is now about recording our Lord's labours in Judea, as He had hitherto been describing His works and labours in Galilee.

52. "*Sent messengers before His face*." Very likely, He was accompanied by a large number of followers, and He thought it right to provide beforehand for their accommodation, in the way of food and lodging. These messengers are generally supposed to be "*James and John*," on account of what is recorded of them (verse 54). "*To prepare for Him*," and those who were with Him, whom no one house could probably lodge or accommodate.

"*Into a city of the Samaritans*." The straight way between Galilee and Judea lay through Samaria (John iv. 4). It is disputed whether the "*city*" here referred to, was the chief city, or some other of minor importance, among the Samaritans.

53. "*And they received Him not, because His face was*," &c. The reason why the Samaritans refused to receive or accommodate our Lord and His followers was, because they perceived, from all the circumstances of His journey, time, manner, &c., that He was going to worship in Jerusalem at the approaching festival. The

messengers sent before Him also may have informed them of it. The Samaritans did not always refuse to extend hospitality to the Jews—as appears from the example of the good Samaritan and the wounded Jew, and also from that of our Lord and the Samaritan woman at the well—but only whenever the latter were going to the Temple of Jerusalem; then, the Samaritans, between whom and the Jews, there existed a deadly enmity, which was particularly awakened by the controversy regarding the proper place for worship, Jerusalem or Garazim—at once refused all intercourse with them in religious matters. For, the Samaritans held, that the Temple erected by them in Mount Garazim was the place where, alone, men could lawfully worship (John iv. 20; Matthew x. 6).

The Samaritans saw from our Lord's whole exterior, His mode of acting and proceeding, that He was going to Jerusalem for the purpose of adoration in the Temple. At this, they felt indignant, as they themselves kept at Garazim the same feasts, which the Jews observed at Jerusalem (3 Kings xii. 32; 4 Kings xvii. 41). There was some difference as to time in both celebrations, in order to prevent collision between those parties, should they meet on their way, at the same time, to the rival Temples of Jerusalem and Garazim. The Samaritans were particularly offended by our Lord going to Jerusalem, passing by their temple; because, He was then regarded as a celebrated Doctor and Prophet; on which account, the Samaritans resented still more the slight, they fancied He put on their temple and worship.

54. "*James and John*" were probably, the messengers sent forward on this occasion, and on their return, resenting the indignity offered their Divine Master, they addressed our Lord, as follows; or it may be, that the people came forward to meet them and prevent them from entering their city, on which occasion, these two disciples, who may have from this been called by our Lord, "*Boanerges*," or "*sons of thunder*" (Mark iii. 17), said, "*Lord, wilt thou . . . and consume them*," to which is added in the ordinary Greek, "*even as Elias did.*" It is evident the Apostles had in mind the act of Elias destroying his enemies, the soldiers of the king of Samaria, by fire from heaven (4 Kings i. 10)—the countrymen of those, who treated our Lord so contumeliously.

55. "*Turning.*" Probably, they walked behind Him, and He turned back to address them. "*He rebuked them*" in the following works, "*You know not of what spirit you are.*" You imagine you are influenced by zeal for God's glory and a feeling of just resentment in imitation of Elias of old. But you seem not to be aware, that the spirit you are influenced by is a human spirit of impatience and vengeance; or, you know not to what spirit you are called. The spirit you manifest is that of the Old Law under which Elias acted—the spirit of retaliation, demanding or permitting "*an eye for an eye,*" &c.; but, My spirit, which you are to imitate— the spirit of my New Law which I inculcate by word and example, is a spirit of meekness; of patient forbearance and forgiveness. Of this you seem to be forgetful, in the present instance. When the Apostles after Pentecost received the Holy Ghost, they then occasionally exercised a spirit of severity in vindication of God's honour They could do so then safely, because they would not be actuated, as they were before receiving the Spirit, by human passions. Although the same spirit dictated the Old Law and the New; still, the effects manifested were different, owing to the difference of circumstances, in both instances. The effects of the spirit of the Old were generally severity and rigour. These were its characteristics, though, occasionally, clemency was shown. The effects of the New were mildness, clemency, though, sometimes,

severity and Christian justice were displayed (as in the case of Ananias and Sapphira, Elymas the Magician; also 2 Cor. x.); but clemency and forgiveness and patient endurance of injuries were its distinguishing characteristics. Our Lord referring to the spirit He wished to inculcate on His followers in cases of personal offences and injuries, adds,

56. "*The Son of Man came,*" at His first coming into this world, "*not to destroy souls,*" that is, *men,* a part being used for the entire man, "*but to save.*" The Apostles wished to destroy the bodies of the offending Samaritans; but they should rather imitate Him who came to save their souls by exhibiting meekness, forbearance, forgiveness of injuries, both on His own part and on that of His followers, and thus entice them to penance and reparation for their misdeeds.

57-60. (See Matthew viii. 19-22.)

61. St. Luke alone mentions this third case; St. Matthew mentions the two former, as above. Whether all the occurrences recorded here by St. Luke in verses 57-61, took place at the same time, of which the third is omitted by St. Matthew, is uncertain. It is conjectured by some commentators, that the third case mentioned by St. Luke alone in this verse did not occur at the same time, with the two preceding ones; but, that St. Luke, seeing they were very similar in their import, narrated them consecutively, as if they occurred in immediate succession.

"*Take leave of them, that are in my house*"—my domestics. In this interpretation, the words, "*them that are in my house,*" are taken to be in the masculine gender, while others understand them to be in the neuter gender (as in Luke xiv. 33), τοις εις τον οικον μου, and to signify, to dispose of all his possessions and divide them among his friends as he might deem fit.

62. "*No man putting his hand to the plough, and looking back is fit for,* &c." The first part should terminate thus, "*No man putting his hand . . . and looking back, is a good ploughman, or fit to plough.*" But our Redeemer concludes the sentence which commenced with a metaphor, by expressing the thing signified by the metaphor, "*fit for the kingdom of God,*" which is the application of the metaphorical allusion. As the man who holds the ploughshare, must always look before him, in order to make straight furrows; so must the disciple of Christ devote himself with a direct, pure intention exclusively to the duties of his calling. The words, "*putting his hand to the plough,*" are probably allusive to Eliseus leaving the plough at the call of Elias and following him (3 Kings xix. 19).

"*Fit for the kingdom of God,*" may mean, fit for labouring in the ministry of the Gospel—for ploughing the field of the Lord. Similar is the idea (2 Timothy ii. 4), "*nemo militans Deo,*" &c.; or, it may be expressive of a general truth regarding all who are determined to follow Christ and embrace the tenets of the Gospel. Such persons must be detached from earthly cares; and must not allow worldly concerns or worldly interests to divide their hearts or turn them aside from the service of God, to whose glory everything in this world should be subservient.

It is clear our Lord saw, that this man had an inordinate hankering after the things of this world, a heart divided between following Christ and solicitude for earthly concerns; as He otherwise would not have censured what would seem to contain nothing deordinate, save, in the supposition made.

CHAPTER X.

ANALYSIS.

Here, we have account of the mission of the seventy-two disciples, and the instructions given them (1-16). Their return, and our Lord's remarks on their having seemingly gloried in their success (17-20). God reveals himself to the humble only (21-24). The Parable of the good Samaritan (25-37). The account of Martha and Mary her sister on the occasion of our Lord's stopping at their house (38-42).

TEXT.

*A*ND *after these things the Lord appointed also other seventy-two: and he sent them two and two before his face into every city and place whither he himself was to come.*

2. *And he said to them: the harvest indeed is great, but the labourers are few. Pray ye therefore the Lord of the harvest, that he send labourers into his harvest.*

3. *Go: Behold I send you as lambs among wolves.*

4. *Carry neither purse, nor scrip, nor shoes; and salute no man by the way.*

5. *Into whatsoever house you enter, first say: Peace be to this house:*

6. *And if the son of peace be there, your peace shall rest upon him: but if not it shall return to you.*

7. *And in the same house remain, eating and drinking such things as they have. For the labourer is worthy of his hire. Remove not from house to house*

8. *And into what city soever you enter, and they receive you, eat such things as are set before you.*

9. *And heal the sick that are therein, and say to them: The kingdom of God is come nigh unto you.*

10. *But into whatsoever city you enter, and they receive you not, going forth into the streets thereof, say:*

11. *Even the very dust of your city that cleaveth to us we wipe off against you. Yet know this that the kingdom of God is at hand.*

12. *I say to you, it shall be more tolerable at that day for Sodom, than for that city.*

13. *Wo to thee, Corozain, wo to thee, Bethsaida: For if in Tyre and Sidon had been wrought the mighty works that have been wrought in you, they would have done penance long ago, sitting in sackcloth and ashes.*

14. *But it shall be more tolerable for Tyre and Sidon at the judgment, than for you.*

15. *And thou, Capharnaum, which art exalted unto heaven: thou shalt be thrust down to hell.*

16. *He that heareth you, heareth me: and he that despiseth you despiseth me. And he that despiseth me, despiseth him that sent me.*

17. *And the seventy-two returned with joy, saying: Lord, the devils also are subject to us in thy name.*

18. *And he said to them: I saw satan like lightning falling from heaven.*

19. *Behold, I have given you power to tread upon serpents and scorpions, and upon all the power of the enemy, and nothing shall hurt you.*

20. *But yet rejoice not in this that spirits are subject unto you: but rejoice in this, that your names are written in heaven.*

21. *In that same hour he rejoiced in the Holy Ghost, and said: I confess to thee, O Father, Lord of heaven and earth, because thou hast hidden these things from the wise and prudent, and has revealed them to little ones. Yea, father, for so it hath seemed good in thy sight.*

22. *All things are delivered to me by my Father, and no one knoweth who the Son is but the Father; and who the Father is, but the Son, and to whom the Son will reveal him.*

23. *And turning to his disciples, he said: Blessed are the eyes that see the things which you see.*

24. *For I say to you that many prophets and kings have desired to see the things that you see, and have not seen them; and to hear the things that you hear, and have not heard them.*

COMMENTARY.

1. "*And after these things,*" that is, after our Lord had left Galilee, and after the other occurrences recorded in the latter part of the preceding chapter, on seeing the spiritual destitution of the people in Judea, where He had hitherto hardly preached at all, save for a very short time after His baptism—His preaching hitherto having been almost exclusively confined to Galilee—

"*The Lord appointed,*" or selected out of the large number of His followers—"*also*" —as He had done in the case of the twelve Apostles, "*other seventy-two,*" or rather, "seventy-two *others,*" as the word "*others*" is allusive to the election and mission of the Apostles who were not seventy-two, but only twelve. Some Expositors maintain, that the mission here referred to was appointed when our Lord was in Samaria on His way to Jerusalem (chap. ix. 51)—Calmet, *hic.*

Almost all the Latin versions have, with the Vulgate, the reading "*seventy-two.*" Most Greek copies and the Syriac have "*seventy.*" The Vulgate "*seventy-two*" seems the most probable reading. For, as our Lord had heretofore appointed twelve Apostles, twelve Patriarchs of the twelve Tribes of spiritual Israel—an apostle for each tribe as its chief and ruler—so it is likely He now appoints an equal number of inferior teachers—six from each tribe—to assist the Apostles. This He did in imitation of Moses, who by the command of God, had chosen seventy-two ancients of the people to bear with him the burden of the government (Numbers xi. 16, 17); and although the number is said to be seventy (Numbers xi. 16-25); still, it is clear there were seventy-two of them, because in addition to the seventy whom Moses brought to the door of the Tabernacle, two remained in the camp on whom the same Spirit descended that was imparted to the seventy (*v.* 26)—Moses selected six from each tribe to avoid jealousy and to beget confidence in their acts. Hence, there were six twelves, or seventy-two. It was not unusual with the Jews to set down round numbers in their calculations even when some more might be counted, as seventy for seventy-two. Thus, speaking of the seventy-two interpreters, who by the command of Ptolemy Philadelphus, rendered the Hebrew Scriptures into Greek, although six from each tribe were selected, as we are informed by Josephus (Lib. Antiq. 12, c. 2); still they are called the *seventy* (*Septuaginta*) even by Josephus himself (*loco citato*). The number, *seventy-two,* might be called *seventy;* but seventy could never be called *seventy-two.*

These *seventy-two* were chosen by our Lord and sent to prepare the way for Him, in every part of Judea where He was to exercise His mission during the short interval that was to elapse before His Passion. They were inferior, in point of rank, to the twelve, as appears from the fact, that one of them, St Matthias, was raised to the rank of Apostle (St. Clement, of Alexan. apud Eusebium, Lib. 1, c. 14 Histor.), and also from the priority of selection and the smaller number of Apostles. The bishops have succeeded the Apostles; and the clergy of the second order, the seventy-two; as is taught by Pope Anacletus, (Ep. 2, St. Jerome ad Marcellam, Bede in Lucam 15, &c.); and though of inferior rank, still, with due subordination to their superiors, the bishops, they share in the work of the sacred ministry. Out of the seventy-two, the Apostles, afterwards ordained some to be Apostles, Matthias (Acts i. 26), Barnabas (Acts xvi. 3); some, deacons (Acts vi. 6), and no doubt, others bishops and priests, who like the ancients above referred to, were formerly termed, *Presbyteri*.

"*He sent them two and two*," for mutual support, protection, and edification; in order also that they might be witnesses of each other's demeanour, and their testimony rendered more credible, "*in ore duorum vel trium testium stabit omne verbum*" (Deut. xix. 15.) Our Lord observed this prudent course in the several commissions confided to His Apostles. He always sent them "*two and two*." The same heavenly prudence has been inculcated in the rules of religious communities when sending any of their members on legitimate business. To religious, in their dealing with the world, will apply, in a particular manner, "*væ soli*" (Eccles. iv. 10).

2. (See Matthew ix. 37, 38, where similar words are employed.)
3. (See Matthew x. 16.)
4. (Matthew x. 10.)

"*And salute no one by the way.*" Our Lord by no means prohibits the exercise of courtesy and urbanity, in returning salutations on the road. He refers to useless and long discourses that might mar the efficiency of their ministry. Similar was the instruction given by Eliseus to his servant Giezi, when putting his staff into his hand, and sending him to raise to life the son of the Sunamitess he said, "*And if any man shall meet thee, salute him not; and if any man salute thee, answer him not*" (4 Kings iv. 29), meaning that he should execute his commission with all possible despatch, without any unnecessary delay.

5, 6. (See Matthew x. 12, 13.)
7. (Matthew x. 10, 11.)

8. Content with whatever may be placed before them, they should not ask for delicacies, superfluities, or good cheer—a line of conduct suited to the Apostolic life, on which they were about entering.

9. (Matthew x. 8.)
10, 11, 12. (Matthew x. 14, 15.)
13, 14, 15. (Matthew xi. 21-24.)

16. (Matthew x. 40.) The honour or contempt shown the legate—the capacity in which the disciples are here considered by our Lord, being sent in the name and by the authority of God—is shown to Him whom he represents.

17. "*And the seventy-two returning*," &c. As St. Mark (chap. vi.) and St. Luke (ix.), after recording the mission of the *Apostles*, subjoin a statement of their return to our Lord, in order to render Him an account of their success, and refer all the glory of it to Him, to whom alone it was due—"*in Thy name*"—so, St. Luke here, also records the return of the "*seventy-two*, after they had discharged their mission, omitting all mention of what they, as well as our Lord Himself, who sent them to prepare the way for Him, had done, save what is said of Him (xiii. 22) "*And He went through the cities and towns teaching, and making His journey to Jerusalem.*" Most likely, He traversed all the country between Samaria and Bethania, near Jerusalem, of which there is mention made towards the close of this chapter (v. 38).

The disciples returned "*with joy*," at the great success of the mission, telling Him, among other things, of which St. Luke makes no mention, "*Lord, the devils also are subject to us in Thy name."* The generality of Commentators understand *" also "* to have reference to the powers expressly given them of *"healing the sick,"* as if they said: Not only have we successfully healed the sick; but, even the very devils went out of the bodies of the possessed, on our invoking your name and authority. Maldonatus, who maintains that the power of casting out devils was given to the seventy-two, as well as to the Apostles, gives *" also "* this signification: Not only have we done the more easy things confided to our power; but, we have accomplished what was even more difficult—we even cast out devils; or it may imply, that not only men, but even devils were subject to them.

18. *" I saw Satan as lightning."* This is commonly understood of the sudden fall of Lucifer in heaven, when the *"third part of the stars of heaven"* (Apoc. xii. 4), that is, of the angels, committed the sin of pride with him, and joined in his rebellion against God (Isaias xiv. 12-15). From bright angels, they were transformed into hideous devils, and, with the rapidity of lightning, hurled from their blissful seats in heaven. Our Lord, according to this interpretation, alluding to His Divine nature, by which He saw and knew all things—*" I saw Satan,"* &c.—refers to the fall of Lucifer, to warn His disciples against the fatal effects of pride, which precipitated Lucifer from his place in heaven. This interpretation supposes that the disciples felt a vain, human complacency in their success, although in words they referred this to Him, *"in nomine tuo."* Hence, in verse 20, our Lord says, *" that spirits are subject unto you,"* without adding, *" in My name,"* as if they took complacency in their own actions. Therefore, he says: Beware of pride, that hurled Lucifer from a state of glory in heaven. I have seen him precipitated in the abyss, with the rapidity of lightning. Take care lest a similar fate—the punishment of pride—should ultimately await you. It is said, that envy caused by the hypostatic union, and the glory to be thereby conferred on human nature, was the cause of Satan's fall and rebellion against God. Thus, our Lord *" saw"* his rebellion and fall. Hence, the disciples should beware of pride and self-complacency. This is St. Jerome's interpretation (contra Jovin), St. Ambrose (de fuga Sæculi, c. 7), St. Cyprian (de Jejunio Christi), St. Gregory (Moral, Lib. 23, c. 7), St. Chrysostom, Bede, St. Bernard, &c.

Others, who exonerate the disciples from all sin and censure, say the words mean: You tell me nothing new, nothing I did not well know before. For, from the instant of my Incarnation, at the very moment I sent you, I saw that Satan's power over this world, and over the children of unbelief, was about being completely shattered. *" Falling from heaven,"* that is, from the high power he exercised over the bulk of mankind. The former interpretation seems preferable; although both might be united, the former being literal, the latter allegorical. *" I, as God, saw fall from heaven, Satan,"* whom I precipitated, as my rival. Also at my Incarnation as man, I saw him precipitated from the places wherein he was adored as God, by the preaching of the Apostles and My disciples, who taught the world to adore the true God (A. Lapide).

19. *" Behold, I have given you,"* &c. As if He said, As it was not from himself Satan derived all his power, and the gifts, which he abused and took vain complacency in, but from God; so, it is to Me, and not to yourselves, you owe all the power and success of which you speak. *" I have given you,"* and I still continue to give you (the Greek is in the present, $\delta i \delta \omega \mu i$, I give) *"power to tread upon serpents and scorpions."* These are understood by some of several species of devils. *" And upon all the power of the enemy,"* and the whole army of the infernal spirits. Others understand the words literally, as in Mark (xvi. 17).

ST. LUKE, CHAP. X.

20. "*Rejoice not.*" This is taken in a comparative sense—"*rejoice not*" (so much) "*in this, that spirits are subject to you.*" He does not censure their rejoicing in the gifts of God, but He tells them not so much to rejoice in this—a power coming to them from without—as in having "*their names written in heaven*"—as in their eternal salvation, which they should hope to be in store for them. The former gift, common to the elect and reprobate (Matthew vii. 22, &c.), is given for the good of others; but, the latter has for object their own personal sanctification, and their enjoyment of eternal glory, should they persevere and die in grace. One's name may be "*written in heaven,*" or "*in the Book of Life,*" to which reference is made (Exodus xxxii. 32, 33; Psalm lxviii. 29; Philip. iv.) in two ways—either in the eternal predestination of God, which is unchangeable and absolute, and one's name thus inscribed cannot be blotted out; or, *conditionally*, on our persevering, in which case we may fall away from justice, and forfeit eternal glory. It is likely it is in this latter sense our Lord speaks here. He wishes His disciples to rejoice in the gifts of grace and friendship of God, now plentifully bestowed on them, as so many pledges of future glory, which they will surely obtain, if they persevere. It is not likely, that our Lord would tell the seventy-two, that they were all, without exception, predestined for glory, when, even among the twelve, there was an exception: "*Have I not chosen you twelve, and one of you is a devil?*" (John vi. 70). It is even said, that the seven first deacons were taken from the seventy-two disciples, of whom one, Nicolaus, was the founder of the Nicolaites (St. Jerome, Ep. 48, c. 3). When our Lord, addressing the twelve, said, they "*would sit on twelve thrones, judging the twelve tribes of Israel,*" He meant to speak conditionally—if they persevered and died in grace. We know that the traitor, Judas, did not persevere, and died miserably by his own hand (Acts i. 18).

21, 22. (See Matthew xi. 25-27.)
23, 24. (See Matthew xiii. 16, 17.)

TEXT.

25. And behold a certain lawyer stood up, tempting him; and saying: Master, what must I do to possess eternal life?

26. But he said to him: What is written in the law? how readest thou?

27. He answering, said: Thou shalt love the Lord thy God with thy whole heart, and with thy whole soul, and with all thy strength, and with all thy mind: and thy neighbour as thyself.

28. And he said to him: Thou hast answered right: this do, and thou shalt live.

29. But he willing to justify himself, said to Jesus: And who is my neighbour?

30. And Jesus answering, said: A certain man went down from Jerusalem to Jericho, and fell among robbers, who also stripped him, and having wounded him went away leaving him half dead.

31. And it chanced that a certain priest went down the same way; and seeing him, passed by.

32. In like manner also a Levite, when he was near the place and saw him, passed by.

33. But a certain Samaritan being on his journey, came near him; and seeing him was moved with compassion.

34. And going up to him, bound up his wounds, pouring in oil and wine: and setting him up on his own beast brought him to an inn, and took care of him.

35. And the next day he took out two pence, and gave it to the host, and said: Take care of him; and whatsoever thou shalt spend over and above, I at my return will repay thee.

36. Which of these three in thy opinion was neighbour to him that fell among the robbers?

37. *But he said: He that showed mercy to him. And Jesus said to him: Go and do thou in like manner.*

COMMENTARY.

25. "*And behold*," at some time when our Lord was delivering instructions. We need not necessarily connect this in consecutive order with the preceding ; and it matters not much in what order the things recorded by the Evangelists were spoken, or in what order they were written by the Evangelists, since the principal object was to record what would serve for our instruction, without too closely attending in some cases to the order of time.

While our Lord was on some occasion engaged in teaching the multitudes, "*a certain lawyer*," νομικος, who is generally supposed to be different from the person of the same profession, referred to in Matthew (xxii. 35), as the circumstances in both cases are quite different. For, in the latter case, our Lord Himself answers the question ; not so, here. "*Stood up*," after having, in a sitting posture, heard our Lord speak of the joys of the life to come, before the multitudes.

"*Tempting Him,*" which some understood in a bad sense, as if the lawyer, from a bad motive, wanted to confound Him, and elicit from Him some reply inconsistent with His former teaching, or at variance with the law of Moses, or the teachings of the expounders of the law ; others, understanding the word in a good sense, suppose, from the respectful tone of His address, "*Master*," that the lawyer only wished to see for himself, if all he heard spoken in praise of our Lord's superior teaching were true.

"*To possess eternal life*" (see Matthew xix. 16). The law of Moses only promised temporal life to those who observed it. But, our Lord frequently spoke of eternal life to His followers. The Jews themselves had hopes of another life, as is clear from several passages of the Scripture, written before and after the captivity. The Pharisees held this doctrine of a future life. The Sadducees, who denied it, were ranked by religious Jews among the Epicureans (Calmet). Hence, the lawyer asks what is he to do, in order to securely possess the promised happiness in the world to come.

26. Our Lord, unwilling to answer directly, interrogating His questioner, refers to the law, and elicits the answer from himself. He asks what are the works he is to do, in order to gain eternal life. Our Lord asks in turn, what are the chief duties prescribed for him to do by the law, in which he was so well versed, without any mention of eternal life, of which the law did not expressly speak. He says, "*quid faciam ?*" Our Lord asks what does the law tell him to do.

27. (See Matthew xxii. 36-40.)

28. Our Lord approving of the lawyer's answer, tells him if he observes the two leading precepts, which are a summary of the entire law, he shall secure eternal life.

29. "*To justify himself*," that is, to clear himself, by proposing a more difficult question, of the imputation of captiously desiring to embarrass our Lord by the question so easily answered by himself—or, wishing to show that he was right in proposing the question now answered, as it would lead to a more difficult one—which he desired to have solved—regarding which, there had been so much controversy and such erroneous notions among the Jews. For, they imagined, that our "*neighbour*," whom we are bound, by the law, to love and serve in his necessities, comprised

only those of the Jewish race, and even among these only the just, and those observant of the law. The above seems to be the most probable meaning of the word, "*justify,*" in this passage, although others understand it to mean, wishing to "*show himself just,*" desirous to know and fulfil the law, in which the justice he wished to show himself anxious about, consisted.

"*And who is my neighbour?*" whom I am to love as myself, to treat as I should reasonably expect to be treated by him in turn, and whom I should be, therefore, bound to serve and relieve in his necessities? The words of our Lord, "*this do,*" &c., conveyed a precept, and delivered instructions more of a practical, than of a speculative character, as the question of the lawyer referred more to a practical duty in regard to our neighbour, than to a speculative point of knowledge.

30. Our Lord shows, by an edifying example of the practical discharge of the duties we owe our neighbour, who our neighbour is, whom we are bound to love. In this example, He is commonly supposed to refer not to an imaginary occurrence, but to a fact, that actually occurred, and, therefore, carried with it more weight. Our Lord's answer (v. 37), supposes it to be a fact. From the example adduced, our Lord means to convey, that our neighbour, in relation to the practical exhibition of charity, comprised not only a co-religionist, or a just man, as the Jews erroneously imagined;—hence, the false gloss on the words, "*diliges proximum, odio habebis inimicum*"—but extended also to all men, even our enemies, as the case of the Samaritan, who was at variance with the Jews, shows here.

"*A certain man,*" generally supposed to be a Jew or Israelite (St. Augustine, Sermo. 37, de Verbis Domini), and also a citizen of Jerusalem (Bede in Commentario).

"*Went down,*" on some business, "*from Jerusalem to Jericho.*" Jerusalem was situated on hilly ground. Hence the words, "*went down.*" We often, for a like reason, hear it said in the Gospel, "*we go up to Jerusalem.*" "*Jericho*" was on the extreme confines of Judea, on the river Jordan. The road between Jerusalem and Jericho was infested with robbers, as we are informed by St. Jerome (in Epist. ad Eustochium Virginem), who tells us, that a certain part of the road was called *Adommin*, or, the *way of blood*, in consequence of the blood frequently shed, and the murders committed there by robbers.

"*Fell among robbers who also stripped him.*" Not only did they capture him and take away his money and means, but they "*stripped him*" of his very clothes. "*Wounded him,*" &c., leaving him in a pitiable plight, unable to succour himself, or seek aid from others, and, therefore, certain to die, unpitied and unaided, by the road-side. This sad picture of his miserable condition, places in a clearer light, the inhumanity of those who refused to succour him. The robbers treated their victims with all this gratuitous inhumanity, probably, to escape pursuit and apprehension.

31. "*It chanced*"—humanly speaking, though, as regards God, it was arranged by His all-seeing Providence—"*a certain priest,*" who was, above all others, bound to succour his neighbour in distress, and give an example in this respect to others. Our Lord here taxes the hard-heartedness of the Jewish priesthood, who placed all their reliance on sacrifices and ceremonies, neglecting the primary dictates of the natural law itself in regard to the exercise of mercy and humanity. "*Passed by.*" The Greek signifies, "*passed to the opposite side.*" This conduct was the more inexcusable, considering the enactment of the law of Moses regarding even the fallen beast of an enemy (Exodus xxiii. 5).

32. The above observations apply to the Levite also, who should give an example of the strictl observance of the law of God.

33. The inhumanity of both is placed in a still stronger light, by the contrast with the charitable conduct of the Samaritan.
"*A certain Samaritan.*" (For a description of the Samaritans, see Matthew x. 5, Commentary on.)
"*Came near him,*" did not turn away in disgust, as the others did. "*Was moved with compassion,*" notwithstanding the deadly hostility of race.

34. "*Pouring in,*" that is, after he had poured in. For he had done so, before binding up his wounds.
"*Wine and oil,*" which he probably carried with him as his viatic for the journey. "*Wine,*" had the effect of cleansing the wounds from the clotted blood with which they were saturated; "*oil,*" soothed his pains. Brought him "*on his own beast,*" after having himself dismo nted, "*to an inn,*" the next he met on the road, and cared him himself, sparing neither expense nor trouble.

35. Being obliged to leave on business, he did not neglect to have provision made for this wretched man, in his absence.
"*Two pence.*" It is not easy to say what was the actual value of these two pence. They were equivalent to a labourer's hire for two days (Matthew xx. 9), and sufficed for the temporary relief of the patient in question.
"*Whatever thou shalt spend over and above,*" &c. While obliged to leave on business, he provides for the wounded man, and conveys that he meant to have him restored to perfect health, before he left him after his return.

The Holy Fathers are fond of dwelling on the clear mystical sense contained in this passage, which, they describe as having reference to the fall of man, and his merciful reparation through Jesus Christ. (Ambrose, Theophylact, Chrysostom, Augustine, &c.) By "*the man who went down,*" they understand, Adam; by *Jerusalem*, Paradise; by *Jericho*, the world; by the *robbers*, the demons; by the *priest*, the Old Law; by the *Levite*, the prophets; by the *Samaritan*, our Blessed Lord; by the *wounds*, disobedience; by the "*beast*" that carried the wounded man, our Lord's Body, in which He, becoming Incarnate, bore our sins and infirmities; by "*the inn,*" the Church, ready to receive all who wish to enter; by the "*wine*" and "*oil,*" the Sacraments of the Church, wine and oil being employed in the administration of the chief Sacraments; by the *master of the inn*, the Sovereign Pontiff, who liberally dispenses the treasures of the Church; by the "*two pence,*" Origen understands the knowledge of the Father and of the Son; St. Ambrose, the two Testaments; St. Augustine, the two leading precepts of charity with which our Lord inspires the pastors of the Church, to exercise pastoral care over their people; by the *return* of the Samaritan, our Lord's second coming to judgment, when he will reward our good actions, especially our care of the poor and afflicted.

36. "*Which of these three in thy opinion was neighbour to him ?*" &c., that is, which of them acted the part of neighbour practically, carrying out the precept, "*thou shalt love thy neighbour as thyself.*" The question of the lawyer "*who is my neighbour,*" whom I am commanded to love as myself? would suggest that our Lord's question would directly be, who is neighbour to these three men referred to? Was it not the man who needed their aid in his extreme distress, bleeding on the road side? But, in

reality, the solution comes to the same. For, as St. Augustine observes, the word "*neighbour*" is a relative term, having its correlative, "*proximi nomen est ad aliquid nec quisquam esse proximus nisi proximo potest*" (St. Augustine de doc. Christiana, chap. 30), and our Lord put the question to the lawyer in the correlative sense, "*who was neighbour to him,*" &c., instead "who was the neighbour of these three men," as in the latter form, the lawyer following the preconceived prejudices of his race, might answer, "their neighbour was confined exclusively to their own race and religion;" whereas, by putting it in the form he employs, our Lord, with wonderful wisdom, forces the lawyer to admit that the two others, while according to the Jews themselves, neighbours of the wounded Jew, neglected their duty in his regard; and the Samaritan acted the part of neighbour towards the distressed Jew, who was his enemy; that, therefore, all mankind, according to his own admission, including our enemies, are our neighbours, in the sense of the Divine precept commanding us to love him as ourselves, and relieve him in his necessities. Hence, our Lord subjoins His approval of the answer, and tells him and us, to act a similar part, that is, to regard and treat all mankind without distinction, our enemies included, as our neighbours.

TEXT.

38. *Now it came to pass as they went, that he entered into a certain town; and a certain woman named Martha, received him into her house.*

39. *And she had a sister called Mary, who sitting also at the Lord's feet, heard his word.*

40. *But Martha was busy about much serving. Who stood and said: Lord hast thou no care that my sister hath left me alone to serve? speak to her therefore, that she help me.*

41. *And the Lord answering, said to her: Martha, Martha, thou art careful, and art troubled about many things.*

42. *But one thing is necessary. Mary hath chosen the best part, which shall not be taken away from her.*

COMMENTARY.

38. "*As they went,*" as Jesus and His Apostles were passing through the several places and cities of Judea, whither He had sent the seventy-two disciples before Him, "*He entered into a certain town*"—in the Greek, κωμη, *a village*—no doubt, accompanied by His Apostles. This is generally supposed to be Bethany, about two miles from Jerusalem, "*the town of Mary and Martha*"—(John xi. 1).

"*And a certain woman named Martha received Him into her house,*" that is, hospitably entertained Him and His Apostles. Unquestionably Martha was duly sensible of the exalted honour conferred on her in being privileged to be the hostess of the Son of God. "*The servant received her Lord; the sick one her Saviour; the creature, her Creator; the one that needed spiritual repast, Him who needed corporal support, owing to the condition he condescended to assume.*"—St. Augustine (Sermon 26, de Verbis Domini).

Although Mary and Lazarus lived in the same house with Martha, the latter only is said to have entertained Him and His followers; probably, because being the elder sister (St. Bernard, Serm. 3 de Assumptione), to whom the house and possessions there belonged as her portion, she exclusively managed the household concerns; whereas, Mary had been away in Galilee, whence she followed our Lord (viii. 2). Hence, her great anxiety on this occasion to prepare everything in a manner worthy of so distinguished a guest.

39. "*Named Mary,*" viz., Mary Magdalen, of whom there is question (chap. vii. 37-48; John xi. 1, &c.; xii. 3, &c.) "*Who sitting also at the Lord's feet,*" &c. "*Also,*" may mean, that she did this in fixed purpose; she not only heard Him in a passing way, but she also with fixed, immoveable determination, "*sat at His feet,*" a phrase denoting that she became an attentive listener to Him as teacher. Disciples are, by a Jewish idiom, said to sit at the feet of their teachers. "*Also,*" may mean, that she, as well as His disciples and other women, listened attentively to His instructions and discourses; or, "*also,*" may have reference to our Lord—He sat teaching, she *also* sat, but it was at His feet, listening as a disciple to His heavenly teaching

"*Heard His word.*" Our Lord omitted no opportunity of imparting instruction. He never lost time; even while food is being prepared for Him, He is engaged in His Father's business. What an example to all who are engaged in the Apostolical ministry. They should be always employed in the business of their calling. "*Hæc meditare, in his esto,*" is the injunction of St. Paul to all ministers of the Gospel (1 Tim. iv. 15).

40. "*Martha was busy,*" or distracted, "*with much serving,*" that is, with the multiplicity of business she had on hands, moving here and there in endeavouring worthily to provide a repast for our Lord and His followers.

"*Who stood and said, Lord, hast thou no care?*" &c. Martha, wearied from work, and possibly finding herself unequal, if unaided, to the task of providing for our Lord and His followers, sweetly appeals to Him in terms of the greatest respect, —"*Lord*"—to advise her sister to come to her assistance. She knew that if she were to appeal directly to her sister, she would do so in vain, so engrossed was she, and so intensely bent on listening to the words of her Divine Lord. "*Hast thou no care?*" &c., is simply intended to arrest our Lord's attention, so that He might see the hardship of her case, and His commiseration might be excited. "*Speak to her, therefore, to help me.*" Martha's anxiety to have everything properly prepared for our Lord was such, that without her sister's aid, be the other attendants ever so numerous, she considered herself to be left alone. She bore testimony to the obedient spirit of her sister; since our Lord had only to say it, and she would comply at once.

41. "*Martha, Martha,*" The repetition of the name indicates affection, or perhaps was meant to invite attention (St. Augustine, Ser. 26, de verbis Domini). "*Thou are careful.*" The Greek word—μεριμνας—means mental anxiety, "*and art troubled about many things,*" distracted with a multiplicity of cares.

42. "*But one thing is necessary.*" The Greek is, "*of one thing, there is necessity.*" Some Expositors explain this to mean, "thou art uselessly and unnecessarily troubling thyself in preparing many dishes; whereas, only one dish, one kind of food alone is necessary." But the comparison evidently conveyed in the following words, "*Mary hath chosen,*" &c., renders this interpretation very improbable. Hence, "*the one thing*" declared to be "*necessary,*" is, seeking and securing the salvation of our souls—the essential end of our creation, of our coming into this world—secure this, all is well; lose or forfeit this, every thing else is lost. This alone is "*necessary.*" Every thing else is useless, save as far as it conduces to secure this end, this priceless good. Every thing else, Every other gain or acquisition is loss, nay, noxious, if it, in any way, mar this essential end. No doubt, Martha, by serving, labouring, and ministering to our Lord, was adopting the means of reaching this great end. But, this multiplicity of occupations was distracting, and exposed her

to the danger of deflecting from the right and straight path, that led thereto. Whereas, Mary while attending to one thing, the sweet converse of her Lord, was not in such danger of going astray or turning aside from the straight path, as was Martha. She found Him whom "*her soul loved; she held Him and would not let Him go.*" (Cant. iii. 2).

"*Mary hath chosen the better part,*" &c. Our Lord does not find fault with the course Martha was pursuing. He only gives the preference to the course Mary followed. She had chosen the part of meditating on the things of God, of attending to His inspirations, of having her mind constantly fixed on Him. This is the more secure way of attaining to heavenly bliss. It is a foretaste of this bliss to come, which consists in the beatific vision, in the knowledge, love, and contemplation of God. Hence, in the life to come, Mary's occupation will continue the same, but in a more intense, exalted, and perfect degree; whereas, worldly cares and interests will pass away with time. The contemplative life is, then, preferred here by our Lord to the active. We are not, however, to infer from this, that those whose duties appertain to the active life, are warranted in abandoning them in order to devote themselves exclusively to contemplation and prayer. The union of the active life with the contemplative is the most perfect of all, such as was followed by our Lord, His Apostles, and all their followers in the ecclesiastical state, and in the ministry of saving souls. Every one should faithfully discharge the active duties of the state of life in which Providence has placed him; and manage so, in the midst of active occupations, as to turn to God by prayer and contemplation, and refer, by a pure intention of pleasing Him, all his actions to His greater glory. Thus, and thus only, will he securely attain the great end of his existence, the "*one thing necessary.*"

CHAPTER XI.

ANALYSIS.

Prayer—the Lord's Prayer. The conditions of prayer, especially perseverance and confidence, illustrated (1-13). The calumnies of the Pharisees regarding the power by which our Lord worked miracles, and His reply (14-23). The return of the unclean spirit, illustrating the evil of the sin of relapse (24-27). Our Lord's teaching on the subject of giving the Jews the sign they sought for (29-32). His teaching on the subject of performing our actions with a good intention, illustrated by the example of light and darkness in the body (33-36). The woes pronounced against the Pharisees (37-54).

TEXT.

*A*ND *it came to pass, that as he was in a certain place praying, when he ceased, one of his disciples said to him: Lord, teach us to pray, as John also taught his disciples.*

2. *And he said to them: When you pray, say; Father, hallowed be thy name. Thy kingdom come.*

3. *Give us this day our daily bread.*

4. *And forgive us our sins, for we also forgive every one that is indebted to us. And lead us not into temptation.*

5. *And he said to them: Which of you shall have a friend, and shall go to him at midnight, and shall say to him: Friend, lend me three loaves,*

6. *Because a friend of mine is come off his journey to me, and I have not what to set before him.*

7. *And he from within should answer and say: Trouble me not, the door is now shut, and my children are with me in bed; I cannot rise and give thee.*

8. *Yet if he shall continue knocking, I say to you, although he will not rise and give*

him, *because he is his friend; yet because of his importunity he will rise, and give him as many as he needeth.*

9. *And I say to you, Ask, and it shall be given you: seek, and you shall find: knock, and it shall be opened to you.*

10. *For every one that asketh, receiveth: and he that seeketh, findeth: and to him that knocketh, it shall be opened.*

11. *And which of you if he ask his father bread, will he give him a stone? or a fish, will he for a fish give him a serpent?*

12. *Or if he shall ask an egg, will he reach him a scorpion?*

13. *If you then being evil, know how to give good gifts to your children, how much more will your Father from heaven give the good Spirit to them that ask him?*

14. *And he was casting out a devil, and the same was dumb; and when he had cast out the devil, the dumb spoke: and the multitudes were in admiration at it:*

15. *But some of them said: He casteth out devils, by Beelzebub the prince of devils.*

16. *And others tempting, asked of him a sign from heaven.*

17. *But he seeing their thoughts, said to them: Every kingdom divided against itself, shall be brought to desolation, and house upon house shall fall.*

18. *And if Satan also be divided against himself, how shall his kingdom stand? because you say, that through Beelzebub I cast out devils.*

19. *Now if I cast out devils by Beelzebub: by whom do your children cast them out? Therefore they shall be your judges.*

20. *But if I by the finger of God cast out devils: doubtless the kingdom of God is come upon you.*

21. *When a strong man armed keepeth his court: those things are in peace which he possesseth.*

22. *But if a stronger than he come upon him and overcome him: he will take away all his armour wherein he trusted, and will distribute his spoils.*

23. *He that is not with me, is against me: and he that gathereth not with me, scattereth.*

24. *When the unclean spirit is gone out of a man, he walketh through places without water, seeking rest: and not finding, he saith, I will return into my house whence I came out.*

25. *And when he is come, he findeth it swept and garnished.*

26. *Then he goeth and taketh with him seven other spirits more wicked than himself, and entering in they dwell there. And the last state of that man becomes worse than the first.*

27. *And it came to pass: as he spoke these things, a certain woman from the crowd lifting up her voice said to him: Blessed is the womb that bore thee, and the paps that gave thee suck.*

28. *But he said: Yea rather, blessed are they who hear the word of God, and keep it.*

29. *And the multitudes running together, he began to say: This generation is a wicked generation: it asketh a sign, and a sign shall not be given it, but the sign of Jonas the prophet.*

30. *For as Jonas was a sign to the Ninivites: so shall the son of man also be to this generation.*

31. *The queen of the south shall rise in the judgment with the men of this generation, and shall condemn them: because she came from the ends of the earth to hear the wisdom of Solomon: and behold more than Solomon here.*

32. *The men of Ninive shall rise in the judgment with this generation and shall condemn it, because they did penance at the preaching of Jonas; and behold more than Jonas here.*

COMMENTARY.

1. "*One of His disciples,*" probably one of the seventy-two, "*said to Him,*" &c. St. Matthew (chap. vi. 6-9), would seem to convey, that our Lord taught us the Lord's

Prayer from Himself, unasked, while delivering the Sermon on the Mount, of which this divine prayer forms a part; whereas, St. Luke conveys here, that he delivered it in quite different circumstances, at the request of one of His disciples, who on seeing Him pray, was induced, by the fervour exhibited by Him, to ask Him how they were to pray. Moreover, the number of petitions given in St. Matthew, is seven; here, five. Hence, some Commentators hold, that our Lord uttered this prayer on two different occasions, as recorded by the two Evangelists. St. Matthew gives the prayer in connexion with our Lord's denunciation of the hypocrisy of the Pharisees, without telling the occasion of its being uttered, as St. Luke does here. Others, hold that the prayer was spoken but once; but that St. Matthew introduced into our Lord's Sermon on the Mount, things spoken by Him on other occasions, and that he wished to give us there consecutively, as much of our Lord's utterances, as he could conveniently describe together. The ordinary Greek copies and the Protestant version have the seven petitions here just as they are given by St. Matthew (vi. 9-13). St. Augustine (Enchiridion, c. 1, tom. 6, p. 240) says, there are *seven* petitions in St. Matthew, and only *five* in St. Luke. It is likely that the form, as in St. Matthew, was inserted here by some copyists in the Greek, who saw the form in St. Luke shorter than that in St. Matthew, or than that in common use among the faithful. It was much easier to add them here than it would be to omit them, as they are omitted in all Latin copies, even the most ancient. If some of the Fathers commented on the whole seven petitions here, they did so, as they wished to give a full exposition of the Lord's Prayer, and to explain the entire of its petitions, handed down by our Lord, as they are fully given in St. Matthew. A similar thing happened in regard to the Beatitudes. St. Matthew gives eight; St. Luke, four. But the *four* substantially contain the *eight*, as the petitions of the Lord's Prayer, recorded here by St. Luke, contain those that are omitted.

"*As John also taught his disciples.*" As John the Baptist had preached to the people, the necessity of penance, so he also composed suitable prayers to be recited by his followers, to excite them to the practice of penance, and inspire them with faith and hope in the Deliverer now at hand, and soon to be manifested to the world. It is not unusual for the founders of new forms of religion to compose prayers for the spiritual benefit and use of their followers. No vestige or record whatever of the prayers composed by John has been preserved. However excellent they may have been, they, still, can bear no comparison with that taught us here by the increated wisdom of God Himself.

2, 3, 4. (See Matthew vi. 9-13.)

5, 6. Having taught them the prayer they ought to employ, our Lord now teaches them how they are to pray; they should pray neither negligently, nor remissly, but fervently and perseveringly.

"*And,*" also, "*He said to them.*" Our Lord illustrates by the following parable—which St. Luke alone records—or familiar comparison, founded on what might occur in daily life to any of themselves, the necessity of fervour and perseverance in prayer. All the circumstances are of a very pressing character—the hour of the night so inconvenient, the urgent necessity of the case, not even the simplest means of meeting the wants of the stranger, fatigued and hungry from his journey. Hence, the petition for "*three loaves,*" one for the host himself, one for the hungry, fatigued guest, and a third in case the two did not suffice. In the East the home-made cakes were small.

7. We need not suppose all these circumstances to have actually occurred—some of them are but the ornamental parts of the parable; nor are they all applicable to the dealings of God with man, when presenting earnest petitions before Him. The application of the several parts is not to be pushed farther than the illustration requires; and the evident scope of the parable is only to show the advantages and efficacy of perseverance in prayer.

8. "*Of his importunity.*" The Greek word, αναιδειαν, means, *shamelessness*, or *shameless persistence* in asking under such circumstances, after having been refused before. "*And give Him,*" not only "*three loaves*" sought for; but, "*as many as he needeth,*" to save himself from further molestation. This, without being literally applicable in all its parts, to the case of the supplicant and God, is intended to prove the advantage and efficacy of preserving prayer. The force of the example consists in this if the prayer of a friend, though unreasonable, so prevailed on account of his importunity, that he received even more than he asked, how much more will our prayers prevail with God, with Whom all times are equally opportune, who even delights in our importunate persistence, and defers hearing us, in the first instance, in order to render the concession in the end more welcome. The parable also conveys the advantages of perseverance in prayer, and inspires confidence; for, if a man relying on the claims of friendship, approaches his fellow-man even at an unreasonable hour, with confidence of being heard, with how much greater confidence ought not we approach a loving Father to obtain all we need from Him.

9-11. This is the application of the foregoing example (see Matthew vii. 7, 10).

12. St. Luke alone gives this example, which means the same thing as the example of the fish and the serpent, viz., it denotes the giving of something not only useless, as a stone for bread; but something noxious, as is "*a scorpion,*" which, by its sting, would harm us. Sometimes a scorpion shut up in the shell of an egg was given in order the more securely to cause injury to the person, who, unsuspecting evil, received this fatal present. It is also said that the body of a scorpion, particularly of the white kind, resembled an egg, as some fishes resembles serpents.

13. (Matthew vii. 11.)
14-23. (Matthew xii. 22-30.)
24-26. (Matthew xii. 43-45.)

27. While our Lord was successfully engaged in refuting the blasphemous calumnies of the Pharisees, a woman in the crowd, admiring our Redeemer's language and miracles, and, probably, under the influence of some divine instinct, raising her voice, cried out, "*Blessed is the womb,*" &c., which simply means, "*Blessed is the mother that gave Thee birth.*" It may be, she was divinely enlightened in regard to His Incarnation, and, like the Angel, who announced it, and Elizabeth who congratulated His Mother upon it, this woman proclaimed her blessed among women, as did the Virgin herself, when, under the influence of inspiration, she cried out, "*Behold, from henceforward, all generations shall call me Blessed.*" But whether the woman in question was enlightened as to the mystery of our Lord's Incarnation, or only spoke from a natural admiration of our Lord's words, and wonderful deeds, she meant to eulogize our Lord Himself, since it is, on account of giving birth to so wonderful a man, she regarded His mother as blessed.

28. *Yea,*" as if He said without denying this, which would be denying the truth, as His mother had been pronounced "*Blessed,*" in several instances (as above), or without asserting or confirming it, which would be praising Himself and His Blessed Mother; this may be, I do not deny its truth; but, "*rather blessed are they,*" &c. The idea conveyed here is the same as in St. Matthew (xii. 50). Our Lord, while giving a preference to spiritual relationship, founded on faith and grace, and on the observance of God's Commandments, over carnal relationship, includes in this latter respect His Blessed Mother, who far excelled in sanctity, and correspondence with divine grace, all the rest of creation together. He gives a preference to spiritual relationship; because, it was more general. It was not confined only to one, but, it extended to all. He does not deny the felicity of her who gave him birth in the flesh; but it was more on account of having first spiritually conceived and begotten Him, by grace and faith in her heart, than on account of having giving Him birth in the flesh, she was happy. He extends this felicity farther, to those who "*hear His word.*" However, this is not sufficient; they must observe "*and keep it,*" carry it out in practice, in word and deed. "*Non auditores verbi justi sunt apud Deum; sed factores verbi justificabuntur*" (Rom. ii. 13).

29. What St. Luke narrates by anticipation (*v.* 16), was, according to St. Matthew (xii. 38), expressed by our Lord, in connection with what is said here.

30-32. (See Matthew xii. 38-42.)

TEXT.

33. *No man lighteth a candle, and putteth it in a hidden place, nor under a bushel: but upon a candlestick, that they that come in may see the light.*

34. *The light of thy body is thy eye. If thy eye be single, thy whole body will be lightsome: but if it be evil, thy body also will be darksome.*

35. *Take heed therefore that the light which is in thee, be not darkness.*

36. *If then thy whole body be lightsome, having no part of darkness: the whole shall be lightsome, and as a bright lamp shall enlighten thee.*

37. *And as he was speaking, a certain Pharisee prayed him that he would dine with him. And he going in sat down to eat.*

38. *And the Pharisee began to say, thinking within himself, why he was not washed before dinner.*

39. *And the Lord said to him: Now you Pharisees make clean the outside of the cup and of the platter; but your inside is full of rapine and iniquity.*

40. *Ye fools, did not he that made that which is without, make also that which is within.*

41. *But yet that which remaineth, give alms; and behold all things are clean unto you.*

42. *But wo to you Pharisees, because you tithe mint and rue and every herb: and pass over judgment and the charity of God. Now these things you ought to have done, and not to leave the other undone.*

43. *Wo to you Pharisees, because you love the uppermost seats in the synagogues, and salutations in the market-place.*

44. *Wo to you, because you are as sepulchres that appear not, and men that walk over, are not aware.*

45. *And one of the lawyers answering, saith to him: Master, in saying these things, thou reproachest us also.*

46. *But he said: Wo to you lawyers also: because you load men with burdens which they cannot bear, and you yourselves touch not the packs with one of your fingers.*

47. *Wo to you who build the monuments of the prophets: and your fathers killed them.*

I

48. *Truly you bear witness that you consent to the doings of your fathers: for they indeed killed them, and you build their sepulchres.*

49. *For this cause also the wisdom of God said: I will send to them prophets and apostles, and some of them they will kill and persecute.*

50. *That the blood of all the prophets which was shed from the foundation of the world, may be required of this generation.*

51. *From the blood of Abel unto the blood of Zacharias who was slain between the altar and the temple. Yea, I say to you, it shall be required of this generation.*

52. *Wo to you lawyers, for you have taken away the key of knowledge: you yourselves have not entered in, and those that were entering in you have hindered.*

53. *And as he was saying these things to them, the Pharisees and the lawyers began vehemently to urge him, and to oppress his mouth about many things,*

54. *Lying in wait for him, and seeking to catch something from his mouth, that they might accuse him.*

COMMENTARY.

33. (See Matthew v. 15.)

34. (See Matthew vi. 22, 23.) "*If the eye be single,*" if the intention be pure, the entire body of the actions will be pure; "*if it be evil,*" if the intention be perverse, all our actions are hateful to God.

35. "*Take heed,*" &c., otherwise, the darkness itself will be very great. "*The darkness itself, how great shall it be?*" (Matthew vi. 23.)

36. "*The whole shall be lightsome,*" not the whole *body*—otherwise there would be a useless tautology—but the whole man, every thing connected with him, all his powers and faculties, every thing emanating from him, will be lightsome. If the body, illuminated by a pure, simple eye, be lightsome, and no part or member darksome; if all the actions and affections be guided and enlightened by a pure intention, so that no part is clouded by passion; then, the whole *man*, both interiorly and exteriorly, shall be lightsome. Then, this "*single,*" or clear eye, "*shall, as a bright lamp,*" which sheds its light on every part of the body, "*enlighten thee,*" enlighten the entire man.

37. "*And as He was speaking,*" or, after He had spoken to the people on some certain occasion. We need not necessarily connect this with the foregoing; for, St. Luke does not say, as He was speaking *these things*, although Maldonatus refers it to the foregoing.

"*A certain Pharisee prayed Him to dine with him,*" manifestly with the view of watching Him and observing, with a sinister motive, His words and actions (*vv.* 53, 54).

"*And He going in, sat down to dinner,*" without further ceremony, or any previous ablutions, or attention to the usual forms observed in this respect, by the Pharisees.

38. "*And the Pharisee began to say, thinking within himself.*" He began silently to revolve within his own mind, murmuring and judging unfavourably of our Lord. The Greek is, "*but the Pharisees seeing, wondered,*" "*Why He was not washed before dinner,*" in accordance with the Jewish traditional usage on such occasions (see Matthew xv. 1; Mark vii. 3).

39. (See Matthew xxiii. 25.)

"*Now,*" (or truly,) "*you Pharisees,*" &c. He charges all the Pharisees, the absent, as well as those present, with washing their bodies, and neglecting to cleanse their souls from moral defilement. Or, "*now,*" the occasion has arisen for approaching you with your crimes and deeds of hypocrisy.

40. "*Ye fools,*" who act so preposterously. This, He says, with a view of correcting their false notions. Hence, He adds, "*Did not He that made that which is without?*" &c. Did not God. the Creator of external things, of cups, of the human person, &c., also create internal things such as the human soul? Now, if out of a feeling of reverence for God, the Creator of external things, you take care to wash and cleanse them, why not, out of respect for Him, be equally solicitous about cleansing the internal, spiritual and invisible things which were also created by Him? Nay, more solicitous; since, the latter effects of His creation approach nearer to Him than mere external things. Is not God more jealous about the cleansing of the heart, and what emanates from it, as they are the effects of man's will, than He is about external things? Our Lord here supposes what was a fact, viz., that all these purifications took place, not from mere social decency and cleanliness; but, from motives of religious worship shown to God, the Creator of these external objects.

41. "*But yet that which remaineth give alms.*" Having above charged them with "*rapine and iniquity,*" He now wishes to convey, that they are not to be despaired of, as if their case were utterly hopeless, and no remedy left. He points out here, the remedy and the means of cleansing their souls from defilement. And, instead of merely cleansing the body, like legal purifications, this remedy prescribed by Him, is a sovereign means for cleansing all, soul and body.

"*That which remaineth*" (Vulgate, "*quod superest*"), is understood by some, of superfluities remaining after our necesssary wants are supplied. Out of these, give alms. Others, following the Greek reading—τα ενοντα—understand the words, to mean: What you possess, or, is in your power; as if he said, Out of the means you possess, and according to your power and ability, "*give alms;*" as in (Tobias iv. 7), "*give alms out of thy substance.*" Others understand the words thus: This remains as my summary and comphrehensive precept and remedy for cleansing you from your iniquities; or, there remains for you one means of cleansing and purifying your souls, viz., "*give alms, and behold all things are clean to you.*" Not that the giving of alms would, of itself, cleanse from sin; but, that almsdeeds, mercy to the poor, would dispose us for obtaining the remission of sin, and would incline God to show mercy to us, in consideration of our showing mercy to the poor. "*Blessed are the merciful, for they shall obtain mercy.*" And, indeed, it rarely happens, as experience tells us, that those who are beneficent and charitable to the poor, do not find mercy in the latter end. "*In die mala liberabit eum Dominus*" (Psalm xl. 2). Nor is it meant, that giving alms alone would suffice; it is said, "*all things are clean unto you,*" on account of it, provided all the necessary conditions be added, just as we hear it said of faith, that it justifies, in which it is implied, provided everything else necessary be superadded.

"*Clean unto you,*" is allusive to the anxiety of the Pharisees for legal and external cleanliness. Almsdeeds will cleanse them from all defilement, both of soul and body. Hence, it should be substituted for their external, useless observances.

42. It may be, that our Lord repeated these denunciations twice, as the circum-

stances are different in Matthew (xxiii.) from those expressed here; or, He may have done so only once, and, likely, St. Matthew gives the order of circumstances.

42-44. (See Matthew xxiii. 23-29.)

44. The idea meant here is the same as that expressed (Matthew xxiii. 27, 28), although conveyed under a different image. In Matthew, it is said, they are like to whitened sepulchres, which may be seen; here, to covered sepulchres, which appear not. But, the idea is the same in both, viz., that the interior is filled with all kinds of defilement.

45. "*One of the lawyers*" or Scribes, answering, said to Him, "*Master in saying these things Thou reproachest us also.*" The Scribes were the teachers and interpreters of the law. The Pharisees observed it rigidly; and that, according to the teaching of the Scribes or lawyers. It might be also, that among the Scribes some were Pharisees, (see Matthew ii. 4; iii. 7). But, as the Pharisees observed all their legal observances in accordance with the teaching of the "*lawyers*" or Scribes, hence, this man says, that our Lord "*reproached them*," or their entire order, "*also*," and spoke contumeliously of them—ὑβρίζεις. These haughty men could not bear correction. The words of our Lord were meant for their conversion and amendment; or, at least, He spoke with a view of protecting the people against the influences of their evil teaching and of marring their wicked endeavours to turn the people aside from faith in Him.

46. This gives our Lord an opportunity of hurling His unsparing denunciations against the Scribes, these false teachers, who led the people astray, and spiritually oppressed them (see Matthew xxiii. 4).

47-51. (see Matthew xxiii. 29-36).

52. The sense is substantially the same—though expressed here under a new image—as that conveyed (Matthew xxiii. 13). "*Taken away*," may be rendered from the Greek, ἤρατε. "*You have taken to yourselves*," you have carried ("*fero*"). You have claimed and arrogated it, as your own exclusive right, and allowed it to no one else. "*The key of knowledge.*" The idea is borrowed from an edifice of which a man retains "*the key;*" and which no one can enter, unless the holder of the key permits him. If we render it, as in our English version, "*taken away*" (*tollo*), the idea is the same. The lawyers have taken away from everyone else the power and authority, and office of teaching, of interpreting the law and the Holy Scriptures, which are the key to bring us to the knowledge of God and Salvation. This authority they have arrogated to themselves exclusively; and grossly abused. For, they themselves refuse to admit Christ as the Messiah; they refuse to enter His Church, and to become associated with His true followers; and by their false teaching and coercive authority, they prevent the people from doing so. They did not themselves, owing to their blindness of heart and perversity, understand the Scriptures, or the sense of the Prophets, which pointed to Christ; and by their false interpretations, which they claimed the right exclusively to make, they kept others from following our Lord. They neither observed the law themselves, nor permitted others to observe it. "*The key of knowledge*," denotes the knowledge of the Sacred Scriptures, to expound which, they sat in the chair of knowledge. "*Entered in*," is allusive to the metaphor of a house. The metaphor and the thing signified are spoken of together.

53. "*Vehemently to urge Him*," with a multiplicity of captious questions. "*And to oppress His mouth about many things.*" "*Oppress His mouth*"—ἀποστοματίζειν, means, to elicit from Him extemporaneous answers, to several questions put all at once, and coming tumultuously from different quarters, without giving time to consider them; and this, with a view of catching Him in His words, of eliciting from Him some answer that might be against the honour of God, the Law, the Traditions of the ancients, or the rights of Cæsar; so that thus they might have matter for accusation against Him, as in following verse.

CHAPTER XII.

ANALYSIS.

This chapter contains an exhortation addressed by our Lord to His disciples, on several subjects, (1-9). He speaks of blasphemy against the Holy Ghost (10). He cautions the people against avarice, the evils of which He illustrates by the parable of the covetous rich man (13-21). He exhorts them not to be too solicitous about earthly things, but to place their confidence in God, and to be liberal in bestowing alms (22-34). He exhorts them to vigilance against His coming to demand an account from them (35-48). He points out the object of His coming on earth, and some of its effects, in the persecutions that are to follow (49-53). The signs of His coming, of which they were wilfully ignorant (54-59).

TEXT.

AND *when great multitudes stood about him, so that they trod one upon another, he began to say to his disciples: Beware ye of the leaven of the Pharisees, which is hypocrisy.*

2. *For there is nothing covered, that shall not be revealed: nor hidden, that shall not be known.*

3. *For whatsoever things you have spoken in darkness, shall be published in the light: and that which you have spoken in the ear in the chambers, shall be preached on the house-tops.*

4. *And I say to you, my friends: Be not afraid of them who kill the body, and after that have no more that they can do.*

5. *But I will show you whom ye shall fear: fear ye him, who after he hath killed, hath power to cast into hell. Yea, I say to you, fear him.*

6. *Are not five sparrows sold for two farthings, and not one of them is forgotten before God?*

7. *Yea, the very hairs of your head are all numbered. Fear not, therefore: you are of more value than many sparrows.*

8. *And I say to you, whosoever shall confess me before men, him shall the son of man also confess before the Angels of God.*

9. *But he that shall deny me before men, shall be denied before the Angels of God.*

10. *And whosoever speaketh a word against the son of man, it shall be forgiven him: but to him who shall blaspheme against the Holy Ghost it shall not be forgiven.*

11. *And when they shall bring you into the synagogues, and to magistrates and powers, be not solicitous how or what you shall answer, or what you shall say.*

12. *For the Holy Ghost shall teach you in the same hour what you must say.*

13. *And one of the multitude said to him: Master, speak to my brother that he divide the inheritance with me.*

14. *But he said to him: Man, who hath appointed me judge or divider over you?*

15. *And he said to them: take heed and beware of all covetousness: for a man's life doth not consist in the abundance of things which he possesseth.*

16. *And he spoke a similitude to them, saying: The land of a certain rich man brought forth plenty of fruits.*

17. *And he thought within himself, saying: What shall I do, because I have no room where to bestow my fruits?*

18. *And he said: this will I do: I will pull down my barns, and will build greater: and into them will I gather all things that are grown to me, and my goods.*

19. *And I will say to my soul: Soul, thou hast much goods laid up for many years, take thy rest, eat, drink, make good cheer.*

20. *But God said to him: Thou fool, this night do they require thy soul of thee; and whose shall those things be which thou hast provided?*

21. *So is he that layeth up treasure for himself, and is not rich towards God.*

22. *And he said to his disciples: Therefore, I say to you, be not solicitous for your life what you shall eat; nor for your body, what you shall put on.*

23. *The life is more than the meat, and the body is more than the raiment.*

24. *Consider the ravens, for they sow not, neither do they reap, neither have they storehouse nor barn, and God feedeth them. How much are you more valuable than they?*

25. *And which of you by taking thought can add to his stature one cubit?*

26. *If then ye be not able to do so much as the least thing, why are you solicitous for the rest?*

27. *Consider the lilies how they grow: they labour not, neither do they spin. But I say to you, not even Solomon in all his glory was clothed like one of these.*

28. *Now if God clothe in this manner the grass that is to-day in the field, and to-morrow is cast into the oven: how much more you, O ye of little faith?*

29. *And seek not you what you shall eat, or what you shall drink, and be not lifted up on high.*

30. *For all these things do the nations of the world seek. But your Father knoweth that you have need of these things.*

31. *But seek ye first the kingdom of God and his justice, and all these things shall be added unto you.*

32. *Fear not, little flock, for it hath pleased your Father to give you a kingdom.*

33. *Sell what you possess and give alms. Make to yourselves bags which grow not old, a treasure in heaven which faileth not: where no thief approacheth, nor moth corrupteth.*

34. *For where your treasure is, there will your heart be also.*

35. *Let your loins be girt, and lamps burning in your hands.*

36. *And you yourselves like to men who wait for their lord, when he shall return from the wedding: that when he cometh and knocketh, they may be open to him immediately.*

37. *Blessed are those servants, whom the Lord when he cometh, shall find watching. Amen I say to you, that he will gird himself, and make them sit down to meat, and passing will minister unto them.*

38. *And if he shall come in the second watch, or come in the third watch, and find them so, blessed are those servants.*

39. *But this know ye, that if the householder did know at what hour the thief would come, he would surely watch, and would not suffer his house to be broken open.*

40. *Be you then also ready: for at what hour you think not, the son of man will come.*

41. *And Peter said to him: Lord, dost thou speak this parable to us, or likewise to all?*

42. And the Lord said: Who (thinkest thou) is the faithful and wise steward, whom his lord setteth over his family, to give them their measure of wheat in due season?

43. Blessed is that servant, whom when his lord shall come he shall find so doing.

44. Verily I say to you, he will set him over all that he possesseth.

45. But if that servant shall say in his heart, My lord is long a coming; and shall begin to strike the men-servants and maid-servants, and to eat and to drink, and be drunk:

46. The lord of that servant will come in the day that he hopeth not, and at the hour that he knoweth not, and shall separate him, and shall appoint him his portion with unbelievers.

47. And that servant who knew the will of his lord, and prepared not himself and did not according to his will, shall be beaten with many stripes.

48. But he that knew not and did things worthy of stripes shall be beaten with few stripes. And unto whomsoever much is given, of him much shall be required: and to whom they have committed much, of him they will demand the more.

49. I am come to cast fire on the earth; and what will I but that it be kindled?

50. And I have a baptizm, wherewith I am to be baptized: and how am I straitened until it be accomplished?

51. Think ye that I am come to give peace on earth? I tell you no, but separation.

52. For there shall be from henceforth five in one house divided; three against two, and two against three.

53. The father shall be divided against his son, and the son against his father, the mother against the daughter, and the daughter against the mother, the mother-in-law against her daughter-in-law, and the daughter-in-law against her mother-in-law.

54. And he said also to the multitudes: When you see a cloud rising from the west, presently you say: A shower is coming: and so it happeneth:

55. And when ye see the south-wind blow, you say: There will be heat: and it cometh to pass.

56. You hypocrites, you know how to discern the face of the heaven and of the earth: but how is it that you do not discern this time?

57. And why even of yourselves do you not judge that which is just?

58. And when thou goest with thy adversary to the prince, whilst thou art in the way endeavour to be delivered from him; lest perhaps he draw thee to the judge, and the judge deliver thee to the exacter, and the exacter cast thee into prison.

59. I say to thee, thou shalt not go out thence, until thou pay the very last mite.

COMMENTARY.

1. "*And when great multitudes*" (the Greek is, *myriads*, signifying great numbers). "*stood about Him, so that they trod on one another, He began, &c.*" The following words are described by St. Matthew, as having been uttered under different circumstances, It may be, that our Lord, on account of their importance, uttered them more than once (see Matthew xvi. 6-12). The Pharisees were the greatest enemies to the spread of the Gospel, and employed every means to turn the people aside from following our Lord. Hence, His unsparing denunciations of these hypocrites. He thus intends to guard the simple people against these wolves in sheep's clothing.

After "*disciples*," the Greek has, πρωτον, *first*. He addressed them first, having afterwards (verse 54) addressed the people, principally, if not exclusively.

2. This has reference to the hypocrisy of the Pharisees, which, one day, will be publicly exposed to the gaze of men; or, it may refer to the Gospel which is now partly concealed and opposed, and shall, one day, overcoming all obstacles, be proclaimed to the entire world. The words contain an adagial meaning, conveying to the Apostles, that the merit of their labours and sufferings for the Gospel, and the hypocrisy of their enemies, shall, one day, be revealed to all men.

3. (See Matthew x. 26, 27.)
4, 5. (See Matthew x. 28.)
6, 7. (See Matthew x. 29-31.)
8, 9. (See Matthew x. 32, 33.)
10. (See Matthew xii. 31.)
11, 12. (See Matthew x. 18-20.)

13. St. Luke does not record the circumstances of this difference among the brothers, nor the merits of the case which our Lord was called upon to settle; nor does he say whether both parties appealed to Him either as umpire, arbitrator, or Judge—or only one party appealed to Him, on account of His influence among the people. We need not suppose the party spoken of regarded our Lord as the promised Messiah, who was to be the protector of the poor (Psalm lxxi. 1, 2). According to the law of inheritance among the Jews, the first born was to obtain a double portion of his father's property (Deut. xxi. 17). Some authors hold that in the case of inheritance by the mother, the property was to be divided equally among all (Selden de Success. in bona, c. 5, 6).

14. Our Lord, seeing that this man was more intent on earthly gain than on heavenly treasures, or, on the attainment of these spiritual joys, of which He had been treating, at once refuses to take up the case; and in His reply, He denies, while reprehending this man for his unreasonable interruption, that it was any business of His to interfere in such matters. They had civil judges to go to, to arrange their differences. "*Man*"—a form of expression used to denote, He knew him not (chap. xxi. 58-60). Our Lord does not here deny His judicial power, or His right, or that of His Church—in which point the Anabaptists err—to interfere if He pleased, since He was constituted "*King of kings and Lord of lords*," &c., and He also gave His Church the plenitude of His authority; but, He here wishes to convey, that the primary end of His mission was not to arrange temporal disputes, or to interfere in secular matters; thus, teaching His followers and the ministers of His Gospel, that spiritual matters should primarily engross all their attention; and temporal matters should be embarked in only as a secondary concern, and subordinate, as means, to the spiritual and eternal welfare of souls. He also desired not to favour the opinions of the carnal Jews, who expected in their Messiah, a powerful earthly Prince and Conqueror. Circumstances do sometimes arise, rendering it imperative on those engaged in the Sacred Ministry, to embark in temporal concerns, as a necessary means of advancing the spiritual welfare of their people, and of averting great spiritual evils and dangers.

He who had come on earth for Divine purposes, properly declined meddling in earthly strife, and having to judge the living and the dead, and to pass sentence on them according to their deserts, He does not vouchsafe to be judge of lawsuits and to act as umpire in regard to possessions (St. Ambrose, Lib. 7, in Luc. n. 121), "*Bene terrena despicit, qui propter divina descenderat,*" says the same Father (*hic*).

15. Taking occasion from this man's petition, which seemed to savour of avarice, He now warns His followers against "*all covetousness,*" not only as regards the desire of other men's property; but, also as regards an excessive attachment to one's own. Hence, the words, "*all covetousness.*" "*He said to them,*" His disciples and the crowd that was present. It may be, He addressed the two brothers, if present, who were contending about the inheritance. "*Take heed and guard against all covetousness.*" From the present case, take a lesson, and beware of all inordinate love for riches and earthly possessions. "*For a man's life,*" &c. The happiness and prolongation of man's life in this world are not brought about by the possession of riches; but, rather the contrary? that is to say, corroding cares and shortening of one's days, owing to the temptations to commit excess, are produced by earthly possessions.

16. To illustrate His precepts on the subject of avarice, and to show the utter folly of excessive attachment to the things of this earth and over-confidence in riches, as the means of prolonging life, or rendering it happy, our Lord proposes a very striking and startling similitude, founded on an event which might have happened, or, at least, which was possible.
"*The land.*" The Greek word means, "*farm,*" or large number of fields, like those of the men reproached by Isaias (v. 8). "*Brought forth plenty of fruit,*" yielded an abundant produce.

17, 18. The increase of riches produced not peace, but anxiety and disquietude. St. Basil (Hom. de Avaritia), observes, that this rich man, in the midst of his riches, felt all the disquietude of the poor, when they are in want of bread or necessary subsistence. He never thought of bestowing his superfluities on the poor. His ears were deaf to their cries. Instead of destroying his granaries to enlarge them, he should have opened them to the poor, to feed the hungry, and like Joseph of old, should have proclaimed to all who were in want to come and receive aid at his hands.
"*And my goods,*" refers to those already stored there. "*All things that are grown to me,*" the increased produce of the present year.

19. "*My soul,*" an emphatic expression for *myself.* It refers to the prolongation of his life. "*My soul.*" The following is the soliloquy of this rich man with himself: "*for many years;*" but who promised him "*many years,*" nay, a single day to enjoy them?
"*Take thy rest,*" &c. Indulge in all kinds of animal gratification, and enjoy all kinds of sensual delight, deny thyself no pleasure. "O, singular, egregious folly," cries out St. Basil, "if you had the soul of a hog, what else could you enunciate?"

20. The rich man thus pondered secretly in his own mind; for, "*he thought within himself*" (v. 17). But, his thoughts were heard and examined in Heaven, which is not slow in pronouncing judgment on him. "*But God said to him,*" either by some secret inspiration, or some sudden mortal stroke, sending him a mortal disease, which was taking him out of life and thus showing his folly; or by an angel, "*thou fool,*" while thou hast not a day which thou canst call thine own, thou promisest thyself many years, on which all thy calculations of long happiness are based. Such is the

judgment, not of man, but of divine wisdom regarding him, and, indeed, it is not difficult even for man, enlightened by faith to pronounce the same.

"*This night.*" This very night on which thou dost calculate on a long life, "*they require*" a form of personal for impersonal, by no means rare, either in Greek or Hebrew signifying, "*shall be required,*" thy soul shall be required. It may also be understood personally, of God and His angels. The angels, as ministers of God's decree, by a just judgment, "*require his soul.*" and cut short the thread of his life, that very night. "*Require that soul,*" about whose enjoyments during many long years to come, the rich man was so solicitous.

"*And whose shall the things be,*" &c. Certainly not thine own, since thy works alone shall accompany thee. They may, possibly, come to some worthless heir; to the very man whom thou abhorrest most. Thou canst not say, to whom they may fall, whether to stranger or relative, friend or foe (Ecclesiastes xi. 19). (Psalm xxxviii. 7), "*He knoweth not for whom he shall gather those things.*"

21. This is the moral conclusion from the above. Such shall be the end and sad fate of him who, engrossed with acquiring and accumulating temporal wealth for his own selfish purposes, for his own pleasure and gratification—"*for himself*" (only), is opposed to "*towards God*"—is regardless of acquiring true riches for himself. "*Not rich towards God,*" rich in good works, which please God, especially in distributing our wealth to the needy poor, His representatives on earth, and thus having our treasures laid up in heaven. "*Rich towards God,*" means rich in good works; "*rich*" in bestowing our goods on God, who will reward us liberally hereafter. The man who makes God his heir, need not fear if suddenly called out of this life; he is prepared; he has sent his treasures before him, securely laid up for him in heaven. The Greek word for "*rich,*" πλουτων, is a participle, signifying "making himself rich in God," by the practice of those virtues, especially charity to the poor, and by the acquisition of merits, which constitute riches in God.

22-28. (See Matthew vi. 25-32.)

29. "*And be not lifted up on high*" (μη μετεωριζεσθε), is understood by St. Augustine and others, to mean, should riches abound with you, be not, on that account, elated or puffed up with pride. Similar is the Apostle's admonition, "*Charge the rich of this world not to be high-minded*" (1 Tim. vi. 17). The Greek word, however, in the latter place is different. It is, μη υψηλοφρονειν. Others give it the meaning of anxiously fluctuating alternately, between hope and fear. The Greek word, which signifies "*to be lifted up,*" or, *suspended*, is allusive to the tossing of vessels high in air on the lofty billows, and then descending to the very depths, an image of great anxiety (Bloomfield). The words represent inconstancy of mind; now, thinking of this; then of that; passing from thought to thought, and always aspiring to something higher, suspended between conflicting hopes and fears.

32. "*Fear not.*" Indulge not in excessive anxiety about your future sustenance, or the necessary means of existence. "*Little flock.*" The disciples of our Lord were then few in number, of lowly condition, of little or no earthly consideration; "*little,*" in comparison with the number of the reprobates; "*little,*" compared with unbelievers, "*little,*" on account of their humility. He terms them "*flock,*" to show that He was their Pastor; they, the objects of His tenderest care and solicitude, and under the special providence of His Heavenly Father.

"*For it hath pleased your Father.*" For, out of His own gratuitous goodness, God, who is, in a special manner, "*your Father,*" and loves you as His dearest children, has been pleased "*to give you a kingdom,*" to make you sharers in the joys and honours of His heavenly kingdom, in case you persevere in serving Him faithfully; now, if He has done what is greater, will He not provide you with what is of less consideration and less value—the necessary means of temporal existence? Let the consideration of this heavenly kingdom destined for you, one day, relieve you, of any inordinate fear of wanting the necessaries of life.

33. And in order to become more fit to inherit this heavenly kingdom in store for you, to the attainment of which earthly possessions are an obstacle and a drawback; disencumbering yourselves of these obstacles, go, and "*sell what you possess, and give alms,*" give the produce to the poor and needy, following My example, and showing you are not anxious about earthly goods, casting your care on God's providence. This is merely a counsel of perfection, but not a strict precept. (Matthew xix. 21, &c.)

"*Bags which grow not old,*" and allow not their contents to slip through and be lost. "*Bags that grow not old,*" are the bosoms of the poor, to whom alms are seasonably given. "*An unfailing treasure,*" &c. By works of piety and charity (see Matthew vi. 20).

34. (See Matthew vi. 21.)

35. Having encouraged His followers to divest themselves of all solicitude about earthly things, He now inculcates on all, constant vigilance in expectation of this kingdom of God, which is not distant, but at hand. During the entire course of your lives, "*let your loins be girt.*" This is allusive to the customs of Eastern people, men as well as women, who wore long flowing garments. They used girdles around the waist, to shorten and draw up their flowing robes, when commencing any work, performing any active service, or setting out on a journey. "*And lamps burning in your hands,*" to be ready at a moment.

36. "*Like men who wait,*" &c. When servants are expecting their master home from the wedding, which took place at night, they always had their garments gathered up, and the lamps at hand, so as to attend to his call at once, without any delay. This is, of course, allegorical. It denotes the constant, never-ceasing vigilance with which we should prepare for our Lord's coming to call us out of life. We should "*have our loins girt,*" being always engaged in *His* service, doing whatever we do, suffering whatever we are doomed to suffer for His glory, keeping Him before our minds in all things, having the lamp of faith trimmed with the oil of good works, unlike the foolish virgins, whose lamps were not properly or sufficiently trimmed in this way, at the last moment, not having their faith enlivened by charity.

37. "*Blessed.*" In the allegorical sense, blessed with an eternal crown of glory, with an abundance of never-ending delights, which it has not been given to the mind of man to contemplate.

"*He shall gird Himself,*" &c. In the literal sense, it is a thing which very seldom occurs, that the master ministers to his faithful servants. However, our Lord supposes it to happen, that a generous master, after having himself enjoyed the pleasures of a banquet, and finding his servants ready to attend to his call on his return, would himself in turn, prepare them a banquet in reward for their fidelity, serve and wait on them. At all events, the parable or illustration is meant to convey the generosity with which God will reward His faithful servants, whom He shall make partakers of His bliss in His heavenly kingdom.

38. "*Second . . . third watch.*" (See Matthew xiv. 25). In the parable, there is no mention of the *first* or *fourth* watch; because, the *first* was too early an hour for returning from a banquet; the *fourth*, too late. The usual hours for returning are mentioned. The example is meant to convey to us, that we may be called to an account at any period of life, and that whenever called, even should He delay His coming, we should be always found watching and ready, persevering in good works, without ceasing or intermission (as in Luke xxi. 34-36).

39. He now, by another parable, points out the necessity of unceasing vigilance, on account of the uncertainty of the time of His coming, and also on account of the punishment of neglect. We should be always ready, owing to the uncertainty of the time of His coming, lest we should be surprised, like the householder, who neglected watching against the attack of the nightly thief. It is supposed in the Greek reading, which is in the past tense, ἤδει—εγρηγορησεν—αφηκεν, "*had known, would have watched, would not have suffered his house,*" &c.—that the house had been robbed, and its goods rifled. His goods were rifled; because not knowing the time of the thief's approach, he did not watch. Hence, we should be constantly on the watch for our Lord's coming, lest we be found unprepared; for, to those, who watch not, He shall come like the nightly thief (see Matthew xxiv. 42-44).

41. "*Peter said to Him,*" &c. Peter knew that he and the other Apostles were appointed as householders in charge of the family of God; that several things were said, which seemed to apply to them exclusively: "*little flock,*" (v. 32); "*He shall gird Himself,*" &c. (v. 37). But the vigilance applied to all; hence, his question. Whether the above exhortations to vigilance did not apply to others as well as to those entrusted with the care of the family, our Lord, without directly answering Peter, conveys in the following, that while it concerned all, it specially applied to the Apostles and prelates of the Church, whose responsibility is greater, and whose accounts are to be demanded with greater exactitude, "*to whom much hath been given,*" &c. (v. 48).

42, 44. (See Matthew xxiv. 45-47.)

45, 46. (See Matthew xxiv. 48-51.)

47, 48. To the above, our Lord subjoins another parable, showing the different degrees of punishment to be inflicted on offenders according to the lights they received and the graces they abused; this served as an answer to Peter, and showed him, that the Apostles were principally concerned, in what He had been saying, owing to their great graces and privileges. "*And did things worthy of stripes.*" This supposes that it is not for voluntary ignorance, but, for positive offences the party is to be punished —offences, no doubt, less grievous than those of the man, who received greater light, and had greater knowledge of his Master's will. No doubt, all have some knowledge of God's will. From the light of reason, all know the leading principles of the law. But, some are favoured with greater lights than others, and the punishment of their crimes, *cæteris paribus*, greater, unless the heinousness of the crimes of the less enlightened, of themselves far exceeded the sins of the enlightened.

"*To whom much hath been given,*" &c. These are general assertions, conveying general truths, easily comprehended even in reference to human affairs. "*Much given*," may refer to gifts conferred for one's own use and sanctification. "*Committed much*," probably, refers to gifts conferred on men, confided to their care and government, for the benefit of others.

49. "*I am come*," &c. These words may have been spoken by our Lord at a different time, from the foregoing; and we need not trouble ourselves, with tracing any consecutive connexion between them; as St. Luke is wont to string together several things spoken by our Lord on different occasions. Others (Jansen. Gandav.) trace a connexion in this way; our Lord had been, in the foregoing, encouraging the Apostles to the faithful performance of their duties, from the consideration that they were His stewards, the dispensers of His goods—an office entailing the heaviest responsibility. He now points out what He expects from them, and how they are to dispense His goods, viz., in propagating the Gospel; in suffering for it; thus, producing abundant fruit.

By "*fire*," some understand the Holy Ghost and His gifts; especially charity, fervour, zeal (Cant. viii. 6), and to this, the Church refers, on the Saturday after Pentecost "*illo nos igne . . . quem Dominus noster, misit in terram et voluit vehementer accendi*," and this fire of Divine love embraces the fire of tribulation also. The Apostles inflamed with Divine love, braved and overcame all tribulations and sufferings, in the cause of the Gospel, of which our Lord forewarned them, as near at hand (A. Lapide). Others understand it, of the fire of Evangelical preaching, which the Holy Ghost inflames. Hence, he descended on the Apostles, about to enter on this duty, in the form of tongues of fire. This Evangelical preaching, unlike the Old Law, or any human doctrine, which is cold and inoperative, set in a blaze the hearts of men; pervading all places, it purged the elect, and fired the impio's with an unjust hatred against the Gospel (Psalm cxviii.) "*ignitum eloquium tuum*," *&c.* "*Sermo Domini ut ignis exestuans in corde meo*" (Jerem. xx. 9). This fire our Lord brought from heaven, and He wished His Apostles to enkindle it on throughout the earth (Jansen. Gandav.).

Others, understand it of the fire of persecution, which they say is more in accordance with the context; "*I have a baptism*," &c. According to these, our Lord wishes to fortify His Apostles against the persecutions they were to be subject to. And to inspire them with greater fortitude, He says, He Himself was the first to pass through the ordeal. In the same sense, He says, He came to bring "*not peace, but the sword*" (Matthew x. 34); and He predicts, that, considering human depravity, the preaching of the Gospel would be the occasion of great divisions, of great sufferings and persecutions, for those who preach and for those who embrace it. It was, however, by such sufferings and persecutions, that, our Lord meant to break down the power of Satan. These alone were the means for securing heaven. This is the meaning of "*fire*" in many parts of Scripture (Psalm lxv. 12; Isaias xliii. 2; Ecclesias. li. 6). This is the interpretation of Tertullian, followed by Maldonatus, Calmet, Lucas, Brugensis, &c.

"*And what will I?*" &c. I am anxious that these embers of charity be enkindled in the hearts of all men, or that these sufferings and persecutions—the portion of my elect—be enkindled everywhere by the preaching of the Gospel, when my Apostles shall enter the lists with the enemies of man, the world, the devil, and the flesh, and shall have to suffer in consequence, persecutions which await myself in the first instance, and await all, who wish to live piously here below (1 Tim. iii. 12). But, it is by means of the sufferings which my followers bravely endure, the powers of the enemy are to be utterly defeated and destroyed.

Instead of, "*what will I but that it be enkindled*" (Vulgate), "*quid volo nisi ut accendatur ?*" in the greek it is, "*what will I, since it has been already enkindled,*" εἰ ἤδη ἀνήφθη. This is interpreted by some, thus: Since it has been already enkindled in the hearts of my disciples and throughout Judea—"*what will I,*" but that it be enkindled still more, throughout the earth? According to this interpretation, adopted by St. Cyril and by Cajetan, the sentence, as it stands, is imperfect till the words, "*but that it be enkindled,*" &c., are added, to complete the sense. By others (Theophylact, &c.), they are interpreted thus: Since it is already enkindled, I have no other wish. In this is implied the desire that it be more and more enkindled. Of the words understood in this sense, the Vulgate "*quid volo,*" &c., is a clear impression. My only desire is, that this fire which I sent upon the earth be enkindled more and more by you in every place. Euthymius interprets it thus: If the fire which I came to send be enkindled, as it really is in you, what more do I desire in this world? What more am I waiting for? The time for returning to my Father is, therefore, just at hand

50. "*And I have a baptism,*" &c. For, "*and,*" the Greek is, δε, *but*, as if He said; but before this fire,—whether understood of Divine love or suffering,—can be fully scattered on the earth, I must first suffer, in order to give an example of suffering to others, and induce them to scatter the fire of persecution throughout the earth after my example—or to scatter this fire of divine love; since it is, by My blood of the cross, that the fire of Divine love and charity is to be lit up, as well by the grace which My suffering merited, as by the considerations which it suggests in the mind of all men. "*Baptism*" signifies suffering; because, our Lord was to be fully immersed in His own blood, as the body in baptism is immersed in water; and He was baptised in another sense; because, He was to be wholly immersed, plunged in suffering, "*as the man of sorrows, and acquainted with infirmities.*" Moreover, water, according to the prevalent notions, was expressive of suffering. (See Matthew xx. 22, &c.)

"*And how am I straitened ?*" &c. These words express not His fears, as is supposed by some, but his anxious, longing desire to redeem mankind by His sufferings and death of the cross. As "*hope deferred afflicts the soul*" (Proverbs xiii. 12); so also, do deferred desires. Our Lord thus anxiously wished for His own death, not for His own sake, but for ours, to save us from sin and to satisfy His Father's justice. His fear of death at His Passion took place in the inferior part of His soul; the present desire, in the superior (see Matthew xxvi. 38).

51. As the fire which our Lord came to scatter on the earth, would be the occasion of disturbances, divisions and persecution, He forewarns His disciples of this in time, lest they should be hereafter disturbed. (See Matthew x. 34, &c.)

52, 53. "*Henceforth,*" After the promulgation of the Gospel, where union reigned, such as can exist among unbelievers. "*Five shall be divided, three against two.*" (53.) "*Shall be divided.*" When three of five embrace the faith, they shall be divided against the two unbelievers; and this will of course reciprocally provoke, or rather entail the division of two against three; or if two embrace the faith, while three remain in a state of infidelity, the result shall be the same. The "*five,*" are "*father,*" "*mother,*" "*son,*" "*daughter,*" "*daughter-in-law.*" For "*mother,*" includes the relation of "*mother-in-law*" towards her son's wife, supposed to be living in the same house. Our Lord here predicts the most dreadful domestic divisions between those most closely united, in consequence of the spread of the Gospel, when one party would give up every earthly feeling and his natural affections sooner than abandon the faith, while unbelievers shall rage against those who, embracing the faith of Christ, have abandoned the false religion of their fathers.

54, 55. "*A cloud rising out of the west*," is a certain prognostic of rainy weather, "*you say*," from observation and past experience, "*and so it happeneth*," generally (see 3 Kings xviii. 44).

56. (See Matthew xvi. 3.) "*Hypocrites.*" In this He points to the Scribes and Pharisees, many of whom, with their followers, were probably among the "*multitudes*" whom our Lord addresses here (*v.* 54). These "*hypocrites*," owing to their voluntary blindness, disguising from themselves the truth of what they saw, and inflated with a vain idea of their Jewish justice, refused to submit themselves to the justice of God, condemning them by the mouth of Jesus Christ, who had only in view their correction. Although well versed in judging rightly of sensible things, they were blind to the important concern, relating to the coming of Christ and its signs, contained in the prediction of the prophecies regarding Him.

57, 58. According to some Expositors (Ven. Bede among the rest), our Lord, in these words, anticipates or answers an objection which the illiterate crowd might raise against their knowing the Messiah from the signs alleged, on the ground, that they were utterly ignorant of Scripture and the prophecies. From their own consciences and from natural reason, aided by grace, which God refuses to none who ask it, they should know, that He who performed the works whereof they were witnesses, which no other man did, was the expected Messiah; and they should judge justly of what is fit and proper regarding Him. According to this interpretation, there is reference here to the foregoing. What follows would be a different argument or subject altogether. From the Greek, however, which runs thus: "*For when thou goest with thy adversary,*" &c., it would seem rather to be connected with what follows, and to have reference to man's reconciliation with God, while there is time, which is illustrated by a human example drawn from the conduct or mode of acting on the part of men when about to appear in judgment before an earthly judge. The example does not seem to have reference to the same thing or occasion spoken of (Matthew v. 25.) For, here, there is question of reconciliation with God; there, with our neighbour. The words would then mean: why do you not judge, from what occurs among yourselves, from what you are wont to do in human transactions, of what it is right and just for you to do in reference to spiritual and eternal interests, in the work of reconciliation with God, which is now presented to you by me. (58). For when there is question of human obligations and debts, real or personal, if about to be brought before a judge, what do you do? Do you not arrange with your adversary on the way to the trial, in order to escape a greater punishment and loss? So should you make peace with God by penance and faith in Me, His Eternal Son, before the day of just retribution and vengeance arrives, and irreparable ruin befal you.

59. (See Matthew v. 25, 26.)

CHAPTER XIII.

ANALYSIS.

In this verse, after referring to a signal punishment inflicted on some Galileans, our Lord explains in what light we are to regard God's judgments, and shows the necessity of penance for all (1-5). The barren fig tree (6-9). The healing of the crooked woman on the Sabbath day, and His crushing reply, on the occasion, to the ruler of the synagogue (10-17). The parables of the mustard seed and of the leaven (18-21). The strait-gate—the rejection from God's kingdom of the Jewish people (22-30). His reply to those who warned Him of Herod's designs (31-34). His lamentation over Jerusalem (34-35).

TEXT.

*A*ND *there were present at that very time some that told him of the Galileans, whose blood Pilate had mingled with their sacrifices.*

2. *And he answering said to them: Think you that these Galileans were sinners above all the men of Galilee, because they suffered such things?*

3. *No, I say to you: but unless you shall do penance, you shall all likewise perish.*

4. *Or those eighteen upon whom the tower fell in Siloe, and slew them: think you that they also were debtors above all the men that dwelt in Jerusalem.*

5. *No, I say to you: but except you do penance, you shall all likewise perish.*

6. *He spoke also this parable: A certain man had a fig-tree planted in his vineyard, and he came seeking fruit on it, and found none.*

7. *And he said to the dresser of the vineyard: Behold for these three years I come seeking fruit on this fig-tree, and I find none. Cut it down therefore; why cumbereth it the ground?*

8. *But he answering said to them: Lord, let it alone this year also, until I dig about it, and dung it.*

9. *And if happily it bear fruit; but if not, then after that thou shalt cut it down.*

10. *And he was teaching in their synagogue on their sabbath.*

11. *And behold there was a woman who had a spirit of infirmity eighteen years; and she was bowed together, neither could she look upwards at all.*

12. *Whom when Jesus saw, he called her unto him, and said to her: Woman, thou art delivered from thy infirmity.*

13. *And he laid his hands upon her, and immediately she was made straight, and glorified God.*

14. *And the ruler of the synagogue (being angry that Jesus had healed on the sabbath) answering said to the multitude: Six days there are wherein you ought to work. In them therefore come, and be healed; and not on the sabbath-day.*

15. *And the Lord answering him, said: Ye hypocrites, doth not every one of you on the sabbath-day loose his ox or his ass from the manger, and lead them to water?*

16. *And ought not this daughter of Abraham, whom Satan hath bound, lo, these eighteen years, be loosed from this bond on the sabbath-day?*

17. *And when he said these things, all his adversaries were ashamed: and all the people rejoiced for all the things that were gloriously done by him.*

18. *He said therefore; To what is the kingdom of God like, and whereunto shall I resemble it?*

19. *It is like to a grain of mustard-seed, which a man took and cast into his garden, and it grew, and became a great tree, and the birds of the air lodged in the branches thereof.*

20. *And again he said: Whereunto shall I esteem the kingdom of God to be like?*

21. *It is like to leaven, which a woman took and hid in three measures of meal, till the whole was leavened.*

22. And he went through the cities and towns teaching, and making his journey to Jerusalem.

23. And a certain man said to him: Lord, are they few that are saved? But he said to them:

24. Strive to enter by the narrow gate: for many, I say to you, shall seek to enter, and shall not be able.

25. But when the master of the house shall be gone in, and shall shut the door, you shall begin to stand without, and knock at the door, saying, Lord, open to us: and he answering shall say to you, I know you not whence you are:

26. Then you shall begin to say: We have eaten and drunk in thy presence, and thou hast taught in our streets.

27. And he shall say to you: I know you not whence you are: depart from me, all ye workers of iniquity.

28. There shall be weeping and gnashing of teeth; when you shall see Abraham and Isaac and Jacob, and all the prophets in the kingdom of God, and you yourselves thrust out.

29. And there shall come from the east and the west and the north and the south; and shall sit down in the kingdom of God.

30. And behold, they are last that shall be first, and they are first, that shall be last.

31. The same day there came some of the Pharisees, saying to him: Depart and get thee hence, for Herod hath a mind to kill thee.

32. And he said to them: Go, and tell that fox, Behold I cast out devils, and do cures to-day and to-morrow, and the third day I am consummated.

33. Nevertheless I must walk to-day and to-morrow and the day following, because it cannot be, that a prophet perish out of Jerusalem.

34. Jerusalem, Jerusalem, that killest the prophets, and stonest them that are sent to thee, how often would I have gathered thy children as the bird doth her brood under her wings, and thou wouldst not?

35. Behold your house shall be left to you desolate. And I say to you, that you shall not see me till the time come, when you shall say: Blessed is he that cometh in the name of the Lord.

COMMENTARY.

1. "*And there were present.*" The Greek—παρησαν—signifies, "*there came up,*" as in Matthew (xxvi. 50), "*at that very time,*" while our Lord was delivering the discourses referred to in the preceding chapter, "*some that told Him of the Galileans, whose blood Pilate had mingled with their sacrifices,*" with the blood of their sacrifices. This is a bold, figurative form of expression, signifying "whom Pilate slew while they were attending at sacrifice," an occurrence of an atrocious nature, generally regarded as a clear manifestation of God's wrath towards sinners, whose guilt must have involved special enormity. Who these Galileans were, or when or wherefore the occurrence referred to took place, is not recorded. Commentators generally understand the Galileans to be certain seditious followers of Judas of Galilee, called the *Gaulonite*, whose chief error was, that the Jews, as being the chosen people of God, owed allegiance to God alone, as their king, and that it was unbecoming in them to pay taxes, or show any marks of allegiance to the Romans, who were Pagans and unbelievers. Judas himself miserably perished in his rebellion; and his adherents were dispersed by Quirinus (Acts v. 37). His followers survived him up to the time

of our Redeemer, as we are informed by St. Jerome (c. 5 ad Titum), and by Josephus; and these gave expression to the seditious sentiments entertained by their founder. It is thought they gave utterance to these disloyal sentiments on the occasion here referred to, while sacrifices were offered up in the Temple, in punishment of which they were put to death in the very Temple by Pilate, who had his soldiers close by in the fort Antonia, and sternly crushed, with a firm hand, such attempts at revolution. This is the interpretation, or, rather, opinion, commonly adopted. Some, however, with Maldonatus, understand the occurrence to refer to the slaughter of some Samaritans at a village named Taribatha, at the foot of Mount Garazim, which they were about to ascend, under the guidance of an impostor, who promised to show them the sacred vessels buried there by Moses. On this occasion, Pilate had possession of the hill before them, with his forces, horse and foot, and slew them (Josephus Antiq. Lib. 18, c. 7; Hegesippus, Lib. 2, do. excid. Jerusalem). But these authors make no mention of sacrifices. However, the people mentioned here are called Galileans, and not Samaritans, and the Galileans were scrupulously exact in offering sacrifice in the Temple of Jerusalem only. Moreover, Pilate's jurisdiction did not comprise Galilee Hence, it is in the Temple of Jerusalem, this occurrence must, on some occasion, have taken place. Others refer it to different occasions; but, the first opinion seems the more probable. It is likely that the event was of very recent date, and that these men who announced it to our Lord, implied that the sufferers must have been guilty of sins of peculiar enormity; or, they may have in view to elicit from Him, as in the case of the man born blind (John ix.), what grievous sins these Galileans had committed to draw down on them such signal punishment. For, from our Lord's answer (next verse), correcting their erroneous notions on this point, they seemed to think, that the infliction of grievous and extraordinary punishment (which, though apparently fortuitous in the course of human events, is fixed and determined by the providence of God), was a proof of enormous and exceptional crime on the part of those so punished (Acts xxviii. 3, 4). The Jews were greatly addicted to these views (John ix. 2, 3). Against this false notion, the argument of the whole book of Job is specially directed.

2. Our Lord combats this false opinion, and shows them, that exceptional punishment is not always a proof of exceptional guilt; that God, out of a large number of sinners equally guilty, selects some for signal punishment, as is often done in the decimation of an army, as a warning and lesson to the rest, although all may be equally deserving of punishment; and from this, He takes occasion to inculcate on all the necessity of penance, if, being equally guilty, they wish to escape the like fate. He admits that these Galileans met with deserved punishment for their sins— although in some cases it happens that the just are visited with great temporal calamities, to test their virtue and increase their merit—and He proclaims that His hearers were equally guilty and deserving of equally great punishment. In truth, God by an effect of His goodness, punishes in this life, those whom He wishes to spare in the next; and, on the other hand, He allows the wicked to enjoy the fruits of their iniquity here, reserving them, as the victims of His everlasting wrath in hell (Job xxi. 9-13; xii. 6).

3. "*Likewise*," all, without exception, shall be punished, if not in this world, most certainly, in the world to come; or, in a most miserable manner, even if different in its mode of execution, "*mors peccatorum pessima*." "*Likewise*," while certainly involving eternal death to all unrepenting sinners, likely, refers to the *same kind of punishment* in

store for many whom our Lord addressed. For, we learn from Josephus (and likely our Lord had this in view), that under the government of Cumanus, 20,000 Jews were destroyed about the Temple (Antiq., Lib. xx. c. 5); that, when the Idumeans were admitted by the Zealots into Jerusalem, 8,500 of the High Priest's party were destroyed; so that "the entire Temple overflowed with blood" (De Bel. Jud., Lib. iv., c. 5); that the three ruling factions, who domineered in the city, before the Romans were admitted, had "everywhere polluted the Temple with slaughter;" that the priests were slain while sacrificing; that several of those who came to worship were slain in presence of their sacrifices; the dead bodies of foreigners and natives were indiscriminately heaped together, and the altar polluted with their blood. (De Bel. Jud., Lib. vi., c. 5, &c.)

4, 5. The occurrence here recorded is not described anywhere else. "*Siloe,*" was a fountain in the south-east of Jerusalem, at the foot of Mount Sion, from which water was supplied to the city (Nehemias iii. 15; John ix. 7). It had a lofty tower quite near it, on the city walls. On some occasion of very recent date, and still fresh in the recollection of our Lord's hearers, this tower fell and killed eighteen men, who were there at the time, manifestly inhabitants of Jerusalem. "*Were they debtors above all the men that dwell in Jerusalem?*" These were signally and justly punished for crimes, in the perpetration of which the other inhabitants of the city were equally guilty. They were punished as a warning and lesson to those who were mercifully spared. Our Lord adduces this second example, to show the Jews that they were debtors to the Divine justice on account of their sins, as well as the Galileans, of whom mention was made above. (5.) He declares, that those punished were not greater sinners, nor were they greater debtors to Divine justice, than the rest of their fellow-citizens, whom God mercifully spared. But unless the latter do penance, they "*likewise,*" shall, without exception, or, in the same way, be punished, certainly hereafter; and, very probably, even in this life. Forty years after this, vast multitudes of the Jews were killed under the falling towers and walls of their city. (Josephus de Bel. Jud., Lib. vi., &c.)

6, 7. Our Lord had menaced them, that unless they did penance, and produced fruits worthy of penance (iii. 8), they would all perish. He illustrates their condition, and the punishment that ultimately awaits them, by the parable of the fig-tree. The fig-tree bore no fruit; neither did they perform good works; the owner waited patiently three years; so does God wait for them; the fig-tree having become utterly useless, is cut down; so shall they.

"*Three years.*" If the fig-tree after failing for two years, brings forth no fruit the *third* year, it never yields. This parable is accommodated by some Commentators to the Jewish synagogue. But, the illustration applies to all unrepenting sinners, whose final doom is represented by that of the fig-tree in the parable.

8, 9. These verses contain the ornamental parts of the parable. They, at the same time, convey to us an idea of the great patience and long-suffering of God in regard to impenitent sinners, with whom He bears, and to whom He repeatedly tenders His graces and loving invitations to return to Him by penance, and by the performance of good works.

10. "*And He was teaching,*" means, He was in the habit of teaching—"*in their,*" or, (as in Greek) "*in one of their synagogues*"—"*synagogue, on the Sabbath.*" On the Sabbath days, the Jews assembled in their synagogues, for the purpose of having the Sacred

Scriptures explained, and of prayer, as Christians frequent their churches, on Sundays and holidays (see Matthew iv. 23). Our Lord avails Himself of the public occasion of their assembling in the synagogue to perform the miracle here recorded.

11. "*A spirit of infirmity*," an inveterate infirmity caused by an evil spirit (v. 16). "*Eighteen years*," of an inveterate nature and incurable by human skill. Evil spirits, by Divine permission, cause diseases and bodily harm in many instances (Job ii.; Psalms lxxvii. 49; xc. 6; Mark ix. 5; Luke iv. 33). "*Bent down*," &c. She almost crept along the ground.

12, 13. Our Lord rarely worked miracles, unasked. Here, with the view of reprehending the superstition of the Pharisees, in regard to Sabbatical observances, for which reprehension He saw that the murmuring about to take place, would furnish a befitting occasion—He calls the woman to Him, and viewing her with the eyes of mercy, lays His hand upon her, which indicates His power, and He pronounces her cured; He Himself, by His Almighty power, curing her, at the same time. "*Loosed from thy infirmity.*" *Loosed*, because her sinews and muscles had been hitherto contracted. "*Immediately she was straight,*" the curvature was gone, and she assumed her natural straightness of body. She "*glorified God*," acknowledging and loudly proclaiming the intervention of Divine power in her favour. No doubt, the multitude present, joined her in doing so.

14. "*The ruler of the synagogue,*" one of the presidents of the synagogue, speaking in the name of the rest. It seems there were several rulers in each synagogue, no doubt, with due subordination (Matthew ix. 18; Mark v. 22; Acts xiii. 5, 15). "*Being angry,*" or affecting to be so.

"*That Jesus had healed,*" miraculously effected a cure, without human appliances, by the sole operation of His power. His anger was ostensibly caused by his great zeal in regard to what he affected to consider as a violation of the Sabbath publicly, in the very synagogue, where the ordinances of the law are inculcated; but, in reality it proceeded from envy, and the knowledge that a miracle thus publicly performed would redound to the glory of our Lord.

"*Answering said to the multitude.*" Our Redeemer had frequently before this chastised the Pharisees for their ignorance and hypocrisy. Fearing a similar castigation, the man addressed not our Lord, but the multitude. He would rather see the wretched woman for ever suffering and bent to the earth, than see our Lord glorified by curing her.

15. "*Ye hypocrites,*" who affect sanctity which you do not possess;—in this case, they affected zeal for the law, when envy alone influenced them (see Matthew vii. 5; xv. 7).—He addresses the Ruler and those who shared in his sentiments. He exposes them by a reference to their own mode of acting, in certain cases, on the Sabbath day.

16. He shows that the cure of the woman was not a servile, but a Divine work, most worthy of the Sabbath, as it tended to glorify God, the Lord of the Sabbath. Every word is emphatic, and shows the indignity of preferring a brute beast to a human being. The antithesis is most marked, between "*the daughter of Abraham,*" and "*an ox or ass;*" the loosing of spiritual bonds in a human being, and the *corporal* loosing of a brute animal; the length of time this woman had been suffering, "*eighteen years,*" and the few hours the brute animal had been bound; the loosing of the animal required time and labour; that of the woman was performed in an

instant; the woman was restored to perfect health and sanctity, the beast was only watered for the time (A. Lapide). "*Loosed from this bond*," so grievous and afflicting.

17. "*Were ashamed*," because, being convicted of calumny, and unable to make any reply, the exposure of their dishonesty and ignorance rendered them subjects of derision.

18, 19. "*Therefore*," being inferential, conveys, that as our Lord after confounding His enemies, inspired the people with confidence, He deemed this a fitting occasion for speaking to them with profit concerning His kingdom, and for proposing illustrative parables to draw them towards it (see Matthew xiii. 31, 32).

20, 21. (Matthew xiii. 33.)

22. It is not necessary to trace a connexion between the several events recorded by the Evangelist. Here, however, the connexion seems to be, that our Lord having in the above referred to the amplitude of His kingdom (*v*. 19), now shows that but few enter it, as appears from the answer given by Him to a certain man, who interrogated Him when passing "*through the cities and towns*" on His way to Jerusalem. Likely, there is reference here to the towns and cities of Judea, whither He had sent His seventy-two disciples before Him. He speaks of the cities, &c., of Judea and Perea also (*v*. 31); for, Herod's jurisdiction lay in Galilee and Perea. Probably, He was making his way to Jerusalem, to attend some festival; it is not known for certain which festival may be referred to.

23, 24. As He was journeying, "*a certain man*," who heard Him discoursing concerning eternal salvation, "*said to Him*." Our Lord declines answering the idle question regarding the number of those saved. He, however, gives a practical and useful reply regarding the mode of securing eternal salvation, and insinuates that but few adopt the necessary means, and, by pursuing the rugged course of penance, enter on the narrow road of virtue; so that but few consequently are saved. "*Strive*." The Greek word, αγωνιζεσθε, is a strong term, implying great exertion. "*Many shall seek to enter*" the kingdom of glory, "*and shall not be able*," because they neglected to enter on the narrow and rugged road of virtue, which alone conducts to it. The few comparatively saved are understood by some, to be spoken of the entire human race, the great majority of whom are infidels, and are thus outside the Church, and consequently outside the way of salvation. But, whether the greater number of the members of the Church are saved or damned, it is hard to say. Some hold the former opinion, because the greater number receive the Sacraments at death; others, the latter, on account of the lives of Christians so little in accordance with their Christian profession. St. Augustine's rule is, as men live, so they die. The views of St. Chrysostom (Hom. 40, ad Populum Antioch), and of St. Augustine (Lib. 4, contra Cresconium, c. 53), are alarming. They seem very harsh and improbable (see Matthew vii. 14, Commentary on.)

25. Our Lord follows up the subject of exclusion from the kingdom of heaven in the subjoined parable, which, in its literal sense, peculiarly applies to the Jews, who saw our Lord on earth. "*Ate and drank in His presence*," &c. In its application, it embraces all Christians, who shall earnestly desire, and shall call in vain for

admittance; and it is conveyed, that calling him Lord, or alleging past relations of familiarity will not avail, if they neglected good works. In that case, He shall neither know nor acknowledge them. In the parable, "*the Master of the house*" represents our Lord Himself; and, although it strictly refers to the Jews in the first instance, it may, by accommodation, be referred to all Christians who, in a still higher sense can say, when they approach the holy table, "*we have eaten and drunk,*" &c.

26. "*But when.*" The Greek means, "but, *from* the time," or, "*when once* He shall be gone in," &c. For, "*shall be gone in,*" the Greek is ἐγερθῇ, "*has risen up,*" to go and see that the doors are properly secured (Matthew xxv. 10).

27. (See Matthew vii. 22, 23.)
28, 29. (See Matthew viii. 11, 12.)
30. (See Matthew xix. 30; xx. 16.)

31. "*The same day,*" on which He delivered the preceding discourse, and alluded to the transferring of the Gospel from the Jews to the Gentiles.

"*Some of the Pharisees,*" who were found scattered through every part of Judea and Galilee. These were the greatest enemies of our Lord, and against them, He never fails to hurl His most unsparing denunciations, publicly reproaching them with their hypocrisy, envy, avarice, &c. (Matthew xxiii. 13-36.) On this occasion, these hypocrites, stung with envy at our Lord's preaching, and maddened at His success among the people, who were becoming alienated from themselves, affect benevolence towards Him, for whose death they were really anxious. They tell him "*to depart.*" "*For Herod hath a mind to kill thee.*" This probably occurred in Perea. Others, with Maldonatus, think it occurred in Galilee. It is, however, to be borne in mind, that the Evangelist had already referred to our Lord's departure from Galilee (ix. 52; Matthew xix. 1). It may be, that the Evangelist here recapitulates his former narrative. Some hold that the Pharisees themselves feigned and concocted this, and that it was utterly untrue; inasmuch as Herod was most anxious to see our Lord, and was greatly pleased when, at His Passion, He was sent to him by Pilate. It may, however, be, that Herod, who was a perfect master of dissimulation, as he seemed to show respect for the Baptist (Mark vi. 20), though he afterwards put him to death, entertained feelings of aversion for our Lord, for having borne testimony to the innocence of John, and would be glad to make away with Him, although affecting respect and a desire to see Him. Some infer from our Lord's answer, telling them to go back and tell Herod his answer (32, 33), that the Pharisees and Herod had a previous understanding on the subject, and that Herod was desirous of sending Him away from his territories without incurring the odium of putting Him to death.

32. "*Tell that fox,*" so called on account of his astuteness and cunning. Our Lord thus shows, He is not afraid of the countenance of the mighty in the discharge of His duty. He, the powerful "*Lion of the tribe of Juda,*" was not afraid of a cunning, timid fox. The Sovereign King of Heaven fearlessly pronounces judgment, and describes the character of a weak creature. Some think, that by "*that fox*" (Greek, "*this fox*"), our Lord meant the man who spoke to Him, regarding Herod's intentions, and the whole of the Pharisees who, assuming the character of Herod, are denounced by our Lord as timid hypocrites and cunning dissemblers. When addressing them, our Lord directly speaks of Herod, of whom He shows He was not afraid.

"*Behold I cast out devils,*" &c. I am engaged in works of beneficence, for which I am deserving of gratitude and good will, rather than hatred or envy. I am under no apprehension of him or of you in the fearless performance of these works of mercy. I mean to continue doing so, for the short time still remaining to Me. "*To-day and to-morrow,*" mean, a short time.

"*And the third day.*" Shortly after that. "*I am consummated.*" My end is come, when I shall have consummated all that had been assigned to Me to do, and fully accomplished the end of My mission here on earth.

33. "*Nevertheless.*" Although the time remaining for Me is but brief, that is no reason why I should remain inactive, or timidly yield to idle threats. In spite of you and Herod, I shall preach and labour. "*I must walk.*" According to the decrees of My Father, I am freely to continue working in the same way, advancing from place to place—"*walk*" means, to work—to the very last moment of My life. Neither need I fear that Herod will kill Me, nor shall I remain here in Perea. I shall push forwards towards Jerusalem, "*because it cannot be,*" looking to the ordinary course of events—looking to what has generally occurred although from time to time, there may be cases of exception—"*that a prophet perish out of Jerusalem.*" It seems to be a sad privilege, almost exclusively reserved for the inhabitants of Jerusalem—to which the following apostrophe has reference (*v.* 34), that they should be the murderers of the prophets in general. And I predict that in the decrees of My Father, they are destined to be the murderers of Me also, the Lord and Chief of all the prophets. Hence, I need have no dread of death at the hands of Herod. This is reserved for the unhappy Jerusalem. Several prophets were killed away from Jerusalem. Some in Samaria by Jezabel (3 Kings xviii. 13; xix. 10). Neither was Jeremias nor Ezechiel killed there; the former was killed in Egypt, the latter in Chaldea, as we are informed by Epiphanius (*in eorum Vita*).

34, 35. (See Matthew xxiii. 37-39.)

CHAPTER XIV.

ANALYSIS.

In this chapter is recorded the cure of the dropsical man by our Lord on the Sabbath-day (1-6). He inculcates humility (7-11), and points out whom we should invite to our feasts, if we expect spiritual remuneration (12-15). The Parable of the great Supper (15-24). The necessity of prudent forethought on the part of His disciples (25-35).

TEXT.

*A*ND it came to pass when Jesus went into the house of one of the chief of the Pharisees on the sabbath-day to eat bread, that they watched him.

2. And behold, there was a certain man before him that had the dropsy.

3. And Jesus answering, spoke to the lawyers and Pharisees, saying: Is it lawful to heal on the sabbath-day?

4. But they held their peace. But he taking him, healed him, and sent him away.

5. And answering them, he said: Which of you shall have an ass or an ox fall into a pit; and will not immediately draw him out on the sabbath-day?

6. And they could not answer him to these things.

7. *And he spoke a parable also to them that were invited, marking how they chose the first seats at the table, saying to them:*

8. *When thou art invited to a wedding, sit not down in the first place, lest perhaps one more honourable than thou be invited by him;*

9. *And he that invited thee and him, come and say to thee, Give this man place: and then thou begin with shame to take the lowest place.*

10. *But when thou art invited, go, sit down in the lowest place: that when he who invited thee cometh, he may say to thee: Friend, go up higher. Then shalt thou have glory before them that sit at table with thee.*

11. *Because every one that exalteth himself, shall be humbled: and he that humbleth himself, shall be exalted.*

12. *And he said to him also that had invited him: When thou makest a dinner or a supper, call not thy friends, nor thy brethren, nor thy kinsmen, nor thy neighbours who are rich: lest perhaps they also invite thee again, and a recompense be made to thee.*

13. *But when thou makest a feast, call the poor, the maimed, the lame, and the blind.*

14. *And thou shalt be blessed, because they have not wherewith to make thee recompense: for recompense shall be made thee at the resurrection of the just.*

15. *When one of them that sat at table with him, had heard these things, he said to him: Blessed is he that shall eat bread in the kingdom of God.*

COMMENTARY.

1. "*And it came to pass.*" St. Luke, who alone mentions this occurrence, does not say when it took place, whether in immediate connexion with what precedes, or on some other occasion.

2. "*One of the chiefs of the Pharisees,*" a man of great consideration, position and influence among them. He was by sect, a "Pharisee," and possessed some authority and dignity among the people; or, the words may mean, He was one of the rulers of the synagogue, and by sect a Pharisee; for, the rulers of the synagogue were not all Pharisees (John vii. 48).

"*To eat bread,*" means, "*to take food.*" The Jews enjoyed better cheer on the Sabbath and festival than on other days (Tobias ii. 9). No doubt, our Redeemer was invited on the occasion; and although He well knew the deadly hostility of the sect towards Him, He still went, wishing to avail Himself of every opportunity of doing good. From the following words, "*they were watching Him,*" many infer that the Pharisee invited Him from the motive of finding something censurable in His conduct.

"*And they were watching Him.*" "*And,*" is superfluous, or it may be used for *then*. "*They,*" viz., those present, "*the lawyers and Pharisees*" (v. 3).

This man, afflicted with the dropsy, was either introduced by the Pharisees on purpose to see if our Lord would cure him on the Sabbath; or, the man himself who, doubtless, was well known to the family of the house, may have presented himself before they sat down to table, in the hope that our Lord, seeing his miserable condition, would of Himself cure him without being asked to do so, as it was the Sabbath day.

3. "*Answering,*" is used to signify, in the Gospel, beginning to speak (see Matthew xi. 25); or, "*answering*" their hidden thoughts and tacit questionings within themselves. "*Is it lawful?*" &c. Our Lord well knew their minds, and that they would censure Him as a violator of the Sabbath; still, He puts the

question to confound them; if they answered affirmatively, then, they would have no grounds for censuring the act of curing; if negatively, then, He would have an opportunity of proving the contrary (as in v. 5).

4. They were afraid, if they answered affirmatively, of contradicting their own teaching; if negatively, of being refuted by Him as contradicting their own practice. *"Taking him,"* touching him with His hand, to show the exercise of Divine power. *"Healed him,"* all of a sudden, *"and sent him away,"* rejoicing in the cure that had been mercifully wrought on him, in the presence of all.

5. *"Answering"* (see above). By an *argumentum a minori ad majus*, He proves, from their own mode of acting in certain cases, the lawfulness of the act He had been after performing. He performs it first, and then justifies it. The taking of an ass or an ox out of a pit involved more servile work and bodily labour than the cure of the dropsical man; and the cure of a human being was of greater value than the preservation of a brute animal. (See xiii. 15, &c.) For *"an ass,"* some MSS., among them the Vatican, have υἱος, *a son*. But, the Vulgate is the most probable—*"ass and ox"* are put for any domestic animal, as they are the domestic animals most common.

6. Although convicted by the evident force of His reasoning, and His reference to their own practical interpretation of the law in cases of less importance than that now in question; still, envy prevented them from giving utterance to what they must have thought regarding our Lord's mode of acting; hence, they held their tongues.

7. Having cured the infirm man of bodily disease, He now wishes to cure them of the spiritual disease under which He saw them labouring, viz., ambition and pride. The Pharisees looked upon themselves as raised above others by their external profession of sanctity, and, therefore, entitled to greater respect. They watched Him. He now, in turn, watches them in a spirit of charity. He spoke to them after they were seated at table, a parable founded on what He witnessed, viz., their anxiety to secure the most honourable places at table; and while adducing this parable or example relating directly to the practice of humility at marriage feasts, under it, He meant to inculcate a lesson of humility for all other occasions as well. This is the moral conclusion pointed out in verse 11. It is not, strictly speaking, a *"parable."* It is rather an example, conveying a lesson of humility in all cases; or, it may be, that our Lord proposed a parable, omitted by St. Luke, of which this is the application (Maldonatus).

10. Similar is the lesson inculcated (Proverbs xxv. 6; Ecclesiasticus iii. 20, &c.) While referring to human glory, which alone influenced the Pharisees, our Lord inculcates true humility, by the external humiliation in this case; self-abasement before God and man (Philip. ii. 3, &c.), which will exalt us before God here and hereafter.

11. This is the general decree of God, raising the humble, depressing the proud, as well in the sight of God as of men, lowering and raising them in their relations towards God and man (see Matthew xxiii. 12).

12. After having inculcated a lesson of humility in regard to His fellow guests,

our Lord now addressing His host, recompenses him by a return of spiritual food, viz., a remedy against avarice, which he much needed—for the corporal food which He deigned to receive at his hands, although He needed no corporal food, as it is He that opens His hand and fills every animal with benediction.

"*Who are rich*," that is, invite not thy rich friends. "*Rich*," affects the preceding. One may invite his poor friends with as much spiritual remuneration as any other poor.

"*Lest they invite thee again*," &c. To be liberal to those who are likely to make a return, is, according to St. Ambrose, a feeling or sentiment of avarice. "*Hospitalem remuneraturis esse affectus est avaritiæ.*" Cicero gives utterance to a similar sentiment (Lib. 1, *de officiis*). So, does Pliny (Lib. 9, Epist. 30). Our Lord does not here forbid our inviting friends, relatives, &c., as this would have the effect of cementing concord and charity, which He Himself wishes on all occasions to promote. He merely counsels us, if we wish to derive the greatest spiritual profit and the greatest amount of merit from the exercise of hospitality, to invite the poor, from whom we expect no return. Thus our motives will be more pure, and our actions performed for God alone, who will not be outdone in generosity at the proper time.

13. "*Call the poor, the maimed, the lame, and the blind*," who are poor. The word "*poor*," affects all. If they were rich, it mattered not whether they were maimed, or lame, &c., so far as the remuneration hereafter was concerned.

14. "*Thou shalt be blessed.*" As regards the full remuneration in the life to come is concerned, since you can expect none in this, as they have it not in their power. Having hidden your goods in the bosom of the poor, you have made God your debtor. Full "*recompense shall be made to thee in the resurrection of the just*," that is, in the everlasting life to come, both as to soul and body. Then, unlike the remuneration received in this life, which is only temporary and transitory in its effects, an eternal weight of glory shall be bestowed on us for the smallest relief given in God's name to the least of our brethren. Our Lord speaks as if the resurrection were for the just alone; because they alone shall rise to glory, and shall receive the reward of good works. The wicked shall rise, but only to receive condemnation.

15. One of those who sat at table, touched with what our Lord had said regarding the rewards to be given in the resurrection of the just, to such as invited the poor, &c., to their banquet, cried out, from an anxious desire of being partaker of these delights, "*Blessed is he that shall eat bread*," &c., that is, partake of food, shall sit down to the banquet prepared for the just, "*in the kingdom of God*," when the just shall be inebriated with the plenty of God's house, and shall drink of the torrents of His delights. It may be, that this man entertained carnal notions regarding the delights of the life to come, and thought they consisted in eating and drinking and all sorts of good cheer. Others, with (Jansenius Gandav.) are of opinion, that he did not entertain such carnal notions; because, our Lord, as appears from the following, would seem to confirm his ideas rather than correct them.

TEXT.

16. *But he said to him: A certain man made a great supper, and invited many.*

17. *And he sent his servant at the hour of supper to say to them that were invited, that they should come, for now all things are ready.*

ST. LUKE, CHAP. XIV.

18. And they began all at once to make excuse. The first said to him, I have bought a farm, and I must needs go out and see it; I pray thee hold me excused.

19. And another said, I have bought five yoke of oxen, and I go to try them: I pray thee, hold me excused.

20. And another said, I have married a wife, and therefore I cannot come.

21. And the servant returning told these things to his lord. Then the master of the house being angry, said to his servant: Go out quickly into the streets and lanes of the city, and bring in hither the poor and the feeble and the blind and the lame.

22. And the servant said: Lord, it is done as thou hast commanded, and yet there is room.

23. And the lord said to the servant: Go out into the high-ways and hedges; and compel them to come in, that my house may be filled.

24. But I say unto you, that none of those men that were invited, shall taste of my supper.

25. And there went great multitudes with him; and turning, he said to them:

26. If any man come to me, and hate not his father, and mother, and wife, and children, and brethren, and sisters, yea and his own life also, he cannot be my disciple.

27. And whosoever doth not carry his cross and come after me cannot be my disciple.

28. For which of you having a mind to build a tower, doth not first sit down and reckon the charges that are necessary, whether he have wherewithal to finish it:

29. Lest after he hath laid the foundation, and he is not able to finish it, all that see it begin to mock him,

30. Saying: This man began to build, and was not able to finish.

31. Or what king about to go to make war against another king, doth not first sit down and think whether he be able with ten thousand to meet him that with twenty thousand cometh against him?

32. Or else whilst the other is yet afar off, sending an embassy, he desireth conditions of peace.

33. So likewise every one of you that doth not renounce all that he possesseth, cannot be my disciple.

34. Salt is good. But if the salt shall lose its savour, wherewith shall it be seasoned?

35. It is neither profitable for the land, nor for the dunghill, but shall be cast out. He that hath ears to hear, let him hear.

COMMENTARY.

16. In the following parable, our Lord shows, that many of the chief men among the Jews who had been invited to the joys of God's kingdom, which He, pursuing the subject, represents under the figure of an earthly banquet, would be excluded from it, owing to their own fault; and, that those whom they contemned among both Jews and Gentiles would be admitted to the places of honour and enjoyment which they forfeited by their sins and neglect, nay more, by their resistance to divine grace and God's gracious calls. Whatever difference of opinion may exist as to the meaning of the several parts of this parable, there is none whatever as to its scope and object. It directly and immediately refers to the reprobation of the Jews and the calling of the Gentile world to the Gospel. The very words of the parable, and the context, evidently convey this; and our Lord employs the parable of the great Supper, as the least offensive way of conveying to that unhappy people, the dreadful sentence of reprobation which they had provoked against themselves, in punishment of their repeated resistance to grace.

Although the present parable is conveyed in different words and under different circumstances of time and place from that (chap. xxii. 1, &c., of Matthew), still, the scope and application of both is substantially the same. The "*certain man,*" refers to Almighty God. The concluding words, "*my supper,*" &c., would show it applies to our Lord, who was God, as well as man. The "*great supper*" is variously interpreted. Some understand it of the Incarnation of the Son of God, when He wedded human nature indissolubly to Himself, and united it personally to the Divine Word.

But, as there is question of a feast, and its accompanying enjoyment, it seems more likely, that the "*great supper,*"—"*great;*" because worthy, of the Sovereign munificence of the King of Heaven—refers to the mystery of man's redemption, and to the manifold and superabundant graces plentifully dispensed in the New Law, as the result of the Incarnation or marriage-union of the Son of God with human nature; and also to the inconceivable glory and heavenly bliss, to which these graces of the New Law securely conduct us. This eternal glory and bliss in the Church triumphant, in the life to come, commences from faith here, where we are members of the Church militant. This primary and literal signification contains, probably, under it another, or mystical signification, a thing by no means uncommon in SS. Scripture (Gal. iv. 24; Hebrews i. 5). The supper may, by accommodation, be applied to the "*great supper,*" of the adorable Eucharist, wherein the Son of God has left Himself to us to the end of time, a perpetual memorial of His love and wonders. This is one of the greatest sources of grace in the New Law, already referred to. The Church accommodates the passage to the adorable Eucharist, in the Gospel of Sunday within Oct. of Corpus Christi.

"*And called many.*" The entire Jewish people. He called them first, through the ministry of John the Baptist. Our Lord Himself next, preached to them in person, employing the same theme as the Baptist, "*do penance,*" &c. Lastly, He sent His Apostles and disciples to invite them and reclaim them. It may be said, with truth, that God had specially and by anticipation called the Jews to a share in this banquet before it actually took place. They were His chosen inheritance, with whom he deposited His oracles. All their privileges having reference to this special invitation, are summed up. (Rom. ix. 4, &c.) They had been occasionally favoured with the ministry of His prophets, whose threats and promises might be regarded in the light of so many invitations to partake beforehand, of that "*great supper,*" in which was to be eaten, "*the Lamb slain from the beginning of the world*" (Apoc. xiii. 8).

17. "*His servant,*" represents the Apostles and preachers of the Gospel. "*At supper time,*" giving a more special and particular invitation to those who previously received a general invitation (see Matthew xxii. 3).

"*Now all things are ready.*" Now they can taste by faith and grace, beforehand, of the joys and bliss of that kingdom thrown open by the death of Christ.

18. (See Matthew xxii. 3.) To the Jews, in the first place, the invitation was confined by Divine appointment. "*Go ye not into the ways of the Gentiles . . . . But go ye rather to the lost sheep of the house of Israel*" (Matthew x. 6), was the injunction given to the Apostles. But the Jews refused coming, on several frivolous pretexts. Inordinate attachment to the things of earth—a characteristic feature of the Jewish people at all times—proved an obstacle to one class, and made them despise the riches of Heaven. "*I have bought a farm, and must needs go see it.*"

19. A feeling of undue curiosity, a sceptical spirit of doubting inquiry, and intellectual pride prevented others. "*I have bought five yoke,*" &c.

20. The gratification of impure passions and sensual delights prevented a third class. "*I have married a wife,*" &c. In a word, the three great leading maxims which rule this world, and domineer over men, viz., "*the concupiscence of the flesh, the concupiscence of the eyes, and the pride of life*" (1 John ii. 16)—the great obstacles to the salvation of the world at all times, and signally at present—prevented the Jews from embracing the Gospel, which inculcated on its followers the opposite principles, viz., the mortification of the flesh, with its vices and concupiscences—the mortification of avarice, in the practice of poverty, and in detachment from the passing goods of this life, in view of those never-failing goods in the life to come; and the mortification of pride, in the practice of humility. These latter are the leading principles of that new life which Jesus Christ came down to renew with His Spirit; the opposite of those cherished by this sinful world which He came down to rescue and redeem.

21. On the servant announcing the result of the invitation, the master of the household becomes exceedingly angry. His servants, the Apostles, are sent out to call in the most abject and despised among the Jews. He himself, His Apostles and disciples execute this commission throughout the whole extent of Judea and Galilee. The haughty, proud Pharisees and priests are rejected. The weak, foolish, and contemptible are called, in order to confound the strong, the wise, and the powerful. "*The Publicans and harlots go before them into the kingdom of God*" (Matthew xxi. 31). According to the most common opinion, the preaching indicated in this verse took place before our Lord's death, and was confined to the poor, ignorant, and repentant sinners among the Jews. "*The streets and lanes of the city,*" indicate the precincts of Jerusalem and Judea.

22. Notwithstanding the number of the Jews who obeyed the call of our Lord and His Apostles, still the supper hall was not filled. It was comparatively empty. Then, the king issues another commission. The Apostles, after they had been endued with strength from on high, and after the fulness of the Spirit had been poured down upon them, go forth, armed with a commission different from that which they received on a former occasion, viz., to confine their labours to the narrow precincts of Judea, and only to look after "*the lost sheep of the house of Israel.*" The plenitude of the Gentiles is now to be admitted. The Apostles are to "*preach the Gospel to every creature,*" to "*go out into the hedges and highways,*" into the neglected and uncultivated regions of the Gentiles, hitherto sunk in vice and error. They are to employ the most cogent of arguments, viz., miracles, together with the example of holy, laborious, unselfish, mortified lives, "*in ostensione spiritus et virtutis,*" to induce them to obey the Divine call, and thus, in a certain sense, "*to compel*" their stubborn wills to bend their necks under the yoke of faith, to offer that holy violence, which alone carries, as it were, by assault, the kingdom of heaven, and thus induce them "*to enter;*" so that, "*the house,*" the Church of God, the ante-room of the banquet hall in heaven, "*may be filled,*" and they may pass, from the Church militant on earth, to the joys of the Church triumphant in heaven. The explanation of "*compel*" above given, which supposes full exercise of free will, strongly influenced by powerfully persuasive external motives, aided internally by the operation of God's efficacious graces, leaves no room for the false charge brought against Christianity, that it is to be embraced against man's will, and that persecution for religious opinions is here sanctioned. The spirit of Christianity is

essentially a spirit of mildness. It allows no other force to be used in bringing Pagans into the Church, save that species of moral persuasion and pressing invitation which we employ in urging men to receive benefits at our hands: as Lot compelled the angels (Genesis xix. 3), and the disciples compelled our Lord, at Emmaus (Luke xxiv. 29. It is in this way the Church wishes to compel men to embrace the faith. (2 Tim. iv. 2, &c.) The "*assent by stripes*," sometimes employed, is denounced by Gregory the Great, when prohibiting the persecution of the Jews at Rome, for refusing to embrace the faith. The Church never approved of the persecution of heretics as such, and if any examples be adduced where violence was used, these are not to be attributed to the Church, any more than other misdeeds of individual members. Heretics are, in many instances, violators of the civil laws; rebels to the constituted authorities. For such crimes, they are justly visited with temporal punishment. There is nothing preposterous in the Church visiting with punishment her rebellious children, and thus endeavouring to bring them back to a sense of duty; any more than there would be for loving parents to reduce disobedient children to a sense of duty by punishing them. It was thus God Himself brought back St. Paul, on the road to Damascus. The Church herself, in her Liturgy, calls on God to force our stubborn wills, leaving us still their free exercise. "*Ad Te nostras etiam rebelles compelle propitius voluntates.*" In this passage, there is no question of heretics at all; but, of Pagans, towards whom the Apostles, who received this commission, never used violence of any sort (Calmet).

24. "*But I say to you,*" &c. This is a dreadful sentence of reprobation pronounced against the Jews, who resisted the call to grace. They shall be for ever excluded from the bliss of God's kingdom—from those ineffable delights, "*which neither eye hath seen,*" &c.; and for ever consigned to the excruciating tortures of hell. "*Because I called, and you refused . . . I will also laugh in your destruction, and will mock when that shall come to you which you feared. When sudden calamity shall fall on you, and destruction . . Then they shall call upon Me, and I will not hear; they shall rise in the morning, and shall not find Me*" (Prov. i. 24-28). "*You shall seek Me, and shall not find Me, and where I am, thither you cannot come*" (John vii. 34). "*I go, and you shall seek Me, and you shall die in your sin*" (John viii. 21). This is true at all times, of obstinate, unrepenting sinners, who are deaf to God's gracious invitations to mercy and penance.

The same excuses are alleged every day, by men who are deaf to God's call and command to approach the Holy Eucharist, which is, indeed, "*a great supper.*" He lovingly threatens them: "*Amen, Amen, I say unto you, unless you eat,*" &c., and graciously invites them, "*He who eats of this bread, shall live for ever;*" still, they are insensible. They are called upon every year to approach. They allege frivolous excuses, and sometimes the same as those mentioned in the Gospel. Would to God the threat of dying in their sins, of being deprived of the Holy Eucharist at death, of calling in vain on God, when too late, of being delivered over to final impenitence, were not so frequently seen verified in regard to such, "*They shall call, I will not hear.*" "*They shall die in their sins.*" Good God! what a dreadful judgment of reprobation.

25. "*Great multitudes went with Him*"—accompanied Him on His way to Jerusalem (chap. xiii. 22), as if proclaiming that they wished to be among His followers and disciples. Taking occasion, from seeing them following Him, our Lord, turning to them, informs them, that in order to be His disciple, it was not enough to approach Him, or follow Him on foot; one must be prepared for crosses and mortifications—for sacrificing, when required, all human affections—to give up all that is nearest and dearest to us.

26. (See Matthew x. 37.) "*Hate*," not simply, but so far as they are opposed to Christ; also, in a *comparative* sense, of loving *less*, of loving them less than Christ, of loving Him more, and this shown in act, when required. Similar is the phrase, "*dilexi Jacob, Esau odio habui.*" The same is expressed by St. Matthew (x. 37), "*He that loveth father or mother more than Me, is not worthy of Me.*" The words of our Lord here are even stronger than those in St. Matthew. We must not only love Him more than them, more than our own lives; but, we must even *positively* "*hate*," not them, but whatever is in them that withdraws us from the love of Christ. We must hate in ourselves, and refuse to ourselves whatever is opposed to Him, and contrary to His law. For, the law of Christ often forbids things contrary to our wicked desires and inclinations.

27-33. (See Matthew x. 38; xvi. 24.) In this verse, our Lord shows how we are to hate our own souls, by adding, "*whosoever doth not carry his cross,*" &c. The word "*disciple,*" is understood by some, of the profession of the Christian faith, the following of our Lord, common to all Christians. In this sense, adopted by Maldonatus, the renunciation, the hatred here mentioned, is strictly preceptive; and means, that sooner than abandon Christ and His faith, we should sacrifice every thing else, be it ever so near or dear to us. Others, with Jansenius, maintain, there is question of being His disciple, like the Apostles and seventy-two disciples, and although the words may, in a general sense, apply to all Christians in regard to giving up all, sooner than abandon Christ, trampling on our own corrupt inclinations, and bearing every kind of persecution and suffering for His sake, still, the words, according to this latter opinion, apply to those who give up every thing in this world, and obey the Evangelical counsels, for the love of Him. In this sense, the words merely convey a counsel. The two following parables, or examples drawn from the ordinary concerns of life, having reference to business of great worldly importance, failure in which would involve great loss and disgrace, would seem greatly in favour of this latter opinion. The case of the builder of the tower reckoning beforehand his resources, and making his undertaking—his difficult and expensive work—dependent on his calculations, clearly enough applies to the Christian who may voluntarily resolve to embrace the state of Evangelical perfection, to which he is not strictly bound. This latter should carefully measure his strength, aided by God's grace, with the difficulties of the state he aspires to, and should he not have good grounds, amounting to a moral certainty, for believing in his power to persevere, he should not embrace it, lest afterwards, if obliged to give it up, he should expose himself to scorn and ridicule, like the builder of the unfinished house. The same is true of the example of the king about to embark in war. The application could not be easily seen in reference to the embracing of Christianity. Our Redeemer would hardly insinuate, that it was free under any circumstances, for any one to decline this important work, to decline the conflict with the enemy of man's salvation, or to enter into any compromise with him in fighting the battle of the Lord. The same is rendered more probable still, by the conclusion and application of the example (*v.* 33), "*So likewise every one of you that doth not renounce all that he possesses, cannot be My disciple,*" as if He said; you are not only to measure your strength in reference to giving up all you hold most dear, for My sake, if you wish to aspire to a state of Evangelical perfection. You must go further still, and renounce all you have in the world, if you aspire to the privilege of being more closely united to Me.

Maldonatus and others, however, who maintain there is question of embracing and retaining the faith, at every sacrifice, say, that our Lord, by the examples adduced, only means to convey, that the embracing of the Christian law, and the observance of its precepts, are not a very easy matter; and hence, as happens in regard to arduous or important worldly business, when men are about to embark on any difficult or expensive undertaking, such as raising an edifice or waging war, they consider their strength and resources; so ought Christians on embracing the law and fai h of Christ, and taking on them His yoke, bear in mind, that it is not a very easy matter, involving no trouble or sacrifice, they are undertaking; that it is not a life of enjoyment, bringing with it great temporal advantages or glory, such as the crowds following our Lord vainly imagined, in regard to our Lord's coming kingdom, which they are embracing; that they should then prepare well for its arduous duties. For, it would be a lesser evil, however enormous, never to have embraced the truth, than after having done so, to turn back (2 Peter ii. 21). Whatever in the examples adduced may serve to illustrate these points, are pertinent; the rest, ornamental. There is no use, therefore, in dwelling on the meaning of the word, "*tower*," nor on the bearing of the compromise, which the king proposes to make. There can be no compromise with the enemy of salvation, no peace or terms with him. Such peace would be utter ruin and destruction. Hence, there can be no application of this portion of the parable in the interpretation of Maldonatus. If the interpretation of Jansenius, who understands it of mere counsel, were adopted; then, there might be some room for application to the subject. It is agreed on all hands, that there are several circumstances in the literal recital of parables of a merely ornamental character, having no reference to the subject, which the parable is intended to illustrate. This observation will save Interpreters much trouble and embarrassment in endeavouring to apply several circumstances in the examples here adduced, since these circumstances are merely ornamental, and not meant to be applied at all, in truth, utterly inapplicable.

34. "*Salt is good*," for seasoning and preserving human food. This would seem to show, that in the above parables, our Lord is primarily and directly treating of the Apostles and disciples who observe the counsels of Evangelical perfection. For, it is in regard to the Apostles, our Lord uses this similitude elsewhere (Matthew v. 13; Mark ix. 49). No doubt, the words apply, in a secondary sense, to Christians at all times, who, by their good example, should entice the infidels to the faith, and confirm their brethren in the faith and practice of good works. This shows the admirable power of our Lord's teaching, which may be suited to different descriptions of men, at different ages, according to their wants and exigencies.

"*But, if the salt shall lose its savour*" (see Matthew v. 13). It is only while it retains its active properties, that salt is "*good*," that is, useful and efficacious for preserving food. But, if it loses its active properties, it becomes unsavoury, and is good for nothing; it even renders the land sterile on which it is cast, at St. Jerome tells us.

CHAPTER XV.

ANALYSIS.

In this chapter, our Lord puts forward three parables, illustrative of the great and tender mercy of God towards sinners. The first, of the lost sheep (1-7). The second, of the lost piece of silver (8-11.) The third, and most affecting of all, of the prodigal son (12-32).

TEXT.

N OW the publicans and sinners drew near unto him to hear him.

2. *And the Pharisees and the Scribes murmured, saying: This man receiveth sinners, and eateth with them.*

3. *And he spoke to them this parable, saying:*

4. *What man of you that hath an hundred sheep: and if he shall lose one of them, doth he not leave the ninety-nine in the desert, and go after that which was lost until he find it?*

5. *And when he hath found it, lay it upon his shoulders rejoicing:*

6. *And coming home call together his friends and neighbours, saying to them: Rejoice with me, because I have found my sheep that was lost?*

7. *I say to you, that even so there shall be joy in heaven upon one sinner that doth penance, more than upon ninety-nine just who need not penance.*

8. *Or what woman having ten groats, if she lose one groat, doth not light a candle and sweep the house and seek diligently, until she find it?*

9. *And when she hath found it, call together her friends and neighbours, saying: Rejoice with me, because I have found the groat which I had lost.*

10. *So I say to you, there shall be joy before the Angels of God upon one sinner doing penance.*

11. *And he said: A certain man had two sons:*

12. *And the younger of them said to his father: Father, give me the portion of substance that falleth to me. And he divided unto them his substance.*

13. *And not many days after, the younger son gathering all together, went abroad into a far country, and there wasted his substance living riotously.*

14. *And after he had spent all, there came a mighty famine in that country, and he began to be in want.*

15. *And he went, and cleaved to one of the citizens of that country. And he sent him into his farm to feed swine.*

16. *And he would fain have filled his belly with the husks the swine did eat; and no man gave unto him.*

17. *And returning to himself, he said: How many hired servants in my father's house abound with bread, and I here perish with hunger?*

18. *I will arise, and will go to my father, and say to him: Father, I have sinned against heaven, and before thee:*

19. *I am not now worthy to be called thy son; make me as one of thy hired servants.*

20. *And rising up he came to his father. And when he was yet a great way off, his father saw him, and was moved with compassion, and running to him fell upon his neck and kissed him.*

21. *And the son said to him: Father, I have sinned against heaven, and before thee, I am not now worthy to be called thy son.*

22. *And the father said to his servants: Bring forth quickly the first robe, and put it on him, and put a ring on his hand, and shoes on his feet:*

L

23. *And bring hither the fatted calf, and kill it, and let us eat and make merry:*

24. *Because this my son was dead, and is come to life again; was lost, and is found. And they began to be merry.*

25. *Now his elder son was in the field, and when he came and drew nigh to the house, he heard music and dancing:*

26. *And he called one of the servants, and asked what these things meant.*

27. *And he said to him: Thy brother is come, and thy father hath killed the fatted calf, because he hath received him safe.*

28. *And he was angry, and would not go in. His father therefore coming out began to entreat him.*

29. *And he answering, said to his father: Behold, for so many years do I serve thee, and I have never transgressed thy commandment, and yet thou hast never given me a kid to make merry with my friends:*

30. *But as soon as this thy son is come, who hath devoured his substance with harlots, thou hast killed for him the fatted calf.*

31. *But he said to him: Son, thou art always with me, and all I have is thine.*

32. *But it was fit that we should make merry and be glad, for this thy brother was dead, and is come to life again: he was lost, and is found.*

COMMENTARY.

1. *Now the Publicans,"* &c. Among the multitudes who followed our Lord (chap. xiv. 25), were to be found "*Publicans*" (see Matthew ix. 10). "*And sinners,*" that is, other public and well-known sinners, who were drawn to Him by His heavenly doctrine, by His promise of pardon on the condition of doing penance, by the experience they had of the merciful meekness displayed by Him towards the most abandoned sinners, while, towards the Pharisees and others reputed just, they knew Him to display the most marked sternness.

The Greek has, "*all the Publicans,*" &c., that is, many of them used to approach Him without reserve, when an opportunity offered.

"*Drew near to Him,*" is interpreted by Maldonatus, were wont to draw near to Him, thus denoting custom, and not referring to any one particular occasion.

2. "*The Pharisees,*" &c. These men were probably among those who were rebuked by our Lord at Simon's feast (xiv. 15). Wherever our Lord appeared in public, in the discharge of His sacred mission, the Pharisees were to be found tracking His steps, for the purpose of narrowly watching all He did and said, with the view of having wherewith to accuse Him.

"*Murmured.*" When they should have praised Him for His clemency, they spoke to the people in terms of censure and reproach (see Matthew ix. 10; Luke v. 30). These hypocrites erroneously supposed that, as in the case of legal defilement caused by contact with any unclean object, their souls were defiled by contact with sinners.

"*This man receiveth sinners, and eateth with them.*" Very likely, our Lord was invited by these men to partake of food, after His discourses. He was pleased to accept such invitations. Hence, the words mean, He takes food with them, on all occasions.

3. In order to refute them, although undeserving of any answer, our Lord, with His accustomed mildness, addresses to them the following parables, or similitudes,

of the lost sheep, of the lost piece of money, and of the prodigal son, with a view of showing how agreeable and pleasing to God is the conversion of sinners; with what great care they should be sought after; with what great clemency they should be received back. He thus justifies His own conduct, and conveys, that if the Pharisees had the least share in the Spirit of God, far from murmuring, they should rejoice at seeing the mercy displayed by our Lord towards sinners, His solicitude and loving condescension in their regard. These examples, or parables, are founded on the daily and ordinary occurrences of life.

4. The straying sheep is frequently employed in SS. Scripture, to represent the sinner straying from the ways of God (Isaias liii. 6; 1 Peter ii. 25). By "*the ninety-nine sheep,*" St. Ambrose understands, the heavenly hosts whom our Lord left in heaven, and came to redeem "*the one that was lost;*" which, according to St. Ambrose—*in hunc locum*—represents human nature, or lost man. This "*sheep,*" though but one, represents many; since we all together, while constituting one body, are many members. "*For, the Son of Man was come to seek and save what was lost*" (Matthew xviii. 11), that is to say, all men. "*For, as all die in Adam; so all shall revive again in Christ*" (1 Cor. xv.) "Let us rejoice, that this sheep which was lost in Adam, is found again, and carried back by Jesus Christ. The arms in which He carries it, are the arms of His cross. . . . This rich Pastor, of whose flock we form only the one hundredth part, has an infinity of other blessed spirits, whom He leaves behind Him in the heavenly mountains, who share in His joy, and rejoice with Him upon the redemption of the human race" (St Ambrose). It, however, more probably refers to an individual sinner, who, by sin against faith or morals, separates himself from the society of the good, as appears from the conclusion, "*one sinner doing penance*" (*v.* 10). Hence, the lost sheep and groat clearly refer to some one sinful man returning to God by penance, rather than to the entire human race. Our Lord, in this example, means to give an idea of the magnitude of the loss of one, since, to recover it, He postpones the care of others for a time.

5. "*Rejoicing,*" with a singular feeling of joy. Not that the lost one is loved or valued more than the ninety-nine, who were free from danger. Our Lord meant only to convey, that the Pastor experiences a sensible feeling of joy, on account of finding this lost one, which he did not experience on account of the others. Men often feel greater joy on account of some unexpected turn of fortune, even of lesser value, than they do on account of their former acquisitions, though far more valuable than what they unexpectedly acquire. Men experience a more sensible feeling of joy on the recovery of an article of inferior value, after it had been lost, than they do for articles of greater value, safely secured. This joy partly arises from the opposite feeling of sorrow which they before sensibly experienced, and which is now removed.

6. From this we see the great, exuberant joy, which he could not confine to himself, but felt forced to communicate to his neighbours, and to all his friends. This, as appears from the following verse, denotes the joy caused by the conversion of a sinner, to the citizens of heaven, viz., our Lord as man, the angels, and souls of the just, who are admitted to the presence and beatific vision of God.

7. This is the application of the above similitude, from which our Lord wishes us to infer, that far from murmuring at His tenderness and mercy towards sinners—

these lost sheep, whom He wishes to bring back to the fold of His Heavenly Father—the Pharisees should rather rejoice with the angels of God on seeing it. The "*one sinner that doth penance*," may refer to the entire human race plunged in sin, before the Incarnation of our Lord. For them, penance is the only means of appeasing God, and sharing in the fruits of His redemption, who bore our sins, and carried us in His arms on the cross. Or, it may denote some individual sinner, converted by the grace of God, and returning by penance, to join the just in the Church, who were preserved from falling into grievous sins, and straying away from God.

7. "*There shall be joy in heaven*," both with Christ, as man, the Supreme Pastor, and the angels and just souls, who are "*his neighbours and friends*" there. The words, "*shall be*," refer to the future abode of our Lord as man, and of the just souls, in heaven, which they did not yet enter; or, "*shall be*," may signify *is*, or, is *wont to be*. By the "*ninety-nine just who need not penance*," are commonly understood, not such men as are altogether sinless, since we all cry out daily, "*forgive us our trespasses*," &c., but, men who are free from mortal sin, and need not a change of heart or life, such as penance implies, and especially need not such penance as those require who are great sinners.

As to the comparison between the feeling of joy in heaven, which is said to be greater in case of one converted sinner, than in that of ninety-nine just men, it is not to be understood, as if the salvation of one were a greater good than that of ninety-nine, or that God loves or esteems one man more than ninety-nine, but that He feels greater actual present and sensible joy from the recovery of the lost one, than for the ninety-nine—first, on account of the unexpected suddenness of the pleasure succeeding the pain which the loss had caused him (see Matthew xviii. 12, 13); 2ndly, because the converted sinner usually displays far greater fervour, owing to his gratitude for the recovery and bestowal of God's friendship, than is displayed by those who do not sensibly feel the sweets of God's returning friendship. The great joy which the conversion of a sinner brings to God and His angels justifies our Lord against the calumnies of His enemies.

This passage furnishes a crushing reply to those who object to the doctrine of the Invocation of Saints, on the ground that they know not what occurs on this earth. In the first place, the assertion that the saints know nothing of what passes on earth, is utterly gratuitous, hazarded without any proof from Scripture or Tradition. Wherever in Scripture there is allusion to absence of knowledge on the part of the dead, there can be no reference whatever to the saints, who *live* with God in glory. For, in proving the Resurrection against the Sadducees, our Lord, by calling Himself the God of Abraham, Isaac, &c., shows that these still live. For, "*He is not God of the dead, but of the living*" (Matthew xxii. 32). The saints, therefore, *live* with God in glory. Again, when it is said in Scripture, that the saints *know* not their children on earth, it means, that they *disown* them on account of their sins, just as God *knows not* the workers of iniquity.

Secondly, we have in this passage the clearest evidence that the saints and angels in heaven do know what occurs on earth. For, they rejoice at the conversion of individual sinners scattered all over the earth. What is said of the angels, applies equally to the just, who "*shall be as the angels of God.*" If they did not *know* of the conversion of the sinners, how could they *feel joy* thereat. In the Book of Tobias (xii. 12), the Angel Raphael tells Tobias that when engaged in acts of mercy he prayed with tears, he (Raphael) offered up his prayers to the Lord. How offer them up unless *he knew* of them?

But, if it be asked *how* can the angels and saints know what passes in different parts of the earth? our only answer is, we cannot say. Whether it be through the medium of visual rays or undulating sounds; or whether, as is more probable, they see all things in God, who makes this knowledge a portion of their beatitude, is perfectly unknown to us. *How* God communicates this knowledge to them we know not, nor does it concern us to know. It is sufficient for us to know and believe the revealed fact, or doctrine. The *mode* in which that fact is accomplished is quite another question, beyond our knowledge and comprehension.

And, let us ask those, who reject the doctrine of the Invocation of Saints—the truth of which is revealed in Scripture, and proposed by the Church—simply because they cannot understand the *mode* of its existence, do they understand the *mode* of the existence of everything else they believe, or affect to believe, before admitting it? The first truth of either *natural* or revealed religion is, that there is one God, existing from eternity, filling heaven and earth with His immensity, in whom "*we live and move and have our being.*" Do they understand God's eternal existence and glorious immensity? The first truth, which is the foundation of the Christian faith, is, the mystery of the Trinity—one God, in three distinct Divine persons—the Nature, in which these persons are one, and the Personality, by which they are distinguished, being one and the same thing. Do they understand *how* this is? Do they understand the mystery of the Incarnation; viz., *how* the Second Person of the adorable Trinity united human nature so perfectly to Him, that you can say of God, that He is man, and of man, that He is God, "*et verbum caro factum est.*" Do they understand this? Do they understand the mysterious and awful doctrine of Original Sin, *how* "*all sinned in one,*" how all were punished with death for the sin of that one, and all rendered liable to be excluded, on account of it, from the beatific vision of God? Do they understand *how* our Lord is really, truly, and substantially present in the Holy Eucharist, in that mode of existence, which, although we can hardly express in words, we still believe through faith, as the Council of Trent expresses it? (§ xiii., c. 1.) Do they understand the mysteries of *nature, how* the soul animates the body? &c., &c.

In truth, without unnecessarily multiplying further instances, if we were to reject everything, the *mode* of whose existence or accomplishment we cannot comprehend, there is scarcely a religious truth or natural phenomenon which we should not reject.

8-10. This second example is also intended to show the joy there is in heaven for the conversion of a sinner. Its scope is the same as that of the parable of the lost sheep. Some Commentators observe, that the parable chiefly regards, not so much the "*groat,*" which was hardly deserving of all the care and anxiety referred to,—since it was but a comparatively trifling coin, upon which was impressed the image of the reigning prince,—as the thing represented by "*the groat,*" viz., the immortal soul of man, impressed with the image and likeness of God. It was meant, like the former similitude, to refute the Pharisees, who, like the angels of heaven, should rather rejoice than murmur, at seeing sinners returning to God by the road of penance.

11. The scope of this third example is the same as that of the two preceding ones, viz., to show the great mercy of God, His joy on the return of the sinner. Hence, the Pharisees should rather commend our Lord for conversing with sinners, with a view to their return to God, than murmur, as they had ungenerously done. In the former examples, we are taught how great is the anxiety and solicitude of God in procuring the conversion of sinners; in the third, viz., that of the prodigal son, so feelingly descriptive of the reckless life of the sinner, of his penance and pardon, we are taught how great

are the benignity and joy with which God receives him on his return; all brought about, whether there be question of seeking the sinner or of receiving him back when divinely inspired to return, by the attracting force and assistance of God's own preventing and efficacious graces, without which the sinner could neither conceive a good thought conducive to salvation, nor advance a single step in the ways of justice.

"*A certain man,*" who represents, according to all, Almighty God; or, what comes to the same, our Divine Redeemer Himself, who became "*man,*" for our sakes.

"*Two sons.*" According to St. Augustine (Lib. 2, Quæst. Evang.), and others, these "*two sons*" represent two peoples, the *Jews and Gentiles*, the "*elder,*" the Jews; the "*younger,*" the Gentiles. But although the parable or example might, in an allegorical sense, apply to these different peoples, the more so, as the murmuring of the Pharisees, represented by the murmuring of the elder brother, might be regarded as the prelude to the indignation of the Jewish people afterwards, on seeing the Gospel transferred to the Gentiles; still, the "*two sons,*" more probably, refer to the just, or those reputed just, such as the Pharisees; and to the public sinners, the Publicans and harlots, whom our Lord graciously received and conversed with. For, besides that the *Gentiles* could hardly be said to be sons of God, having been estranged from Him, it was in reference to the murmuring of the Pharisees at our Lord's condescension towards sinners, who were Jews; and for the purpose of justifying His conduct, that this and the two preceding parables were introduced. Some parts of the parable would better suit those who are really just; while other parts of it, such as, for instance, the murmuring and envy of the "*elder brother*" (verses 27-29), would hardly suit these, who could not be properly represented, as feeling anger or jealous envy at the reconciliation of sinners. Unless, perhaps, it might be said, that this latter part of the parable, from verse 21, to the end, was merely ornamental, having no place in the application, which, as Tertullian observes, we need not trouble ourselves in explaining "*nec valde laboramus omnia in expositione torquere*" (Tertullian de Pudicitia, chap. 8, 9); or, that the jealousy expressed, merely signifies that such is the benignity of God towards sinners, such the abundance of graces, such the happiness He mercifully bestows, that it would be calculated to beget feelings of jealousy and envy even among the very elect.

12. "*The younger,*" borne forward by the impetuosity of youthful passions, becomes impatient of paternal restraint.

"*The portion of the substance,*" a fair and equitable portion, that would fall to me, in case of your death, or my marriage engagement. According to the Roman and Jewish laws, a man's property was entailed on his children after his death in equal portions, save that the first-born received a double portion. Hence, the father was not permitted to dispose of his property arbitrarily. Sometimes, a father during his lifetime, distributed his property in the above proportions, with certain reservations in regard to his own and his wife's support.

"*And he divided to him his substance.*" The Greek word, $\beta\iota o\varsigma$, signifies *life*, or the substance, necessary for the support of life. He gave them their respective portions of his substance, to be freely used by them. It is not said, if the elder received his; but it is understood from the parable, that having received his portion also, he left it to be wisely administered, with the rest of his father's goods, under the guardianship and care of his father.

The words of this verse convey, that God, having created man, and having endowed him with several gifts of nature and grace, "*left him free in the hand of his own counsel*" (Ecclos. xv. 14), to the full exercise of free will, which He, if invoked, will assist by

His grace. They also convey that there are some who foolishly imagine, that they can employ their goods and gifts without any further need of God's protection or dependence on His providential care, as is conveyed here in the case of the prodigal.

13. "*Not many days after.*" His youthful impetuosity hurried him headlong, to carry out without delay his purpose of gratifying his passions.

"*Gathering all together.*" Converting into money, all the property at his disposal.

"*Went abroad into a far country,*" to be far away from paternal admonition and vigilance, the more to indulge in unrestrained gratification. Applied to the sinner, this does not mean distance of place; but, of affection, "*sciendum non locorum spatiis, sed affectu, aut nos esse cum Deo aut ab eo discedere*" (St. Jerome, Ep. 146). It is "oblivion of God" (St. Augustine, Lib. Quæst. Evang. c. 33).

Of Cain, it is said, that "*he went out from the face of the Lord, and dwelt as a fugitive on the earth*" (Gen. iv. 16), after he had committed the unnatural crime of slaying his brother.

"*And there wasted his substance by living riotously;*" "*devouring his substance with harlots*" (v. 30). This conveys to us, that the sinner abused all the gifts of nature and grace, and turned them against their very Author. This abuse embraces not only carnal sins, strictly so called, but all kinds of sins, whereby man perverts the gifts and graces of God.

14. This unhappy young man having squandered all the gifts of nature and of grace; with his intellect rendered darker; his will, more and more inclined to evil; living among wicked associates, now falls into great want of spiritual bread, viz., the Word of God, and of the virtues whereby the mind is nourished and strengthened. Now destitute of everything, he finds that a great famine prevails in the country, which renders it hard even for the rich to preserve life, and, therefore, much more difficult for this destitute young stranger. This renders the subsequent part of the parable more probable, relating to his having hired himself to one of the citizens of the country, and having submitted to the most menial and revolting occupation to sustain life.

In its application to the sinner, St. Augustine understands the famine of the want of the Word of Truth (Lib. 2, Quæst. 33, in Quæst. Evangel.; so do Bede and Theophylact). St. Ambrose, St. Jerome, Euthymius—of the want of all virtues. In the region of luxury, of lust and pleasure, there is no room for virtue. In the pressure of spiritual famine, this wretched young man felt the want of the Word of God, exhortation, admonition, also of the sacraments, to help him to correct his depraved morals; hence, he is sent to feed swine.

15. We here see the dreadful condition he was reduced to, and the pressure of want which forced him to join himself to "*one of the citizens of the country.*" No employment, ever so menial or degrading, is too low for him, in order to avert death from famine. He becomes more and more estranged from God. This "*citizen*" is generally understood of the Prince of demons, of whom he becomes the slave. What an exchange for the miserable sinner, who cannot bear to be dependent on God, his loving Father, to become the slave of impure demons, bound over hand and foot, to them, and still more estranged from God. What masters compared with the loving Father whom he left! What slavery in comparison with the liberty of the children of God!

"*He sent him into his farm to feed swine.*" The most degrading condition in all countries to which a man could be reduced; but particularly degrading among the Jews, on account of their peculiar abhorrence of these unclean animals, and the provisions of the Jewish law in reference to them.

In their application to the sinner, these words show the utter degradation of those who commit sinful deeds, and glory in their shame; and the deep feeling of humiliation they should experience in considering their state, is compared by the Son of God with that of the man who was reduced to the degrading condition of feeding swine.

16. "*He would fain,*" &c., shows the extreme want to which the sinner is reduced. To this the Holy Ghost refers, according to St. Jerome, when he describes the wretched condition of the sinner under the figure of Jerusalem, that had gratuitously prostituted herself and received no recompense (Ezechiel xvi. 34).

"*And no one gave unto him.*" Here are probably understood the words, *nutritious food*, or *bread*, or *food fit for human use;* since, he needed not, that any one would give him of "*the husks*" which he was dealing out to the swine, unless it be meant that the husks should be distributed according to measure, to the swine; and that even of these he had not remaining what he would wish to use for satisfying the cravings of hunger; it may be, that this cruel master was more concerned for the wants of his cattle than of his domestics—a thing not altogether uncommon in this hard world. The former seems the more probable, since, of the *husks*, no one could give him or allow him any save the master himself. What a just retribution on him who squandered his property luxuriously on others, now to find no one to stretch him in his dire distress, a morsel of bread.

These "*husks,*" according to some, meant the rind or outward covering of grain, given to swine, and utterly unfit for human use; according to others, a kind of pulse or acorn, usually given to swine. Considering the dire famine above referred to, the former is the more probable. In their application to the case of the sinner, they denote the hollow emptiness and utter worthlessness of sinful gratification to satisfy the craving of the human soul for that happiness for which it was created, since God alone can satisfy the human heart. "Thou hast made us for Thyself, and our heart is not at rest till it rest in Thee " (St. Augustine).

17. Like one recovering from an unconscious state of drunkenness or sleep, the prodigal, "*returning to himself,*" remembers his father's house. This is very intelligible in the parable, inasmuch, as it usually happens, that temporal privations and misfortunes have the effect of making men enter into themselves and consider the foolish and extravagant conduct that caused all the misery and want that came upon them. "*Vexation alone shall make you understand what you hear* " (Isaias xxviii. 19). In its application to the sinner, it means that although the prolonged habit of sin generally renders men more insensible and more callous in regard to their miserable condition; still, God sometimes employs great spiritual destitution and want, particularly in the case of those who before had tasted His heavenly sweetness, to make men enter into themselves, aided by His heavenly grace, without which they could not entertain a single thought conducive to salvation. Here God, by His preventing grace, rouses the sinner from the lethargic sleep of spiritual death in which he was sunk, and brings him back to himself to consider his miserable state. This opening of his eyes to a consciousness of his own condition and to a sense of the Divine mercy, was the first grace, the first motion of penance which God mercifully accorded to him, and thus stimulated him to further exertions to go forth

from his miserable state and seek reconciliation with his offended and outraged father.

"*How many hired servants in my father's house,*" &c. "*By hired servants*" (*mercenarii*), are meant, those who work for daily wages. The contrast or antithesis here is very striking. "*Hired servants.*" Strangers to the household, having bread in abundance and to spare in the father's house, while the son of that household, far away in a strange land, is perishing from hunger, in want of the commonest food.

By "*hired servants,*" or, mercenaries, St. Jerome (Ep. 146) understands, those among the Jewish people who observed the law from love of temporal goods; and who, being just, by the justice of the law, and also merciful, were such, not from the love of justice or mercy; but from the motive of receiving from God, according to promise, a long and happy life in this world. What is said of the Jews, St. Jerome observes, might generally apply to those in the Church, the house of God, our Father, who act well, not from love, as dutiful children should do, but, from a a mercenary fear of punishment and a desire of temporal recompense.

As the prodigal in the application of the parable to sinners, who departed from God, suffered from spiritual want, from a privation of the blessings of grace and spiritual gifts, the abundance "*of bread,*" therefore, which the mercenaries enjoyed in His Father's house, must refer to spiritual blessings; and these must be, in one sense, sons of God, but of an inferior class, who acted principally from the hope of remuneration, as mercenaries do, and not from the pure and more exalted motives of filial love. They are of that class referred to by David, "*Inclinavi cor meum ad faciendas justificationes tuas . . . propter retributionem.*" Whereas, the children in the more exalted sense are represented by those of whom he speaks, "*Quomodo dilexi legem tuam, tota die meditatio mea est?*" "*Levavi manus meas ad mandata tua quæ dilexi.*" It may be, the words have no application at all, in the parable, and are only introduced ornamentally, to convey the deep consciousness of his degradation and misery on the part of the prodigal, contrasting his own miserable degraded condition with the happiness of those who were his inferiors; or, if applied, it may designate those, who were of no consideration in the Church compared with him, before he fell away from God. The first step in the prodigal's recession from God was oblivion of God. Hence, his first step in returning is remembrance of God and of the things of His house.

18. Now that the grace of God has opened his eyes and touched his heart, he does not tarry long, aided by the same grace, in taking a firm resolution. He determines at once to abandon the wretched condition and place he was in, and to throw himself on the mercy and forgiveness of Him whom he knew to have still for him the bowels of tenderness and the compassion of a Father.

"*I will arise*"—a Hebrew form of expressing the commencement of energetic action, or it may be allusive to the sluggish state of sin, in which he lay, the mire in which he was wallowing. I will leave this wretched country—these gloomy shadows of death.

"*And will go to my father.*" I will hasten to cast myself at the feet of "*my father,*" who has still the patient bowels of mercy for me. "*I shall confess my injustice to him*" (Psalm xxxi. 5), humbly acknowledge my innumerable offences against God and man; against heaven and earth.

"*Father, I have sinned against heaven.*" In the mouth of the prodigal, looking on his father as a mere earthly parent, whom he offended, the words will mean,

I have committed sins against God in heaven, and offended thee, and scandalized my fellow-creatures on earth. I have committed innumerable sins against heaven and earth. But, viewed in reference to God, "*against heaven and before thee*," mean the same. Or, "*before thee*," might mean, I have sinned against heaven; and, to aggravate my fault, I committed it in thy very presence, who fillest all space, and art everywhere present, with Thy glorious immensity.

19. "*No more worthy to be called thy son*," to be reinstated in the same place of exalted dignity I forfeited. The parable supposes him to occupy the most dignified place in his father's household. He now only asks to be admitted into his father's house, and restored to his favour, on any terms, be they ever so humble. "*Make me one of thy hired servants.*" Let me now be admitted back into the ranks of the humblest of the faithful within Thy holy Church. These humble sentiments, inspired by God's grace, this resolution to confess his iniquity, were pleasing to God, who looks to the humble. "*Humilia respicit et alta a longe cognoscit;*" "*Exaltat humiles.*" The prodigal entertained feelings of humble sorrow in his heart, with a determination to confess his sins, as he afterwards did (v. 21). But he had not yet done so, as is observed by St. Augustine (Quæst. Evangel. 23, Lib. 2).

20. "*And rising up, he came to his father.*" He was not long in carrying out his resolve under the inspirations of Divine grace.

"*And when he was yet a great way off,*" &c. This represents to us, in vivid colours, the infinite mercy and amiable condescension of God in dealing with sinners. This beneficent Father does not wait at home till His son appears before him, humbled to the earth and crying for forgiveness and confessing his faults. No, His bowels of paternal affection are moved. "*He saw him*" coming. He beheld the miserable plight, the sad condition he was reduced to. Far from rejecting or spurning him from his presence, "*he was moved to compassion.*" All his parental love is now excited, and he has compassion on his fallen, degraded son. He gives him the most sensible proof of his affection. Although the parable may be understood of the general fruits of Redemption, resulting from the Incarnation of our Lord, when "*God so loved the world, as to give up for it His only begotten Son*" (John iii. 16), and gave us the kiss of peace, when "*afar off*" (Ephes. ii.), reconciling us through Jesus Christ, who, on His part, came from afar, descending from heaven, for that end; still, it in a more special way, vividly represents the infinite mercy and loving condescension of Almighty God in regard to particular sinners whom He inspires to return to Him by penance. By His preventing graces, He attracts them: infuses into them the spirit of true contrition; thus admitting them to His loving, paternal embraces, and giving them the kiss of reconciliation and peace.

21. His sincere sorrow now finds vent in the humble confession of his guilt, on which he had already resolved (v. 18, 19). St. Augustine observes (Lib. 2 Quæst. Evangel. c. 33), that the prodigal stops short in the confession he proposed making. He now omits saying, "*make me as one of thy hired servants.*" This may have arisen from his seeing the great love manifested by his father now receiving him back once more as his son; and hence, the prodigal would not undervalue it by seeking a lower place. Overpowered by his father's beneficent goodness, he thinks it unnecessary. St. Augustine says, he omitted it from a feeling of generosity. He disdains to exhibit a servile spirit towards him, who exhibits loving signs of paternal affection; or, it may be, his father interrupted him, before he came to that part, by telling his servants, "*Bring forth quickly the first robe*" (v. 22). Some hold that the

prodigal did utter those words; but, that St. Luke omits recording them, as being easily perceived from what preceded. Unmindful of his former outrages, this good father with wonderful celerity pardons him, and clothes him in the robes suited to his original dignity.

22. "*The first stole*," "*the ring*," "*and shoes*," indicate that he was admitted to his former place of dignity, which he had forfeited. "*The first*," that is, excellent, "*stole*," a robe worn only by the children of distinguished houses. The particle, "*the* stole," would point to the garment he wore in his father's house, and left behind him, on his departure for the journey to the distant country, in which he wrecked his fortune and character. This robe represents charity, which covers a multitude of sins, and sanctifying grace, the chief ornament of the soul, now once more restored to him—the distinctive robe of the sons of God, with which those who are "*baptized are clad*" (Galatians iii. 27), being clothed "*with the new man*," &c. (Ephes. iv. 24.)

The "*ring*," which was a mark of dignity among the Easterns, an ornament of the rich, and a pledge of solemn engagements, denotes the indwelling of the Holy Ghost in the soul. "*In hoc cognoscimus quoniam in eo manemus et ipse in nobis quoniam de spiritu suo dedit nobis.*" (John iv.) "*In quem credentes signati estis spiritu promissionis sancto.*" (Ephes. vi.)

The putting of "*the ring on his hand*," denotes, according to some Expositors, the performance of good works, consequent on his conversion.

"*Shoes on his feet*," which servants or slaves were not allowed, denote promptitude and readiness to walk in the way of virtue, and to preach the glad tidings of reconciliation and its sweets to others. (Ephes. vi.) The "*shoes*" were given to guard his feet in the way of virtue, from impinging against a stone, or any scandalous obstruction, that might cause him to fall. Among the ornaments with which the Lord promised to adorn Jerusalem in crowning her with gifts, was to have her magnificently shod (Ezech. xvi. 10); and the Jews were ordered by Moses, to have their feet shod, as a preparation for eating the Paschal lamb (Exod. xii. 24), which was a figure of the "*fatted calf*," mentioned here. They are a part of the spiritual ornaments necessary to render a soul pleasing to God. By the grace which they typify, we may "*now walk according to the Spirit, and not according to the flesh*" (Rom. viii. 4), and with it, under the protection of the Most High, "*walk upon the asp and basilisk, and trample under foot the lion and the dragon*" (Psalm xc. 13), unto the preparation of the Gospel of peace. It is necessary to be clothed with the virtues typified by the above ornaments, suited only to the sons of the household, in order to be allowed to partake of "*the fatted calf*" (v. 23).

23. "*The fatted calf.*" The article, in the Greek, would indicate that there is question of a "*calf*" fattened and reserved for some occasion of special rejoicing like the present. Some understand this, of the fulness and abundance of heavenly graces, peace, and interior joy in the Holy Ghost, which God plentifully bestows on sinners after their conversion and return to Him. Others understand it, of the Holy Eucharist, of which St. Augustine says: "Although God be omnipotent, He can do no more; although infinitely wise, He can contrive nothing greater; although infinitely rich, He can give nothing greater." Regarding which, the Council of Trent also declares (§ 13, c. 2), "that in it our amiable Saviour poured forth all the riches of His love for man." This is the greatest gift, the most precious pledge of His love that God can give to men. It was the last proof of his affection, that he ordered his servants to bring forth on the occasion of the rejoicings for his lost child.

24. All this denotes the great joy there is in heaven over the conversion of a penitent sinner. "*My son.*" He does not disdain to bestow on him the original title—so endearing—of "*son.*" "*Was dead,*" reputed such, owing to his long absence; and in its spiritual application to the sinner, *really* dead to God and to grace, "*and is come to life again,*" by a spiritual resurrection from the grave of sin. "*Was lost,*" &c. This clause is but an explanation of the preceding, expressed in different words and in a different form.

"*And they began to be merry.*" The whole household. This indicates the great joy there is in heaven over the conversion of a sinner.

25-27. This refers to an imaginary detail of the parable, which naturally fits into the literal narrative, as a thing that might occur; and it well suits, as a natural introduction to the cause of the jealous feelings expressed in *v.* 28, by the elder brother.

28. If by the elder brother, we understand those really just; then, the jealousy expressed only conveys, that such is the abundance of gifts which God bestows on converted sinners, that it would be calculated to excite the jealousy of the just themselves, although this cannot be, since the just always rejoice at the conversion of sinners. But the words taken in the above sense, convey the magnitude of the graces conferred on the penitent sinner (Euthymius).

If the words refer to those only reputed just, such as the Scribes and Pharisees, in reference to whose murmurs at our Lord's condescension to sinners, they are introduced; then, the passage conveys a deep reproach to the Scribes and Pharisees. For, as no one would censure the benevolent father referred to in the parable, for his great kindness and loving condescension and merciful forgiveness towards his lost child, whom he went half way to meet, and feasted with; so, neither should the Pharisees murmur at the like conduct on the part of our Lord when eating with sinners with a view to reclaim them; and as the elder son was blameable for these feelings of murmuring jealousy; so were the Pharisees, who were typified in him.

The elder son may be said, under different respects and circumstances, to typify the really just and the reputed just, such as the Scribes and Pharisees. He represented the really just, inasmuch as he remained with his father and observed his mandates. But, inasmuch as he spoke disparagingly of his father, looking on himself as just, and his brother a sinner, he represented the murmurs and scornful arrogance of the Pharisees. It was only as representing these latter, he is said, in the parable, to express murmurs and jealousy. How admirably the amiable condescension of the loving father is depicted here. He goes out to this jealous son. He gently remonstrates with him (*v.* 31), pointing out the great advantage he always possessed in enjoying the plenty of his father's house, and in being made partaker of all his goods.

So, those whom God by His grace preserved from sin—for without His grace and assistance, any one, no matter how just, would commit, at times, the greatest crimes—should always be grateful to their good God, who wonderfully preserved them, and should compassionate those who were not equally blessed.

CHAPTER XVI.

ANALYSIS.

This chapter contains the parable of the unjust Steward, with its suggestive lesson of the prudence of salvation (1-9). It also contains instructions on the subjects of covetousness, fidelity to grace, the indissolubility of marriage (10-18); and concludes with the history of the life, hard-heartedness, and the frightful torture and despair of the rich glutton condemned to the everlasting fire of hell (19-31).

TEXT.

AND he said also to his disciples: *There was a certain rich man who had a steward: and the same was accused unto him, that he had wasted his goods.*

2. *And he called him, and said to him: How is it that I hear this of thee? give an account of thy stewardship: for now thou canst be steward no longer.*

3. *And the steward said within himself: What shall I do, because my lord taketh away from me the stewardship? To dig I am not able; to beg I am ashamed.*

4. *I know what I will do, that when I shall be removed from the stewardship, they may receive me into their houses.*

5. *Therefore calling together every one of his lord's debtors, he said to the first: How much dost thou owe my lord?*

6. *But he said: An hundred barrels of oil. And he said to him: Take thy bill and sit down quickly, and write fifty.*

7. *Then he said to another: And how much dost thou owe? Who said: An hundred quarters of wheat. He said to him: Take thy bill, and write eighty.*

8. *And the lord commended the unjust steward, forasmuch as he had done wisely: for the children of this world are wiser in their generation than the children of light.*

9. *And I say to you: Make unto you friends of the mammon of iniquity, that when you shall fail they may receive you into everlasting dwellings.*

10. *He that is faithful in that which is least, is faithful also in that which is greater: and he that is unjust in that which is little, is unjust also in that which is greater.*

11. *If then you have not been faithful in the unjust mammon; who will trust you with that which is the true?*

12. *And if you have not been faithful in that which is another's; who will give you that which is your own?*

13. *No servant can serve two masters, for either he will hate the one, and love the other: or he will hold to the one, and despise the other. You cannot serve God and mammon.*

14. *Now the Pharisees who were covetous, heard all these things: and they derided him.*

15. *And he said to them: You are they who justify yourselves before men, but God knoweth your hearts; for that which is high to men, is an abomination before God.*

16. *The law and the prophets were until John; from that time the kingdom of God is preached, and every one useth violence towards it.*

17. *And it is easier for heaven and earth to pass, than one tittle of the law to fall.*

18. *Every one that putteth away his wife, and marrieth another, committeth adultery: and he that marrieth her that is put away from her husband, committeth adultery.*

19. *There was a certain rich man, who was clothed in purple and fine linen: and feasted sumptuously every day.*

20. *And there was a certain beggar named Lazarus, who lay at his gate, full of sores.*

21. *Desiring to be filled with the crumbs that fell from the rich man's table, and no one did give him; moreover the dogs came and licked his sores.*

22. *And it came to pass that the beggar died, and was carried by the Angels into Abraham's bosom. And the rich man also died: and he was buried in hell.*

23. *And lifting up his eyes when he was in torments, he saw Abraham afar off, and Lazarus in his bosom:*

24. *And he cried, and said: Father Abraham, have mercy on me, and send Lazarus that he may dip the tip of his finger in water, to cool my tongue, for I am tormented in this flame.*

25. *And Abraham said to him: Son, remember that thou didst receive good things in thy life-time, and likewise Lazarus evil things: but now he is comforted, and thou art tormented.*

26. *And besides all this, between us and you there is fixed a great chaos: so that they who would pass from hence to you, cannot, nor from thence come hither.*

27. *And he said: Then, father, I beseech thee that thou wouldst send him to my father's house, for I have five brethren,*

28. *That he may testify unto them, lest they also come into this place of torments.*

29. *And Abraham said to him: They have Moses and the prophets; let them hear them.*

30. *But he said: No, father Abraham, but if one went to them from the dead, they will do penance.*

31. *And he said to him: If they hear not Moses and the prophets, neither will they believe if one rise again from the dead.*

COMMENTARY.

1. It is disputed among Commentators, whether the following parable was spoken immediately after the three preceding ones, at the same time and in the same place. The common opinion, to which the adversative and connecting particle, δε (*but*), adds much force, is, that it was uttered immediately after them. By a very natural connexion, our Lord, after having reproved the Pharisees, who murmured at His mild treatment of sinners, now directly addressing His followers in general, unto the end of time, points out, how wealth should be employed; that almsdeeds are to be added to penance, in order to obtain the grace of repentance for sinners, and perseverance for the just, almsdeeds being obligatory on all. This was, no doubt, indirectly intended for the Pharisees, whose griping avarice, which made them "*deride Him*" (v. 14), He censures in this parable. By the example of the unjust steward, He wishes to show the avaricious Pharisees and all rich men, to the end of time, the prudence they should practise in regard to spiritual matters, the alacrity with which they should shut up "*alms in the heart of the poor, as it shall obtain help against all evil*" (Eccles. xxix. 15).

The word, "*steward*," as appears from the Greek—οικονομος—means, a dispenser, who has charge of all his master's goods. The Vulgate term, "*villicus*," would refer to a land-steward in charge of the farm. Here it is taken in a wider signification (*vv.* 5-7). "*Was accused.*" The Greek word means, *denounced, charged.*

"*Wasted,*" by luxurious living; or, by ill-conceived generosity in bestowing presents and the like. It need hardly be remarked that, in their spiritual application, the words, "*the rich man*" denotes Almighty God, the Sovereign Lord and Master of all, to whom belongs every thing, the earth and its fulness.

By "*the steward,*" is meant, man, His creature, to whom He confided His goods, whether gifts of fortune, of nature, or of grace, to be employed, not for man's own individual advantage; but, for the benefit of His Master, whose steward he is, in the manner He enjoins, and for His honour and glory. From this entire passage, we can clearly see, that in relation to God, whatever may be said of rights secured by human law—no man is absolute proprietor or master of anything he possesses. He is a mere steward or dispenser, and in order to discharge the first duty of every steward, viz., fidelity (1 Cor. iv. 2), he must employ his master's goods solely for his master's profit. From this, we may also see, that the more God has entrusted to us, the greater the goods of fortune, the gifts of nature or grace confided to our stewardship, the greater shall be the return we must make Him, the heavier our accountability, and the stricter the account demanded at our hands ; so that, instead of glorying in the magnitude or multitude of the talents bestowed on us, we should rather tremble at the account we are one day to render of them.

2. The master summons his accused steward, states the charge made against him, and calls for an account of his stewardship.

"*For, now thou canst be steward no longer,*" which may mean, that unless, after due investigation, he cleared himself of these charges, in the act of rendering an account, he shall be discharged—Justice would demand he should not be condemned, before due inquiry—or, it may mean, that the notoriety and certainty of his guilt involved dismissal on the spot, and the feelings of the steward himself (verse 3), would convey that, he knew his own guilt, which involved consequent dismissal. In their spiritual application, these words refer to the dread summons issued to every one at the hour of death, to part for ever with their temporal goods, and render an account of their administration. What a dreadful summons to us all! What a momentous account, on the issue of which will depend an eternity of happiness or woo !

3, 4. Here we have, without any very direct bearing or significance in the aim of the parable,—what, probably, should be regarded as ornamental,—the ingenious contrivance which occurred to the steward for providing against the evil day, when dismissed from the office of steward, upon which, most likely, his livelihood depended. He promptly resolves on a course which, although a fresh proof of his dishonesty, shows, at the same time, his worldly prudence and tact in providing against the evil day. "*They may receive me,*" that is, give me support and maintenance in my necessities.

How applicable are the words, "*To dig I am not able ; to beg I am ashamed,*" to the sad, desolate condition of those who, from their own misconduct and misuse of God's gifts, spiritual and corporal, are painfully deprived of those occupations, as well sacred as profane, on which their livelihood depended. Having been once "*the salt of the earth,*" and having "*lost savour,*" they are cast out and utterly degraded, being trodden under the feet of men.

5-7. This shows he had general charge of his master's goods. "*Every one of his lord's debtors.*" So that his fraudulent conduct would be less liable to suspicion than if he only called some, and that all might be under obligation to treat him kindly and generously in the day of need. These two debtors mentioned in verses 5-7, are only examples of all the rest; for he called "*every one of his lord's debtors,*" and, no doubt, treated all in the same way, proportionally, as he treated these two. "*An hundred barrels of oil.*" "*Barrels,*" Greek—βαρους—a word derived from the Hebrew; in Syriac, *Matreion,* derived from the Greek. "*Barrel*"—*Batus*—was of equal measure with an *Ephi*—*Batus,* for *liquids ; Ephi,* for *solids*—and each contained the tenth part of a *corus,* or *quarter,* as in next verse (Ezechiel xlv. v. 11).

7. "*An hundred quarters of wheat.*" "*Quarters,*" in Greek, κορους. Every *corus* ("*quarter*") was equivalent to ten *cadi* ("*barrels*") in liquids, and ten *Ephi,* in solids. Hence, the stewards remitted more to the second debtor, to whom he remitted but twenty quarters out of the hundred, than he did to the former, although he remitted fifty out of the hundred, since twenty *cori,* or "*quarters,*" contained far more than was contained in fifty *cadi* or "*barrels.*"

"*Take thy bill,*" in Greek, γραμμα, his note of hand, the written instrument securing payment, kept in the hands of the steward. This note of hand, the steward hands back to each debtor, for the purpose of destroying it and writing out a new one containing a lesser amount. He tells him to do that "*quickly,*" implying *secrecy*, and every one to do it, implying, that it was done by each one separately.

"*And the lord commended,*" &c., that is, "*the lord*" of the unjust steward, whose goods were squandered, on learning how prudently he acted from a worldly, selfish point of view, although naturally indignant at the injustice committed against himself, and this fresh proof of his steward's dishonesty, still could not help commending the dexterous cunning—"*acted wisely*"—displayed by him with a view to his own future interests. "*The lord,*" refers to the injured master of the steward, and not to our Lord Jesus Christ, as appears from the next verse, where our Lord speaks of Himself "*I say to you,*" &c., in pointing out the moral of the parable.

The force of the conclusion would be greater in the interpretation, which understands "*Lord,*" of the injured master of the steward. For, then it would be an argument *a minori ad majus*, as St. Augustine understands it to be (Lib. 2, Quæst. Evangel. Quæst. 34), conveying, that if the rich man praised the dexterity of his unjust steward, how much more will God commend and reward His faithful servants, who dispense the goods He confided to them according to His good will and pleasure.

Observe, the commendation of the master has not for object the dishonest *act* of his unjust servant. It is exclusively confined to the *p udence* he displayed in it. He commended him, "*because he had done wisely.*" "What is commended, then, on the part of the unjust steward, is his *cunning*, his cleverness, and this by his temporal lord only. If it be said that at least his example is proposed by our Lord, for our imitation, we answer, not in all respects, and only inasmuch as he showed great prudence and zeal in gaining his end. The steward acted *unjustly ;* and no one was less likely to praise him for that, than the master whose goods he wasted; but he acted also *prudently, cleverly*, according to the wisdom of the flesh, determined, as far as he could, not to lose all when deprived of his place ; and for that foresight, he is praised even by his injured master. When St. Paul calls on the Romans to serve justice unto sanctification with the same zeal with which they served iniquity before (Rom. vi. 19), does he thereby approve of the object of their former zeal ? We may praise the actor's skill without approving the play, or the robber's courage without extolling felony, or even the duellist s aim without extenuating the fearful guilt of murder. It is the *prudence* of the steward, and that alone, and not his unjust conduct, that is eulogized. The *wisdom* of the children of this world is praised, not the *end* to which that wisdom is directed, as is more evident still from what follows. The enemies of Christianity labour, therefore, in vain to find in these words any commendation of injustice" (Dr. MacCarthy, *in hunc locum*).

"*For the children of this world,*" a Hebrew phrase, as are also the words, "*children of light.*" These are the words of our Redeemer, conveying to us, that the votaries of this darksome world, and those who live according to its ideas and maxims—so opposed to truth and "*light*"—"*are wiser in their generation,*" in adopting means for attaining their worldly ends, and securing perishable riches—the only thing worldlings value and esteem—"*than the children of light,*" the sons of God, who profess to live by the light of the Gospel, which God has mercifully shed upon them, are, in the adoption of proper means for securing their end, the enjoyment of imperishable goods and eternal happiness. Our Lord adds this, lest He might appear to commend the dishonest conduct of the steward. He only refers to the steward's conduct, in order to stimulate His followers to greater zeal in attaining their end, than worldlings do in attaining theirs. By contrasting the prudence of worldlings, "*the wisdom of the flesh, which is death*," with the prudence of His followers; or "*the children of light*," which is "*the wisdom of the spirit, which is life and peace*" (Rom. viii. 6), our Lord wishes His followers to display greater zeal in their way, than worldlings do in theirs. Here naturally suggests itself the solemn reflection on the wisdom of salvation. As the wise man refers the sluggard to the industry of the little ant, so our Lord refers us to the industry and care which worldlings employ in their business in attaining their worldly ends. What is every other wisdom, but folly, unless it conducts us to the end of our creation? What can everything else avail, if we miss this? "*Quid prodest homini si universum mundum?*" &c. What comparison between the passing gratification of the brutal passions of the body, in which we are become like the brute beasts, "*the horse and mule that have no understanding*"—gratification, which lasts but a moment, and is succeeded by bitterness and remorse—and the eternal enjoyment of the spiritual and heavenly delights, for which the immortal soul of man is made?

9. "*And I say unto you.*" This is the conclusion drawn from the above parable by our Lord for the guidance of His followers at all times. "*I*" and "*you*," are very emphatic. The *steward* said to *himself*, I know what I shall do; I shall make friends for myself of my master's debtors. *I* say also to *you*, imitating the steward's cunning and prudence, do you also make friends for yourselves out of the unjust, unrighteous mammon, which your Sovereign Master has deposited in your hands, to be dispensed by you, as faithful stewards, according to His will, by laying up your riches in the bosom of the poor, "*that when you shall fail*," and shall be deprived of the stewardship at the hour of death, when you shall be called upon to render an account of your dispensation, "*they*," like the master's debtors, whom the steward desired to conciliate in order to be admitted into their houses, "*may receive you into*" their houses, in the kingdom which is properly theirs (Matthew v. 3; Luke vi. 20), houses, or "*tabernacles*," which are to endure for ever.

"*Mammon of iniquity*," a common Hebraism for unrighteous, *iniquitous mammon*. "*Mammon*" is a Syriac word, signifying *riches* (Matthew vi. 24). Riches are termed iniquitous or unjust—μαμμωνα της αδικιας—for several reasons, either, because they are, generally speaking, the fruit of injustice on the part of our forefathers, by rapine, plunder, &c., or, on our own part. Hence, the common phrase, "*dives aut injustus aut hæres injusti*," quoted by St. Jerome (Ep. 1, ad Hebridiam, Quæst. 1), and as the heir of injustice knows not precisely to whom he should make restitution, he should give it to the poor; or, because they occasion injustice in their possessors, unless greatly on their guard, such as pride, avarice, luxury. In this way St. Paul terms concupiscence "*sin*," being the cause and effect of sin, "*quod habitat in me peccatum*" (Rom. vii. 17); or, because, it is the unrighteous or unjust alone, that regard riches as their sovereign good, place their whole trust in them, and value them unduly, although false, deceitful, and transitory, never satisfying the human heart; the just, on the other hand, in possessing riches, regard them as transitory, and value heavenly riches alone; or, because, men often regard the riches they possess as absolutely their own, whereas, in reality they are God's, to whom belongs the earth and its fulness. Men, in reference to God, hold them by the mere title of dispensation or stewardship. This latter meaning well suits the parable, in which God is signified by the "*rich man.*" We are only stewards, who unjustly employ for our own selfish ends what belongs to Him. Riches are not unjust or unrighteous of themselves, but only in their abuse.

"*When you fail.*" When at death, you are called upon to render an account of your stewardship, now to be taken away from you.

"*They may receive you*," or, rather, God shall admit you, owing, in some cases, to their intercession, into His heavenly kingdom, which is peculiarly the inheritance of the poor; but He shall do so, especially in consideration of the pure motive of charity, which dictates the giving of alms to the poor, which are, therefore, given to Himself, whom they represent. This latter reason will hold, whether there be question of the faithful and just poor, themselves occupants of heaven, or of the unjust poor excluded from it, when we relieve them for God's sake, whom in their poverty they represent.

"*Into everlasting dwellings*," which peculiarly belong to the poor, as such. No doubt, many among the poor shall be excluded, who die impenitent, and many among the rich admitted, who shall merit by their charity the graces necessary to fulfil the other precepts of God. For, mere alms-giving will not save; but, alms-giving will move God to grant forgiveness of sin and the graces necessary for salvation. The rich have great difficulties in gaining heaven; and from this passage, it is clear, that unless they discharge the duty of alms-giving they shall be excluded from God's everlasting kingdom. "*Everlasting*," solid, enduring mansions, in opposition to these dwellings "*made with hands*" in this world, whose duration is but temporary.

From this entire passage is clearly seen the duty of relieving the poor by alms-giving, under pain of exclusion from the kingdom of heaven. We are *mere stewards* of the goods we possess in this world. If we appropriate them to our own use, instead of dispensing them according to the will and for the interests of our Master, we act the part of unjust, unfaithful stewards; and we shall be excluded from God's everlasting mansions, when the accounting day arrives.

The precept of alms-giving may be also clearly seen from the providence of God in the present order of things. While arranging the unequal distribution of earthly goods, He appoints the rich as His own stewards and representatives in regard to His poor. In order to bind together more firmly the several members of the great human *family*, He has ordered that they should mutually depend on each other, as He had done in regard to the several members of the human *body;* and He has made the reciprocal exhibition of love, the great bond of indissoluble union. When the rich, then, neglect to succour their indigent brethren, and follow not the example of Him whose place they hold, Who "*opens His hand and fills every animal with benediction;*" Who "*makes His sun from heaven rise on the good and bad, and rains upon the just and the unjust,*" they become instrumental in subverting the order of Providence, established by God. Through them His name is blasphemed; and an order of things established directly at variance with His divine ordinances; and their neglect made chargeable, with wicked men, on His infinite goodness and wisdom. Hence, our Lord regards the salvation of a rich man as so very difficult; because, it is so hard to find a rich man who complies, to the requisite extent, with the precept of relieving the poor.

The same precept is clearly referred to (1 John iii. 17), where He condemns those who, having a knowledge of their neighbour's wants, and the means of relieving him, still neglect doing so. Also, James i. 13-27; ii. 15; Matthew xxv. 34-46. The same may be also clearly seen from the fate of the hard-hearted rich man, whose history and miserable end are given towards the close of this chapter, *vv.* 19-31.

10-12. Our Redeemer would seem to have for object in these three verses, to inculcate charity towards the poor, and the faithful discharge, on the part of the rich, of their office as stewards, in the dispensation of the goods of this world, which, properly speaking, are God's. This He inculcates, on the ground, that infidelity in the discharge of their office, of properly dispensing temporal goods, would entail the withholding or withdrawal from them, of spiritual goods, and their final exclusion from the eternal bliss, for obtaining which spiritual gifts and graces are indispensable. He also inculcates due correspondence with spiritual graces, and the proper use of them.

"*He that is faithful in that which is least,*" &c. This is an adagial expression, founded on the common opinion of mankind and experience, conveying what generally happens. It is understood of fidelity or want of fidelity in small things, arising from an innate principle of honesty or dishonesty. Men who find their servants honest in small things regard them as deserving of credit in regard to great things. Hence, we find the reward given in the Gospel, "*quia super pauca fuisti fidelis, super multa te constituam,*" &c. "*The least*" and "*little,*" are generally understood of temporal matters, which are "*little*" compared with spiritual treasures; and "*greater,*" of the more precious treasures of the spiritual life. The man, who is not faithful in the administration of temporal goods, according to the will of God, shows that he does not deserve to be intrusted with the spiritual treasures of grace, which he would be sure to employ unprofitably. "*Si quis domui suæ præesse nescit, quomodo Ecclesiæ Dei diligentiam habebit?*" (1 Timothy iii. 5.)

11. This is an inference from the foregoing adage "*If you have not been faithful,*" in the dispensation of "*unjust mammon,*" the goods of this world, which are fugitive, uncertain, deceitful and never satisfy the cravings of the human heart, "*who will trust you with that which is true?*" He refers to the spiritual treasures of grace, which are in reality "*true*" riches, alone capable of satisfying the heart, alone conducting to the true and permanent end for which we were created. This may be understood of all men, to whom God commits His treasures of grace, to be employed by them for their own sanctification and final salvation. Our Lord here threatens the rich and avaricious, that by the misuse of temporal wealth, they will deserve to be refused spiritual graces, or, to have the graces which they possess, withdrawn from them. In verse 9, He proposes the reward of alms-deeds; in these verses, the punishment of neglecting it.

12. "*Another's,*" temporal wealth, which belongs to God—like that which the steward squandered—given as His own to us for administration. We have merely the use of it from Him. Riches were never ours; we brought none of them into this world, nor shall we bring any out of it. They are external to us, and by no means belong to us, foreign to the rational and spiritual nature of man. "*Your own,*" the spiritual treasures of grace, which may be called "*our own,*" because they remain with us; they adhere to us, and conduct us to our last end, for which we were destined and created, and which we cannot lose. "*Who will give?*" &c. No one; God will withhold or take away spiritual goods in punishment of our abuse or maladministration of the temporal goods confided to our stewardship (Psalm xlviii. 17, 18; Job xxvii. 19).

13. Our Lord in this verse employs an adage founded on experience, regarding the impossibility of serving two masters of opposite characters, demanding opposite and contrary things, in order to dissuade His followers, and the Pharisees, also, whom He specially censures, from the pursuit of avarice. (See Matthew vi. 24, Commentary on.) The adage is suggested by the idea, that those who neglect alms-deeds, show an

inordinate attachment to riches, which they serve as an idol. Now, such service is incompatible with the service of God. We can serve only one or the other.

14. "*Now the Pharisees, who were covetous*"—fond of money—"*heard all these things.*" The Greek has, "*the Pharisees also,*" as well as the disciples, whom He addressed, "*heard all these things.*"

"*And they derided Him.*" The Greek word for "*derided,*" εξεμυκτηριζον, conveys the external expression of their contempt—literally, *they turned up their noses* at Him—a common metaphor, denoting derision—"*naso suspendere adunco*" (Horace). They sneered derisively at our Lord—Himself poor and bereft of all earthly riches—for inculcating on the rich the duty of distributing their wealth among the poor. Not considering the selfish accumulation of wealth, opposed to the teaching of Moses, and to the high standard of legal perfection they proposed to follow, they sneered at the doctrine, that they were mere stewards of their earthly wealth; that riches were unjust "*mammon;*" that the amassing of wealth was incompatible with the service of God, especially as the law of Moses promised temporal blessings to its faithful observers. Hence, these men sneered at our Lord's teaching, just as, now-a-days, we find the haughty, the libidinous, &c., despise the Evangelical teaching regarding humility, charity, &c., so opposed to their loose, dissolute morals. "*The sensual man perceiveth not these things that are of the Spirit of God*" (1 Cor. ii. 14).

15. Having observed their sneers, our Lord, in order to cover them with confusion, reproaches them publicly, with vainly affecting to be just, though not so in reality, and forces them to enter into themselves, that they might discover what God sees in their interior, viz., hypocrisy, secret injustice, avarice, and envy. He conveys, that while they affected to be just, they were abominable in the sight of God.

"*You are they who justify yourselves before men*"—that is, affect legal justice, and wish to be regarded as just before men, putting on the appearance of sanctity and disinterestedness.

"*But God knoweth your hearts.*" By this, Our Lord conveys, that He clearly saw into their interior, and knew the vices with which they were tainted; but, as these vices were too great to be exposed, He insinuates so much by saying that God, "*the searcher of hearts,*" saw how their hearts were tainted with avarice and other corrupt passions. "*For,*" is a proof of the assertion tacitly conveyed in the words, "*God knoweth your hearts,*" viz., that their secret vices, with which they were stained, were well known to God, and their acts prized at their proper value. "*What is high to men*"—what is held in esteem by men, riches, station, and apparent sanctity, which men can only judge of from what they see—"*is an abomination before God,*" "*abominatio Domini est omnis arrogans,*" &c. (Proverbs xvi.) Sometimes God approves of what men approve; but, oftentimes what men approve of is detested by God, if avarice, pride, hypocrisy, reign in the heart, and sincerity be wanting. The sentence here uttered by our Lord has reference to the pride and hypocrisy of the Pharisees, whose external sanctity men prized and valued, but, God hated and detested, as the interior dispositions were wanting. All their external show was the sheerest hypocrisy, which is an abomination before God.

16. Lest they might allege that the law of Moses proposed worldly wealth and prosperity, as the reward of the observance of the law, our Lord says, "*the law and the prophets*" (see Matthew xi. 12-14) "*were until,*" the time of "*John,*" the Baptist. Earthly goods were then promised as rewards to men, but only as figures of the heavenly goods in store for them. But since His time, "*the kingdom of God is preached,*" without

shadow or figure, "*and every one,*" without distinction, the greatest sinners, including the harlots and publicans, who shall go before the Pharisees into the kingdom of God, "*useth violence towards it,*" by mortifying their passions and renouncing all inordinate attachment to earthly goods. Hence, those held in disrepute, who are an abomination with men, may be very precious with God ; as, on the other hand, as above stated, those in repute with men, are often an abomination with God.

17. (See Matthew v. 19.) Lest the Pharisees might imagine this teaching to be contrary to the law, our Lord asserts that the reverse is the case ; since the solid and abiding riches of heaven, alone capable of satisfying the human heart, were in reality typified by the goods promised in the law—goods, which were mere figures of ours, held out in the New Law. The evangelical perfection, inculcated in the preaching of the kingdom of God is the very term and end, to which the law conducts us.

18. See Matthew xix. 9, &c., where the words of this verse uttered absolutely, and without any exception, in reference to the re-marriage of any whose repudiated wife may still live, are adduced in proof of the Catholic doctrine, which teaches, that such re-marriages are invalid ; that the parties so united are guilty of adultery by co-habitation. The words here recorded by St. Luke would be absolutely false, if adultery or any other cause should dissolve the *vinculum* of the marriage of Christians once consummated, as long as either party is still alive. Indeed, if it were otherwise, any one reading St. Luke, unless he chanced to fall in with St. Matthew, would be necessarily led into error—an error, too, which would entail an unfair restriction, and a burthen too heavy in certain contingencies, if the partner of an adulterous party were free to re-enter the marriage state with another. It is held by some, that the words of our Lord here, were uttered, as St. Luke records them, on an occasion different from that mentioned in St. Matthew, chap. xix.

19. Very likely, this is to be connected with the portion of this chapter (v. 1-18), in which our Lord speaks of the duties of the rich in regard to the distribution of their wealth to relieve the necessities of the poor. Many Commentators hold, that the intermediate portion, from v. 13 to this, was spoken on a different occasion, and inserted here by St. Luke, as it occurred to him in writing his Gospel, without any immediate connexion with the subject of this chapter. In the preceding, our Lord shows the reward attached to the faithful dispensation of the goods of this world (v. 10), the punishment of privation of grace and glory attached to their abuse ; and here, in order to strike terror into the Pharisees, who sneered at Him (v. 14), and all others whom it might concern, He shows, by a frightful example, in which, He vividly depicts the tortures of the damned, the dreadful punishment of neglecting to employ the goods of this world in relieving the known necessities of the poor.

"*A certain rich man,*" &c. Our Lord, while mentioning the name of the beggar, Lazarus, "*honorabile nomen eorum corum illo*" (Psalm lxxi. 14), suppresses the name of the rich man condemned to hell, "*nec memor ero nominum eorum per labia mea*" (Psalm xv. 4), out of a feeling of consideration for himself and *his five brethren*, whom he left after him, and also to convey, that his name was blotted out of the book of the living. Moreover, He conveys by this, how different God's judgments are from those of men, who blazon forth the names of the rich and powerful, and regard the names of the poor as undeserving of mention.

"*He was clothed in purple,*" the dress worn by kings, and by such as kings authorized to wear it (Daniel v. 7, 16, 29 ; 1 Machabees x. 20 ; xi. 58 ; xiv. 43, 44). Hence, some interpreters conjecture, that reference is made to Herod, or some prince of the time. The Roman Senate used to bestow it on such as they saluted as kings. In course of time, however, the nobles and the rich used to wear it. Hence, of the valiant woman, it is said, "*Purpura, etc. . . indumentum ejus.*" This rich man, whoever he may have been, lived in royal splendour and magnificence.

"*And fine linen.*" Linen of the finest texture, worn next his person, thus showing his effeminate luxury. The purple he displayed externally.

"*And fared sumptuously.*" He enjoyed at table the most delicate food, wine, music, &c., and all the other accompaniments of luxury, and this not merely on festal, but, "*every day.*" With him it was one continuous round of enjoyment of all the pleasures which this world could afford.

Whether our Lord, to whom, as God, the occurrences in the other world were thoroughly known, records a true historical fact; or a mere parable, a mere imaginary case, typifying realities, is disputed among Commentators. The preponderance of authority favours the former view; and the mention of names, Lazarus, and the *five brothers* of the rich man, corroborates the latter. Moreover, parables are generally founded on events and objects visible to the senses, employed to illustrate moral truths; but, not on invisible things. It would have more force, if a real occurrence of an awful nature, such as this, were adduced in proof of the sinfulness of abusing or not properly using riches. There are certain things contained in the narrative of our Lord, which would seem parabolical, such as, the conversation of the rich man with Abraham regarding his sending Lazarus to him; the torture of his tongue, &c. Hence, it seems more likely, while it may have been a real event, that certain circumstances are mixed up with it, of a parabolical nature.

20. In the preceding we have a picture of supreme earthly happiness. We now have depicted an instance of excessive human misery, want, and suffering. While the rich man was thus enjoying himself, there lay at his gate a wretched beggar. Our Lord gives the proper name of the beggar—"*Lazarus*"—while suppressing that of the rich man, for the reasons already assigned. There are, however, interpreters who understand Lazarus to be a common name, denoting, according to Etymology, as the Hebrew word, *Lazaur*, signifies, "*unto help,*" that is, one exposed as an object to be helped.

"*Lay,*" prostrate, helpless, devoid of all human aid, exposed to the vicissitudes of the weather.

"*At his gate,*" outside the vestibule of the rich man, exposed to the vicissitudes of the weather, but so that his condition and appearance were well known to the rich man (v. 23).

"*Full of sores,*" his body covered all over with ulcers. Some hold, that he was suffering from leprosy. It is not so easy to reconcile this opinion with the Mosaic ordinance prohibiting lepers to reside near human habitations. For, this "*rich man*" was manifestly a Jew. He calls Abraham, "*Father,*" and is, in turn, addressed by him, as "*Son.*"

21. "*Desiring to be fed,*" he did not exhibit any importunity in asking; however, his wretched condition loudly appealed for help.

"*With the crumbs that fell from the rich man's table.*" He desired to be treated like the whelps that eat of the crumbs that fall from their master's table.

"*And no one did give him.*" The servants shared in their master's inhumanity. These words, though not found in the Greek, are understood in the narrative. The poor beggar had no one to comfort or relieve him. While the rich man fared sumptuously, Lazarus had not a morsel to eat; while the rich man was gorgeously apparelled in purple and fine linen, Lazarus was covered over with ulcers.

"*Moreover, the dogs came,*" &c. Some understand this to mean, that the dogs showed more humanity than man, by licking away the putrid matter issuing from his sores, thus affording him some relief. Others, that he was so well known there, that the very dogs, that are in the habit of scaring away strangers, recognised him well. Hence, the rich man could not but be aware of his misery. Others, however, looking to the word, "*moreover,*" which would seem to denote an additional feature of his wretched condition—for, everything mentioned regarding his condition in this life only exhibits his misery—say, the words mean, his condition was so weak, he was so destitute, that he was unable to drive off the dogs—wandering dogs, the pest of Eastern cities—that caused him additional torture by licking his wounds.

22. Death makes a great change, in the condition of both. The wretched beggar, Lazarus, who had no one to give him the very crumbs he craved, by a spirit of holy patience, resignation, and conformity to God's holy will—mere poverty without practising virtue would not do—merited to be "*carried by angels,*" the officers of God's heavenly court, "*into Abraham's bosom,*" the Limbo, or place of rest for the just of old, before the death of Christ had thrown open the gates of heaven to the Saints. Our Lord calls this, "*Abraham's bosom,*" founded on the ancient custom of reclining at feasts,—because, Abraham having merited, by the heroism of his faith, to be called, the Father of all the faithful, received, as it were, into his arms and paternal embraces and fondly cherished,—as an earthly parent, receives into his bosom the children of his love,—the just who, enjoying his company, were detained with him in the place of rest until the death of Christ. Some hold, that the words, "*Abraham's bosom,*" imply, that even in that abode of rest, Lazarus occupied a very high place, next to Abraham himself, reclining, as it were, on his Father's bosom. From this passage we see that, after death, the souls of the just are carried by angels into a place of rest, in which sense of, *carrying,* David says, "*in manibus portabunt te,*" &c. Hence, holy Church prays, "*Jubeas eam a sanctis, angelis suscipi, et ad patriam Paradisi perduci, signifer, sanctus Michael representet,*" &c. This place, designated "*Abraham's bosom,*" is generally supposed to be in the bowels of the earth, but is in a higher position than hell. (*v.* 23), "*He lifted up his eyes.*" In this place, all the just were detained as in a place of rest, and refreshed by Abraham with the hope of heavenly bliss in due time, promised to Abraham and his seed.

"*And the rich man also died; and he was buried in hell.*" In the Greek, the punctuation and construction are different. It runs thus, "*The rich man also died and was buried.*" (*v.* 23.) "*And in hell, lifting up his eyes,*" &c. According to this construction, the words mean, "*he was buried,*" with much pomp and external show, in the tomb he may have himself previously prepared. The burial of Lazarus, being private and of no note, is passed over in silence. The construction in our Vulgate better carries out the antithesis between the carrying of Lazarus by angels to Limbo, and the burying of the rich man in the bottom of hell. Moreover, the description of the condition of both on earth having been given in the preceding verses, it seems more natural, as is clearly conveyed in our version, that now we have a description of the changed condition of both in the other world.

The condemnation of the rich man to the torments of hell suggests a most fearful lesson to the rich of this world. Why was this rich man condemned? Was it on account of his riches? Surely, not. Many among the saints possessed in abundance the riches of this earth. Many of them reached the highest honours and dignities with their accompanying wealth, that this world could bestow. Riches, if properly employed, may bring us to salvation, and may contribute to an increase of glory. Out of *"the mammon of iniquity,"* we may raise up powerful advocates before the throne of grace by hiding our alms in the bosom of the poor, who, after death, may receive us into everlasting tabernacles; and this, in many instances, is the merciful design God has in view in bestowing them.

Was he a heartless oppressor, a wholesale exterminator, who mercilessly ground down the countenance of the poor, against whom the cry of distress, the wail of the widow and the orphan, ascended before the throne of a just God? Was he guilty of the unnatural crime of creating a widespread misery, which he afterwards refused to alleviate—a thing by no means uncommon? Our Redeemer charges him with no such crime. Nor do we find him charged with being a rock of scandal, a stumbling block of offence, by his public immoralities, spreading the odour and infection of spiritual death everywhere around him.

Neither have we any reason for doubting the sincerity of his faith; for Abraham addresses him as his *"son"* (v. 25), and the reference which Abraham makes to *"Moses and the Prophets"* (v. 29), would lead us to suppose, that the unhappy man offered no public resistance to the teaching or the ordinances of the ruling authorities of the Jewish Church, who sat in the chair of Moses. Why then was he *"buried in hell"?* Our Redeemer, in the foregoing passage, conveys, that it was for a mere sin of omission, for his inhumanity, for his neglect to succour the miseries of the poor.

23. *" And lifting up his eyes,"* &c. Here our Lord, who commenced this narrative, regarding the conditions of *Dives* and Lazarus, while in this life, composed of soul and body, continues to speak of them in the other world, as if invested with bodies and corporal senses, as He could not otherwise convey to us an idea of spiritual things in the invisible world to come. Thus, God is oftentimes represented as having limbs, though a pure Spirit. The rich man was, by Divine revelation, or some ray of Divine light, made aware of the happy condition of Lazarus, of whose sufferings in this life, and his own criminal neglect to succour him, his present tortures—the punishment of this criminal neglect—reminded him. As the sight of the rich man's happiness and worldly enjoyment formerly aggravated the sufferings of Lazarus; so, now, the sight of the bliss of Lazarus seems to have aggravated the rich man's tortures.

24. *" And he cried and said."* By this cry is understood his earnest desire for relief, which God made known to Abraham.

" Father Abraham." This unhappy man must have been a Jew, descended from Abraham, whom all Jews addressed as *Father*. Abraham, for the same reason, addresses him as *"Son"* (v. 25). He hopes by addressing him, as Father, to move him to compassion.

" Have mercy on me, and send Lazarus," &c. He entreats Abraham, whom he supposes to be the chief person vested with authority in that place, to send Lazarus, whom alone he knew among those who were in Limbo, to afford him some relief, and refreshment, by giving him even one drop of water to cool his tongue. He refused Lazarus a crumb of bread; now he, in turn, is a suppliant, and asks in vain for a drop of water *"to cool his tongue,"* which shall never be given him, *"petiit guttam qui*

negaverat micam," observes a Holy Father. His tongue, thus tortured, was probably the member that offended most, not only in the sensual enjoyment of good things, but, also in the utterance of obscene words and improper language of all sorts. In what things a man sins, in the same also is he tortured. *"Quantum in deliciis fuit, tantum illi date tormentum et luctum"* (Apoc. xviii. 7). The soul of the rich man being in hell, the word *"tongue"* is therefore used here, metaphorically, and the words convey, that owing to God's power, he felt the same torture as if his tongue were really burning. Indeed, men oftentimes seem to feel the same sensation of pain, after a limb is amputated, as they would feel if the limb had not been removed.

"For I am tormented in this flame." The power of God could effect that material fire, as the instrument of Divine justice, would act on a spiritual substance, as it does on the demons—*"depart into everlasting fire, prepared for the Devil and his angels"* (Matthew xxv. 41). So, in like manner, might it happen in regard to the disembodied souls of men, on whom He might act directly, as He produces sensations through the bodily senses. All this shows the excessive and excruciating tortures this damned man was enduring, not only from fire acting on him by the Divine power ; but, from perpetual remorse of conscience, arising from the recollection of his past guilt, from a knowledge of the felicity he forfeited, from the company of hideous devils, from the constant consideration of his doom, unceasingly forced on his intellect, and the horror and maddening resistance to his fate unceasingly forced on his will.

25, 26. *" And Abraham said to him."* Instead of an oral conversation between Abraham and the damned man, most likely, the things here uttered were made known on both sides by God. *"Son."* Abraham addresses him blandly, and abstains from reproaching him with his crimes. He was his *"son,"* being a Jew, although he was far from following his father's example in the exercise of mercy and hospitality ; and this appellation of *"Son"* forcibly reminds this wretched man of that privilege, and, prabably, adds to his torments.

"Remember that thou didst receive," &c. Abraham's reply conveys—first, that the condition of both was the just retribution due to their deeds in this life; and, secondly, that it was impossible, on the part of Lazarus, to give him any relief. *"Good things."* The Greek has, *"thy good things,"* by which Abraham conveys, that the condemnation of the rich man was owing to the luxurious life he had led, in making his own of the goods of which he was a mere steward, and not dispensing them to the poor according to God's will. *" And likewise Lazarus evil things,"* in which are implied, patience under suffering, conformity to God's holy will, and the practice of all other virtues required from him.

"But now he is comforted," in reward for the virtues he practised, and the holy life he led. *"And thou art tormented."* By a just judgment of God, thou art now enduring, and shalt endure for ever—and this you cannot but *"remember"*—the punishment and torture due to thy wicked life and hardhearted insensibility towards the distressed poor.

26. *" Besides all this"*—that is, besides the just judgment of God, to which the just must ever bow, in a spirit of conformity to His adorable will—compliance with your request is impossible, owing to the eternal separation, which by a Divine, unchangeable decree exists between the just and the reprobate. *"Between us and you there is fixed a great chaos."* The Greek for *"chaos"* means, a chasm, a *gulf,* or *hiatus.* This chasm is *"fixed"* immoveably for all eternity by the Divine decree ; it is utterly impassable, both on account of the eternal separation between just and reprobate, and on account of the distance, which was very great, although both places were under the earth. Hence, there was no passing to and fro, even though they wished it. It

is a hypothetical assertion; for, the just, who must ever conform to God's will, cannot wish any such intercourse, since He has fixed an eternal barrier to any such communication, and the elect have the same feelings and sentiments regarding the reprobate, that God shall ever have.

27, 28. "*And he said.*" The thoughts on both sides were communicated by God to Abraham and to the unfortunate rich man. It is the common opinion, that there was no actual oral conversation between them.

"*Then, father, I beseech thee, that thou wouldst send him to my father's house.*" As if he said; the impassable gulf, firmly established between the just and the condemned reprobate, does not exist between the departed just and those still living on earth. "*I have five brethren.*" "*Five,*" may denote any indefinite number. These my brethren now living in my father's house, are pursuing the same reckless course of luxurious living, strengthened in this by my wicked example, and of utter insensibility to the wants of the famishing poor, that I pursued; and I pray you to send him to them, "*that he may testify to them.*" "*Testify,*" means, to admonish, to warn them of their impending doom. Or, it may mean, to give testimony—the literal signification of the word—that, as an eye witness, he may bear testimony regarding the condition of things in the other life, a point on which sensual and luxurious men, blinded by present enjoyment, express doubts, on the ground, that no one ever came back to tell us of it.

"*Lest they also,*" following the example I gave them, "*may come into this place of torments.*" He made the request, rather from a feeling of self-love, than from love of his brethren, as he felt, that their damnation, which he, to a great degree, occasioned, would increase his own. St. Gregory (Dialog. Lib. iv. c. 33), observes that as the happiness of the saints is increased on seeing those whom they loved, sharers in glory, so, also, is the sufferings of the reprobate, on witnessing the tortures of those whom, with a natural and worldly love, they loved on earth. St. Augustine and St. Chrysostom think he was influenced by a feeling of natural affection; not that he could elicit any act of virtue, owing to his hatred of God and of all good, and the dreadful despair he was in; but, the damned may wish for some natural good, such as the happiness of their parents and friends. Since nature is not extinguished in them, they may wish for such, as a natural blessing, just as animals nourish their young.

That the dead, by Divine permission, sometimes appear to men on earth, not only in sleep, but in their waking, is held by St. Augustine (Libro de Cura Mortuorum, c. 15), where he proves this from several examples, some of them known to himself. He says, it would savour of impudence to deny it. But, how this occurs; whether the dead themselves appear in their proper person, or angels assume their appearance, St. Augustine says, exceeds his powers to give any opinion on. He seems, however, more inclined to think it was effected by angels assuming the appearance that dead men had, when on earth. However, not to speak of diseased imaginations, there should be great reserve as to believing in every apparition; for, sometimes the devil might appear in the shape of deceased persons, to lead them into error.

29. Abraham's stern reply is, "*They have Moses and the prophets.*" They have the testimony of Sacred Scripture, the inspired and infallible Word of God, bearing witness on this subject. "*They have*" them, explained in their synagogues. They can expect no higher authority than God's own Word, contained in the Books of "*Moses and the prophets,*" every week explained to them. "*Let them hear them.*"

What further testimony do they want? Our Lord divides the Old Testament into the Books of "*Moses and the prophets,*" including also, the *Hagiographa*. It is evident, from this passage, that the Old Testament teaches what is necessary, regarding the rewards and punishments of a future life, and the means for attaining eternal life, and escaping everlasting torments, by observing God's precepts, as laid down in the Books of "*Moses and the prophets.*" No doubt, this is more fully and more explicitly developed in the New Testament. The Evangelists refer to the testimony of the law and the prophets (Matthew vii. 12; xi. 13; Luke xvi. 16-29; John i. 45). As the Gospel is testified to by the law and the prophets, if the Jews believed them, they would believe in the Gospel, which is a fuller and a more perfect development of the law and the prophets (John v. 46.)

30. "*No, Father, Abraham*" "*No;*" it is not sufficient for them to have "*Moses and the prophets;*" or "*no,*" they won't believe "*Moses or the prophets,*" but if Lazarus returned, they would do penance. This was the common error which worldlings affected to labour under. They rejected the teaching of SS. Scripture as unreal. They said, no one ever came back to teach us concerning the rewards or punishment of the other life; and our Redeemer, in order to silence the cavils of the avaricious Jews, on the subject of the future life, and the punishment entailed by a neglect to dispense their wealth among the needy poor, introduces Abraham, their father, whom they all revered, as teaching them, and removing their erroneous notions on this subject.

31. "*If they hear not Moses,*" &c. This is founded on reason and experience. On reason; for, surely, the authority of God is greater than that of any individual witness returning from the grave; since they might at once say, it was a mere phantom and delusive apparition; on experience; for, they did not believe Lazarus, after he was resuscitated. They rather sought to put him to death (John xii. 10). Nay, when our Lord raised himself, by His omnipotent power, from the grave, after having repeatedly predicted it—thus clearly proving His Divinity—they altogether rejected His testimony, and did not believe Him after it, any more than before it. And, if they did not believe Him, whose resurrection was foretold by the law and the prophets, much less would they believe any one else, who would return from the grave to bear testimony.

The latter portion of this sad history of the reprobate rich man consigned to hell, is calculated to fill the hardhearted rich with feelings of terror and alarm; "*if they hear not Moses and the prophets,*" &c. It shows them, that, in many instances, the passion, or rather demon of insatiable cupidity, blinds the eyes, and steels the hearts of such men against the threats and promises of Heaven; so that, if a witness were to come back from the grave, and in solemn tones of warning, borrowed from the tomb, to depict the awful doom in store for them, they would pay no heed to him. They would risk all, sooner than part with the idol on which their hearts are unchangeably centered. Oh, if the veil were withdrawn, and an Angel of the Lord were to disclose to our view the gloomy mansions of the damned, how many a wretched father or mother, or near relative, might we find presenting themselves to their surviving heirs, now enjoying their possessions, having been consigned, in punishment of their hardhearted insensibility to the poor, to those devouring flames, which burn without consuming, where "*their fall is without honour, and they are an eternal reproach among the dead,*" crying out for mercy; and, because they themselves never showed mercy, now, no mercy is shown to them in turn. How many may not there be at this moment in hell, who, like the rich man referred to, may be calling on the angels of heaven, to warn their unreflecting heirs, now pursuing the same course of hardhearted insensibility towards the poor, of the awful doom in store for them. But, what could an angel from heaven, what could the solemn accents of a man returning from the grave, reveal to them, that they have not already, on still higher authority—an authority greater than Moses and the prophets—the direct authority of an infinitely veracious God? For, heretofore, "*God, who, at sundry times, and in divers manners, spoke in times past, to the fathers by the prophets, last of all, in these days, hath spoken to us by His Son, whom He hath appointed heir of all things, by whom, also, He made the world*" (Heb. i. 1, 2). We should, then, "*See not to refuse Him that speaketh. For, if they escaped not to refuse Him that spoke upon earth, much more shall not we that turn away from Him that speaketh to us from heaven*" (Heb. xii. 25.)

CHAPTER XVII.

ANALYSIS.

In this chapter, our Lord inculcates the avoidance of scandal, the forgiveness of injuries, and He points out the great power of faith (1-6). He next inculcates the virtue of humility on our part, by describing the unprofitable servant (7-10). We have next an account of the cure of nine lepers, and our Lord's remarks on their want of gratitude (11-19). He next treats of the coming of the Kingdom of God, and of the final coming to judgment of the Son of Man (20-37).

TEXT.

*A*ND *he said to his disciples: It is impossible that scandals should not come: but wo to him through whom they come.*

2. *It were better for him, that a mill-stone were hanged about his neck, and he cast into the sea, than he should scandalize one of these little ones.*

3. *Take heed to yourselves. If thy brother sin against thee, reprove him: and if he do penance, forgive him.*

4. *And if he sin against thee seven times in a day, and seven times in a day be converted unto thee, saying, I repent: forgive him.*

5. *And the apostles said to the Lord: Increase our faith.*

6. *And the Lord said: If you had faith like to a grain of mustard-seed, you might say to this mulberry-tree, Be thou rooted up, and be thou transplanted into the sea: and it would obey you.*

7. *But which of you having a servant plowing or feeding cattle, will say to him when he is come from the field: Immediately go, sit down to meat:*

8. *And will not rather say to him; Make ready my supper, and gird thyself, and serve me whilst I eat and drink, and afterwards thou shalt eat and drink?*

9. *Doth he thank that servant, for doing the things which he commanded him?*

10. *I think not. So you also, when you shall have done all these things that are commanded you, say: We are unprofitable servants; we have done that which we ought to do.*

11. *And it came to pass, as he was going to Jerusalem, he passed through the midst of Samaria and Galilee.*

12. *And as he entered into a certain town, there met him ten men that were lepers, who stood afar off;*

13. *And lifted up their voices, saying: Jesus, master, have mercy on us.*

14. *Whom when he saw, he said: Go, show yourselves to the priests. And it came to pass, as they went, they were made clean.*

15. *And one of them when he saw that he was made clean, went back, with a loud voice glorifying God,*

16. *And he fell on his face before his feet, giving thanks: and this was a Samaritan.*

17. *And Jesus answering, said: Were not ten made clean? and where are the nine?*

18. *There is no one found to return and give glory to God, but this stranger.*

19. *And he said to him: Arise, go thy way; for thy faith hath made thee whole.*

20. *And being asked by the Pharisees: when the kingdom of God should come? he answered them and said: The kingdom of God cometh not with observation:*

21. *Neither shall they say: Behold here, or behold there. For lo, the kingdom of God is within you.*

22. *And he said to his disciples: The days will come when you shall desire to see one day of the son of man; and you shall not see it.*

23. *And they will say to you: See here, and see there. Go ye not after, nor follow them:*

24. *For as the lightning that lighteneth from under heaven, shineth unto the parts that are under heaven, so shall the son of man be in his day.*

25. *But first he must suffer many things, and be rejected by this generation.*

26. *And as it came to pass in the days of Noe, so shall it be also in the days of the son of man.*

27. *They did eat and drink, they married wives and were given in marriage, until the day that Noe entered into the ark: and the flood came and destroyed them all.*

28. *Likewise as it came to pass in the days of Lot: They did eat and drink, they bought and sold, they planted and built.*

29. *And in the day that Lot went out of Sodom, it rained fire and brimstone from heaven, and destroyed them all.*

30. *Even thus shall it be in the day when the son of man shall be revealed.*

31. *In that hour he that shall be on the housetop, and his goods in the house, let him not go down to take them away: and he that shall be in the field, in like manner let him not return back.*

32. *Remember Lot's wife.*

33. *Whosoever shall seek to save his life, shall lose it: and whosoever shall lose it, shall preserve it.*

34. *I say to you: in that night there shall be two men in one bed: the one shall be taken, and the other shall be left.*

35. *Two women shall be grinding together; the one shall be taken, and the other shall be left: two men shall be in the field; the one shall be taken, and the other shall be left.*

36. *They answering say to him: Where, Lord?*

37. *Who said to them: Wheresoever the body shall be, thither will the eagles also be gathered together.*

COMMENTARY.

We need not labour to trace any connexion between this and the preceding chapter, as some Commentators endeavour to do. It is very likely St. Luke notes down what is recorded in the beginning of this chapter, from memory, of course under the influence of inspiration, without any reference to the preceding. It may be that the words of this and the following verses were spoken on two different occasions by our blessed Lord (Matthew xviii.), and here.

1-4. (See Matthew xviii. 6-8, 21, 22.)

5. The words of this verse may be a detached and independent narrative, having

no immediate or direct connexion with the preceding. Probably, they were uttered on the occasion of the fruitless attempt on the part of the Apostles to cast out a devil, which our Lord ascribes to their want of the necessary faith (Matthew xvii. 19, &c.), and the allusion to the example of the mustard seed in both places, here as well as there, renders this probable. On many other occasions, our Lord reproaches them for their weak faith (Matthew viii., xvi., xvii.; Luke viii. 25). He attributed their failure to their unbelief, or want of faith; they, therefore, ask Him to increase their faith (xii. 28).

It may be, that on one of these occasions to which St. Luke refers here without mentioning it, these words were uttered by the Apostles, in reply to these reproaches. Although the words may be inserted here independently by St. Luke, without any reference to the context, they can be connected with the preceding, thus: The precepts enjoined in the preceding chapter and here, regarding self-denial in parting with riches and giving abundant alms, contempt of pleasures, forgiveness of injuries, etc., were very hard to flesh and blood, impossible even to our corrupt nature of itself. It required no small amount of confidence in God, founded on faith, and of Divine supernatural grace to comply with them. Hence, they pray for an increase of this confidence and grace to enable them to accomplish His holy will in all things. While humbly acknowledging the weakness of their faith, the Apostles, at the same time, profess their belief in our Lord's Divine power, since God alone could give or increase faith; and in commending their petition, He increases, to some degree, their faith, reserving its fullest increase till after His Ascension and the descent of the Holy Ghost on them.

6. (See Matthew xvii. 20.) In St. Matthew, our Lord speaks of removing a mountain, which probably was in view; here, He speaks of a "*mulberry tree*," probably within immediate reach. The Greek is "*sycamine tree*," which is said to be found in Egypt and Palestine, resembling a *fig-tree* in its fruit, and the mulberry in its leaves (Bloomfield). The Black-mulberry tree is called Sycamine in Greece (Kitto, Encyclopedia).

"*Be thou rooted up*," etc. A natural impossibility, requiring a miracle for its accomplishment; so, also in the spiritual order, although the forgiveness of injuries as enjoined in the above, and the other duties prescribed by our Lord, be impossible to corrupt nature; still, grace and faith shall achieve all. They shall remove mountains of pride and obstinacy, and tear up by the roots confirmed habits of sensuality and sinful selfishness.

7-10. Some Expositors say there is no immediate connexion between this and the preceding; others, however, trace a direct connexion thus:—Our Lord having enjoined the performance of arduous precepts, now wishes to eradicate every feeling of pride and corrupt complacency which His followers might be tempted to entertain from the observance of these precepts; and He does this by introducing an example from the ordinary occurrences of human life, from the treatment which a faithful servant, who carries out the wishes of his master, receives. While he receives the wages due to his labours, he is entitled to no special thanks for having discharged his duty. Our Lord applies the example to the case of His servants at the conclusion of the parable (v. 10), "*So you also*," etc.

"*Plowing or feeding cattle*," are expressive of any of the ordinary occupations of servants. They, most likely, have no other application in the parable. "*Go and sit down to meat . . . and afterwards thou shalt eat and drink*," convey, that those who labour in God's service, must not forthwith expect the rest and reward in store for them. They must labour in their Heavenly Master's service to the end, and accomplish God's will not only in one point, but in all things. They must not only fulfil one precept, but all God's precepts, and labour faithfully and unceasingly in whatever works He may enjoin on them to the end like the servant in question, who was obliged to attend his master on his return in the evening after having laboured in the field during the day.

"*Doth he thank that servant?*" &c. As in human affairs, the master does not "*thank*" or give any special mark of appreciation to the servant who discharges the prescribed duties, beyond the hire, the payment or remuneration, due to his labours; so, in the service of God, if we merely discharge the duties assigned to us, the omission of which would entail eternal woe, we are not to expect any special remuneration—"*thanks*"—any more than St. Paul expected (1 Cor. ix. 18, &c.), if he merely preached the Gospel, the neglect to do which, would involve him in eternal woe. It was only for a work of supererogation, the preaching of the Gospel gratuitously, he expected a special reward; and in this only had he any cause for glorying in the Lord. But, although the master does not "*thank*" his servant, or show any special recognition for his discharge of the prescribed duties, it by no means follows, that he does not reward him for his services, or that he fails to give him the stipulated hire or payment. So, in like manner, God rewards us for the observance of His Commandments, by giving us eternal life, which out of His infinite goodness He promises to those who, aided by His grace, keep the Commandments—"*If thou wilt enter into life, keep the Commandments*"—but we can expect no "*thanks*" or special reward, on account of the mere performance of what is prescribed; as we had done nothing extraordinary or singular, deserving of special and cumulative reward. This is attached to the observance of the Evangelical counsels, of which our Lord speaks, when addressing the young man in the Gospel (Matthew xix. 19, &c.), He says, "*If thou wilt be perfect, go sell what thou hast,*" &c.

"*So, you also, when you shall have done . . . unprofitable servants,*" &c. The word "*unprofitable*" is opposed to deserving of "*thanks*" as appears from the foregoing. What deserving of "*thanks*" means, has been explained in the foregoing, and illustrated by the conduct and teaching of St. Paul, in reference to the gratuitous preaching of the Gospel. It is observed, that our Lord does not say, "*you are unprofitable servants;* but, "*say you; we are unprofitable servants*" and, although our Lord would not tell us to say, what is not the truth, still He employs this form to commend humility, and make us acknowledge our worthlessness in His sight, even after having observed all His commandments.

He prefers this conclusion, "*say you*" &c., and this application of the parable, before, that, which the parable would naturally suggest, viz.: So neither shall God thank you, after you shall have performed all that is commanded you. This latter conclusion, our Lord does not use, because God renders great thanks, bestows great remuneration on His servants, after doing what they are bound to do, unlike earthly masters, who do not thank their servants in such cases. He uses the form employed here, to inculcate a lesson of humility, and make us acknowledge our unworthiness, in his sight, so far as we ourselves are concerned. He Himself would say to us, considering what we are, owing to His own grace, as He said of Job, "*Vir simplex et rectus ac timens Deum, et recedens a malo*" (Job i. 1); also, "*Well done, good and faithful servant, because thou hast been faithful over a few things,*" &c. (Matthew xxv. 21.) "*Come, ye blessed of my Father, possess you the kingdom prepared for you . . . for, I was hungry and you gave me to eat,*" &c. (Matthew xxv. 35.)

"*Unprofitable*," is differently understood by different Commentators. Some interpret it, we are *unprofitable*, because we bring no profit to our Master, who "*stands not in need of our goods*" (Psalm xv. 2); and we owe Him all our services on the titles of Creation, Conservation, Redemption, &c., even although he proposed no reward at all. Hence, a motive for us not to glory in our acts, and to practise humility. In St. Matthew (xxv. 30), the word has a different meaning, where he, whom our Lord designates as an "*unprofitable servant*," is consigned to outer darkness. In this latter passage, he is expected to bring some profit to his master, for the talent confided to him. Instead of that, violating his master's injunctions, he allows that talent to remain unemployed, and his master's wealth thus to become unproductive. In the former case our Lord himself calls him "*unprofitable;*" here, we call ourselves such, out of humility.

Others, understand it, we are "*unprofitable*," of ourselves, without God's grace, left to our own weak nature, which would be of itself incapable of fulfilling our prescribed duties.

The most probable interpretation is that given in the preceding verse, where it is opposed to receiving "*thanks*," or being entitled to any special recognition, as instanced in the case of St. Paul. This is the reason assigned here. We are "*unprofitable servants*," in the sense, that we have done nothing extraordinary, nothing that we were not bound to, under pain of eternal woe; nothing, therefore, in which we should have special cause for glorying; nothing that we did not owe on many titles of justice, to God. In this interpretation, it is opposed to the utility arising from the performance of works of supererogation, of carrying out the counsels of Evangelical perfection. This is not opposed to the Catholic doctrine of *merit*, which is abundantly proved from several passages of SS. Scripture. When we, looking at our own natural weakness, call ourselves "*unprofitable servants*," then it is, that our Lord, regarding in us the fruits of His own grace, regarding us as sons of God (1 John iii. 2); as heirs of God, and His own co-heirs (Romans viii.), will address us, "*Well done, good and faithful servant . . . enter into the joy of thy Lord,*" thus giving us the stipulated reward He promises us, as in the case of the labourers in the vineyard. (Matthew xx.)

11. We cannot determine for certain, to which journey of our Lord from Galilee to Jerusalem reference is made here. Nor, indeed, does the context here afford us any clue for ascertaining it. It may, possibly, refer to the journey mentioned (chap. ix. 42, &c.), on which he had been treated so inhospitably by the Samaritans, towards whom he returned good for evil, by curing one of their countrymen of a loathsome leprosy. For of the ten cured, one was a Samaritan. And His having passed through the midst of Samaria and Galilee, is mentioned in allusion to the cure of the Samaritan leper with the nine others. This was His direct route to Jerusalem, through the confines of both provinces, by the road which passes between both.

12. "*As He entered*," or was about to enter, "*a certain village,*" which was on the confines of both provinces. The cure here referred to took place outside the village, from which, by the law of Moses, those infected with leprosy were excluded. Hence, "*they stood afar off*" as they were not allowed to come too near, for sanitary and mystical reasons, contemplated by the law of Moses. At what distance, lepers were obliged to keep aloof cannot be ascertained.

13. "*They lifted up their voice.*" As they could not approach too near (Leviticus

xiii, 46), in order to be heard by Him, and also to show the earnestness and fervour of their supplication. They also joined in one common cry, in the hope that their joint cry for relief would be more efficacious. Jews and Samaritans, between whom there was no communication (John iv. 9), cast aside their mutual religious differences, and became united from a sense of their common misery, and a strong desire of a cure, of which all were equally in quest.

"*Jesus, Master.*" The Greek word for "*Master*"—επιστατα—which is peculiar to St. Luke, and applied by him in several parts of his Gospel to our Lord only, (v. 5; viii. 24-45; ix. 33-49), signifies, not merely a teacher, but a teacher vested with authority. It conveys, You can command all things, command this disease to depart from us. Comparing Luke ix. 49, with Matthew xvii. 4; Mark ix. 5, it signifies the same as κυριε, *Lord*, and *Rabbi, Master*. In Luke (ix. 49), it corresponds with διδασκαλε, *Master, Teacher*, in Mark ix. 38.

"*Have mercy on us.*" They don't specify in what they hoped to have Him exercise mercy. But, firmly believing in His power, they confided in His beneficent will to restore them to health, and remove their bodily leprosy.

14. "*Whom when He saw,*" not only with the eyes of the body, but also with the eyes of mercy, "*He said: Go, show yourselves to the priests.*" (See Matthew viii. 4, &c.) Our Lord sends them to the priests, before He actually cures them, as He cured the leper (Matthew viii.), in order to try their faith and test their obedience, and also make it clear, to whom they were indebted for their cure. Understanding our Lord's command to contain an assurance that He would cure them—the priests had no power to cure, their part simply was to attest the cure and offer a sacrifice of thanksgiving as prescribed in the law of Moses, and restore them to society (Leviticus xiii. 14)—they obeyed at once, and were miraculously cured on their way. It is said by some, that, as our Lord could not recognise the Samaritan priests—priests of a false faith and worship—He meant that even the Samaritan would go to Jewish priests. Others say, that the "*priests*" meant, those belonging to each one's religion. The Jewish priests, for the Jews; the Samaritan priest, for the Samaritan leper. Without raising any question as to our Lord's sending the Samaritan to his own priest, as a minister of a schismatical worship, the advocates of this latter opinion might say, he was sent merely for a certificate of his restoration to health, which, likely, the Jewish priests would not give; and even, if given by them, it would not avail him. This did not necessarily entail a journey to Jerusalem on the part of the Jewish lepers. The priests of any locality could give the required attestation of the cure; and thus enable a cured leper to return to his house and kindred.

15. Whether he returned, after having shown himself to the priest, as our Lord commanded, and received the required certificate of his cure, or before it, when on his way he saw himself cured, is not quite clear from the context, although the words, "*when he saw that he was made clean, he went back,*" would seem in favour of the opinion that he returned the moment he saw himself cured. Having gone some distance, and probably out of our Redeemer's sight, they perceived their cure. Most likely, they were also cleansed from the leprosy of sin. Our Redeemer, it is thought, usually conferred the grace of justification on those on whom He wrought a bodily cure, inspiring them with sentiments of true contrition.

"*With a loud voice,*" showing the intensity of his grateful feelings.

"*Glorifying God,*" who displayed His power and goodness in his cure, through Christ.

16. "*And fell down on his face*," in prostrate adoration, "*at His feet*." Before, he kept aloof; now, seeing himself cured, he ventured to approach nearer, even to His very feet.

"*And he was a Samaritan*." The Evangelist adds this, to contrast the gratitude of this stranger, who belonged to a people who were not so favoured as the Jews, with the ingratitude of the nine others who were Jews.

(For the history of the Samaritans, see Matthew x. 5.)

17, 18. This interrogatory form is a more forcible way of enunciating the fact of their cure.

Our Lord would seem to reproach the nine others for their want of gratitude in not imitating the example of the Samaritan, who returned and gave thanks to his benefactor. "*To give glory to God*," by openly proclaiming the exercise of His power and goodness in their cure through Christ. He does not say, "*give glory to Me*," to convey, that the glory of every thing should be given to God alone, and that He sought His Father's glory in all He did.

"*But this stranger*," alien in religion and extraction. The circumstance of this man being a stranger to the Jewish religion, a member of a false and schismatical Church, between which and the Synagogue there was no communication, not even civil intercourse, only set forth, in a clearer light, the ingratitude of the Jews, God's chosen people, on whom He bestowed so many and such signal favours; to whom the Son of God was sent to preach first, and by them ungratefully rejected.

"*Where are the nine?*" How applicable is not this question, in many instances, to Christians, who, after receiving wonderful cures of their bodily ailments and spiritual distempers from God, ungratefully forget all, and insult and outrage afresh the best of benefactors, relapsing into sin, like the swine wallowing in the mire, or the dog returning to his vomit; thus, crucifying again the Son of God, and making a mockery of Him.

19. "*Arise*," from the posture in which he lay prostrate at His feet. "*Go thy way*." Thou hast shown thy gratitude, in which the nine others were signally wanting.

"*Thy faith*," whereby thou didst unhesitatingly believe in My power; and, confiding in My implied assurance of curing thee, on thy way to the priest, didst obey My mandate. "*Hath made thee whole*," restored his bodily health, and most likely, cured him of the spiritual leprosy of sin, signified by the corporal leprosy from which he suffered. Our Lord, by ascribing the cure to faith, which concurred as a necessary disposition for effecting it, showed His great modesty, in not ascribing it to Himself, who accomplished it.

He, as usual, commends the great virtue of faith, as it was the foundation of the whole system of spiritual life, and of the religion He was about to establish. It was the virtue most needed to bring man back to God. For, as man first departed from God by pride of intellect, the affectation of knowledge like unto that of God; so, his first step in his return to God must be, by humbling that proud intellect, and rendering it captive to faith in embracing, on the sole authority of God, truths which it could not understand, since faith is the "*argumentum non apparentium*" (Heb. xi. 1). (See 2 Cor. x. 4, 5.)

20. "*And being asked by the Pharisees*," on some occasion or other. We need not trouble ourselves too much in tracing a connexion between this and the preceding. St. Luke oftentimes describes consecutively, in the same passage, events and occurrences that took place only at different times, on different occasions, and in different places.

"*When the kingdom of God,*" &c. Our Lord and the Baptist had, several times, spoken of the near approach of the kingdom of God. The Pharisees, who, in common with the great bulk of the Jewish nation, formed certain false carnal notions on this subject—expecting that the kingdom of this long-expected Messiah would be all earthly, exceeding in external splendour that of Solomon, subjecting all the nations of the earth to the power of the Jews—not having seen any signs of this long-desired state of things, now derisively ask Him when His kingdom, His glorious reign, would make its appearance.

Our Lord, seriously replying to their derisive taunts, tells them, "*the kingdom of God cometh not with observation,*" that is, with such signs as they expected, viz., the precursory manifestation of earthly pomp, or regal power and magnificence, which usher in earthly royalty; in other words, He tells them, that His kingdom is not earthly, but all spiritual; although, indeed, it might be said, that the first coming, too, of the Messiah, had its proper precursory signs, viz., prophecies fulfilled, miracles performed, heavenly manifestations, angels appearing at His birth, the Magi at the stable, the prophecies of Simeon and Anna, His wonderful doctrine, preaching, &c. The coming of the Son of God, as well as His reign, is twofold—the first, in humility and hidden privacy; the second, in majesty, which shall show itself in splendour and power all at once, "*Deus manifeste veniet*" (Psalm xlix. 3), so that there will be no mistake regarding it. Our Lord treats, in the first place, of His first coming, which was a preparation for the second, and, speaking of this first reign, He says:

21. No one can say regarding it, that the seat of royalty is here or there, in this city or that; and He shows the utter folly of His derisive interrogators, in looking for what is present with them. "*For, lo, the kingdom of God is within you.*" It is in your own power to embrace it. You need not mount to heaven to bring it down, nor cross the sea to fetch it (Deut. xxx. 11-14; Rom. x. 8, 9). Or, "*within you,*" may mean, it is all spiritual, in the hearts of good men, in which God reigns spiritually by faith, hope, and charity; and in yours, too, if you wish to correspond with God's grace. In saying to the Pharisees, "*it is within you,*" our Lord does not mean, that they are of the kingdom of God; but that their contemporaries, who had grace and faith, and practised obedience and humility, were of it; that it was of such a nature as to be in the souls of men, and that they could be of it, if they pleased. Hence, it is said elsewhere, "*the kingdom of God is come upon you*" (Matthew xii. 28); the word, "*you,*" denoting all men who wished to embrace it. Some understand "*within you,*" to mean, in the midst of you. "*Where hath stood one in the midst of you, whom you know not*" (John i. 26). Our Lord, in answering their question, passes from treating of the future kingdom to the present, as (in Matthew xvii. 11, 12; Mark ix. 11) when asked about Elias, the Thesbite, He treats of the Baptist, his type or figure.

22. Turning from the unbelieving Pharisees, who derided Him, to His disciples, ever docile and respectful, He tells them that in the embarrassments, that they shall have hereafter to encounter, they will eagerly desire, even for one day, His society, such as they now enjoy, in order to receive advice and counsel how to act; but owing to His having ascended into heaven, they shall not have that advantage. To His disciples, He speaks of His glorious coming, typified by His coming to destroy Jerusalem by the hands of the Romans. Some understand the words to mean, that in the midst of the trials of this life, they would anxiously long to see our Lord's coming on His own day in majesty to judge the world, and punish the enemies by whom they are now oppressed.

23. Between My ascension and final glorious coming, false prophets will arise, saying, "*See here and see there.*" Some understand this, of the time preceding the destruction of Jerusalem; others, of His final glorious coming in majesty, to take vengeance on His enemies, of whose unutterable woes at the end of the world, those endured at the taking of Jerusalem were an expressive type and figure (see Matthew xxiv., *passim*). There is no opposition between the words of this verse, and of verse 21. For, here, He speaks of false prophets; there (*v.* 21), of men in general, the purposes referred to in both places being different.

24. This may refer to His second coming in majesty; or, to His coming suddenly to destroy Jerusalem, and utterly extirpate, on account of their crimes and resistance to grace, the ungrateful Jewish nation. He shall come upon the Jews suddenly, like the lightning of heaven—an image of His unexpected coming at the end of the world, when He shall appear suddenly in His awful majesty (see Matthew xxiv. 25-27).

25. But, before He comes in His glory and majesty, "*He must first suffer many things, and be rejected by this generation,*" of Jews now alive, who shall crucify Him and put Him to death. The same treatment is in store for all His followers. "*Through many tribulations we must enter into the kingdom of God*" (Acts xiv. 21).

26, 27. (See Matthew xxiv. 37-39.)

28. This example is recorded by St. Luke only, with a view to the lesson inculcated (*v.* 32).

30. "*Even thus,*" that is, after the examples of the unexpected suddenness with which God visited the sinful Antediluvians and the Sodomites, shall the Son of Man come suddenly and unexpectedly.

31. (See Matthew xxiv. 17, 18.)

32. "*Remember Lot's wife*" (Genesis xix. 26). She was commanded by the Angel not to look back, while Sodom, &c., were being destroyed. Disobeying the Angel's command, she, from a lingering longing and love for what she left behind her in Sodom, or from an undue anxiety about her friends and relations, looked back, and was turned into a pillar of salt, "*a monument of an incredulous soul*" (Wisdom x. 7). Our Redeemer here cautions His followers, by the examples of the terrible fate of Lot's wife, not to imitate her in looking back with an inordinate desire for earthly goods, or a desire to return to past sinful pursuits; but rather, to look forward to the goods to come, lest, when the day of the Lord shall have arrived, we may find ourselves irreparably involved in the punishment of the wicked.

33. (See Matthew xvi. 25; x. 39.)

34-36. (See Matthew xxiv. 40, 41.)

"*Where, Lord?*" Our Lord had been speaking of the mysterious separation of the good and the bad; some to be taken, and others left. Not understanding all He had been saying in a style of almost prophetic mysteriousness, they ask Him, "*where*" those taken shall be brought to; or, "*where,*" the events He had been speaking of would take place. He answers in a general mysterious manner.

37. "*Wheresoever,*" &c. (See Matthew xxiv. 28.)

CHAPTER XVIII.

ANALYSIS.

In this chapter, our Lord proposes the parable of the unjust judge and the importunate widow, to show the necessity and advantages of continuous persevering prayer, offered up with confidence (1-8). He illustrates the vices of pride and the virtue of humility by the parable of the Pharisee and the Publican (9-14). After blessing the little children who were presented to Him, and having given salutary instructions on the subject of detachment from earthly possessions, to a ruler who would fain become His follower, but was prevented from doing so by his riches (15-30), He foretells His future Passion and Resurrection (31-34). He cures a blind man at Jericho (35-43).

TEXT.

AND he spoke also a parable to them, that we ought always to pray, and not to faint.

2. Saying: There was a judge in a certain city, who feared not God, nor regarded man.

3. And there was a certain widow in that city, and she came to him, saying: Avenge me of my adversary.

4. And he would not for a long time. But afterwards he said within himself: Although I fear not God, nor regard man,

5. Yet because this widow is troublesome to me, I will avenge her, lest continually coming she weary me.

6. And the Lord said: Hear what the unjust judge saith.

7. And will not God revenge his elect who cry to him day and night: and will he have patience in their regard?

8. I say to you that he will quickly revenge them. But yet the son of man when he cometh, shall he find, think you, faith on earth?

9. And to some who trusted in themselves as just; and despised others, he spoke also this parable:

10. Two men went up into the temple to pray: the one a Pharisee, and the other a publican.

11. The Pharisee standing prayed thus with himself: O God, I give thee thanks that I am not as the rest of men, extortioners, unjust, adulterers, as also is this publican.

12. I fast twice in a week: I give tithes of all that I possess.

13. And the publican standing afar off would not so much as lift up his eyes towards heaven; but struck his breast saying: O God, be merciful to me a sinner.

14. I say to you, this man went down into his house justified rather than the other: because every one that exalteth himself, shall be humbled: and he that humbleth himself, shall be exalted.

15. And they brought unto him also infants, that he might touch them. Which when the disciples saw, they rebuked them.

16. But Jesus, calling them together, said: Suffer children to come to me, and forbid them not, for of such is the kingdom of God.

17. Amen I say to you: Whosoever shall not receive the kingdom of God as a child, shall not enter into it.

18. And a certain ruler asked him, saying: Good master, what shall I do to possess everlasting life?

19. And Jesus said to him: Why dost thou call me good? None is good but God alone.

20. Thou knowest the commandments: Thou shalt not kill: Thou shalt not commit adultery: Thou shalt not steal: Thou shalt not bear false witness: Honour thy father and mother.

21. Who said: All these things have I kept from my youth.

22. *Which when Jesus had heard, he said to him: Yet one thing is wanting to thee: sell all whatever thou hast, and give to the poor, and thou shalt have treasure in heaven: and come, follow me.*

23. *He having heard these things, became sorrowful: for he was very rich.*

24. *And Jesus seeing him become sorrowful, said: How hardly shall they that have riches enter into the kingdom of God.*

25. *For it is easier for a camel to pass through the eye of a needle, than for a rich man to enter into the kingdom of God.*

26. *And they that heard it said: Who then can be saved?*

27. *He said to them: The things that are impossible with men, are possible with God.*

28. *Then Peter said: Behold we have left all things, and have followed thee.*

29. *Who said to them: Amen I say to you, there is no man that hath left house, or parents, or brethren, or wife, or children, for the kingdom of God's sake,*

30. *Who shall not receive much more in this present time, and in the world to come life everlasting.*

31. *Then Jesus took unto him the twelve, and said to them: Behold we go up to Jerusalem, and all things shall be accomplished which were written by the prophets concerning the son of man.*

32. *For he shall be delivered to the Gentiles, and shall be mocked, and scourged, and spit upon:*

33. *And after they have scourged him, they will put him to death, and the third day he shall rise again.*

34. *And they understood none of these things, and this word was hid from them, and they understood not the things that were said.*

35. *Now it came to pass, when he drew nigh to Jericho, that a certain blind man sat by the way-side, begging.*

36. *And when he heard the multitude passing by, he asked what this meant.*

37. *And they told him that Jesus of Nazareth was passing by.*

38. *And he cried out, saying: Jesus, son of David, have mercy on me.*

39. *And they that went before, rebuked him, that he should hold his peace. But he cried out much more: Son of David, have mercy on me.*

40. *And Jesus standing commanded him to be brought unto him. And when he was come near he asked him,*

41. *Saying: What wilt thou that I do to thee? But he said: Lord, that I may see.*

42. *And Jesus said to him: Receive thy sight: thy faith hath made thee whole.*

43. *And immediately he saw, and followed him, glorifying God. And all the people when they saw it, gave praise to God.*

COMMENTARY.

From verse 8, it would appear, that the following was spoken at the same time and in connexion with the preceding teaching respecting the final coming of our Lord. "*And He spoke to them,*" viz., His disciples, "*a parable.*" He adduced a proof, *a fortiori*, or indeed, rather, *a dissimili*, as St. Augustine says (Sermo 36, de Verbo Domini), namely, from an example the very opposite of the subject to which it is applied, to show the necessity of continuous persevering prayer, full of confident assurance, that in His own good time, God will come to our relief.

"*That we ought always to pray.*" The Greek will mean, He spoke a parable "*for this,*" that is, a parable showing this. "*That it is necessary always to pray.*" The word "*always,*" does not of course convey, that men should be ever on their knees engaged in vocal prayer. This would be unreasonable and incompatible with the duties of life, and the wants of human society. It only means, that we should be always ready for prayer, frequent and attentive in its exercise, particularly at stated times, and in seasons of temptation and trial, persevering, and "*not fainting*," till we obtain our requests; that we should always walk in the Divine presence, by a spirit of prayer, love, and sorrow for sin; that we should refer our actions to God's glory, and by frequent aspirations, be constantly in communication with Him. This every fervent Christian can and ought to do, without any interference with other duties. Thus, it is said of David, "*Semper baculum in manibus*," &c. (1 Kings xvii.); our Redeemer, "*Semper docui in synagoga*." Even the widow in question did not always worry the judge; but, "*often*."

"*And not to faint*." The Greek, μη εκκακειν, means, to become faint-hearted, or desponding in difficulties and trials of life, owing to human infirmity, particularly, if we fail to obtain at once the object of our petitions. We should not, on that account, give up, but rather persevere, until even our importunity and perseverance succeed in obtaining our requests, as was the case with the importunate widow in the subjoined parable.

2. The example of a judge, who was cruel and inexorable, and who had a character for impiety and impudence, adds greatly to the force of the argument. If such a man could be prevailed upon by importunity, how much more, will not a just and merciful God be influenced by the persistent entreaties of His beloved children (*v.* 7), (Matthew vii. 11; Luke xi. 13).

"*Feared not God.*" An impious atheist. "*Neither regarded man.*" An impudent scoffer of his fellow-men, reckless of public opinion, who had neither conscience nor character. Sometimes impious, wicked men, are deterred from evil by fear of human opinion. This man had not even that redeeming quality—a man of the most defiant effrontery. Such a character is still fresh in the memory of men. For a true portrait, see Matthew xxvi. 62.

3. The helpless condition of the "*widow*," whom he was, in virtue of his office, bound to protect, adds force to the parable. "*Avenge me.*" The Greek word, εκδικησον, means, not to take vengeance, but to do justice, to rescue her by a just judgment from the unjust prosecution of her "*adversary*"—αντιδικου—her powerful legal opponent, who sought, by his influence and wealth, to crush her, in a suit at law.

4. "*And he would not for a long time.*" Likely, owing to his innate perversity, and hope of receiving a bribe.

"*Although I fear not God, nor regard man.*" I am dead to all stings of remorse of conscience, and deaf to the reproaches of men, utterly reckless, as regards character.

5. "*I will avenge her.*" I will render her justice, in the suit in which she is involved, against her powerful opponent.

"*Lest continually coming she weary me.*" The Greek word for "*weary*," υπωπιαζη, means, literally, as happens pugilists, to bruise one under the eyes, and leave livid marks —υπωπιον—to render them black and livid from hard fists and severe blows. The same as the Latin, *obtundo* (as 1 Cor. ix. 27). Here, it means, "*to worry him to death.*" The unjust judge now takes action, from a selfish feeling of consulting for his own ease, by being freed from the discomfort of constant worry. Similar are the conduct and sentiments of the man importuned at midnight (xi. 8). The judge might pretend to apprehend, from her continuous reproaches and injurious language, that she would at last assault him personally.

6. Our Lord wishes to direct their attention to the parable and its several circumstances and features, in order to see the contrast in its application more clearly.

7. "*God*," a just and merciful Judge, a beneficent Father, contrasted with an impious, impudent, heartless judge.

"*Avenge*." Vindicate the cause of "*His elect*," His chosen children, whom He loves with an infinite love; whom He loved from eternity; to whose good He makes everything else subservient; who, moreover, cease not, "*day and night, to cry unto Him*," offering Him a holy violence. Will He not be moved by their pious importunity, their filial confidence, their unceasing, persevering entreaties?

"*And have patience*"—μακροθυμων—which means, "*long suffering*"—"*in their regard*," referring to the elect. The meaning is, will God patiently permit them to be afflicted, or will He defer too long to vindicate and right His chosen servants? According to the Greek reading, the word "*and*," will signify *even*. Will God not avenge His elect . . . even when He is patient, or long-suffering in allowing them to be harassed and persecuted? St. Chrysostom reads, και μακρωθυμει. The Vulgate reading better suits the assertion in next verse, "*I say to you, He will quickly avenge them.*"

8. "*Quickly.*" When, after bearing long, and showing long-suffering in their regard, according to the decrees of His providence, He sees it expedient, not "*quickly,*" or immediately, on our petitioning Him. He often defers listening to our petitions, in order to try our patience and perseverance in prayer. For, it is to inculcate perseverance in prayer that the present parable is introduced.

"*Nevertheless,*" nothwithstanding My unfailing promise to succour My faithful followers, who, believing in My words and confiding in My promise, should persevere in prayer as a condition of obtaining relief and their liberation in due time; how few are there, comparatively, who, at My last coming, and during the preceding ages, when men should be ever ready for My coming, will be found to retain, under the pressure of persecution and suffering, the faith, which alone can insure persevering prayer, as well as the hope and firm confidence of being rescued by Me in due time. How few, therefore, who entitle themselves and have a claim to be delivered. The fault will be theirs, and not Mine; since they did not fulfil the conditions on which I promised to relieve them. This is understood by many interpreters of the general defection which, under the persecuting reign of Antichrist, shall take place at the end of the world (Matthew xxiv. 12-24; 2 Peter iii. 3). It may also be said to refer to the several defections which, at all intervening periods of time, shall take place, owing to the pressure of temporal evils, in consequence of which persevering and hopeful appeals to God will be given up by a comparatively large number of Christians. All this shall proceed from a want of firm faith in God's words, and of unhesitating reliance on His promises. For, from faith proceeds prayer, and from the magnitude and constancy of faith, proceeds perseverance in prayer. If we look to the present state of the world, the prevailing infidelity, the indifference even of professing Christians, in regard to their religious duties, and especially prayer, have we not grave reasons to apprehend that we are approaching, nay, almost surrounded on all sides, by that general apostasy referred to here by our Blessed Lord?

9. It is likely, the following parable of the Pharisee and the Publican, addressed not, like the foregoing, to His disciples, but to those whom He meant to reprove

and correct, was introduced by our Lord, not only to repress the pride and boasting of the Pharisees, and others such, and to inculcate the virtue of humility in general (*v.* 14), but also to point out its necessity as a condition of prayer, no less than perseverance, as inculcated in the preceding parable.

"*Those who trusted in themselves*," or, as the Greek has it, "were persuaded regarding themselves," would seem, from the parable, to refer to the Pharisees in a special manner, whilst including haughty men of every class at all times, who taking a vain complacency in themselves as possessing virtues of which they were in reality destitute, despised all others as devoid of such virtues.

"*He spoke also this parable.*" It may be a history of a real occurrence; or, it may be a mere imaginary occurrence—as seems most probable—intended by our Lord for the illustration of His subject. Whether real or imaginary, it is called a "*Parable;*" because, it serves to illustrate the general truth referred to by our Lord at the close.

"*Every one that exalteth himself,*" &c. The Greek for "*despised,*" means, *made nothing*, or, *thought nothing*, of others.

10. "*Went up,*" in allusion to the position of the Temple built on a hill. This is symbolical of the elevation of the soul, when addressing God in prayer. They went to pray; for, His "*house is the house of prayer.*" "*Pharisee*" (see Matthew iii 7). "*Publican*" (see Matthew ix. 11).

11. "*The Pharisee standing prayed thus with himself.*" The word, "*standing,*" according to some Expositors (Maldonatus, &c.), who hold that the Jews usually observed a kneeling posture at prayer, means, being present or placed in the Temple. These interpreters adduce in proof of their opinion the case of Solomon, who prayed on bended knees (3 Kings viii. 54; 2 Paralip. vi.), of Daniel (vi. 10), Micheas (vi. 6), the Apostles and disciples (Acts vii. 59; ix. 40; xx. 36), from whom the Christian custom of praying on bended knees was borrowed or derived. Others, however, maintain that whilst on certain solemn and exceptional occasions, such as those referred to, the Jews knelt at prayer, the rule usually practised was, to pray in a standing posture (Matthew vi. 5; Genesis xviii. 22; Job xxx. 20; Jeremias xvi.; xviii. 20; 2 Esdras ix. 2-5; 1 Kings i. 26). This latter seems to be the opinion generally adopted, which is corroborated by the word, "*standing,*" taken here in its literal signification. For the King alone, and the High Priests, had their seats in the Temple; they alone could sit; all others, generally stood at prayer and sacrifice, at which it would be very fatiguing to assist, during the long time spent at, on bended knees.

The Pharisee took his position in a prominent place, high up in the Court of the Temple, near the Court of the Priests, the Altar of Incense and the *Sanctum Sanctorum*, while the Publican stood afar off (*v.* 13) from the Court of the Priests, in some private place, from an humble sense of his unworthiness. The word, "*standing,*" conveys a different idea determined by the language used in both cases. As regards the Pharisee, it conveys—as appears from the language employed—that he stood with head erect and lofty mien, and boastful, as if to discuss with God, the question of His justice and personal merits.

"*Prayed thus with himself.*" The word, "*prayed,*" may refer to, "*I give thee thanks,*" thanksgiving being a form of prayer, as the Canticle of Anna is called (1 Kings ii. 1, 2, &c.), although St. Augustine would regard the words as spoken ironically. "*He went up to pray;*" he would ask nothing of God, but only praise himself.

"*With himself,*" is understood by some, thus: he prayed with himself, since he did not pray to God, who neither heard nor approved of his address; others thus: he prayed with himself, because it was not inspired by God, but proceeded from himself; others, because it was an act of self-complacency, in every respect selfish.

"*I give Thee thanks, O God,*" &c. "*Superbe gratias egit*" (St. Augustine, Psalm cxlvi). If this were a sincere act of thanksgiving to God, referring to Him as to its source, all that He possessed, an humble acknowledgment, that every good comes from Him—our Lord would not hold up the act of the Pharisee, as a subject for reproach and condemnation; but, it is because, it was a mere hollow expression of his lips, not a sincere act, proceeding from his heart, as his haughty language, condemning the rest of men, and the Publican, in particular, implies; it is because he gloried in his supposed good acts, and in his avoidance of gross sins, as if his fancied superiority over others were attributable to himself, to his own personal deserts, to his own industry, and not to God, "*per meus justitias, quibus iniquus non sum*" (St. Augustine), that our Redeemer condemns him. It is clear, from his contempt of others, his scornful allusion to the Publican, and rash judgment regarding him; his considering himself so perfect, as to ask nothing further of God, that this unnecessary allusion to his own good works, was the result of pride, and of his attributing all to his own merits only. Owing to the subtlety of pride, we often thank God, in order to praise ourselves. Had he a particle of humility, a knowledge that all he possessed was a gratuitous gift emanating from God, he would not unnecessarily boast of the gratuitous gift of another; nor would he despise others on whom the Author of every good gift did not think well to bestow so many blessings. How often do we find men speculatively declare they are utterly unworthy of the gifts God has bestowed upon them; but, in almost the same breath, they begin to boast of their superiority over their less favoured brethren, whose faults they at once proclaim. When subjected to humiliation, they practically deny what they asserted before, regarding their own unworthiness and the gratuitousness of God's gifts; thus in act belying their professions.

"*Touch the mountains,*" subject those haughty men to the slightest humiliation, and at once "*they shall smoke*" (Ps. cxliii). Then, indeed, the emptiness of their hollow professions becomes publicly manifest. We sometimes read of great saints—St. Paul and others—recounting their works and labours in the cause of God; but they did so from necessity, in order to protect the faith, and advance the cause of God against wicked impostors. In every case, they ascribed all the merit to God, and not to themselves.

"*The rest of men.*" This is qualified by the following, as if he were not so foolish as to prefer himself to all mankind, but to "*extortioners,*" who use violence; to the "*unjust,*" who employ fraud and deceit in order to take away one's property, &c. He thus takes a vain complacency in himself, compared with the greater part of mankind, though St. Augustine (Serm. 36), thinks he refers to the whole mass of mankind. "*Quid est,* "*cæteri homines,*" *nisi omnes præter ipsum? ego justus sum, cæteri peccatores.*"

"*As also is this Publican.*" He not only blindly expressed his opinion of the rest of men, but he descends to particulars, and rashly condemns the poor Publican, whom God justifies. This shows his pride, and makes it clear that, while thanking God in words, he was really, and in his heart, only boasting of his own superiority. If he were just, and the Publican, a sinner, should he not have acknowledged that his justice would be the gratuitous gift of God? And why despise or condemn any one else whom God might not have treated so bountifully? It was the effect of pride, attributing his fancied superiority to his own industry and innate excellence. It is likely, that these words were not heard by the Publican, who "*stood afar off*" (v. 13).

Having boasted of his having "*avoided evil*," the Pharisee, in next verse, boasts of the other quality of justice, viz., that "*he did good.*"

12. He not only fasted on the days appointed, but he boasted of having gone further; he, unlike these adulterers, "*fasted twice in the week.*" "*I give tithes,*" not only of corn, wine, and oil, as enjoined in the law, but of "*all that I possess,*" even to the smallest herbs, "*mint, anise, and cummin*" (Matt. xxiii. 23), unlike these "*unjust extortioners.*"

13. "*Standing afar off,*" in the furthermost part of the court of the people, without venturing to approach where the Pharisee stood, near the Court of the Priests and the Altar of Holocausts. The Publicans were prohibited by no law to enter the Temple, unless they were Pagans, in which case, they stood in the Court of the Gentiles. The Publican referred to here would seem to have been a Jew.

"*Standing,*" conveys a different posture here, from that in the case of the Pharisee. There, as the context shows, it denoted haughty demeanour; here, humble, downcast humility.

"*Would not so much as lift up his eyes to heaven.*" With these eyes, that had been hitherto wholly intent on the things of earth, he considers himself unworthy of looking up to heaven, to God, whom he had hitherto so grievously offended, much less of raising up his hands, like the Pharisee, who, probably, raised up his hands and eyes, from a proud consciousness of his deserts in the sight of heaven. By this, the Publican conveyed, that he sinned against the whole host of heaven. St. Augustine remarks, "*Ut aspiceretur, non aspiciebat, sursum respicere non audebat; premebat conscientia, spes sublevabat.*"

"*But, struck his breast,*" to show his sorrow of heart; to confess, and punish sin which proceeds from the will. He thus showed outward marks of penance, of his internal sorrow, and his resolve to chasten himself for his sins. The striking of the breast, at all times, with Jews and Christians, denoted sorrow for sin, humility of heart, and resolution to do penance. This striking of his breast was an external confession, a sign of contrition and satisfaction.

"*Saying, O God, be merciful to me a sinner.*" Literally, "to me, *the* sinful one." This is an humble confession of sin and a petition for pardon of the same; a very brief, but efficacious form of prayer, to be imitated at all times, by truly humble penitents, who should ascribe all the malice of sin to themselves, without extenuation of it from circumstances, or without throwing the blame on others. This brief, but comprehensive petition, is more fully expressed and developed in Psalm l.—"*Miserere mei Deus,*" &c. While the Pharisee scornfully singled out the Publican as an object of contempt, he, in his humility, singles himself out as the chief sinner on earth, surpassing in wickedness all other sinful men.

14. "*Went down,*" in allusion to the position of the Temple on a hill (*v.* 10). "*Justified,*" rendered really just by the grace of God, who Himself had inspired him with the necessary dispositions, consequent on which He remits sin and infuses the grace of justification. "*Rather than the other,*" whose boastful contempt and rash judgment regarding the Publican, and proud conduct before God, rendered him deserving of condemnation. That one was really justified, and the other condemned, is clearly shown from the general reason assigned (*v.* 14). The Vulgate is, "*ab illo,*" that is, *præ illo, in preference to the other.* The Greek reading is different in several manuscripts. That followed by the Vulgate, which is the reading of the Vatican MS.,

is παρ' ἐκεῖνον, *rather than the other*. Most of the ancient codices have ἢ γαρ εκεινος, *quam enim ille*, which it is very hard to explain. Some understand it thus: *Surely*, more than the other. Some codices have, ἢ εκεινος (μαλλον), being understood, as in Matthew (xviii. 8), Luke (xv. 7), more than the other. It is thus the Syriac version has it, and St. Augustine so quotes it in several places. (Epist. 86, ad Casulanum; Serm. 36, de Verbis Domini, &c., &c.)

"*Because, every one*," &c. (See Matthew xxiii. 12; Luke xiv. 11.) This is the general reason assigned for saying, that one was justified and the other condemned; and thus our Lord rebuked those who proudly trusted in their own fancied justice, and despised every one else (*v.* 9). These haughty Pharisees, and such like, were to be humbled here and hereafter, publicly rejected and abandoned by God; the most notorious sinners to be received by God in preference. "*The publicans and harlots to go before them,*" &c. (Matthew xxi 31.)

15, 16. (See Matthew xix. 13-15.)
17. (See Matthew xviii. 3.)
18-27. (See Matthew xix. 16-26.)
28-30. (See Matthew xix. 27-29.)
31-33. (See Matthew xx. 17-19.)

34. (See Mark ix. 31). The words of our Lord here were so utterly incompatible with their preconceived and cherished notions regarding the temporal glory and splendour of the Messiah's reign, in which they hoped to be sharers, that the allusion to His Passion they could never endure nor understand. (See also Matthew xx. 19.)

35-43. (See Matthew xx. 29-34.)

CHAPTER XIX.

ANALYSIS.

In this chapter, we have an account of our Lord's becoming Zaccheus' guest, and His instructions on the occasion (1-10). The Parable of the pieces of money given out to traders in order to derive profit therefrom. The rewards given to the faithful servants, and the punishment of the unprofitable (11-28). Our Lord's triumphal entry into Jerusalem (28-40). He weeps over Jerusalem. He drives the buyers and sellers out of the Temple (41-46). He teaches in the Temple. His enemies are prevented, through fear of the people, from destroying Him (47, 48).

TEXT.

*A*ND entering in, *he walked through Jericho.*

2. *And behold there was a man named Zacheus: who was the chief of the Publicans, and he was rich.*

3. *And he sought to see Jesus who he was, and he could not for the crowd, because he was low of stature.*

4. *And running before, he climbed up into a sycamore tree that he might see him: for he was to pass that way.*

5. *And when Jesus was come to the place, looking up, he saw him, and said to him Zacheus, make haste and come down: for this day I must abide in thy house.*

6. *And he made haste and came down, and received him with joy.*

7. And when all saw it, they murmured, saying that he was gone to be a guest with a man that was a sinner.

8. But Zacheus standing said to the Lord: Behold, Lord, the half of my goods I give to the poor: and if I have wronged any man of anything, I restore him four-fold.

9. Jesus said to him: This day is salvation come to this house: because he also is a son of Abraham.

10. For the son of man is come to seek and to save that which was lost.

11. As they were hearing these things, he added and spoke a parable because he was nigh to Jerusalem, and because they thought that the kingdom of God should immediately be manifested.

12. He said therefore: A certain nobleman went into a far country to receive for himself a kingdom, and to return.

13. And calling his ten servants, he gave them ten pounds, and said to them: Trade till I come.

14. But his citizens hated him, and they sent an embassage after him, saying: We will not have this man to reign over us.

15. And it came to pass that he returned, having received the kingdom: and he commanded his servants to be called, to whom he had given the money; that he might know how much every man had gained by trading.

16. And the first came, saying: Lord, thy pound hath gained ten pounds.

17. And he said to him: Well done, thou good servant, because thou hast been faithful in a little, thou shalt have power over ten cities.

18. And the second came, saying: Lord, thy pound hath gained five pounds.

19. And he said to him: Be thou also over five cities.

20. And another came, saying: Lord, behold, here is thy pound, which I have kept laid up in a napkin:

21. For I feared thee, because thou art an austere man: thou takest up what thou didst not lay down, and thou reapest that which thou didst not sow.

22. He saith to him: Out of thy own mouth I judge thee, thou wicked servant. Thou knewest that I was an austere man, taking up what I laid not down, and reaping that which I did not sow:

23. And why then didst thou not give my money into the bank, that at my coming I might have exacted it with usury?

24. And he said to them that stood by: Take the pound away from him, and give it to him that hath the ten pounds.

25. And they said unto him: Lord, he hath ten pounds.

26. But I say to you, that to every one that hath shall be given, and he shall abound: and from him that hath not, even that which he hath shall be taken from him.

27. But as for those my enemies, who would not have me reign over them, bring them hither; and kill them before me.

28. And having said these things, he went before going up to Jerusalem.

29. And it came to pass, when he was come nigh to Bethphage and Bethania unto the mount called Olivet, he sent two of his disciples,

30. Saying: Go into the town which is over against you, at your entering into which, you shall find the colt of an ass tied, on which no man ever hath sitten: loose him, and bring him thither.

31. And if any man shall ask you: Why do you loose him? you shall say thus unto him: Because the Lord hath need of his service.

32. And they that were sent went their way, and found the colt standing, as he had said unto them.

33. *And as they were loosing the colt, the owners thereof said to them: Why loose you the colt?*

34. *But they said: Because the Lord hath need of him.*

35. *And they brought him to Jesus. And casting their garments on the colt, they set Jesus thereon.*

36. *And as he went, they spread their clothes underneath in the way.*

37. *And when he was now coming near the descent of mount Olivet, the whole multitude of his disciples began with joy to praise God with a loud voice, for all the mighty works they had seen.*

38. *Saying: Blessed be the king who cometh in the name of the Lord, peace in heaven, and glory on high.*

39. *And some of the Pharisees from amongst the multitude said to him: Master, rebuke thy disciples.*

40. *To whom he said: I say to you, that if these shall hold their peace, the stones will cry out.*

41. *And when he drew near, seeing the city, he wept over it, saying:*

42. *If thou also hadst known, and that in this thy day, the things that are to thy peace: but now they are hidden from thy eyes.*

43. *For the days shall come upon thee: and thy enemies shall cast a trench about thee, and compass thee round, and straiten thee on every side,*

44. *And beat thee flat to the ground, and thy children who are in thee: and they shall not leave in thee a stone upon a stone: because thou hast not known the time of thy visitation.*

45. *And entering into the temple, he began to cast out them that sold therein and them that bought,*

46. *Saying to them: It is written: "My house is the house of prayer." But you have made it a den of thieves.*

47. *And he was teaching daily in the temple. And the chief priests and the scribes and the rulers of the people sought to destroy him.*

48. *And they found not what to do to him. For all the people were very attentive to hear him.*

COMMENTARY.

1. As our Lord was approaching Jericho, He cured "*the blind man*" (xviii. 35) Here, is a continuous description of our Lord's journey. Near Jericho, He cured the blind man; in Jericho, He converts Zaccheus; He wastes not a moment of His time; He seizes every opportunity, and seeks for every befitting occasion of doing good.

"*He walked*," that is, walking, He was passing through Jericho.

2. "*And behold*." This calls attention to what follows, as a great and wonderful occurrence. "*There was*," &c. He describes the man by name, Zaccheus; by his profession, "*chief of the Publicans;*" by his possessions, "*he was rich*."

Some say, that Zaccheus was a Gentile, which they infer from *v.* 9, "*he also is a son*," &c. Others hold he was a Jew. The very name itself is Hebrew, signifying, *pure, just*. This seems more probable. The reason for the opposite opinion will be explained in *v.* 9.

"*Chief of the Publicans.*" (See Matthew ix. 11.) If Zaccheus was a Gentile, he may be regarded as one of the Roman knights, or *Mancipes*, who farmed the public revenues. This class was held in high estimation (Cicero, Oratio 9, pro Plancio).

These had under them, in the several provinces, a class of inferior collectors, generally natives of the country. The latter were regarded with the greatest horror among the Jews (*loco citato*). If he was a Jew, then, the designation, "*chief of the Publicans*," denotes that, while he shared in the odium of the local collectors, he might be looked upon as a kind of middleman—or contractor—(Ellicott), between the Roman knights, who farmed the revenues, and the lower class of Publicans, who actually collected them, and in doing so harassed and oppressed the people. It denotes what we might term a Commissioner of the Customs (Kitto).

"*And he was rich.*" This is added, to denote the sacrifices he made in giving up his profession, and the difficulty in effecting his conversion (xviii. 24).

3. "*He sought to see Jesus, who He was.*" The fame of our Lord was everywhere spread abroad. Zaccheus, having never seen Him, was anxious to know Him by personal appearance, and see what kind of person He was. But as our Lord was accompanied by a large crowd of people, who pressed closely around Him, Zaccheus could not succeed on account of his lowness of stature. His anxious desire to see our Lord arose, probably, not from curiosity. He seemed quite disposed and prepared to believe in Him, of whose miracles and marvellous works he heard so much.

4. Hence, "*running before*" Him, forgetful of his dignity, his riches, and the ridicule with which, no doubt, the crowd would be glad to overpower a "*chief of Publicans*," he climbed up a Sycamore tree, which grew on the public road, by which our Redeemer was to pass, in order to get a glimpse at Him. "*Sycamore*," which differs from Sycamine (xvii. 6), denotes a species of tree, called "*the Egyptian fig tree*," composed of a *fig tree* 'συκος) and a *mulberry tree* (μωρος). It partakes of the nature of both; of the mulberry in its leaves, and of the fig tree in its fruit, which is like a fig in its shape and size. The fruit grows neither in clusters, nor at the end of the branches, but sticking to the end of the tree (Calmet—Pliny, Lib. 13, c. 7). Sycamore trees were very common in Palestine, especially in the low-lying valleys of the Jordan, where they grew to a considerable height. (3 Kings x. 27; 2 Paralip. i. 15; Amos vii.)

5. "*Looking up*," not casually, but by a lofty decree of Divine counsel, "*He saw him*," not merely by the eyes of the body, but with the eyes of Divine mercy, which penetrated His inmost soul, and inspired Him with sentiments of true compunction and sorrow. Addressing him by name, whom He never saw before, He says: "*Zaccheus, make haste and come down*," as if to say, thou hast ascended the tree in great haste; come down with the same haste.

"*For, this day, I must abide*," in virtue of My benevolent charity towards yourself and your entire household. I have decreed to select your "*house*," in preference to all the others in Jericho for My dwelling place this day. Zaccheus had, in soul and affection, offered Him a cordial invitation and welcome. "*Promittit Christus se ad ejus domum venturum cujus desiderantis jam possederat animum*" (St. Chrysostom, Hom. de Zaccheo); "*Etsi vocem invitantis Jesus non audierat, viderat tamen affectum*" (St. Ambrose). How long our Lord remained as Zaccheus' guest, we cannot know for certain. Likely, He remained there for the greater part of the day, if not for the night.

6. "*He makes no delay;*" "*tarda molimina nescit gratia spiritus sancti*" (St. Ambrose). "*Joyfully,*" with great spiritual joy, on account of the unspeakable honour bestowed on him, which fully satisfied his longings to receive his Lord.

7. "*When all,*" &c., that is the crowd, among whom, doubtless, were some Pharisees and their adherents, also some Scribes. All held Publicans in unutterable horror and aversion. "*They murmured,*" as was their wont, from a feeling of self-righteousness and pride.

"*A man that was a sinner,*" a leader in the traffic of iniquity—a man of infamous profession. The Publicans were regarded in this light by the Jews. Zaccheus' profession, or calling, was regarded as disgraceful among the Jews, and placed men on a level with the unbelieving heathens. Zaccheus, it would seem, was not above the temptations to rapacity and injustice, which the exercise of his office presented (*v.* 8).

8. "*Standing,*" that is, commencing suddenly to speak—similar is the phrase "*stetit et ait*" (x. 40)—he thus addressed our Lord, in refutation of the crowd, who, probably, may have overheard him thus speaking, when our Lord entered his house, or, when He was leaving it. Others, take "*standing,*" literally, to denote his respectful and earnest attitude in presence of His Master. It is likely, that our Lord had, on entering the house of Zaccheus, delivered heavenly maxims, as was His wont, on all occasions, regarding the several obligations of life, and the practice of all Christian virtues, uprightness and honesty amongst the rest, and that this elicited from him the following declaration.

"*Behold,*" as if to solicit attention to a matter deserving of admiration. He divides his goods into *two* parts, the first half to the poor; and thus, he would redeem his sins by mercy to the poor. "*The half of my goods, I give to the poor.*" "*I give,*" that is, am prepared and determined to "*give,*" to relieve the wants of the "*poor,*" and I now assign them for that purpose. This shows the thorough conversion of Zaccheus, and his resolution to practise the counsel of perfection, which, doubtless he heard, was given to the rich young man (chap. xviii. 22), a few days before. The remaining half of his property he reserves for the purpose of making the amplest restitution.

"*And if I have wronged any man of any thing.*" The Greek word for "*wronged*"—εσυκοφαντησα—means, to injure by false information, under threat of which money was often extorted (see chap. iii. 14). He reserves the second half of his goods, not for himself, but to discharge amply the obligation of restitution, which the Publicans were generally liable to, owing to unjust exactions. "*If,*" does not imply doubt; it signifies, whatsoever injury I have done fraudulently to any man.

"*I restore him fourfold.*" So as not only to give back the amount taken, but more than amply compensate for any loss that may accrue to him from loss of property, *lucrum cessans et damnum emergens.* From his giving one-half his property to the poor, which must have been justly acquired—this is contradistinguished from the substance acquired fraudulently—and his giving back, restoring four times more than he unjustly possessed, it is clear, the most part of Zaccheus' goods were justly acquired. His disinterestedness in divesting himself of the most of his property, to which men of his class were so inordinately attached, shows the thorough sincerity of his conversion. The law of Moses commanded restitution to a fourfold amount, only in case of stealth of sheep, and fivefold in case of the stealth of oxen (Exodus xxii. 1). But this did not apply to Zaccheus, whose unjust acquisitions were in money. In cases of voluntary restitution in other matters, the law required restitution of one-fifth in addition to the value of the principal (Leviticus vi. 5; Numbers v. 6, 7). But Zaccheus went far beyond the requirements of the law, and proved by his acts the sincerity of his conversion. His words have not reference to the past. They contain no boasting of his past merits, as in the case of the proud Pharisee. They merely express his present resolve, as the effect of God's grace and our Saviour's visit, in regard to the future; and they convey an atonement for the blasphemies of the proud Pharisees, and tend to justify our Lord's act, in dwelling with him, who shows himself to be different from what they charged him to be. Hence, he speaks only of his future acts, inspired by God's grace, and out of necessity, in reply to the taunts of the proud Pharisees

9. "*Jesus said to him.*" The particle "*to*" is interpreted by many to mean, *of*, or *regarding* him, to those present, as in Rom. x., "*ad Israel dicit*," that is, *de Israel;* "*multi dicunt animæ meæ*," that is, *de anima mea;* "*non est salus ipsi in Deo ejus.*" "*This day is salvation come to this house.*" "*This day*," shows that it was not of his past acts, but his present resolves, Zaccheus was speaking. "*Salvation,*" the fulness of faith, abundance of grace, thorough perfect conversion, not alone to Zaccheus himself, but to the entire family, in reward for the disinterested charity, and truly generous conduct of the head of the family, whose example they followed. Our Lord made his entire household, who, probably, may have been sharers in his sins of injustice, partakers of his abundant justification. They, too, received the grace of faith and justification, with the chief of the house.

"*Because he also is a son of Abraham.*" This may mean, that being one of Abraham's carnal descendants, our Lord, who was sent first to the lost sheep of the house of Israel, felt He was only exercising the duties of His office, in visiting him and converting him, the unjust murmurs of the crowd notwithstanding. According to this interpretation, the proximate reason of his conversion is not assigned. His conversion was not caused by his being one of the carnal descendants of Abraham, many of whom were left in their sins; in these words, a reason is assigned only for our Lord's visiting and staying with him.

It may mean, that whether Jew or Gentile, he has proved himself to be a real spiritual son of Abraham, one of the sons of promise, for whom alone the inheritance of justification is reserved.

Some hold, that Zaccheus was a Gentile. But besides, that the word is of Jewish origin, signifying, *pure*, the crowd would have loudly reproached our Lord with having chosen the house of an unbelieving Gentile for His abode, if he were such, as was done in regard to Peter, even by the faithful, after having received the Holy Ghost. Nor are the words of this verse, "*because he also, &c.,*" opposed to this; "*also,*" although a Publican, and seeming outcast from religious society; or, "*also,*" as well as the others who believed in Me, and imitated the faith of Abraham. Moreover, if he were a Gentile, our Lord would hardly say in the presence of the multitude at this stage, when they were not prepared for it, that a Gentile was a son of Abraham, although he might be such, in a true spiritual sense (Gal. iii. 9).

10. "*For the Son of Man,*" &c. In this, our Lord, redargues the murmuring crowd, by referring to His office, in coming into this world. He came to save the lost one especially, and in the first place, the lost ones of the house of Israel, such as Zaccheus was. This passage is read very appropriately in the Mass of the Dedication of Churches, to which it is very applicable. To churches dedicated and set apart for the oblation of the adorable sacrifice, the words will literally apply; "*this day I must abide*" (and abide permanently) "*in thy house.*" "*This day, salvation is come to this house,*" where the Lord of Glory deigns to dwell, in order to bestow on all who approach Him there, the abundance of all spiritual blessings.

11. "*And as they were hearing these things,*" viz., His disciples and the crowd, who were at the door awaiting our Lord's exit from Zaccheus' house, and had been attentively listening to the words spoken by our Redeemer and his host.

"*He added and spoke a parable.*" He proceeded to speak the following parable. The Evangelist assigns the reason, "*because He was nigh to Jerusalem,*" the capital city of Judea, only about eleven miles distant, or a few hours' journey from Jericho. "*And because they thought the kingdom of God should be immediately manifested.*" Only one reason is assigned, though there are apparently two. The words mean, because being nigh Jerusalem, "*they thought,*" &c. The disciples of our Lord and others imagined that our Lord, who on former occasions went up comparatively alone, but, on this occasion, accompanied by vast crowds, increasing as He went along, was now on His way to inaugurate His long promised reign, so ardently expected by the Jewish nation. This reign, they imagined, would be a temporal kingdom, far exceeding, in point of splendour and magnificence, the temporal kingdom of Solomon, as is apparent, from several occurrences in the Gospel, and, especially from the request of the mother of the sons of Zebedee (Matthew xx. 20). Hence, He is now saluted on entering Jerusalem, as the promised son of David, in whose regard the prophecies, both as to time and other circumstances, were literally fulfilled. Any thing uttered by our Lord, that clashed with their preconceived notions, was to them unintelligible and disheartening. It was to dissipate these notions, that our Lord spoke the following parable, in which He conveys, that until He returned again to earth, His glorious reign would not be manifested; that, in the interval, His servants should labour hard, by the good employment of the talents confided to them, to amass treasures of merits in expectation of it. Although this kingdom of His Church would be visibly established on earth—a light on a candlestick, a city on a hill, to which all nations would flock—still, the glorious ruler of that kingdom would be invisible, seen only through His visible Vicar, until, at the end of time, He would appear in glory, to reward His faithful servants, and trample on His enemies.

12-27. Some hold the following parable to be substantially the same as that referred to by Matthew (xxv. 14-30), although there may be some immaterial points of difference, both as to the time and place at which both were uttered. Others hold, they are different parables, uttered on two different occasions: this, *before* our Lord's final approach to Jerusalem; that in St. Matthew, *after* it. Doubtless, the scope and object of both parables are substantially the same (see Matthew xxv. 14, &c.), although some Expositors, even in this, note a difference; in St. Matthew, the apparent object being to indicate the proportion that should exist between the amount of goods confided to us, and the gains secured by us; in this, to show that the different degrees of glory and reward to be bestowed on us, will be in proportion to our labours and to the gains secured for our Master.

Calmet observes, that in the following parable, two parts are to be carefully distinguished. The first, contained in *vv.* 12, 14, 15, 27, regards the rebellious subjects of a prince, who went abroad to secure a kingdom. The example was fresh in the memory of the Jews. *Archelaus*, about thirty-three years before this time, had gone to Rome to obtain the kingdom from Augustus, as was then required in the case of the rulers of Judea, who were at this time, the creatures of the Romans, and, therefore, independently of personal demerits and cruelty, hated by the Jews (*v.* 14). The Jews held Archelaus in special hatred and petitioned Augustus against him on account of his cruelties (Josephus, Antiq. Lib. 14, c. 11). Augustus paid no heed to their remonstrance, and he returned to inflict punishment on those who would not have him reign over them. Whether our Lord had Archelaus in view, or only spoke generally, the circumstances admirably suit his case. And so far as his going to receive a kingdom was concerned, it was a type of our Lord's departure for heaven, to receive a kingdom and glory from His Father, as was his rejection a type of the rejection of our Lord by His people, and their dreadful punishment, shortly afterwards, at the hands of the Romans. This latter was a figure of the punishment to be inflicted at the last day, when our Lord shall come in majesty to judge the world. The second part of the parable has reference to the depositing of a certain amount of money by the prince in the hands of his servants, for the purposes of gain (*vv.* 13, 15 . . . 26).

"*A certain nobleman went into a far country.*" This chiefly refers to our Lord's Ascension, to receive the kingdom and glory from His Father, whence He is to return in majesty at the last day. (See Matthew xxv. 14, &c.)

13. "*Calling his ten servants, gave them ten pounds,*" denotes the gifts, both natural and supernatural, bestowed on us by God, in order that we should employ them usefully, for His glory, as a means of receiving a reward at His coming. "*Trade till I come.*" There is a difference clearly perceptible here between this and the parable in St. Matthew, in which latter parable the sums given are unequal. The "*pound,*" in Greek—μνα— is supposed, by some, to equal in value the sixtieth part of a talent, which, in weight equals 3000 sicles. According to others, it was equal to 25 sicles, or 100 drachmæ, or denaria (£4, 1s. 3d.) The Hebrew *mina* was equal to 60 sicles, or 240 drachmæ. Whatever may have been its precise value, the "*pound,*" or *mna*, denoted the gifts for the use and proper employment of which, we are to render an account to God hereafter.

17. "*Over ten cities.*" A mode of remunerating faithful governors, common at this time (Matthew xxv. 20-23). It is meant to represent the glory bestowed in judgment, on God's faithful servants.

19. "*Five cities,*" shows the different degrees of glory in store for the elect, proportioned to the different degrees of merit; one having gained ten; another, five; each being representative of different classes among the elect.

21. "*Austere.*" The Greek is αυστηρος—*griping*, grinding, heartless. The word in Matthew xxv. 24, is σκληρος—signifying the same.

27. This denotes the slaughter and utter ruin of the Jews at the taking of Jerusalem, and the dreadful punishment of the reprobate at the last day, when our Lord will trample on His wicked enemies.

28. "*Having said these things, He went before,*" &c. After having spoken the foregoing parable, which derived special significance from His being on His last journey to Jerusalem, where, by His death and sufferings, He was to earn for Himself, the kingdom of glory, in search of which He was afterwards to ascend. "*He went before,*" to show His alacrity in going quickly to the scene of His Passion.

Ascending up to Jerusalem." The entire journey from Jericho to Jerusalem was an ascent.

29-37. (See Matthew xxi. 1-10.)

37. The multitude of His followers began to praise God with a loud voice,

saying, "*Hosanna to the Son of David*" (Matthew xxi. 9). "*For all the mighty works they had seen*," the miracles, evidences of mighty power they saw performed by our Lord, such as that at Jericho (xviii. 35, &c.; Matthew xx. 29, &c.), but especially the resuscitation of Lazarus, on which account the crowd came to meet Him (John xii. 18.)

38. "*Peace in heaven.*" May Heaven offended by sin be reconciled to men on earth, through the redemption and satisfaction to be made by this Son of David, who is destined to take away the enmity that existed between them owing to sin; whose sacred destined office it is to "*make peace though the blood of His cross, both as to the things on earth and the things that are in heaven*" (Coloss. i. 20; ii. 14, 15). Thus appearing in heaven and presenting his wounds, He intercedes with His Father for us (Hebrews ix. 24). Hence, the words will not differ much from those uttered by the Angels at His nativity, "*Peace on earth to men ;*" because, Earth is one of the terms of reconciliation—Heaven the other, between which peace is to be established.

"*And glory on high.*" The consequence of this peace and reconciliation of man with God is, that the angels and saints shall, for ever, render thanks to God, and proclaim His boundless attributes of justice, mercy, goodness, &c., thus rendering Him glory.

39, 40. "*The stones will cry out*"—an hyperbolical form of expression, denoting it to be imposible, that His praises would not be proclaimed, since, if these were rebuked, God would miraculously animate the very stones to celebrate His triumph (see Matthew xxi. 11). Similar is the language (Habacuc ii. 11), "*For the stone shall cry out of the wall; and the timber that is between the joints of the building, shall answer,*" addressed by the prophet to Joakim, King of Judea, who built great palaces from the unjust exactions wrung from his people; thus menacing him, that the buildings and their component parts shall proclaim his injustice and heartless exactions practised on his people. The stones did, in point of fact, bear witness to our Lord's Divinity at His crucifixion, "*vere filius Dei erat iste*" (Matthew xxvi.), and also when, in accordance with His prophecy (verse 44), a stone was not left upon another, the whole city being razed to the ground by Titus (see Matthew xxiv. 2).

41. The only instances in which it is mentioned in the Gospel, that our Lord wept, are here, and at the resuscitation of Lazarus. No doubt, in both instances, He had mystical reasons in view. The impenitent Jerusalem and the dead Lazarus were both expressive figures of souls obstinately bent on their eternal ruin, being dead in sin.

We can here see how indifferent our Lord was to the acclamations He received; and how little He valued them, when He burst into tears while receiving them. We can also see His great charity for this wretched city, when seeing its obstinacy and unbelief, regardless of His own sufferings soon at hand, He wept, not over Himself; but "*over it,*" in view of the terrible destruction that was soon to overtake it, "*si oblitus fui tui Jerusalem, oblivioni detur dextera mea,*" &c. (Psalm cxxxvi. 5.)

42. "*If thou also hadst known, and that in this thy day, the things that are to thy peace,*" &c. Should "*if,*" be taken in its strict meaning, then the sentence would be suspensive, and no corresponding part expressed to finish it. Hence, some add, "*if, &c.,*" "*thou would be careful to embrace this favourable opportunity of securing peace,*" or, "*thou wouldst, by no means, perish.*" These authors say the sentence is suspensive, and broken by an aposiopesis, by no means uncommon in the language of grief.

expressive of the sorrowful feelings and deep emotion of our Lord, who burst into loud sobs and cries before completing it, as is usual with men who begin to speak, while overwhelmed with grief, which chokes their utterance. Others give the Greek, ει (*if*) the meaning of ειθε, *utinam, would!* or, *O!* in which case, the sentence is complete, thus; O! or would! that thou hadst known, "*thou also*," as well as I, or, rather, as well as this crowd, that now follow Me, singing joyous "*Hosannas*," and attending to My teachings and doctrines.

"*And that in this thy day.*" "*Thy day*"—on which is verified, in thy presence, the prophecy of Zachary, regarding the advent of thy long expected Messiah, and deliverer—or, "*thy day*"—the entire term of My preaching in thy midst, given to thee as a special favour, crowning all the other special favours and privileges bestowed on thee from Heaven, preferably to all the other nations of the earth. "*Thy day,*" of My gracious visitation (*v.* 44).

"*The things that are to thy peace.*" That would establish and consolidate thy temporal prosperity, thy lasting, abiding spiritual felicity, instead of the terrible destruction which is speedily on its way to overwhelm thee. The things that would establish peace for thee, are faith in Me, as thy long expected Messiah, obedience to My teachings, repentance, conversion from thy sinful ways. These would be the means of securing peace with God, of warding off the fury of the Romans, when they would find that My kingdom, all spiritual, would not clash with their legitimate rights or pretensions.

"*But now,*" or *in reality,* "*they are hidden,*" or *were hidden* "*from thy eyes.*" Wilfully blind, obstinate, and impenitent, you cannot open your eyes to the light, which from heaven has beamed upon you.

Maldonatus says, the objective case, governed by "*if thou hadst known,*" is not, "*the things that are to thy peace;*" but, the words, "*For, the days shall come upon thee,*" &c. If thou hadst known the misfortunes that are in store for thee, but which are now hidden from thy eyes, even "*in this thy day, which is for thy peace,*" that is, in which thou enjoyest such peace and security, thou wouldst not rejoice, but wouldst rather weep, even as I now weep on thy account. This would be a very smooth interpretation; but the Greek, τα προς ειρηνην σου, "*the things that are for thy peace,*" is opposed to it. And Maldonatus, without any authority, changes τα into τῇ, as if to agree with ημερα σου. No doubt, his interpretation would be very smooth, if there were any grounds for the change he makes in the original text, to suit it to his own notions of the meaning of the passage. Against his views, it might be said, that while weeping over Jerusalem, our Lord reproaches it with its blindness in not seeing what was placed before it; obstinately closing its eyes against the divine light; whereas, it could hardly be expected to see or know the evils that were hidden in the dark womb of futurity. And our Lord assigns, as the cause of this visitation, that they did not, as doubtless they should, know the day of His gracious visitation (*v.* 44), which seems to be the same as the words of this verse. In truth, all Maldonatus' reasoning is founded on a groundless supposition, that the words should be changed, and on a dangerous tampering with the sacred text, to suit his own preconceived notions.

43. "*For, the days shall come upon thee and thy enemies,*" &c. A Hebrew form for saying, the days shall come upon thee, in which thy enemies shall, &c.—just as, "*Ecce dies veniunt et suscitabo David,*" &c., that is "*dies, in quibus, suscitabo.*" (Jerem. xxxiii.)

"*Shall cast a trench,*" that is, as the original Greek means, a *rampart,* or *stockade,* such as Titus afterwards raised.

"*And compass thee round, and straiten thee on every side.*" This was actually done by Titus, when he blockaded Jerusalem, by finally building round it—after the stockade had failed—a wall that could not be burnt. unlike the rampart or stockade.

44. "*And beat thee flat to the ground, and thy children.*" Shall level the city with the dust, demolish the buildings, and destroy her inhabitants, by putting them to the sword, as applied to "*children,*" and dashing them against the very stones.

"*And they shall not leave in thee a stone,*" &c. (See Matthew xxiv. 2.)

"*Because thou hast not known the time,*" &c. All these evils will come upon thee, because thou hast not attended to My gracious visitation—the offers of reconciliation and pardon I have made thee. Therefore, shall God justly punish thee. The word, "*visitation,*" though sometimes used to denote the exercise of justice, and due chastisement (Exod. xx. 5; xxxii. 34; Isaias xxxii. 17), is here taken to denote a merciful "*visitation,*" such as our Lord's, on His entrance, this day, into Jerusalem, and His entire life among men, "*visitavit et fecit redemptionem plebis suæ; visitavit nos oriens ex alto.*"

45. (See Matthew xxi. 12, &c.) This was the second time our Lord vindicated the sanctity of His Temple. The first occasion is recorded by St. John (ii. 14), as having occurred at the commencement of His sacred mission. The second, as recorded here, occurred at its close. Almost His first and last public acts were the driving out ignominiously of the profane traffickers from the Temple. St. Luke here omits our Lord's retirement into Bethania, and the cursing of the barren fig-tree (Matthew xxi. 18-22; Mark xi. 12-14), as these occurrences were already mentioned by Matthew and Mark.

47. In this we have a brief account, left us by St. Luke only, of the manner in which our Lord passed the few days between Palm Sunday and Good Friday. By night, He retired from the city to Mount Olivet, where He spent the whole night in prayer (xxi. 37). He retired the first night to Bethania (Mark xi. 11).

The Pharisees, &c., sought every opportunity of making away with Him.

48. "*They found not,*" &c. They could devise no effectual means for destroying Him, as the people hung upon His words.

"*Very attentive.*" The Greek means, "*hung upon Him,*" being charmed and captivated with His divine eloquence, the wisdom of His answers, and the commanding excellence of His teaching, on which account, the chief men, Scribes and Pharisees, dreaded His boundless influence (St. Mark xi. 18).

CHAPTER XX.

TEXT.

*A*ND *it came to pass that on one of the days, as he was teaching the people in the temple and preaching the gospel, the chief priests and the scribes with the ancients met together,*

2. *And spoke to him, saying: Tell us, by what authority dost thou do these things? or, Who is he that hath given thee this authority?*

3. *And Jesus answering, said to them: I will also ask you one thing. Answer me:*

4. *The baptism of John was it from heaven, or of men?*

5. *But they thought within themselves, saying: If we shall say, From heaven: he will say: Why then did you not believe him?*

ST. LUKE, CHAP. XX.

6. But if we say, Of men, the whole people will stone us: for they are persuaded that John was a prophet.

7. And they answered that they knew not whence it was.

8. And Jesus said to them: Neither do I tell you by what authority I do these things.

9. And he began to speak to the people this parable: A certain man planted a vineyard, and let it out to husbandmen: and he was abroad for a long time.

10. And at the season he sent a servant to the husbandmen, that they should give him of the fruit of the vineyard. Who beating him sent him away empty.

11. And again he sent another servant. But they beat him also, and treating him reproachfully, sent him away empty.

12. And again he sent the third: and they wounded him also, and cast him out.

13. Then the lord of the vineyard said: What shall I do? I will send my beloved son: it may be, when they see him, they will reverence him.

14. Whom when the husbandmen saw, they thought within themselves, saying: This is the heir, let us kill him, that the inheritance may be ours.

15. So casting him out of the vineyard, they killed him. What therefore will the lord of the vineyard do to them?

16. He will come, and will destroy these husbandmen, and will give the vineyard to others. Which they hearing, said to him: God forbid.

17. But he looking on them, said: What is this then that is written, The stone which the builders rejected, the same is become the head of the corner?

18. Whosoever shall fall upon that stone, shall be bruised: and upon whomsoever it shall fall, it will grind him to powder.

19. And the chief priests and the scribes sought to lay hands on him the same hour: but they feared the people, for they knew that he spoke this parable to them.

20. And being upon the watch, they sent spies, who should feign themselves just, that they might take hold of him in his words, that they might deliver him up to the authority and power of the governor.

21. And they asked him, saying: Master, we know that thou speakest and teachest rightly; and thou dost not respect any person, but teachest the way of God in truth.

22. Is it lawful for us to give tribute to Cesar, or no?

23. But he considering their guile, said to them: Why tempt you me?

24. Show me a penny. Whose image and inscription hath it? They answering said to him, Cesar's.

25. And he said to them: Render therefore to Cesar the things that are Cesar's; and to God the things that are God's.

26. And they could not reprehend his word before the people: and wondering at his answer, they held their peace.

27. And there came to him some of the Sadducees, who deny that there is any resurrection, and they asked him,

28. Saying: Master, Moses wrote unto us, If any man's brother die having a wife, and he leave no children, that his brother should take her to wife, and raise up seed unto his brother.

29. There were therefore seven brethren: and the first took a wife, and died without children.

30. And the next took her to wife, and he also died childless.

31. And the third took her. And in like manner all the seven, and they left no children, and died.

32. Last of all the woman died also.

33. *In the resurrection therefore, whose wife of them shall she be? For all the seven had her to wife.*

34. *And Jesus said to them: The children of this world marry, and are given in marriage:*

35. *But they that shall be accounted worthy of that world and of the resurrection from the dead, shall neither be married, nor take wives.*

36. *Neither can they die any more: for they are equal to the angels, and are the children of God being the children of the resurrection.*

37. *Now that the dead rise again, Moses also showed, at the bush, when he calleth the Lord: "The God of Abraham, and the God of Isaac, and the God of Jacob."*

38. *For he is not the God of the dead, but of the living: for all live to him.*

39. *And some of the scribes answering, said to him: Master, thou hast said well.*

40. *And after that they durst not ask him any more questions.*

41. *But he said to them: How say they that Christ is the son of David?*

42. *And David himself saith in the book of psalms: "The Lord said to my Lord, sit thou on my right hand,*

43. *Till I make thy enemies, thy footstool."*

44. *David then calleth him Lord: and how is he his son?*

45. *And in the hearing of all the people, he said to his disciples:*

46. *Beware of the scribes, who desire to walk in long robes, and love salutations in the market-place, and the first chairs in the synagogues, and the chief rooms at feasts.*

47. *Who devour the houses of widows, feigning long prayer. These shall receive greater damnation.*

COMMENTARY.

1-8. (See Matthew xxi. 23-27.)
9-16. (See Matthew xxi. 33-41.)
17-19. (See Matthew xxi. 42-46.)
20-26. (See Matthew xxii. 20-26.)
27-40. (See Matthew xxii. 23-33.)
41-44. (See Matthew xxii. 41-46.)
45-47. (See Matthew xxiii. 5, 6-14.)

CHAPTER XXI.

ANALYSIS.

In this chapter, our Lord commends the generosity of the poor widow (1-4). He foretells the destruction of Jerusalem and of the Temple (5-24). He describes the precursory signs that are to usher in the Day of Judgment (25-33). He exhorts all to be watchful (34-38).

TEXT.

AND looking on, he saw the rich men cast their gifts into the treasury.

2. *And he saw also a certain poor widow casting in two brass mites.*

3. *And he said: Verily I say to you, that this poor widow hath cast in more than they all.*

4. *For all these have of their abundance cast into the offerings of God: but she of her want, hath cast in all the living that she had.*

5. *And some saying of the temple, that it was adorned with goodly stones and gifts, he said:*

6. *These things which you see, the days will come in which there shall not be left a stone upon a stone that shall not be thrown down.*

7. *And they asked him, saying: Master, when shall these things be: and what shall be the sign when they shall begin to come to pass?*

8. *Who said: Take heed you be not seduced; for many will come in my name, saying, I am he: and the time is at hand: go ye not therefore after them.*

9. *And when you shall hear of wars and seditions, be not terrified: these things must first come to pass, but the end is not yet presently.*

10. *Then he said to them: Nation shall rise against nation, and kingdom against kingdom.*

11. *And there shall be great earthquakes in divers places, and pestilences and famines, and terrors from heaven, and there shall be great signs.*

12. *But before all these things they will lay their hands on you: and persecute you, delivering you up to the synagogues, and into prisons, dragging you before kings and governors for my name's sake.*

13. *And it shall happen unto you for a testimony.*

14. *Lay it up therefore in your hearts, not to meditate before how you shall answer.*

15. *For I will give you a mouth and wisdom, which all your adversaries shall not be able to resist and gainsay.*

16. *And you shall be betrayed by your parents and brethren, and kinsmen and friends: and some of you they will put to death.*

17. *And you shall be hated by all men for my name's sake.*

18. *But a hair of your head shall not perish.*

19. *In your patience you shall possess your souls.*

20. *And when you shall see Jerusalem compassed about with an army: then know that the desolation thereof is at hand.*

21. *Then let those who are in Judea flee to the mountains: and those who are in the midst thereof, depart out: and those who are in the countries, not enter into it.*

22. *For these are the days of vengeance, that all things may be fulfilled that are written.*

23. *But wo to them that are with child, and give suck in those days; for there shall be great distress in the land, and wrath upon this people.*

24. *And they shall fall by the edge of the sword: and shall be led away captives into all nations: and Jerusalem shall be trodden down by the Gentiles: till the times of the nations be fulfilled.*

25. *And there shall be signs in the sun, and in the moon, and in the stars: and upon the earth distress of nations, by reason of the confusion of the roaring of the sea and of the waves.*

26. *Men withering away for fear, and expectation of what shall come upon the whole world. For the powers of heaven shall be moved:*

27. *And then they shall see the son of man coming in a cloud with great power and majesty.*

28. *But when these things begin to come to pass, look up and lift up your heads: because your redemption is at hand.*

29. *And he spoke to them a similitude. See the fig-tree, and all the trees:*

30. *When they now shoot forth their fruit, you know that summer is nigh.*

31. *So you also when you shall see these things come to pass, know that the kingdom of God is at hand.*

32. *Amen I say to you, this generation shall not pass away, till all things be fulfilled*

33. *Heaven and earth shall pass away, but my words shall not pass away.*

34. *And take heed to yourselves, lest perhaps your hearts be overcharged with surfeiting and drunkenness and the cares of this life: and that day come upon you suddenly.*

35. *For as a snare shall it come upon all that sit upon the face of the whole earth.*

36. *Watch ye therefore, praying at all times, that you may be accounted worthy to escape all those things that are to come, and to stand before the son of man.*

37. *And in the day-time he was teaching in the temple: but at night going out, he abode in the mount that is called Olivet.*

38. *And all the people came early in the morning to him in the temple to hear him.*

COMMENTARY.

1-4. (See Mark xii. 41-44.)

5. "*Some saying of the Temple.*" We are informed by St. Mark (xiii. 1), that our Lord uttered the words recorded here (v. 6), "*as He was going out of the Temple*"—after having paid it His last visit—there is no record of His having visited it afterwards—being spoken to on the subject by "*one of His disciples*" (see Matthew xxiv. 1, &c.), who pointed out to Him, with a view of averting the threatened destruction, the magnificence of the structure, its "*goodly stones*," and the costly votive offerings "*and gifts*" with which it was adorned and enriched. These votive offerings, presented by kings and others to the Temple, were very costly and numerous (2 Machabees iii. 2; v. 16; ix. 16).

The Greek for gifts, αναθημα, having the penultimate long (with an η, as here), signifies a thing set apart, and as the etymology of the word conveys, *hung aloft*, as a gift or votive offering. This is the only place where the word is found in the New Testament. In the Old (2 Machabees ix. 16), it denotes a votive offering. Having the penultimate short (with an ε), it is found in several parts of the New Testament (Rom. ix. 3; 1 Cor. xii. 3; xvi. 22; Gal. i. 8, 9). It always denotes an accused person or thing, set apart for destruction, as an object of divine malediction (see Rom. ix. 3).

6. "*These things which you see*," signifying, "*of these things which you see*" (and admire as deserving of immortality) "*. . . there shall not be left a stone,*" &c. By prefixing "*of,*" we would complete the sentence, which the vehemence of our Redeemer's feelings left incomplete. Others complete it thus, by putting the words interrogatively, as they are put by Matthew and Mark—"*Are these the things which you see*" and admire? Others, among whom Beelen (Græc. Gram., N.T., § 28, 3) say, ταυτα, "*these things,*" is a nominative absolute, representing emphatically the subject of the whole sentence. It is an example of a *Rhetorical Anacoluthon*. For the remainder, see Matthew xxiv. 2.

7-12. (See Matthew xxiv. 2-14.)
13-18. (See Matthew x. 17-22.)

18. "*But a hair of your head shall not perish.*" This is a proverbial expression, the same as "*the hairs of your head are numbered*" (Matthew x. 30), signifying, that no material evil or loss will befal them; that notwithstanding the number of enemies foreign and domestic, that may assail them, the providence of God will protect them, and turn all wicked attempts to their good account.

19. "*In your patience.*" By patiently enduring evil to the end, in the hope of future retribution, they "*shall possess their souls,*" shall gain and save their souls.

The idea conveyed is the same as in Matthew x. 39; xvi. 35, viz., that by suffering patiently and perseveringly for His sake, they shall gain their souls. *Perseverance* in patient suffering is of course implied, as in Matthew xxiv. 13.

20-24. "*And when you shall see Jerusalem compassed about with an army.*" This is what St. Matthew (xxiv 15) calls "*the abomination of desolation.*"

25-33. (See Matthew xxiv. 29-35.)

34. Our Lord here points out how we are to prepare for His coming; and cautions us against the chief obstacles to due preparation; He inculcates continual vigilance, which is in several places of Sacred Scripture (see 1 Thess. v. 6, &c.), recommended as the chief means of due preparation. What is said here to those who may be alive at our Lord's second coming, is intended for all men at all times; since, the second coming of our Lord to judgment virtually takes place at death, when each one is to be presented before the tribunal of Christ at the particular judgment, "*to receive the proper things of the body, according as he hath done, whether it be good or evil*" (2 Cor. v. 10). Hence, our Lord says, speaking on this subject, "*What I say to you, I say to all: Watch*" (Mark xiii. 37).

The exhortation to vigilance, with which our Lord closes His description of His coming to judgment, is recorded in the Gospels of Matthew (xxiv. 36-42); Mark (xiii. 32-37), as well as here, in different words. The lesson of instruction is substantially the same in the three.

"*And take heed to yourselves,*" be ever watchful and on the alert, "*lest any time*"—not alone your bodies, but—"*your hearts be overcharged,*" and weighed down "*with surfeiting and drunkenness.*" These words should be transposed, as "*surfeiting,*" follows, and is the effect of "*drunkenness.*" Excessive indulgence in drink and food, not only depresses and weighs down the body; but the soul, and renders it unfit for spiritual exercises, and prayer. Under "*drunkenness,*" are included all the other illicit pleasures of the body.

"*And cares of this life,*" excessive cares. The Greek, μεριμναῖς, denotes excessive, absorbing anxiety (see Matthew vi. 25).

"*And that day come upon you suddenly,*" unprepared for it, while sunk in the sleep of sin, and overcharged with carnal indulgences, which prevent spiritual vigilance and prayer.

35. "*For, as a snare,*" &c. The day of the Lord shall insnare unto ruin and destruction, those men who "*sit,*" in idleness and unconcern, absorbed in the enjoyment of sensual and illicit pleasures, with all their thoughts on earth, just as a snare catches those birds, that settle on the earth when they least expect it, while the birds that are borne aloft in air escape it. Similar are the words of St. Paul (1 Thess. v. 2, 3); Isaias (xxiv. 17); Psalm x., "*Pluet super peccatores laqueos.*"

36. Having refrained from these illicit enjoyments, which are an obstacle to vigilance, they should, then, be watchful (see Mark xiii. 33; Matthew xxiv. 42), and in order to succeed in this, as their own weak powers are unequal to it, they should invoke aid from on high, by constant and persevering prayer. Thus, avoiding sin by practising vigilance and good works, through the help of God's grace, which prayer will secure for them, they may escape "*the snare,*" and be preserved from all the evils, which God shall pour out on the wicked, and may be

worthy to stand with firm confidence and hope before the tribunal of the Son of Man, to receive favourable judgment of mercy.

37. From the time of His triumphal entry on Palm Sunday, our Lord devoted the day-time to preaching and to the service of the people, who, He knew, would shortly put Him to a cruel death—and most part of the night to prayer and communication with His Father.

"*In the day-time,*" literally, "*the days.*" He was preaching on Sunday, Monday, Tuesday, and Wednesday. It is not likely He went to the Temple on Thursday (see Matthew xxvi. 2-30). For the most of the "*nights,*" after preaching during the day, He retired to Mount Olivet, and there spent the chief part of the night in prayer, and in communing with His Heavenly Father, in order to prepare for His coming struggle. "*He abode in the Mount of Olives.*" He certainly went one of the nights to Bethania (Matthew xxi. 17). But whether He went there the other nights, is, by no means, clear. The words of this verse could be verified even in that view, as Bethania lay quite close to the Mountain of Olives. It may be, that our Lord spent the greater part of the night in the open air.

38. All the people came early in the morning to hear Him preach in the Temple, so attracted were they by His heavenly discourses.

CHAPTER XXII.

ANALYSIS.

In this chapter, we have an account of the conspiracy of the Jews against our Lord—the treason of Judas—the preparation for the Pasch (1-13). The last Supper, and the institution of the Blessed Eucharist (14-23). Our Lord's discourse on the occasion, among other things, His prediction of Peter's fall, and the promise to him of Primacy over the entire Church, and infallibility in guiding and governing her (24-38). His agony in the garden (39-46). His betrayal by Judas (47-53). The denial of our Lord by Peter (54-62). The mocking of Him by the servants (63-65). His intrepid declaration of His Divinity before the Council (66-71).

TEXT.

NOW the feast of unleavened bread, which is called the pasch, was at hand.

2. And the chief priests and the scribes sought how they might put Jesus to death: but they feared the people.

3. And satan entered into Judas who was surnamed Iscariot, one of the twelve.

4. And he went, and discoursed with the chief priests and the magistrates, how he might betray him to them.

5. And they were glad, and covenanted to give him money.

6. And he promised. And he sought opportunity to betray him in the absence of the multitude.

7. And the day of the unleavened bread came, on which it was necessary that the pasch should be killed.

8. And he sent Peter and John, saying: Go and prepare for us the pasch, that we may eat.

9. But they said: Where wilt thou that we prepare?

10. And he said to them: Behold, as you go into the city, there shall meet you a man carrying a pitcher of water: follow him into the house where he entereth in:

11. And you shall say to the good man of the house: The master saith to thee: Where is the guest-chamber, where I may eat the pasch with my disciples?

12. And he will show you a large dining-room furnished: and there prepare.

13. And they going, found as he said to them, and made ready the pasch.

14. And when the hour was come, he sat down and the twelve apostles with him.

15. And he said to them: With desire I have desired to eat this pasch with you before I suffer.

16. For I say to you, that from this time I will not eat it, till it be fulfilled in the kingdom of God.

17. And having taken the chalice he gave thanks, and said: Take, and divide it among you.

18. For I say to you, that I will not drink of the fruit of the vine, till the kingdom of God come.

19. And taking bread, he gave thanks, and brake: and gave to them, saying: This is my body which is given for you. Do this for a commemoration of me.

20. In like manner the chalice also, after he had supped, saying: This is the chalice, the new testament in my blood, which shall be shed for you.

21. But yet behold, the hand of him that betrayeth me is with me on the table.

22. And the son of man indeed goeth, according to that which is determined: but yet wo to that man by whom he shall be betrayed.

23. And they began to inquire among themselves which of them it was that should do this thing.

24. And there was also a strife amongst them, which of them should seem to be greater.

25. And he said to them: The kings of the Gentiles lord it over them ; and they that have power over them, are called beneficent.

26. But you not so: but he that is the greater among you, let him become as the younger: and he that is the leader, as he that serveth.

27. For which is greater, he that sitteth at table, or he that serveth? Is not he that sitteth at table? but I am in the midst of you, as he that serveth:

28. And you are they who have continued with me in my temptations:

29. And I dispose to you, as my Father hath disposed to me, a kingdom:

30. That you may eat and drink at my table in my kingdom : and may sit upon thrones judging the twelve tribes of Israel.

31. And the Lord said: Simon, Simon, behold satan hath desired to have you that he may sift you as wheat.

32. But I have prayed for thee that thy faith fail not: and thou being once converted, confirm thy brethren.

33. Who said to him: Lord, I am ready to go with thee both into prison and to death.

34. And he said: I say to thee, Peter, the cock shall not crow this day, till thou thrice deniest that thou knowest me. And he said to them:

35. When I sent you without purse and scrip and shoes, did you want anything ?

36. But they said: Nothing. Then said he unto them: But now he that hath a purse, let him take it, and likewise a scrip: and he that hath not, let him sell his coat, and buy a sword.

37. For I say to you, that this that is written, must yet be fulfilled in me, "And with the wicked was he reckoned." For the things concerning me have an end.

38. But they said: Lord, behold here are two swords. And he said to them: It is enough.

39. And going out he went according to his custom to the mount of Olives. And his disciples also followed him.

40. And when he was come to the place, he said to them: Pray, lest you enter into temptation.

41. *And he was withdrawn away from them a stone's cast: and kneeling down he prayed,*

42. *Saying: Father, if thou wilt, remove this chalice from me: But yet not my will, but thine be done.*

43. *And there appeared to him an Angel from heaven, strengthening him. And being in an agony, he prayed the longer.*

44. *And his sweat became as drops of blood trickling down upon the ground.*

45. *And when he rose up from prayer, and was come to his disciples, he found them sleeping for sorrow.*

46. *And he said to them: Why sleep you? arise, pray, lest you enter into temptation.*

47. *As he was yet speaking, behold a multitude: and he that was called Judas, one of the twelve, went before them, and drew near to Jesus for to kiss him.*

48. *And Jesus said to him: Judas, dost thou betray the son of man with a kiss?*

49. *And they that were about him, seeing what would follow, said to him: Lord, shall we strike with the sword?*

50. *And one of them struck the servant of the high-priest, and cut off his right ear.*

51. *But Jesus answering, said: Suffer ye thus far. And when he had touched his ear, he healed him.*

52. *And Jesus said to the chief priests and magistrates of the temple, and the ancients that were come unto him: Are you come out, as it were against a thief, with swords and clubs?*

53. *When I was daily with you in the temple, you did not stretch forth your hands against me: but this is your hour, and the power of darkness.*

54. *And apprehending him, they led him to the high-priest's house. But Peter followed afar off.*

55. *And when they had kindled a fire in the midst of the hall, and were sitting about it, Peter was in the midst of them.*

56. *Whom when a certain servant maid had seen sitting at the light, and had earnestly beheld him, she said: This man also was with him.*

57. *But he denied him, saying: Woman, I know him not.*

58. *And after a little while another seeing him, said: Thou also art one of them. But Peter said: O man, I am not.*

59. *And after the space as it were of one hour, another certain man affirmed, saying: Of a truth, this man was also with him; for he is also a Galilean.*

60. *And Peter said: Man, I know not what thou sayest. And immediately as he was yet speaking, the cock crew.*

61. *And the Lord turning looked on Peter. And Peter remembered the word of the Lord, as he had said: Before the cock crow, thou shalt deny me thrice.*

62. *And Peter going out wept bitterly.*

63. *And the men that held him, mocked him, and struck him.*

64. *And they blindfolded him, and smote his face. And they asked him, saying: Prophesy, who is it that struck thee?*

65. *And blaspheming, many other things they said against him.*

66. *And as soon as it was day, the ancients of the people, and the chief priests, and scribes came together, and they brought him into their council, saying: If thou be the Christ, tell us:*

67. *And he said to them: If I shall tell you, you will not believe me:*

68. *And if I shall also ask you, you will not answer me, nor let me go.*

69. *But hereafter the son of man shall be sitting on the right hand of the power of God.*

70. *Then said all they: Art thou then the Son of God? Who said: You say, that I am?*
71. *And they said: What need we any farther testimony? For we ourselves have heard it from his own mouth.*

COMMENTARY.

1-23. (See Matthew xxvi. 1-29.) The Apostle having said that there was a question raised as to who was to be the traitor (v. 24), now states that there was a contention also as to which of them seemed greater to our Lord (Jans.), some of them at this time apparently enjoying greater privileges than others (see Matthew xviii. 1). Very likely, as the prediction of His death and resurrection was the occasion of a like contention on the former occasion, so also was it on this.

24. "*And there was also a strife,*" &c. Some Expositors—among them Maldonatus —conceiving that it was utterly improbable that the Apostles, after having received the Blessed Eucharist, and witnessed our Lord's humility in washing His disciples' feet, &c., would, under such solemn circumstances, indulge so inopportunely in an unseemly strife for pre-eminence, in the very presence of their Divine Master,—are of opinion that there is question here of the same contention that took place on their journey to Jerusalem (Matthew xx. 20), and that it is inserted here, out of the order of events, by St. Luke. The lesson of humility given here is the same as that given in the passage of Matthew referred to. Against this opinion it is held, that St. Luke had already (ix. 46, &c.), referred to the former contention.

Others, with Venerable Bede, hold, that the contention here mentioned, had for object, to yield the more honourable places to one another—each trying to occupy the lower place, so that it is rather a contention of humility than of pride—"*non est incredibile, quia honore se invicem præveniendo certaverint.*" The following words of our Lord do not well accord with this view.

By others, it is maintained, that on hearing our Lord say He was to leave them (v. 22), they began, in suppressed accents, to inquire, who was to exercise His authority and superiority after He had gone—"*which of them should seem to be greater*"—which many understand for "*greatest,*" some contending for this party, others, for that. Very likely they did not fully understand our Lord's words, addressed to Peter. (Matthew xvi.) Hence, our Lord addressed to them the admonition contained in verses 25-28, which is in sense very like that delivered on the occasion of the similar contention which formerly took place, if the present be not the same.

Some maintain, that this strife and the subsequent words occurred before the institution of the Eucharist, and in connexion with the washing of the disciples' feet (John xiii. 4-12). The exhortation which He gives them there (John xiii. 14-16) to practise humility, of which He Himself gave an example, is, in substance, very like the exhortation delivered here.

25. (See Matthew xx. 25, &c.) "*Are called beneficent,*" rejoice in high-sounding titles, chiefly in titles commending their goodness and beneficence to their people Whether they deserve these titles or not, they haughtily claim them, and aspire to be addressed by them. Some say the word, "*beneficent,*" is the same as princes. The Hebrews termed their princes, *Nebedim,* beneficent; thus the words will mean, they are desirous to be called princes, that is, "*beneficent.*"

26, 27. (See Matthew xx. 25-28.) "*I am in the midst of you, as he that serveth,*" may be allusive to the washing of the feet, or to the general course of life and humility pursued by our Lord in the company of His followers. The words of these two verses are substantially, though somewhat varied, the same as in Matthew xx. 25-28.

28. "*And you are they,*" &c. Our Lord represses their desire of primacy, not only by inculcating a lesson of humility, which, after His own example, they should practise, as in the preceding verses, but also by pointing out to them, as here, that instead of a miserable priority in this world, each shall attain a very high degree of honour and enjoyment in His kingdom in the world to come. After having rebuked them, He now blandly consoles them, and praises them for their persevering adhesion to Him, when others deserted Him, in the midst of trials and sufferings. "*Temptations,*" means "*trials,*" contradictions, and persecutions, which He endured at the hands of the Jews.

29. "*And,*" therefore, in reward for your past constancy, "*I dispose to you a kingdom,*" which can be reached only through the road of suffering. This is the condition on which I can enter into glory; this is the condition laid down for Me by the will of My Heavenly Father. "*As my Father hath disposed to me.*" My Father has transferred all things to Me, has given all power into My hands, and by the same power with which He has disposed a kingdom for Me, and on the same conditions, "*as,*" so do I dispose it for you.

30. The kingdom prepared for you consists in two things—first, ineffable enjoyment, typified by what men most relish in this world, magnificent repasts, "*that you may eat,*" &c; secondly, honour and power, "*that you may sit,*" &c. (See Matthew xix. 28.) That passage is very like this. "*Amen, I say to you, you who followed Me,*" &c., are similar to the words, here, "*who have continued with Me in My temptations;*" there, "*shall receive an hundred fold;*" here, "*that you may eat,*" &c.; there, "*you also shall sit,*" &c.; here, "*and may sit upon thrones,*" &c.

31. "*And the Lord said,*" &c. After having consoled His Apostles with the promise of ineffable delights in store for them, He now, in order to turn their thoughts from contentions regarding pre-eminence, foretells the trials and temptations which they will have to encounter, and, at the same time, by addressing Peter, and saying, that He prayed for him, in particular, in order that he would confirm his brethren, he insinuates who it is that is to hold the Primacy amongst them.

The words of this verse, peculiar to St. Luke, are supposed to be addressed to Peter, immediately after his declaration (John xiii. 36, 37), that he would lay down his life for his Divine Master.

"*Simon, Simon,*" repeated for emphasis' sake, and to arrest attention, "*behold, Satan,*" the adversary of the human race, the enemy of God and man, "*hath desired to have you.*" "*Desired*" (ἐξῃτήσατο), means to "*demand,*" and has special reference to demanding a criminal to be delivered up. As formerly, in the case of Job, to which this seems to be allusive, he asked permission to tempt Job, so now does he ask God, without whose permission he cannot tempt man—hence, the words, "*lead us not into temptation*"—to be allowed to employ all his cunning and strength to tempt the Apostles ("*you*" in the plural). "*That he may sift you (winnow you), as wheat,*" shows the violence of the temptation, with which those who had hitherto remained with our Lord, and adhered to Him in His trials, were to be tossed and agitated. Under this temptation they succumbed for a time, but only afterwards to be endued with greater strength from on high, after the humiliation of a temporary defeat. It is clear, from our Lord's words, that the chief assault was to be made on their faith. They were, no doubt, of themselves too weak to resist Satan successfully; but our Lord provided a permanent remedy, a permanent support, against these enduring assaults on their faith, *enduring*, because, once repulsed, Satan would not give over. That permanent support was in the indefectible faith, for which He prayed His Father on behalf of Peter. It was through Peter, their faith was to be supported and strengthened in the day of need and trial.

32. "*But I have prayed for thee.*" This prayer being absolute, from the very form of expression—no condition is even insinuated—must be infallibly efficacious. It had for object, not that Peter would be free from temptation, but that his "*faith fail not*," or be utterly destroyed. The word, "*confirmed,*" shows the strength of temptation, which would cause him for a time to waver. "*Thee,*" is in the singular number—περι σου—as there is special personal reference to Peter, for whose unyielding, indefectible faith the Son of God absolutely addresses His Father, who always heard Him. "*And I know that Thou hearest Me always*" (John xi. 42). Although, Peter afterwards sinned against the external profession of his faith, many hold, he retained it in his heart. At all events, his faith did not utterly "*fail,*" strictly speaking; for, he recovered it, at once, if lost.

"*And thou being once converted.*" Having been, after thy temporary fall and infidelity, in regard to the external profession of faith, converted to God by sincere penance, and then permanently rendered firm and immoveable thyself, by My heavenly grace and assistance. According to this interpretation of "*converted,*" our Lord gently insinuates Peter's future fall and repentance. Others say, the word, "*converted,*" is a Hebraism, signifying, *in turn*, as if our Lord said: I have prayed for the indefectibility of thy faith, and do thou, *in turn*, confirm thy brethren, as I confirm thee. Others hold, that "*converted*" is to be immediately connected with the words, "*brethren,*" thus: And thou at some time, when it becomes necessary, being turned towards thy brethren, strengthen them in the faith.

"*Confirm*"—(στηρισον—as I now command thee, and in commanding, authorize thee)—in that faith in which thou shalt be firmly founded and established.

"*Thy brethren,*" the other Apostles—who were all his brethren, all to be assaulted by Satan, and confirmed by Peter—and their successors to the end of time, who needed to be strengthened against the assaults of hell, no less than the Apostles themselves, together with the entire Church built upon him, which, being destined to survive to the end of time, may require to be confirmed and strengthened in the faith by thee, in the persons of thy successors, at every period of its existence. "In confirming the Apostles, Peter really confirmed those whom the Apostles confirmed" (Murray).

From the command and commission given here to Peter, and to him only, by the Son of God, is proved his Primacy of jurisdiction and authority over the entire Church. For, in thus vesting Peter with authority, our Lord must have imparted to him, whatever was necessary for its full and effective exercise against the wiles and persecutions of wicked men, whom Satan employs at all times, to "*sift*" and agitate the members of God's Church. The full and effective discharge of this arduous commission requires not merely that faith be imparted, through the ordinary channel of preaching and instruction; but, also, full legislative and executive authority to repress effectively every attempt at leading men astray, to condemn contrary errors, and all doctrines tending to obscure it, to curb all attempts at undermining it, and punish by the arms of the Spirit, all men of whatever order, rank, station, or degree, who may be made instrumental in tarnishing its purity. Nothing short of this power could suffice for the effective discharge of the lofty commission given to Peter; nothing short of it, was, therefore, given by Him, to whom belongs *"all power in heaven and on earth."* What is this but the Primacy of jurisdiction and authority?

This passage is commonly quoted, and very properly so, as containing a proof of the dogma of the Pope's Infallibility. It order to avoid misconception, it may not be amiss to explain precisely what this dogma of Infallibility means. This will best be done by explaining—first, what *it is not;* and, secondly, what *it is*. It does not imply, by any means, that in his private capacity, as a writer or preacher, even on doctrinal points, the Pope may not utter unsound or erroneous doctrine. The Pope has never done so; but so far as the belief in the defined doctrine of the Infallibility is concerned, he may. Secondly, it is not to be confounded with *impeccability*. No promise of exemption from sin was ever made to St. Peter, or his successors; nor did it ever enter into the head of any Catholic, to claim such exemption for them. Thirdly, it is not to be confounded with the power of deposing temporal rulers, or of absolving their subjects from due allegiance. Whatever may be said of the rights of the Pontiff to such power, or of its actual exercise, we can freely admit, that the Sovereign Pontiff may even exceed bounds and commit sin, and act unjustly in its exercise, without trenching, in the slightest, on the defined doctrine of the Infallibility. It may be right to observe on this subject, that if the Pope exercised such power, he exercised it, independently of any other claim, in virtue of the international laws of Christendom in force at the time, and the voluntary concession of Christian Princes themselves; and when these Princes infringed the contracts entered into, they, according to the existing laws, rendered themselves liable to the stipulated penalties of such infringement.

Having seen what the dogma of Infallibility *is not*, let us now see what *it is*. It is clearly expressed in the Dogmatic Constitution of the Vatican Council thus: "We, therefore, faithfully adhering to Tradition, which dates from the commencement of Christianity . . . teach and define as a dogma divinely revealed, that the Roman Pontiff, when he speaks *ex cathedra*—that is to say, when discharging the functions of Pastor and Doctor of all the faithful, by virtue of his Apostolic authority, he *defines* a doctrine of faith and morals, to be held by the *universal Church*—he enjoys, by the Divine assistance promised to him in blessed Peter, the same infallibility with which our Redeemer intended His Church should be endowed, when defining any thing concerning faith and morals; and, that, consequently, such definitions of the Roman Pontiff are irreformable of themselves, and not from the Church. If any one should presume—which, may God forbid—to contradict this our definition, let him be Anathema." From the above, we clearly see, what every Catholic is bound to believe on this point, under pain of heresy. It is simply this—that, whenever the Sovereign Pontiff, as head of the Church—as Supreme Pastor and Teacher—"*defines*," or, clearly declares, that any point of doctrine is to be held by the universal Church, as contained in the deposit of revelation left by God to His Church, or, is opposed to the same; in other words, whenever he teaches the universal Church the faith of Christ, he cannot go astray, in virtue of the promises of Christ, and the gratuitous gift of God attached to his sacred person and office.

The above doctrine is clearly revealed in this passage. This follows—first, from the office divinely assigned to Peter only—"*for thee,*" "*thy faith,*" &c.—of protecting and strengthening the faith of all his brethren, and of the entire Church, which is to be confirmed in the faith through them. This office he has to exercise against the assaults of most powerful and wily enemies—all the powers of hell, represented by "*Satan.*" This he could not effectively discharge—if, on the one hand, we consider his furious, malignant enemies; on the other, the nature of the several points of faith, in many cases surpassing the human understanding, which he must defend and explain—unless he was gifted with Infallibility; nor, could he otherwise supply the inquisitive and learned portion of mankind with sufficient motives of credibility, so as to bow down their proud intellects in obedience to faith. How could he confirm others in the true faith, if he himself could err? Hence, his Infallibility.

Secondly, from the absolute and efficacious prayer of the Son of God, that the faith of Peter, while confirming his brethren and the entire Church in the doctrine of Christ, both regarding faith and morals—proper notions of both being essential for salvation—would never fail. Now, what is this but securing for him the gift of Infallibility, whenever addressing the Church, he defines doctrines of faith or morals, as declared in the dogma above explained? And as this privilege, of confirming the faith of the entire Church, was granted to Peter not merely on his own behalf, but for the good of others, and in his capacity of Chief Pastor, having charge of the entire flock, "*lambs and sheep,*" it is clear this same privilege— the means divinely instituted for preserving the faith, equally necessary at every period of the Church, as the powers of hell never relax their efforts to ruin souls, to destroy their faith and morals—was meant for his successors in the Roman See to the end of ages, to whom all the privileges of Peter, as Pastor, have been fully transmitted. The gift of Infallibility was granted to the other Apostles, as such; and, hence, being merely a personal privilege, was not transmitted to their successors, the Bishops. But to Peter it was granted, not alone as Apostle, in which case, it would cease with his own life; but as Chief Pastor, to "*confirm his brethren*"—a pastoral function—in which latter respect, it was to descend to his successors in the Primacy of authority and jurisdiction over the entire Church.

33, 34. (See Matthew xxvi. 34.)

35, 36. Our Lord, turning to the rest of the Apostles, now predicts the impending storm—a state of things immediately awaiting them, different from what they hitherto experienced—and He thus wishes to fortify them against it. Heretofore, when sent on the mission, bereft of the necessaries of life, without any viatic, or provision for their journey, God's secret providence so arranged it, that all their wants were supplied, and they enjoyed the blessings of peace.

"*But now,*" they will find it quite otherwise—a different condition of things will arise. Now, like men in time of war, they must provide themselves with the necessary means of support and defence to sustain and protect life, which shall be in imminent peril, from extreme penury and the sword of their persecutors. The words of this verse, about purchasing a sword, and taking a purse with them, which was not formerly allowed by Him (Luke ix.); but, now allowed, on account of the change in circumstances—because, formerly, men helped them; now, they persecute them— are not to be understood in their strict, literal sense, as conveying a precept to buy a sword, &c.

"*Buy a sword,*" is a proverbial expression, conveying, that a thing was to be done, *at any cost.* The words are only meant by our Lord to convey, in allegorical language, the great privations and dangers to which the Apostles would be subjected after *He*— in whose society and paternal care lay their support, and exemption from all harm—

was visibly taken away; and for the purpose of inspiring them with confidence in God, in the midst of their trials. Far from meaning that they should buy a sword, He does not allow Peter to use the one he had; and, in His previous teaching, He told them when struck on one cheek, even to turn the other to the striker. The meaning seems to be, that such will be their perilous condition hereafter, that if they had to depend on human aid alone, a sword would be necessary to rescue them. As for Himself, He was soon to be put to death; He needed no provision. He also wished to convey, that He voluntarily underwent the sufferings He predicted beforehand. Similar is the meaning of several passages of the Prophets (Jer. ix. 17, 18; Ezech. iv. 2), in which they prefigure dangerous times, by representing what men do in order to guard against impending evils.

Our Lord spoke rather obscurely, so as to leave the Apostles under the erroneous idea that He really wanted to have swords for His defence. This He did, with the view of showing His followers and the Jews, as has just been remarked, that He voluntarily underwent His Passion, while His disciples were inflamed with a desire of defending Him, and also with a view of eradicating all desires of revenge out of their hearts, by severely rebuking Peter, and curing the man whose ear he cut off.

37. He assigns a reason why His Apostles should be prepared for adversity and persecution. A disciple cannot be above his master; they must share His fate and the odium and opprobrium in store for Him. Now, among the other prophecies regarding Him, the prophecy of Isaias (liii. 12) is yet to be fulfilled, and soon to be accomplished. "*And with the wicked*," &c. He was to be tortured, crucified, as a malefactor, and to be suspended on an ignominious gibbet, between two notorious thieves, as if He were the greatest malefactor of the three, and thus put to a shameful death.

"*For the things*," &c. *i.e.*, all the prophecies that concerned Him, are sure to be fulfilled, and are now on the point of their full accomplishment, and, therefore, this one regarding My sufferings and ignominious death, must be fulfilled among the rest. Hence, when expiring, He exclaimed, "*Consummatum est.*"

38. The Apostles, misunderstanding our Lord's words in this passage, as in Matthew (xvi. 6, 7), or, rather, their allegorical meaning, and His purpose in using them, take His words literally to refer to material swords. Hence, seeing He was not understood, He, as it were, abruptly, as is quite commonly done by men when they find their hearers incapable of understanding them, and dont wish to rectify the mistake, terminates the subject by saying, "*It is enough*," which is the same as, *that will do, let us drop the subject at present.*

The scornful sneers of Ellicot, insultingly uttered in his Commentary on this passage, while alluding to some out-of-the-way mystical interpretation, given of this passage by some obscure Catholic—an interpretation seldom or never referred to by Catholic writers—are undeserving of notice. He might very well have reserved taunting sneers for the ridiculous jargon caused by the outlandish opinions of some of his own co-religionists.

How it happened that the Apostles had *two* swords, is differently accounted for. The most probable way of accounting for it is, that as the road between Galilee and Jerusalem was notoriously infested with robbers, travellers, as a matter of precaution, carried swords with them. Others say, the words only convey that there were two swords in the house when the conversation took place. "Behold, *here* are two swords" (Grotius). Others, understand them of large knives, used in the immolation of the Paschal lamb (St. Chrysostom).

39-65. (See Matthew xxvi. 36-75.)
66-71. (See Matthew xxvii. 1-7.)

CHAPTER XXIII.

TEXT.

*A*ND *the whole multitude of them rising up, led him to Pilate.*

2. *And they began to accuse him, saying: We have found this man perverting our nation, and forbidding to give tribute to Cesar, and saying that he is Christ the king.*

3. *And Pilate asked him, saying: Art thou the king of the Jews? But he answering, said: Thou sayest it.*

4. *And Pilate said to the chief priests and to the multitudes: I find no cause in this man.*

5. *But they were more earnest, saying: He stirreth up the people, teaching throughout all Judea, beginning from Galilee to this place.*

6. *But Pilate hearing Galilee, asked if the man were of Galilee?*

7. *And when he understood that he was of Herod's jurisdiction, he sent him away to Herod, who was also himself, at Jerusalem in those days.*

8. *And Herod seeing Jesus, was very glad, for he was desirous of a long time to see him, because he had heard many things of him: and he hoped to see some sign wrought by him.*

9. *And he questioned him in many words. But he answered him nothing.*

10. *And the chief priests and the scribes stood by, earnestly accusing him.*

11. *And Herod with his army set him at nought: and mocked him, putting on him a white garment, and sent him back to Pilate.*

12. *And Herod and Pilate were made friends that same day: for before they were enemies one to another.*

13. *And Pilate calling together the chief priests, and the magistrates, and the people,*

14. *Said to them: You have presented unto me this man, as one that perverteth the people, and behold I, having examined him before you, find no cause in this man touching those things wherein you accuse him.*

15. *No, nor Herod neither. For I sent you to him, and behold, nothing worthy of death is done to him.*

16. *I will chastise him therefore, and release him.*

17. *Now of necessity he was to release unto them one upon the feast-day.*

18. *But the whole multitude together cried out, saying: Away with this man, and release unto us Barabbas.*

19. *Who for a certain sedition made in the city, and for a murder, was cast into prison.*

20. *And Pilate again spoke to them, desiring to release Jesus.*

21. *But they cried again, saying: Crucify him, crucify him.*

22. *And he said to them the third time: Why, what evil hath this man done? I find no cause of death in him: I will chastise him therefore, and let him go.*

23. *But they were instant with loud voices requiring that he might be crucified: and their voices prevailed.*

24. *And Pilate gave sentence that it should be as they required.*

25. *And he released unto them him who for murder and sedition had been cast into prison, whom they had desired: But Jesus he delivered up to their will.*

26. *And as they led him away, they laid hold of one Simon of Cyrene, coming from the country: and they laid the cross on him to carry after Jesus.*

27. *And there followed him a great multitude of people, and of women who bewailed and lamented him.*

28. *But Jesus turning to them, said: Daughters of Jerusalem, weep not over me, but weep for yourselves, and for your children.*

29. *For behold the days shall come, wherein they will say: Blessed are the barren, and the wombs that have not borne, and the paps that have not given suck.*

30. *Then shall they begin to say to the mountains: Fall upon us: and to the hills: Cover us.*

31. *For if in the green wood they do these things, what shall be done in the dry?*

32. *And there were also two other malefactors led with him to be put to death.*

33. *And when they were come to the place which is called Calvary, they crucified him there; and the robbers, one on the right hand, and the other on the left.*

34. *And Jesus said: Father, forgive them, for they know not what they do. But they dividing his garments, cast lots.*

35. *And the people stood beholding, and the rulers with them derided him, saying: He saved others, let him save himself, if he be Christ, the elect of God.*

36. *And the soldiers also mocked him, coming to him, and offering him vinegar.*

37. *And saying: If thou be the king of the Jews, save thyself.*

38. *And there was also a superscription written over him in letters of Greek, and Latin, and Hebrew:* THIS IS THE KING OF THE JEWS.

39. *And one of those robbers who were hanged, blasphemed him, saying: If thou be Christ, save thyself, and us.*

40. *But the other answering, rebuked him, saying: Neither dost thou fear God, seeing thou art under the same condemnation.*

41. *And we indeed justly, for we receive the due reward of our deeds: but this man hath done no evil.*

42. *And he said to Jesus: Lord, remember me when thou shalt come into thy kingdom.*

43. *And Jesus said to him: Amen I say to thee, this day thou shalt be with me in paradise.*

44. *And it was almost the sixth hour: and there was darkness over all the earth until the ninth hour.*

45. *And the sun was darkened; and the veil of the temple was rent in the midst.*

46. *And Jesus crying with a loud voice, said: Father, into thy hands I commend my spirit. And saying this, he gave up the ghost.*

47. *Now the centurion seeing what was done, glorified God, saying: Indeed this was a just man.*

48. *And all the multitude of them that were come together to that sight, and saw the things that were done, returned striking their breasts.*

49. *And all his acquaintance, and the women that had followed him from Galilee, stood afar off beholding these things.*

50. *And behold there was a man named Joseph, who was a counsellor, a good and a just man:*

51. *(The same had not consented to their counsel and doings,) of Arimathea, a city of Judea, who also himself looked for the kingdom of God.*

52. *This man went to Pilate, and begged the body of Jesus.*

53. *And taking him down, he wrapped him in fine linen, and laid him in a sepulchre that was hewed in stone, wherein never yet any man had been laid.*

54. *And it was the day of the Parasceve, and the sabbath drew on.*

55. *And the women that were come with him from Galilee, following after, saw the sepulchre, and how his body was laid.*

56. *And returning they prepared spices and ointments: and on the sabbath-day they rested according to the commandment.*

COMMENTARY.

1-26. (See Matthew xxvii. 11-32.)
27-32. (See Matthew xxvii. 32, Commentary on)
33-56. (See Matthew xxvii. 33-66.)

CHAPTER XXIV.

ANALYSIS.

In this chapter we have an account of our Lord's Resurrection, and the announcement of it by two angels to the pious women that came to the sepulchre, who in turn announce it to others (1-12). Our Lord's apparition to the two disciples on their way to Emmaus, and the conversation that mutually took place (13-35). His apparition to the twelve Apostles assembled together, and His discourse relative to the truth of His Resurrection and the reality of His person (36-43). His commission to them to preach the Gospel (44-48). His promise to send down the Holy Ghost (49). His Ascension 50-53).

TEXT.

AND on the first day of the week very early in the morning they came to the sepulchre, bringing the spices which they had prepared.

2. *And they found the stone rolled back from the sepulchre.*

3. *And going in, they found not the body of the Lord Jesus.*

4. *And it came to pass, as they were astonished in their mind at this, behold two men stood by them in shining apparel.*

5. *And as they were afraid and bowed down their countenance towards the ground, they said unto them: Why seek you the living with the dead?*

6. *He is not here, but is risen. Remember how he spoke unto you, when he was yet in Galilee,*

7. *Saying: The son of man must be delivered into the hands of sinful men, and be crucified, and the third day rise again.*

8. *And they remembered his words.*

9. *And going back from the sepulchre, they told all these things to the eleven, and to all the rest.*

10. *Now it was Mary Magdalen and Joanna, and Mary of James, and the other women that were with him, who told these things to the apostles.*

11. *And these words seemed to them as idle tales: and they did not believe them.*

12. *But Peter rising up ran to the sepulchre; and stooping down he saw the linen clothes laid by themselves, and went away wondering in himself at that which was come to pass.*

13. *And behold, two of them went the same day to a town which was sixty furlongs from Jerusalem, named Emmaus.*

14. *And they talked together of all these things which had happened.*

15. *And it came to pass, that while they talked and reasoned with themselves, Jesus himself also drawing near went with them.*

16. *But their eyes were held that they should not know him.*

17. *And he said to them: What are these discourses that you hold one with another as you walk, and are sad?*

18. *And the one of them, whose name was Cleophas, answering, said to him: Art thou only a stranger in Jerusalem, and hast not known the things that have been done there in these days?*

19. *To whom he said: What things? And they said: Concerning Jesus of Nazareth, who was a prophet, mighty in work and word before God and all the people.*

20. *And how our chief priests and princes delivered him to be condemned to death and crucified him.*

21. *But we hoped that it was he that should have redeemed Israel: and now besides all this, to-day is the third day since these things were done.*

22. *Yea and certain women also of our company, affrighted us, who before it was light were at the sepulchre,*

23. *And not finding his body, came, saying that they had also seen a vision of angels, who say that he is alive.*

24. *And some of our people went to the sepulchre: and found it so as the women had said, but him they found not.*

25. *Then he said to them: O foolish, and slow of heart to believe in all things which the prophets have spoken.*

26. *Ought not Christ to have suffered these things, and so enter into his glory?*

27. *And beginning at Moses and all the prophets, he expounded to them in all the scriptures the things that were concerning him.*

28. *And they drew nigh to the town whither they were going: and he made as though he would go farther.*

29. *But they constrained him, saying: Stay with us, because it is towards evening, and the day is now far spent. And he went in with them.*

30. *And it came to pass, whilst he was at table with them, he took bread, and blessed and brake, and gave to them.*

31. *And their eyes were opened, and they knew him: and he vanished out of their sight.*

32. *And they said one to the other: Was not our heart burning within us, whilst he spoke in the way, and opened to us the scriptures?*

33. *And rising up the same hour they went back to Jerusalem: and they found the eleven gathered together, and those that were with them,*

34. *Saying, The Lord is risen indeed, and hath appeared to Simon.*

35. *And they told what things were done in the way: and how they knew him in the breaking of bread.*

36. *Now whilst they were speaking these things, Jesus stood in the midst of them, and saith to them: Peace be to you; It is I, fear not.*

37. *But they being troubled and frighted, supposed that they saw a spirit.*

38. *And he said to them: Why are you troubled, and why do thoughts arise in your hearts?*

39. *See my hands and feet, that it is I myself; handle, and see: for a spirit hath not flesh and bones, as you see me to have.*

40. *And when he had said this, he showed them his hands and feet.*

41. *But while they yet believed not and wondered for joy, he said: Have you here anything to eat?*

42. *And they offered him a piece of broiled fish, and a honey-comb.*

43. *And when he had eaten before them, taking the remains he gave to them.*

44. *And he said to them: These are the words which I spoke to you while I was yet with you, that all things must needs be fulfilled, which are written in the law of Moses, and in the prophets, and in the psalms, concerning me.*

45. *Then he opened their understanding, that they might understand the scriptures.*

46. *And he said to them: Thus it is written, and thus it behoved Christ to suffer, and to rise again from the dead the third day:*

47. *And that penance and the remission of sins should be preached in his name unto all nations, beginning at Jerusalem.*

48. *And you are witnesses of these things.*

49. *And I send the promise of my Father upon you: but stay you in the city, till you be endued with power from on high.*

50. *And he led them out as far as Bethania: and lifting up his hands he blessed them.*

51. *And it came to pass, whilst he blessed them, he departed from them, and was carried up to heaven.*

52. *And they adoring went back into Jerusalem with great joy.*

53. *And they were always in the temple praising and blessing God. Amen.*

COMMENTARY.

1-12. For a full account of the order in which things occurred, in connexion with the visits of the holy women, and their announcement to the Apostles and disciples— the apparitions of Angels, and of our Lord Himself—the visit of the Apostles to the tomb (see Commentary, Matthew xxviii. 3-8; Mark xvi. 9-13).

1 "*Now upon the first day of the week.*" With us, Sunday, or the Lord's day, *Dies Dominica*, on account of our Lord having risen from the dead on this day. "*Very early in the morning.*" The Greek conveys, "*at deep, or early dawn,*" before daylight actually appeared. The women came to the sepulchre for the purpose of embalming our Lord's body, with the spices they had prepared. In the ordinary Greek, the words are added, "*and certain others with them.*" These words are wanting in the best MSS., among others, the Vatican MS. They were very probably introduced from verse 10, where this is said of Mary Magdalen, Joanna, &c.; and also to make the passage harmonize with Mark xvi. 1. There were, doubtless, other women besides these. But these are mentioned as the more prominent among them. Hence, in Matthew xxviii., Mary Magdalen and the other Mary alone are mentioned for the same reason, and John xx. 1, Magdalen alone.

2. "*The stone.*" St. Luke said nothing hitherto in his narrative of a "*stone*" having been rolled to the mouth of the sepulchre. It is stated (Matthew xxvii. 60). In Mark (xvi. 4) it is said to be "*very great.*" This stone was rolled back by the Angel of the Lord, who sat on it (Matthew xxviii. 2).

3. "*And going in,*" at the invitation and under the guidance of the angel, whom they found sitting on the stone which he had rolled back (Matthew xxviii. 6). St. Luke omits all mention of the appearance, in the first place, of one angel.

"*They found not,*" &c. They saw the place perfectly empty. St. Luke makes no mention of the angel that spoke to them outside, as in Matthew (xxviii. 2-6).

4. "*As they were astonished in their mind at this.*" The Greek for "*astonished,*" conveys doubt, hesitation. After leaving the monument, they were thrown into consternation and perplexity of mind on account of the vision of angels, the removal of the stone, and the absence of our Lord's body, not being able to comprehend what it all meant.

"*Two men,*" angels in human form, "*in shining apparel.*" This indicates their heavenly origin. Perplexed at what they saw, and seemingly not paying sufficient attention to the testimony of *one* angel who had conducted them to the tomb; *two* other angels—the number of witnesses required in law—appeared outside, to dissipate their doubts and fears, regarding the taking away of our Lord's body. No wonder the glorious sepulchre of the Son of God should be filled with angels in honour of their Lord and Master. Hence, two others appeared to Magdalen, one sitting at the head, another at the feet, where the body of Jesus had been laid (John xx. 12).

5. Terrified at this new miraculous apparation, and not daring to look at the dazzling appearance of the angels, they "*bowed down their countenance towards the ground,*" partly from a feeling of fear, and partly from a feeling of modesty, as the angels appeared in the form of young men. No doubt, they acted similarly in regard to the angel that first appeared to them, although this is omitted by St. Matthew.

"*They said,*" probably one of the two, with the concurrence of the other. As they did not seem to have attached due weight to the words of the one angel who had already addressed them in the blandest manner, and as they still seemed in doubt as to what had become of our Lord's body, these angels, therefore, addressed them in a form somewhat more stern, "*Why seek you*"—why persevere in seeking—"*the living with the dead?*" Why seek among the dead Him who is essential life? "*The living*"—τον ζωντα—the living one—"*the resurrection and the life*"—the Source of life in all that live—(Apoc. i. 18).

6. "*Remember how He spoke to you.*" Our Lord had told His disciples and the holy women, among the rest, while in Galilee, before He came to Judea, that after having suffered death, He would rise again.

"*Yet in Galilee,*" whence the holy women came with our Redeemer to Jerusalem (xxiii. 55). St. Luke here records what is not mentioned by the other Gospel writers, that when our Lord told His disciples of His death and resurrection, the women were amongst His hearers on that occasion, and they remembered His words, but, like His other followers, they did not fully understand them at the time.

9. This was the first return of the holy women, when they hastened to announce to the Apostles and the disciples what they saw and heard. They said nothing about it on the way. This is the same announcement referred to by St. John (xxi. 2), who only mentions Magdalen, because she was the most prominent among the women. He does not, however, assert that she alone came, nor does he deny that others were with her, which is stated here (v. 10), any more than he asserts that she made the announcement to Peter and John only, or deny that the announcement was made to all the Apostles, as is stated here, "*and the rest,*" viz., disciples. They observed a profound silence, in regard to externs, on their return, probably for very prudential reasons (Mark xvi. 8).

10. "*Joanna,*" the wife of Chusa, Herod's steward (viii. 2).

"*Other women.*" St. Mark (xvi. 1), says, Salome, the wife of Zebedee, was one of these (Matthew xxvii. 56). These holy women followed our Lord from Galilee, accompanied Him on His journey, and ministered to His wants, as was usual among the Jews (1 Cor. ix. 5).

11. "*Idle tales*"—ληρος—babbling, silly talk—"*and they believed them not,*" on which

account, our Lord afterwards upbraided them with their incredulity (Mark xvi. 14). They considered, that owing to the infirmity of the female character, these took mere spectral illusions and phantoms for realities. Our Lord allowed His Apostles, as well as the pious women, to be slow in believing, in order that the faith in His resurrection might be strengthened by more numerous proofs, "*Sic eorum infirmitas nostra facta est firmitas*"—St. Gregory (See Mark xvi. 10, 11).

12. "*Then arose Peter*," &c. This is manifestly the visit described by St. John (xx. 3-10); from which it appears, although not mentioned here by St. Luke, that John accompanied Peter, and that being younger and more active, he outran Peter, and arrived first at the sepulchre, but did not go in; whereas, Peter not only "*stooped down*," as described here, but actually went into the sepulchre, and then John also, who on arriving, only stooped down and looked in, followed Peter into the sepulchre, and saw the linen cloths, and the napkin that bound our Lord's head, "*lying in a place by itself*" (John xx. 7, 8).

"*And departed*," returned back to Jerusalem. The women also returned a second time. It was at this latter return our Lord appeared to them (Matthew xxviii. 9).

13. "*And behold*," conveying, that the following was a sudden and unexpected manifestation.

"*Two of them*," generally supposed to refer to two of the seventy-two disciples. Our Lord had several followers besides the seventy-two, of whom some, like Nicodemus, who came to Him by night, did not publicly profess their adherence and attachment to Him. That these two were of the seventy-two, is the more common opinion of the Fathers. That they were not of the Apostles, is clear from verse 33, where it is said, "*they found the eleven gathered together*."

"*Went the same day*," Easter Day, on which our Lord had risen.

"*To a town*." St. Mark (xvi. 12) has, "*into the country*." The common opinion is, that St. Luke here, and St. Mark, refer to the same occurrence, which is fully detailed by St. Luke alone. The objection to this opinion, derived from the assertion of St. Mark, that those to whom they announced it, "*did not believe;*" whereas, St. Luke (v. 34) would seem to say the contrary, is of no weight; since it might be said that among those, of whom St. Mark speaks, some did not believe, while others did, and among the latter were the Apostles.

"*Sixty furlongs*," or about seven and a half miles "*from Jerusalem*." "*Named Emmaus*." After the total subjugation of the Jews, it was called Nicopolis, as we are informed by Sozomen (Lib. 5, Hist. c. 21); St. Jerome (ad Eustoch. de Epitaph. Paulæ Ep. 27).

14. The occurrences which took place in regard to our Lord, viz., His sufferings, death, and the announcement made by the holy women on that morning, formed the subject of their conversation.

15. "*And it came to pass*," seemingly by mere chance, so far as it concerned them, but not so, as regarded our Lord, by whom it was deliberately arranged beforehand.

"*Talked and reasoned with themselves*," talked over the events that occurred, "*and reasoned*" about the conclusions to be deduced, as to whether He had really risen, as He had promised, and the consequences of His having risen or not risen, &c.

"*Jesus Himself also*"—the very person of whom they were speaking. This is the force of "*also*," unexpectedly, His approach being unobserved till He actually joined them as a fellow-traveller, journeying the same way; thus illustrating His promise, as Ven. Bede, in *hoc loco*, observes—that "where two or three are assembled in His name, He is in the midst of them."

16. "*But their eyes were held*," &c. Our Lord did not wish to be recognised by them. St. Mark (xvi. 12), says, "*He appeared in a different shape.*" Both may have happened. Whilst remaining substantially the same as He had been before in His mortal form, His glorious and immortal body presented in some features a different appearance, owing to the natural qualities of a glorified body, from what it had before presented, just as shall be the case with our bodies after the Resurrection (1 Cor. xv. 41, 42); and, as happened to our Lord Himself after His resurrection, when Magdalen took Him for the gardener, and the Apostles for a Spirit (v. 37), although it is not said that in either case their eyes were held. His glorious body may have assumed the appearance of a stranger travelling homewards. The eyes of the disciples were held so as not to recognize Him in His altered and glorified shape. So were their ears also in regard to His voice, which probably was changed as well as His outward appearance. Our Lord held their eyes by a supernatural influence, so that although seen, He might not be recognized by them, in order that their faith and testimony might be more firm, when after laying bare the wounds of unbelief, a suitable remedy might be more effectually and more abidingly applied—"*ut ulcus suum (dubitationis et tristitiæ) discipuli aperirent et pharmacum susciperent*"— (Theophylact).

17. "*What are those discourses that you hold one with another ?*" The Greek for "*hold*," conveys the idea of *tossing backwards and forwards like a ball*. Hence, it means, to interchange.

"*And are sad*," show a sad and mournful countenance. Our Lord Himself well knew the subject of their conversation, and the cause of their sorrow—He may also have on His near approach, overheard what they were speaking about. He wishes, however, to ascertain it from themselves, in order to apply the remedy, of which their own admissions would be naturally suggestive. In some MSS.—the Vatican among the rest—after, "*as you walk*," are inserted the words, "*they stood still*,"—εσταθησαν— "*sad in countenance.*"

18. "*Cleophas*," probably, a native of Emmaus, as is inferred from the pressing invitation given to our Redeemer to receive hospitality from him (v. 29).

"*Art thou only a stranger ?*" &c., that is, art thou the only stranger among the crowd of strangers, that came to Jerusalem on the occasion of the great Paschal solemnity, that is ignorant of these things, of which we are speaking? They took Him for one of the strangers who came to celebrate the Pasch at Jerusalem. "*And hast not known,*" &c. "*And,*" has the meaning of "*who*, knoweth not," &c. "*Only*," or rather "*alone*," directly affects the verb, "*knowest not*," in the meaning of the passage. These disciples are so full of their subject, that they can think of nothing else, and cannot conceive, how it could be supposed, that there was any thing else to engage the attention of any one in Jerusalem, save the great events they were discoursing about. Beelen (Gramm. Græcit, § 3) observes, that the finite verb, παροικεις, is put for παροικων, and one sentence expressed by two, connected by και, συ μονος παροικων Ιερουσαλημ, ουκ εγνως.

19. Our Lord, without denying that He knew all the events, designedly conceals all cognizance of them, and, in order to ascertain from their own admission the thoughts of their minds, the weakness of their faith and their hesitancy, which He meant to remedy, asks, "*what things?*" What are the things you refer to as having happened? They reply, the things that happened, "*concerning Jesus of Nazareth*," &c.

The disciples here refrain from expressing their belief in our Lord's Divinity, if they had such belief, not knowing the stranger with whom they were conversing. It might be perilous to express such faith, on account of the persecution they might suffer from the Jews (Ven. Bede). Or, it may be, that being in a state of doubt and perplexity on account of recent events, they knew not what to call our Lord, beyond what was almost universally believed regarding Him, viz., that He was a distinguished Prophet, who, with miraculous wonders, united a doctrine all heavenly "*before God*" (Acts ii. 22), "*and all the people*," God and man testifying to His merits. The power and sanctity of God were wonderfully displayed in Him, and the whole people, the envious Pharisees excepted, always revered Him as a Prophet. They then convey to this stranger, that such a man should rather be treated with honour, than be ignominiously put to death.

20. "*And crucified Him*," by the hands of the Romans, to whom they delivered Him for this purpose (see Acts ii. 36; iv. 10). The disciples prudently refrain from expressing their own convictions regarding the injustice of the treatment He received, as they were speaking to an unknown stranger, who might denounce them to the Jewish authorities.

21. "*We hoped that it was He who should have redeemed Israel*"—the promised, long-expected Messiah, who would rescue the Jewish people from the odious yoke of the Romans. But, now recent events have considerably perplexed us, and served to lessen this hope. The disciples shared in the common error of their countrymen, who imagined that the Messiah would effect the temporal deliverance of the Jews. Even up to His ascension, they expected this (Acts i. 8). In this verse, is shown the perplexity or fluctuation between hope and fear, under which the disciples were now labouring.

"*And besides all this*," besides the perplexity caused by His death and ignominious sufferings, our embarrassment and want of confidence and belief regarding Him, are still more increased, when we remember—what was calculated to raise our hopes still higher—that He promised to rise again on the third day, and now, "*to-day is the third day since these things happened*," that is, since His betrayal and death; and still, there is no clear evidence of His having risen. Even if the disciples remembered our Lord's promise, they did not clearly understand what it meant. The disciples probably remembered the promise and prediction regarding His resurrection on the third day, as is conveyed in the above explanation, but in their confusion and perplexity, they omit all allusion to such promise, and express themselves in an incoherent form, or, it may be, they purposely suppressed any distinct allusion to this prediction, when addressing a stranger whom they knew not, lest they might expose themselves to ridicule, for their credulity in attending to a promise, in which they were apparently disappointed.

22. And even to add to our perplexity, and cause us to linger still between hope and doubt, "*certain women also of our company, affrighted us*," threw us into an ecstasy, or threw us into amazement—such is the force of the Greek verb.

24. "*And some of our people.*" Hence, more than one went, more than Peter (*v.* 12); John also is included, so that there is reference here to the visit made by Peter and John. (John xx. 3, &c.) "*But Him they found not.*" Hence, between the disappearance of the body, and their ignorance as to where He is, our doubts and perplexity are further increased.

25. Hitherto, our Lord had patiently heard them out, and having fully ascertained from themselves the spiritual malady of religious doubt and hesitation, they were suffering from, He now prudently applies the proper remedy. "*O foolish*"—the Greek word, ανοητοι, means devoid of mind or intelligence—"*and slow of heart to believe in all things,*" or, to believe all things—"*the prophets have spoken.*" "*All things.*" They believed and fully appreciated what the prophets had said regarding the glories of the future Messiah; but the other things, that regarded His humiliations and sufferings, they were slow to believe, and could not be brought to comprehend.

26. "*Ought not Christ to have suffered these things?*" "*Ought not.*" Looking to the predictions of the prophets, to His own voluntary, free action, arranging all beforehand, and to the decree of God, ordaining that His Son should redeem mankind, by His voluntary sufferings and ignominious death, it was necessary He should suffer. There was nothing about which the prophets and the Books of Moses were more explicit than regarding the sufferings and humiliations of the Messiah, therefore called "*the end of the law*" (Rom. x. 4). Hence, our Lord shows the disciples that the very thing that weakened their faith and made them lose all hope—for by saying, "*we hoped,*" they insinuate that such hope was lost at present—should be the very thing to increase their faith, and confirm their hope. For if He did not suffer, He would not be the Messiah of whom the prophets spoke.

"*And so,*" through the predicted ordeal of sufferings, and no other way—this being an indispensable condition—"*enter into His glory,*" viz., the glory of His resurrection, ascension—the exalted name He received in reward for His humiliation (Philip. ii. 6). "*His glory*"—"*His,*" singly merited by Him—"*His,*" by the preordinating decrees of God (Heb. ii. 9). This is His ordination regarding all His followers, "*per multas tribulationes,*" &c. (Acts xiv., &c.)

27. "*Moses.*" The Books of Moses, "*and the writings of the prophets,*" "*He expounded to them in all the Scriptures the things that were concerning Him.*" Commencing with the very beginning of Sacred Scripture, the Books of Moses, He fully explained the texts that chiefly regarded Him, and also the types that foreshadowed Him, the Brazen Serpent, the Paschal Lamb, the Sacrifice of Isaac, and the rest which are found in the several books of Sacred Scriptures regarding Him.

28. "*The town*" of Emmaus, "*whither they were going*"—"*and He made as though He would go farther.*" Although He wished to remain and reveal Himself, still in order to give them an opportunity of pressing Him to partake of their hospitality, and thus render them worthy of hearing more of His heavenly doctrines, He acted as if He meant to proceed farther. He only showed by act what He meant to do; He meant to go farther, if they did not press Him to remain. There is nothing, therefore, savouring of a practical falsehood in seeming to do what He was about doing. His action, when seeming to proceed, was equivalent to the question, "shall we now part?" There was no more in this than in His appearing in the form of a stranger travelling homewards, and His apparent motion forwards was only carrying

out this notion; or in His assuming the form of the gardener, when He first appeared to Magdalen. Although He knew, as God, they would press Him to remain; still, acting as man, He made an experiment of their hospitable feelings towards Him, whom they regarded as a stranger.

29. "*They constrained Him, saying,*" &c. They eagerly pressed Him, whose society and words had caused them such pleasure. "*Because it is towards evening.*" The sun had already passed the meridian. Some hours of day, however, still remained For they returned that very day to Jerusalem, and announced to the Apostles, that they saw the Lord (v. 33). It is supposed by many that Cleophas lived at Emmaus, and entertained our Lord at his house, which, St. Jerome says (Ep. 27 Epis. ad Paulam, c. 3), *our Lord made into a church*, from which it is inferred, that St. Jerome held that our Lord administered the blessed Eucharist on this occasion. Wherever the Eucharist is celebrated, there is a church.

30. It is a subject of dispute among Commentators whether our Lord celebrated the blessed Eucharist on this occasion, or not. Some who hold the affirmative (St. Augustine, Sermo. 140, de Tempore; St. Jerome, Ep. 27; Theophylact, Bede, A. Lapide, Maldonatus, &c.), prove their view: first, from the words used here, "*took bread,*" "*blessed,*" "*broke,*" "*gave to them,*" which, being precisely the same as those in which the institution of the Eucharist is described (Matthew xxvi. 26), would imply that the same thing took place in both cases. Again, the words of the disciples (v. 35), "*the breaking of bread,*" are the terms in which the blessed Eucharist was designated in the days of the Apostles (Acts xi. 42; 1 Cor. x. 16; *panis quem frangimus*); 2nd, from the effect produced. "*This breaking of bread*" had the miraculous effect of opening the eyes of the disciples, so as to know our Lord. It was, therefore, a very solemn, religious act. These disciples, probably, having heard from the Apostles of the ceremony observed by our Lord at the last supper, seeing it repeated here, and remembering His words a year before this (John vi.), when He spoke of Himself as the Bread that came down from heaven—the Bread that gave life to the world—at once, owing to the miraculous effect of the Eucharist, recognised Him in this adorable mystery of His love; 3rd, the blessing here is different from the ordinary blessing at meals, for it was given, not at the commencement, but at the end of supper, "*eum cœnasset,*" for our Lord immediately after vanished.

These Commentators, therefore, hold that our Lord gave Himself to these two disciples under one species, in the form of bread only, as we have no account of the chalice, our Lord having suddenly disappeared on being recognised in the breaking of bread. Others, however (Jansenius, Estius, Calmet), are of a different opinion, whilst Bellarmine, Natalis, Alexander, &c., give no positive opinion on the subject either way.

31. "*Their eyes were opened.*" The following words explain what this means, not that they were blind before, but that some veil, some obstacle, supernaturally impeded their clear vision, so that they could not see Him. Hence, it is added, "*and they knew Him.*" This was the miraculous effect of "*the breaking of the bread,*" as they themselves afterwards explain (v. 35). They were opened in the same way as were those of our fallen first parents (Genesis iii.), of Agar (Genesis xxi. 19).

"*And He vanished out of their sight.*" He rendered Himself invisible to them, by an effect of His Divine power, and passed away from them, after He had shown Himself visibly to them in His glorious body, and after He had been recognised by them. This circumstance of suddenly rendering Himself invisible and disappearing, was of itself calculated to confirm their faith and belief that it was Christ, and Christ only, they saw.

32. "*Was not our heart burning,*" &c. These words are understood by some to mean, that they reproached themselves for not having known Him before, owing to the fire which His conversation kindled in their hearts. Others understand the words to be confirmatory of their assured recognition of our Lord, just seen by them, as if to say, surely it must be He, for we could not account otherwise for the burning heat we felt during the entire time He was expounding the Scriptures, and conversing with us on the way. The effect of God's Word properly received is, to enlighten us and inflame us with Divine love, "*ignitum eloquium tuum vehementer.*" (Psalm cxviii. 140; Proverbs xxx. 5; Deut. xxxii. 2; Luke xii. 42; Ezechiel i. 13, &c.) No wonder that the pious reading of, and meditation on, the Word of God, should stimulate and inflame us to advance more and more in the road of perfection. If it fail, the fault is entirely our own.

33. "*The same hour,*" without a moment's delay. Although now it was "*towards evening,*" &c., they rose up, at once, from table, in their anxiety to impart to the Apostles and other disciples the glad tidings regarding our Lord's resurrection and appearance to themselves. Probably, they meant before this occurrence to spend the night at Emmaus; but now, they make no delay in returning in haste to Jerusalem.

"*The eleven.*" It is thus the Apostolic College is styled subsequent to our Lord's death. Thomas was absent on this occasion (*v.* 36), *hic,* when the two approached, and being incredulous, left before our Lord spoke to the eleven (John xx. 19-24). It may be, Thomas was present. "*And those that were with them,*" viz., the holy women and the other disciples—our Lord's disciples of either sex—who then stopped at Jerusalem, and were assembled together in the same house with the Apostles, conversing about the wonderful manifestations both to the women and Peter regarding His resurrection.

34 "*Saying,*" that is, the eleven, and the others, first informed the two disciples, who imagined they were the first to announce the glad tidings of our Lord's resurrection, so that when the two announced the apparition vouchsafed to themselves, they had nothing new to impart, that the others had not already known.

"*The Lord is risen indeed,*" that is, truly and undoubtedly.

"*And hath appeared to Simon.*" It would seem that our Lord appeared to Peter first, before He manifested Himself to any other man, out of regard for his ardent love, to console him for his fall—as He appeared first to the fallen, loving Magdalen before other women—and as a privilege intended for the head of His Church (1 Cor. xv. 5). When He appeared to Peter we cannot ascertain. But it is commonly believed He appeared to him, before He appeared to the two disciples referred to here. It would seem the Apostles and disciples placed more reliance on the declaration of Peter than they did on that of the women; although still some among them doubted (Mark xvi. 13).

35. After hearing from the assembled Apostles and disciples of our Lord's apparition, the two disciples relate in turn what occurred to themselves on the road and at table, and furnished further evidence, to an audience already prepared to believe, of the truth of our Lord's resurrection.

36. Whilst the two disciples were engaged in relating all in connexion with our

Lord's apparition at Emmaus, as in the preceding verse, "*Jesus stood in the midst of them*," without any previous notice or intimation, in a way conspicuous to all assembled, "*the eleven, and those that were with them*" (*v.* 33). In virtue of the glorious gift of subtilty, passing into the apartment, the doors remaining closed, "*He came and stood in the midst of them;*" He came from without, "*the doors were shut.*" There is clearly question of the same apparition here, and John xx. 19. St. Luke mentions some circumstances omitted by John; whilst John, in turn, states circumstances omitted by Luke.

"*And saith to them: Peace be to you.*" Addressed to them the form of salutation which among the Jews was expressive of all good things; as much as to say: My advent is pacific; I mean to impart to you abundance of benedictions, as a friend and benefactor, by no means, an enemy.

"*It is I*," your Divine indulgent Master, who so often rescued you from dangers and difficulties. "*It is I*," whose well-known form, and familiar tone of voice, you can easily recognise. "*It is I*," whose ignominious death you have lately bewailed; but who, now rising from the dead, wishes to console you, by the announcement of His glorious Resurrection.

"*Fear not;*" therefore, when you know who I am, My sudden and unexpected visit, in My glorified state, at this late hour, need cause no alarm.

37. "*Troubled and frightened*" at our Lord's apparition, suddenly and unexpectedly, at that late hour of the night, while the doors remained closed, they imagined, owing to these fears, "*that they saw a spirit*," or, it was rather, the idea of a spectre or spirit from the other world appearing among them, that caused their trouble and fright. Men naturally feel terror at any supernatural apparition, at any intercourse with the beings of the invisible world. The disciples, therefore, fearing the object they saw might have assumed our Lord's body and appearance, be it angel, or demon, were thrown into fright and confusion, by the suddenness of His appearance in a way peculiar to a spirit, leaving the doors still closed.

38. "*Why do thoughts*," anxious, strange, perplexing thoughts, regarding the reality of My presence, as to whether you see a real body or a spirit, "*arise in your hearts*"—occupy your minds and hearts? Our Lord, in this, shows them He knows their very interior, the very thoughts that agitate them.

39. Not only does He give a proof of the truth of His resurrection, by showing Himself to be the Searcher of hearts; but He also adds further evidence to confirm their faith and dispel their fears. If the sight of My well-known form, and the familiar tones of My voice, do not convince you, look at My hands and feet, and—what is a still stronger proof of the reality of My body—handle them; feel and touch My real, solid flesh; feel the traces of my wounds in those hands and feet that were nailed to the cross.

"*For a spirit*," coming back from the other world, as you suppose Me to be, "*hath not flesh and bones.*" St. Augustine (Lib. de Cura pro Mortuis, c. x., xi., xvi., xvii.), says, it would be temerity to deny that spirits, viz., angels, demons, souls of the departed, sometimes appear. This seemed to be the impression of the Jews. Our Redeemer rather confirms that tradition here; or, at least, He strongly countenances it. These occurrences are, no doubt, rare, nor can we suppose that, without some grave reason connected with the departed soul or its surviving friends, the Almighty would suspend or change the established laws of nature.

40. "*He showed them His hands and feet*," retaining the traces of the wounds. Whether they touched them, as He invited them to do, is not stated here, any more than in John xx. 27, regarding Thomas, who is generally supposed to have felt them, and then exclaimed (v. 28), "*My Lord and my God.*" It is likely the disciples did touch Him, and to this, St. John (1 Ep. i. 1), refers, "*quod manus nostræ contrectaverunt de verbo vitæ,*" &c. This opinion derives confirmation from this verse. Our Lord wished them to touch Him, as a further proof of His reality, not only to them, but to all nations, to whom they were to preach the Gospel to the end of time. St. Jerome, however, is of a contrary opinion (Ep. Adversus Errores), and maintains, they did not touch Him. Therefore, it is, he says, our Lord called for food (v. 41). This testimony of the senses, although, of itself, only a morally convincing argument would, conjointly with all the circumstances, viz., the miracles of our Lord, the prophecies regarding the Resurrection, and considering His object in exhibiting His hands and feet, namely, to prove the Divinity of the Messiah, &c., furnish an undoubted argument (St. Thomas, 3 p., q. 55, Art. 6). "Wherefore, the language, figure, shape, countenance, wounds, touch of our Lord, His eating and drinking, His conversation, assertions, predictions, miracles, the testimony of angels, the oracles of prophets, all these conjointly, most assuredly demonstrated our Lord's Resurrection" (A. Lapide).

41. Our Lord addresses another argument to confirm their faith. "*Believed not,*" applies only to some. Surely, Peter, Magdalen, and the two disciples to whom He appeared, firmly believed; but, others, from the very excess of joy ("*for joy,*" as in the Greek, is to be joined to "*believed not*"), and their wonder at the suddenness of the event, were afraid to believe in such joyous tidings, lest in case of possible error, their disappointment and chagrin would be the greater. It was this feeling of wonder, and this excessive sense of joy, that made them not believe with a firm Divine faith, as if they thought it too good to be true—we cannot believe our eyes. The words, "*not believing,*" do not convey a positive resistance to faith; but a want of firmness in faith, arising, not from obstinacy of will, but from the magnitude of their joy, from the unexpected nature of the occurrence, and from the vehemence of their anxiety, about its truth, as in the case of Jacob, on hearing Joseph was still alive (Genesis xxv. 26); of Peter liberated from prison (Acts xii. 7). Leo (Serm. I. de Assum.). Our Lord permitted all this hesitancy and doubt, in order still to elicit stronger proofs of His resurrection, and thus leave us no grounds for diffidence

He asks, "*Have you here anything to eat?*" He knew well they had, as they were at their repast (Mark xvi. 13). Likely, He came in at the close of it, in order not to interrupt them before; since, probably, on His appearance they rose up, out of respect. He asks the question, in order to receive the food from themselves, to eat it in their presence, and thus supply the strongest proof of His being alive, viz., His consuming food. He did the same in the case of the girl whom He raised to life. So did Lazarus, in Bethania (John xi.) Our Lord did really eat, not from necessity, but dispensatively; just as He retained the traces of the wounds in His body.

42. This piece of broiled fish and the honey-comb had, probably, remained after the repast. In this description of plain food, we see the simple frugality of the Apostles and the other followers of our Lord.

ST. LUKE, CHAP. XXIV.

43. He had eaten "*before them*," in their presence, while they looked on. This was a real manducation and reception of food into the stomach without nutrition, which was not needed in a glorified body. It was then consumed by the Divine power, and reduced to nothing. "*Futuræ resurrectionis corpus, imperfectæ potestatis erit, si cibos sumere non potuerit, imperfectæ felicitatis, si cibis eguerit*" (St. Augustine. Ep. 49, Quæst. 1); and elsewhere he says, "*Non enim potestas, sed egestas edendi ac bibendi immortalibus corporibus aufertur*" (De Civ. Deis. Lib. 13, c. 22). "*Ad exhibendam fidei veritatem in corpore dignatus est etiam non necessitate sed potestate cibum sumere*" [St. Augustine, Sermone olim 147, tempore nunc 142, n. 12].

"*Taking the remains He gave to them.*" He did so in order to make the fact of His having really eaten more manifest, and also that they might testify that they partook of food in common with Jesus, resuscitated from the dead. Thus were fulfilled the words of St. Peter (Acts x. 41), "*Nobis qui manducavimus et bibimus cum illo*," &c. This was the last argument our Lord added to the preceding, to prove the truth of His resurrection. So that the Apostles and disciples after that joyfully believed, without hesitation in the truth of His resurrection. No doubt, we find angels eat with Abraham (Genesis xviii. 9), with Lot (xix. 5), with Tobias. But, besides that their act of eating could not be regarded as the natural action of living bodies, they did not partake of food, in order to prove to doubting men that they were not spirits, as Jesus asserted regarding Himself.

The words, "*He gave them the remains*," are wanting in the extant Greek and Syriac versions. They are found in the Arabian and in the Greek copy, from which our Vulgate was translated. They are also quoted by many ancient writers (see Mills).

44. "*And He said to them.*" After having abundantly demonstrated from several sources of argument, the truth of His resurrection, He now adduces further proofs, viz.: First, that all they saw happening Him, His sufferings, death and resurrection, had been often foretold to them by Himself, when He lived continually in their company, during His mortal life; and secondly, they were also predicted of Him in the several oracles of the prophets. *These are the words (or things), which I spoke to you when I was yet with you,*" before My death, sojourning commonly with you—I am with you even now; but, My presence now is exceptional; this is not the permanent sojourn of a glorified body. The things *He* spoke are these, viz.:— "*that all things written in the law of Moses, and in the prophets, concerning Me, must be fulfilled.*" Our Lord, during His mortal sojourn, pointed out the several passages in the Pentateuch, and other books of Scripture, that had reference to the mysteries of His life, death, and glory. We have no full record of His allusion to these books, when instructing them; but these prophesies should be fulfilled. Now they see them fulfilled in all that happened Him. Now they have experimental knowledge of their fulfilment. Nothing, therefore, new or unexpected has occurred to cause them surprise, or unsettle their faith. Our Lord refers to the books of the Old Testament, following the division which, according to St. Jerome in his Prologus Galeatur, then obtained among the Jews:—First, "*Moses,*" or the Pentateuch; second, "*the Prophets,*" the prophetical books (Daniel excepted), including not only the greater and lesser prophets—of the latter, making only one book—but also the historical books—Josue, Judges, Ruth, Kings; thirdly, "*the Psalms,*" which stand for the *Hagiographa*, or sacred writings, of which part, the Psalms was the most conspicuous book. This part also included Job, Books of Solomon,

Books of Paralipomenon, Daniel, Esdras, Esther (see Dixon, Prolog., vol. i., p. 60). Some Expositors think the words of this and following verses are by anticipation recorded here by St. Luke, as spoken on Easter Day; whereas, in reality, they could have been spoken only on the Ascension Day, since at the close, our Lord adds, after promising the Holy Spirit, "*but stay you in the city*," &c. Now this could not refer to Easter Day; since, as we learn from St. Luke (Acts i. 1-11), and other sources, He appeared often, and ordered them to meet Him in Galilee, when He showed Himself to a large number on a mountain. It may be that our Lord spoke the words of this verse to *v*. 48, twice, that is, on Easter Day and Ascension Day. For, the words of these verses, 44-46, addressed to the body of the Apostles, are very similar to what is told of the two disciples at Emmaus, *vv*. 25-27; and, not unlikely, He may have spoken similarly to the assembled Apostles and disciples.

45. "*He opened their understanding*"—enlightened their minds by His grace—"*so that they might understand the Scriptures.*" We know that the Scriptures contain difficult and obscure passages, which it is not given to all to understand, without God's heavenly light and grace. Our Lord opened their minds in a degree necessary to understand the Scriptures which He quoted as having reference to Himself, and thus firmly established their faith in all the mysteries regarding Him, as He did already to the two disciples at Emmaus; but, the full enlightenment of their minds in all truth was reserved for Pentecost Day, when the promised Spirit of Truth was to descend on them.

46. Having opened their minds, so as to be enabled to understand Him, then He quoted the several passages which had reference to the four following chief mysteries of His life and death:—First, "*Thus, it is written, and thus it behoved Christ to suffer.*" Very likely, He said this after quoting the texts of Sacred Scripture and the Scriptural types that regarded His death. It is written in the Psalms, the Prophets—Isaias, Jeremias, &c., that Christ should suffer. Secondly, "*and rise again from the dead.*" He also quoted the several texts and types in which this article was contained.

47. The third point, which He likely quoted Sacred Scriptures and types to elucidate is, the result of His passion and death, viz., that "*penance*" and its immediate spiritual effect, "*remission of sin,*" the end for which Christ suffered and rose again—for "*He died for our sins, and rose again for our justification*!"—should be preached, not to one nation, as hitherto, but to the ends of the earth—"*to all nations in His name,*" by men acting as the dispensers of His mysteries, and as His legates and ministers. Our Lord places "*penance*" before "*remission of sins,*" which is the fruit of penance; without penance sin is not remitted—"*nisi pœnitentiam egeritis omnes similiter peribitis.*" And, fourthly, that this preaching, in accordance with the decrees of God, should commence with Jerusalem (Isaias ii. 3; iv. 1; Micheas iv. 2). "*Beginning,*" that is, those who were to act in His name, should begin their preaching in Jerusalem. It was God's will, that salvation should be first offered to the Jews, and only after them, to the Gentiles. The Greek is in the genitive, αρξαμενων, by those "*beginning at Jerusalem.*" St. Peter did so (Acts ii. 38); the Apostles, even St. Paul, began with the Jews. According to this reading, "*beginning*" is dependent on and connected with "*be preached,*" κηρυχθηναι αρξαμενων. The Codex Vat. has, αρξαμενοι. The common reading is αρξαμενον, which is preferred to the others by Beelen, chiefly on account of the preponderance of authorities (Gram. Græcit, § 32, 7). He regards

it as a specimen of the accusative absolute, meaning, *facto initio a Hierosolymis* He says it is usual with the Greeks to use impersonally in the accusative case, participles of the neuter gender and singular number, as in the present instance.

48. "*And you are witnesses of these things.*" The present "*are*" has a future sense, "*shall be*," as is said in Acts (i. 8), "*and you shall be witnesses of Me in Jerusalem, and in all Judea,*" &c., just as in the words, "*and I send the promise,*" &c. The word, "*send,*" means, "*shall send.*" It may be that "*are*" has a present signification, as if He said: You have had ocular evidence of these leading events and mysteries connected with Me, so as to be able to preach them with confidence hereafter. They preached what they saw, heard, looked upon, and their hands had handled (1 John i. 1). "*Of these things*"—of all that is to be preached regarding Me. You shall preach My Passion, Resurrection, penance, remission of sin, in accordance with the prediction of the prophets, through all nations, after having first commenced at Jerusalem.

49. They might allege their own weakness, ignorance, and inability, to enter on so arduous and exalted a mission; our Lord removes those apprehensions, by assuring them, He would fill them with the spirit of power and strength. "*And, behold, I send*" you on Pentecost Day just at hand, "*the promise of My Father.*" By Metonomy, the promise is used for the thing promised, viz., the Holy Spirit, whom My Father promised through the prophets, especially Joel, "*effundam de Spiritu Meo super omnem carnem,*" &c., and whom I promised to send from My Father (John xiv. 16; xv. 26; xvi. 17). "*But, stay you in the city*" of Jerusalem (Acts i. 4), where your preaching is to commence, "*till you be endued with power from on high,*" until the Spirit of fortitude, who shall strengthen you against all temptation and fear, and shall enable you to resist all the powers of earth and hell, descends on you from above. Hence, not from earth is your aid to be derived, but from heaven. The same is called by Gabriel, "*virtus altissimi obumbrabit tibi*" (i. 35). "*Endued*"—clothed, penetrated, filled, &c.; covered, as with a garment, so that His power alone would be seen in them, and not their own weakness. The compendious narrative given here by St. Luke is more diffusely narrated. (Acts i. 1-10, &c.) Hence, these words were not spoken till after He returned from Galilee, where He showed Himself to a large multitude (Matthew xxviii. 16; 1 Cor. xv. 6). For, here He tells them to remain in the city till the descent of the Holy Ghost. From other sources, we learn that He told them to repair to Galilee and meet Him there, which they did (Matthew xxviii. 16). The words from *v.* 44-49 were spoken shortly before His Ascension, since the promised Spirit was to be sent down "*not many days*" afterwards, viz., on Pentecost Sunday, which shortly followed Ascension Day. Our Lord had chosen Jerusalem as the place for sending down His Holy Spirit on the Apostles, because it was in Jerusalem He wished to found His Church, which He did on Pentecost Sunday. "*De Sion exibit lex et verbum Domini de Jerusalem*" (Isaias ii. 3). It was there He wished to promulgate the New Law; it was there a greater number of spectators were present to witness the effects of the descent of the Holy Spirit; and as it was there He underwent the greatest humiliation, so there He wished to display His glory and power.

50. After having remained with them forty days (Acts i. 3, &c.), proving His Resurrection, and instructing them in everything relating to the government of His Church, both as to faith, morals, and discipline, to the end of time, "*He led them out from Jerusalem, as far as Bethania*" (the eleven and those that were with Him—*v.* 33).

Bethania was about fifteen furlongs from Jerusalem. It lay at the foot of Mount Olivet, on the eastern slope, farthest from Jerusalem. Mount Olivet lay between Bethania and Jerusalem. It was from this place, He proceeded to the scene of His Passion. He was, therefore, determined to proceed from the same place, which, as the native village of Lazarus and Mary, was very dear to Him, to enjoy the glory of His Father. He also wished to convey that in the same place, or in the valley of Josaphat, that lay between Mount Olivet, from which He ascended (Acts i. 11), and Jerusalem, He would display the splendour of His majesty in judging the living and the dead (Acts i. 11; Joel. iii. 12; Zacharias xiv. 3, 4, 5).

"*Lifting up His hands*," a ceremony commonly used among the ancients in giving a benediction (Leviticus ix. 22). Such was also the usage observed by the Patriarchs (Genesis xxvii. 4; xlviii. 9; xlix. 1); so, also, by Moses (Exodus xvii. 11). The same ceremony has been constantly in use in the Christian Church, with the addition of the sign of the cross—partly the source of all blessings—which is surely of Apostolic origin. Nay, some authors—Suarez—St. Jerome (in Isaias lxvi. 19), believe that our Lord Himself, on this occasion, made the sign of the cross in the air, while, with uplifted hands, He blessed His Apostles. What wonder if He did so, since it is most likely He carried into heaven, to plead for us, the very scars of His Passion, which He retained after His resurrection (v. 40). Heb. ix. 36.

"*He blessed them*." The Patriarchs of old blessed their children when departing from them at death (Genesis xxvii. and xlix.), so used the Priests bless the people under the Law of Nature (Genesis xiv. 19), and the Mosaic Law (Numbers vi. 23). Hence, our Lord, Father and Priest of the Church, the Author of the Law of Grace, on leaving the earth, blesses His friends and followers, and gives them an earnest of His heavenly gifts.

51. It was in the act of of blessing them, "*He departed from them.*" He raised Himself up by His own power, the Apostles looking on, as He gradually ascended, until He vanished. "*A cloud received Him out of their sight*" (Acts i. 9), "*and He was carried up into heaven.*"

52. "*Adoring*," falling prostrate, and paying Him, as God, supreme worship, the *cultus latriæ*, due to the sovereign majesty of God only. Hitherto, they had known our Lord in the flesh; and, owing to their familiar intercourse with Him whom they knew to be God, He vouchsafed not to exact, at least, externally, as far as we know, this exhibition of Divine worship; but, now they knew Him no longer in the flesh, but in the spirit (2 Cor. v. 16). Very likely, before this act of prostrate adoration, and while they were gazing on Him ascending, the two men in white garments addressed them (Acts i. 10), and after this testimony, coupled with the evidence of His Divinity afforded in His Ascension, they fell down, and adored Him, sitting at the right hand of His Father.

Having adored, "*they went back* (from Mount Olivet) *to Jerusalem,*" not in sadness, but, "*with joy,*" on seeing this last crowning proof of their Lord's Divinity, and of the glory in store for Him—whom they so ardently loved—(John xiv. 28), at His Father's right hand, and the exaltation of His name, at the sound of which every knee in creation must bend (Philip. ii. &c.), together with the assurance they felt of the fulfilment of His promise, to send them the Comforter, the Spirit of Truth, to remain with them for ever.

53 "*They were always*" (*i.e.*), every day, and often at seasonable times, "*in the*

temple praising and blessing God. Amen." It is generally supposed this refers to the time after the descent of the Holy Ghost, which accords with the account given by St. Luke (Acts ii. 46; v. 21, 42) of the occupation of the Apostles after Pentecost, who were described as continually in the Temple, engaged in prayer and preaching Jesus Christ; for, before the descent of the Holy Ghost, in the interval between Ascension and Pentecost, they are represented as withdrawing to an upper room, where they persevered in prayer with Mary, the Mother of Jesus, with the women, and the brethren (Acts i. 13, 14). At the same time, the context here would favour the opinion, that even in the interval between Ascension and Pentecost, they frequently visited the Temple, the scene of their Master's labours at the close of His life—the house of prayer—the house of His Father. Nor is the account left us of their having abode in an upper room, necessarily opposed to this opinion.

"*Amen,*" for meaning (see Matthew v. 18; vi. 13). Here, it is wanting in some of the best MSS.

Ven. Bede observes, that as St. Luke commenced his Gospel with the ministry of the Temple in the Priesthood of Zachary; so, he very appropriately closes it with an account of the ministry of the Apostles, not in the oblation of legal victims, but in the praising and blessing of God.

GENERAL INDEX OF CONTENTS.

Abias, 4.
Abraham, bosom of, 183.
Absolution (by Priests), meaning of, 104.
Alms, advantage of, 131; duty of, 174, 178.
Angels (praises of God), 54.
Anabaptists, 136.
Annas, 75.
Annunciation, 13.
Aposiopesis, example of, 212.
Anna, Prophetess, 65.
Archelaus, 74, 210.
Augustus (Cæsar), 43, 73, 210.
Avarice, evils of, 137, 138.

Baptist, conception, birth, office of, 9, 25, 33.
—— circumcision of, preaching of, 59, 75, 79. 180.
Benedictus (Canticle), 40.
Bethania, 246.
Bethlehem, 48.
Boanerges, 113.
Book (of life), 119.

Caiphas, 75.
Cyrinus, 46.
Churches, dedication of, 209.
Christ, Incarnation, 21, 23; birth, 49; circumcision, presentation, 53, 59.
—— finding in Temple, 67, 70; obedience, temptation, 81.
—— judicial character, 136.
Church, infallibility of, 216, 217.
Cross, sign of, 246.
Compulsion of faith, 158.

David, 14; city of, 48.
Disciples (seventy-two), 116.
Drachmæ, 211.

Elias, Eliseus, 86.
Elizabeth, 5
Emmaus, journey to, 235, &c.
Eucharist, 171, 239.

Faith (perseverance in), 200.
"*Full of grace*," explained, 16.

Gabriel, 13.
Garazim, 113.
Ghosts, 186, 241.
God, Omnipotent, 22, 32.
Heretics, treatment of, 158.
Herod, 4, 74.
High Priest, 75.
Humility, 203, 204.
Hyperbole, 212.

Incarnation, 21, 23.
Infallibility of Pope, 226, 227.
Isaias, 83, 84.

Jerusalem, menaced destruction of, 213, 214
John, meaning of, 7.
Joanna, wife of Herod's steward, 107.
Joseph, 13, 71.
Jubilee year, 84.
Judge (unjust), picture of, 199, 200.

Kingdom of God, meaning of, 195, 196, 210.
Knowledge (key of), 132.

Lepers, cured, 193, 194.
Lazarus and Dives, parable of, 181, 187.
Life, contemplative, active, 125.
Limbo, 183.
Lot's wife, 196.
Lysanias, 74.

Moses, law of, on stealth, 208.
Magdalen, 100, 102, 106, 107.
Magnificat, 28, &c.
Martha, Mary, 123, 124.
Marriage, *vinculum*, 181.
MARY, ever Virgin, 14, 24, 26, 30, 58, 129. 180.
Mammon, 177.
Mina, 211.
Merit, 192.
Military life, 78.
Naim, 97.
Nazareth, 16.

Obedience, 71
Orient, 43.
Olivet, 246.

Plough, 114.
Peace (of good will), 54, 212.
Pharisees, 162, 180.
Pilate, 74.
Pride, example of, 201.
Prayer, 127, 128, 199, 200.
Prodigal Son, parable, 166, 172.
Publican, 78, 207.
Publican and Pharisee, parable of, 200.
Primacy (of Pope), 227.

Restitution, example of, 208.
Resurrection (of our Lord), 219, 220, &c

Sicles, 211.
Samaritans, 112, 113; (good), 121, 122.
Simeon, 60, 64.
Sinners, joy at their conversion, 163, 164
Simon (Pharisee), 100.
Self-denial, 159.
Soldiers, 78.
Servant (*unprofitable*), 192.
Shepherds, 56, 57.
Saints, invocation of, doctrine, 164, 165.
Sycophant, 78, 208.
Supper (great), 156, 158.
Steward (unjust), 174, 176.
Sycamore, 207, 190.

Temple, beauty of, 215.
Testament, (old), division of, 187, 243
Theophilus, 1.
Tiberius (Cæsar), 73.
Tower, 159; in Siloe, 147.

Vigilance, 140.

Widow, 199.

Zaccheus, 204, 209.

www.ingramcontent.com/pod-product-compliance
Lightning Source LLC
Chambersburg PA
CBHW032221230426

43666CB00033B/451